The European Illustrated Press and the Emergence of a Transnational Visual Culture of the News, 1842–1870

This book looks at the roots of a global visual news culture: the trade in illustrations of the news between European illustrated newspapers in the mid-nineteenth century. In the age of nationalism, we might suspect these publications to be filled with nationally produced content, supporting a national imagined community. However, the large-scale transnational trade in illustrations, which this book uncovers, points out that nineteenth-century news consumers already looked at the same world. By exchanging images, European illustrated newspapers provided them with a shared, transnational, experience.

Thomas Smits is Postdoctoral Researcher at the University of Utrecht, the Netherlands.

Routledge Studies in Modern European History

Food and Age in Europe, 1800–2000
Edited by Tenna Jensen, Caroline Nyvang, Peter Scholliers and Peter J. Atkins (Durham University)

Utopia and Dissent in West Germany
The Resurgence of the Politics of Everyday Life in the Long 1960s
Mia Lee

Mobility in the Russian, Central and East European Past
Edited by Róisín Healy

Circles of the Russian Revolution
Internal and International Consequences of the Year 1917 in Russia
Edited by Bartłomiej Gajos and Łukasz Adamski

Strange Allies
Britain, France and the Dilemmas of Disarmament and Security, 1929–1933
Andrew Webster

1989 and the West
Western Europe since the End of the Cold War
Edited by Eleni Braat and Pepjin Corduwener

Margins for Manoeuvre in Cold War Europe
The Influence of Smaller Powers
Edited by Laurien Crump and Susanna Erlandsson

The European Illustrated Press and the Emergence of a Transnational Visual Culture of the News, 1842–1870
Thomas Smits

For more information about this series, please visit: www.routledge.com/history/series/SE0246

The European Illustrated Press and the Emergence of a Transnational Visual Culture of the News, 1842–1870

Thomas Smits

LONDON AND NEW YORK

First published 2020
by Routledge
2 Park Square, Milton Park, Abingdon, Oxon OX14 4RN

and by Routledge
52 Vanderbilt Avenue, New York, NY 10017

Routledge is an imprint of the Taylor & Francis Group, an informa business

© 2020 Thomas Smits

The right of Thomas Smits to be identified as author of this work has been asserted by him in accordance with sections 77 and 78 of the Copyright, Designs and Patents Act 1988.

All rights reserved. No part of this book may be reprinted or reproduced or utilised in any form or by any electronic, mechanical, or other means, now known or hereafter invented, including photocopying and recording, or in any information storage or retrieval system, without permission in writing from the publishers.

Trademark notice: Product or corporate names may be trademarks or registered trademarks, and are used only for identification and explanation without intent to infringe.

British Library Cataloguing-in-Publication Data
A catalogue record for this book is available from the British Library

Library of Congress Cataloging-in-Publication Data
Names: Smits, Thomas, author.
Title: The European illustrated press and the emergence of a transnational visual culture of the news, 1842–1870 / Thomas Smits.
Description: London ; New York : Routledge, 2020. | Series: Routledge studies in modern European history | Includes bibliographical references and index.
Identifiers: LCCN 2019042842 (print) | LCCN 2019042843 (ebook) | ISBN 9780367247867 (hardback) | ISBN 9780429284380 (ebook)
Subjects: LCSH: Journalism, Pictorial—Europe—History—19th century. | Illustrated periodicals—Europe—History—19th century. | European newspapers—Illustrations—History—19th century. | Art and society—Europe—History—19th century.
Classification: LCC PN4784.P5 S65 2020 (print) | LCC PN4784.P5 (ebook) | DDC 070.49—dc23
LC record available at https://lccn.loc.gov/2019042842
LC ebook record available at https://lccn.loc.gov/2019042843

ISBN: 978-0-367-24786-7 (hbk)
ISBN: 978-0-429-28438-0 (ebk)

Typeset in Times New Roman
by Apex CoVantage, LLC

Contents

List of figures	vii
List of tables	viii
Acknowledgements	ix

Introduction 1

A Russian girl and a French illustrated newspaper 1
The first visual news medium? 4
Historiography: in a national context 6
Theory: the transnational nineteenth-century
 illustrated press 9
Methodology: working in between print and digital formats 11

1 Readers all over the world: the audiences of the *Illustrated London News*, *l'Illustration*, and the *Illustrirte Zeitung*, 1842–1870 21

Introduction 21
Historiography and methodology: readership and digital
 newspaper archives 22
Different audiences 23
Conclusion 57

2 The transnational trade in illustrations of the news, 1842–1870 67

Introduction 67
Historiography: transnational networks 68
Methodology: networks 71
Preconditions of the transnational trade in illustrations 72
Three phases of the transnational trade in illustrations
 of the news 91
Conclusion 116

vi   *Contents*

3   Foreign images of war: *L'Illustration's* images of the Crimean War in *Cassell's Illustrated Family Paper*   131

Introduction 131
Historiography: the Crimean War and visual reportage 132
Methodology 135
The Crimean War 136
Cassell's Illustrated Family Paper *138*
The original corpus 143
French illustrations in Cassell's Illustrated Family Paper *153*
Conclusion 162

4   Images of the world: the transnational trade in illustrations and the visual representation of the Universal Exposition of 1867   171

Introduction 171
Historiography 173
Methodology 174
The Universal Exposition of 1867 176
The transnational network 179
Mediation 190
Conclusion 207

Conclusion   218

Bibliography   224
Index   235

Figures

0.1	Entrenched *tirailleurs* before Sevastopol	3
1.1	A crowd in front of the London office of the *Illustrated London News*, 1851	25
1.2	The office of the *Illustrirte Zeitung* in 1862	26
1.3	Office of *l'Illustration* in 1844	27
1.4	Kiosk of *l'Illustration* in 1850	28
1.5	News store selling the *Illustrated London News* in the Australian goldfields	36
1.6	Front page of the German version of the *Illustrated London News* in 1851	46
1.7	Images of the Great Exhibition in the German version of the *Illustrated London News* in 1851	47
2.1	A special artist of *l'Illustration* in 1867	74
2.2	A Parisian barricade taken on the spot in 1848	78
2.3	*Skizzen aus dem Leben einer Frühverblühten* (1847)	94
2.4	The Thames embankment and subterranean London (1868)	112
3.1	Henri Durand-Brager (1856)	147
3.2	In the rain (1856)	150
3.3	The peace (1856)	153
3.4	The French emperor and empress and the Algerian flag (1854)	160
3.5	Imaginative uniforms of English officers at Scutari (1854)	161
3.6	Disembarkation of Russian prisoners at the Île d'Aix (1854)	162
4.1	Network visualization: the transnational trade in illustrations of the 1867 exposition	177
4.2	Rimmel's pavilion in the park (1867)	185
4.3	US exhibition at the exposition (1867)	189
4.4	The pavilion of the emperor (1867)	198
4.5	The Russian *isbah* (1867)	199
4.6	The Portuguese and Spanish pavilions (1867)	201
4.7	The saltwater aquarium (1867)	207

Tables

0.1	Illustrated newspapers mentioned in this book	15
0.2	Abbreviations of keyword searches in digital collections used in this book	17
3.1	Most common draughtsmen of illustrations concerning the Crimean War in *l'Illustration*, 1853–1858	144
3.2	Subjects of the original and re-published images of *l'Illustration* concerning the Crimean War	149
3.3	The main nationalities shown on images in the original and the re-published corpus	151
4.1	Original and copied illustrations concerning the 1867 exposition in 31 European and American illustrated newspapers	176
4.2	Illustrated newspapers of which images were copied in other publications	180
4.3	The percentage of square metres allotted to all participating countries on the exhibition ground and the percentage of space allotted to them in the illustrated press	191
4.4	Percentage allotted to different categories in all the illustrated newspapers, the five main suppliers and the smaller illustrated newspapers	193

Acknowledgements

This book began its life as a PhD thesis submitted to the Radboud University in Nijmegen, the Netherlands. I would like to thank my thesis supervisors, Sopie Levie and Lotte Jensen, for their excellent guidance. Besides providing constructive criticism on the many different versions of my thesis, Professor Levie also proofread countless proposals and articles, for which I am very grateful. I would also like to thank my colleagues at the cultural studies department in Nijmegen and at the history departments of the universities of Amsterdam and Utrecht, where I taught classes during my PhD. On an international level, I would like to thank the Research Society for Victorian Periodicals, not only for awarding me a Curran fellowship, which enabled a research stay at the British Library, but also for providing a forum where the study of the nineteenth-century periodical press and young researchers can blossom. I would like to thank Rob Langham and the wonderful editorial assistants at Routledge for guiding me through the process of publishing this book. Finally, I would like to thank Boudien de Vries at the University of Amsterdam, whose inspiring course on nineteenth-century magazines cured me of my previous obsession with the Second World War and firmly endeared me to the world of the illustrated press. On a personal level, I could not have written this book without the love, support, and critical insight of my partner Clara. You truly are my 'rock in the surf,' as the Dutch proverb goes. Thank you.

Introduction

A Russian girl and a French illustrated newspaper

In the aftermath of the Battle of the Alma (20 September 1854), the first clash of Crimean War (1853–1856), the allied columns became increasingly and dangerously overextended. Discipline broke down, and troops started to plunder abandoned Russian farms, estates, and palaces in the vicinity of Sevastopol. During the chaotic episode, a group of Zouaves, a French military unit raised to fight in colonial North Africa, feasted on expensive champagne and burgundy from the cellars of the Bibikov Palace. Their commander, Jacques Leroy de Saint Arnaud, did not call his troops to order; instead, he gladly accepted a looted pedestal table, which he shipped off to his wife in Constantinople. The published diary of one of the Zouaves records the looting of the palace, vacated by its noble Russian owners only hours before:

> I went into a small boudoir. . . . Fresh cut flowers were still in vases on the mantelpiece; on a round table, there were some copies of *l'Illustration*, a writing box, some pens and paper, and an uncompleted letter. The letter was written by a young girl to her fiancé who had fought at the Alma; she spoke to him of victory, success, with the confidence that was in every heart, especially in the hearts of young girls. Cruel reality had stopped all that – letters, illusions, hopes.[1]

Aside from the obvious poignancy of the situation this letter discloses to us, the passage also reveals that a young Russian girl, living on the outskirts of Europe, had access to *l'Illustration*, the most famous French illustrated newspaper of the time. The entry does not mention whether the publications on the table were recent ones; nonetheless, it is entirely possible that she would have seen images of the soldiers who would soon be looting her very house. From June 1853, *l'Illustration* extensively covered the 'affairs in the Orient,' as both the run-up to the Crimean War and its duration was called. In the issue from 6 May 1854, a full-page illustration showed the landing of the Zouaves and a regiment of British Highlanders on the beaches of Gallipoli. Only a couple of weeks later, these hardened troops posed an immediate threat to the safety of the girl and, more acutely, her fiancé.[2]

2   *Introduction*

Today, *l'Illustration* is generally considered to be thoroughly French. However, just like the Bibikov family, many of its subscribers lived in other countries. In 1863, Paul Schmidt, a German printer who worked for the famous French periodical in Paris, described how the newspaper sent around 12,000 copies – 55 per cent of its entire print run – abroad each week. The Netherlands and Britain received a substantial number of these copies, but the publication had subscribers all over the world.[3] In 1845, *l'Illustration* could already claim the 'most distinguished' citizens of Europe among its readers, that is to say, the French-speaking upper classes.[4] Even if they did not speak French, international elites still liked to receive the French publication, if not for its articles, then for the prestige it bestowed on the reader. In 1863, a travel account in Charles Dickens' magazine *All the Year Round* noted:

> The king of Persia is said to dislike Europeans generally, and to believe that the emperor of France and himself are the only two great sovereigns in the world. He has formed this opinion chiefly with the aid of a French illustrated newspaper, which he receives, and of which such parts as are likely to please him are translated for his edification. The French have, therefore, great influence over his mind.[5]

In 1854, *l'Illustration* could boast around 24,000 subscribers, all of whom would have seen the images of the Crimean War embedded in the publication's pages. However, they were not the only ones to be exposed to these illustrations.[6] In January of that year, the *Kerry Examiner and Munster General Observer*, the provincial newspaper of the south-eastern Irish city of Tralee, published a review of *Cassell's Illustrated Family Paper*.[7] Its low cost dazzled the reviewer: 'Several shops in town' sold it for one penny, making it available to 'every member of every grade of society.'[8] How could John Cassell, the owner of the periodical, provide his readers with the truly beautiful illustrations 'of many of the scenes referred to in the present war between the Russians and the Turks'?[9] The answer to this question is simple: he bought practically all of them from *l'Illustration*. *Cassell's Illustrated Family Paper*, printing an astonishing 500,000 copies in 1854, served its British readers *French* images of the Crimean War.

L'Illustration's Crimean War images were disseminated even further. In November 1854, it published an image of French sharp-shooters entrenched in the lines before Sevastopol (Figure 0.1). Three weeks later, on 9 December 1854, the German *Illustrirte Zeitung* published exactly the same image. After the illustration also appeared in *Cassell's Illustrated Family Paper* on 22 December, it crossed the Atlantic Ocean to the United States, where the Bostonian illustrated newspaper *Ballou's Pictorial Drawing-Room* published it on 13 January 1855. Finally, the readers of Madrilean *la Ilustracion* could also see the image in its issue of 20 January 1855. It is highly likely that the illustration even reached as far as the British Australian colonies. John Cassell resold or re-used a large number of the French images for the Australian version of his publication: *Cassell's Illustrated Family Paper and Melbourne Advertiser*.

Figure 0.1 Entrenched *tirailleurs* before Sevastopol. 'Tirailleurs retranchés – D'après un croquis de M. Dulong,' *l'Illustration* (18 November 1854). The Hague, Royal Library of the Netherlands, T 1788 (1854-24).

In the end, several million people saw *l'Illustration*'s images of the Crimean War: among them, a Russian princess, scared for her life and that of her fiancé; a French *bourgeois*, following the first large military campaign of Napoleon III in Paris; a German industrialist, pondering over the implications of the war for international relations; a labourer in London, deciding if he should volunteer for the British army; an Irish farmer, looking eagerly at the military failures of his colonizer; a recently immigrated citizen of Melbourne, feeling patriotic and homesick; and maybe even the king of Persia. Readers all over the world from diverse social and cultural backgrounds formed an opinion about the Crimean War based on the same group of images. Images and readers alike had become a part of a transnational visual news culture.

The dissemination of *l'Illustration*'s coverage of the Crimean War exemplifies the two central lines of inquiry of this book. First, famous illustrated newspapers were distributed beyond the national level. Just like *l'Illustration*, other titles, such as the *Illustrated London News* and the *Illustrirte Zeitung*, had subscribers all over the world, making their audiences far less national than scholars have previously assumed. Second, the images themselves were transnational products. In the mid-nineteenth century, illustrated newspapers in Europe and the United States sold and resold images of the news to each other on a large scale.

On the basis of these two observations, this book argues that the dissemination of famous illustrated newspapers and their images led to the formation of a transnational visual culture of the news. Although it is often presumed that a transnational visual news culture, fuelled by widely distributed news photographs, originated in the twentieth century, the dissemination of illustrations of the news makes clear that this phenomenon has its roots in the nineteenth century. From the early 1840s, the establishment of the *Illustrated London News* (1842), *l'Illustration* (1843), and the *Illustrirte Zeitung* (1843) paved the way for a large number of readers to start looking at the same images of the news and, in a way, at the same world.

4   *Introduction*

The first visual news medium?

When the *Illustrated London News* published its first issue on 14 May 1842, it altered the relationship between the media, the public, and the news. Although newspapers had informed readers about current events since the early seventeenth century, they mainly contained articles, and images were rarely used to represent the news.[10] This situation changed when the *Illustrated London News* began to 'depict' the world to its readers on a regular weekly basis, becoming the 'first newspaper to make pictorial reportage its dominant feature.'[11] Reflecting on the *Illustrated London News*'s coverage of the Great Exhibition of 1851 in London, the *Economist* remarked that its main innovation lay in the fact that it spoke not only to the ears, with texts, but also 'to the eyes' of its readers.[12] Its images conveyed knowledge 'immediately,' speaking a new visual language that could be 'universally comprehended.'[13]

This was by no means an accidental effect, but a deliberate focal point for the newspaper. In its opening address, the *Illustrated London News* promised its readers to 'keep continually before the world a living and moving panorama of all its actions and influences.'[14] The historian Arthur Bryant, who wrote for the periodical himself, observed that the 'wonderful week-by-week record of the past contained in the pictures and letter-press of [its] Victorian volumes spans an epoch of both human progress and human crisis unparalleled by any comparable one in the annals of mankind.'[15] Despite such high praise, the illustrated press could hide as much as it revealed. Publications constantly made choices concerning the elements of modern life they presented to their readers; for example, horrible railway accidents fascinated both newspaper and reader alike, but images of the wretched living conditions of the urban poor found neither public nor publisher interest.[16] Similarly, illustrated newspapers used wars to boost their sale figures, but the victims of these wars – the corpses of dead soldiers – were often conspicuously absent on their pages.[17] Significantly, although these newspapers used every opportunity to underline the objective and truthful nature of their images, they nonetheless depicted non-Western 'others' in a stereotypical and racist manner.[18] It may come as no surprise that our words *stereotype* and *cliché* derive their meaning from the nineteenth-century techniques used to make metal copies of wood-engraved images.

After its launch, the *Illustrated London News* quickly became a huge success. Starting with a circulation of 23,000 copies in 1842, regular sales grew to an astounding 130,000 copies by 1855. The print run of special issues enjoyed even greater successes. The *Illustrated London News* printed 300,000 copies of the double issue, containing images of the funeral of the Duke of Wellington in 1852, and the supplement on the Indian Rebellion (1857) reportedly sold as many as 500,000 copies.[19] Publishers all over the world quickly copied the successful British format. After the establishment of *l'Illustration* and *Illustrirte Zeitung* in 1843, publishers began printing periodicals modelled on the example of the *Illustrated London News* in the Netherlands (1844), Portugal (1844), Russia (1845), Spain (1845), Italy (1847), Hungary (1848), the United States (1851), Sweden (1855), Poland (1859), and Denmark (1859) (Table 0.1). In 1885, Mason Jackson, the first historian of the illustrated press, counted 36 illustrated newspapers published outside Britain, but he acknowledged that his list could only 'convey some idea of the extent to which pictorial journalism has spread during the last 40 years.' *Hubbard's Newspaper and Bank Directory of the World*, published by the American advertisement agency of the same name in 1882, supports this statement: it lists 98 illustrated newspapers, appearing in 21 different countries. Hubbard could arrange advertisements in the *Illustrated Tasmanian News* (1873–1882), the *Vsemirnaya Illyustratsiya* (World Illustrated) (1869–1889) in St. Petersburg, the *Illustração do Brazil* (1876–1882) of Rio de Janeiro, and the Tōkyō eiri shinbun (Tokyo Illustrated News) (1875–1889).[20]

From the early 1840s onwards, illustrated journalism became a common, and maybe even defining, feature of modern day-to-day life. In 1851 the *Economist* noted: 'Our great authors are now artists. . . . The events of the day or week are illustrated or described by the pencil; and so popular is this mode of communication that illustrated newspapers are becoming common all over Europe.'[21] In 1859, the French illustrated newspaper *le Monde Illustré* boasted: 'The taste for illustrations has penetrated the ranks of the masses and is now prevalent everywhere. We do not only want stories that speak to the mind, we want images that speak to the eyes. The engraving has become the indispensable complement to the text.'[22] Even if they did not supersede all newspapers in circulation, they certainly surpassed them 'in public favour.'[23] In 1873 Frederic Hudson, the famous editor of the *New York Herald* and one of the first American press historians, wrote in *Journalism in the United States*:

> Illustrated papers have become a feature. Every newspaper stand is covered with them. Every railroad train is filled with them. They are 'object-teaching' to the multitude. They make the battlefields, the coronations, the corruptions of politicians, the balls, . . . familiar to everyone. They are, in brief, the art gallery of the world. Single admission, ten cents.[24]

The years between 1842 and 1870 can be described as the heyday of the illustrated newspaper. During this period, illustrated newspapers were the most important shapers of the visual culture of the news. Major developments in reproduction technology and communication networks resulted in a dramatic decrease in the production time of images and, likewise, an increase in the dissemination of illustrated newspapers. From the early 1870s onwards, their importance diminished as their monopoly on visual representation was broken. Ironically, the same developments in reproduction technology that permitted a dramatic reduction of production costs for illustrated newspapers also enabled all sorts of print media, such as daily newspapers, to use images. More importantly, during the 1880s, the reproduction of photographs in print media became feasible, which meant that realistic illustrations of the news had to compete with this new visual medium.

Despite the success and omnipresence of mid-nineteenth-century illustrated newspapers, historians have mostly connected the visual representation of the news to photography.[25] The 'half-tone revolution' of the early 1880s, described

6   *Introduction*

by Ulrich Keller as the 'second invention of photography,' made it possible to reproduce photographs in print media on a massive scale. As a result, the invention of this technique is generally regarded as the origin of our current visual news culture.[26] Similarly, the transnational distribution of images of the news is often tied to other technological developments. For example, in his *magnum opus* on visual culture, German historian Gerhard Paul notes that the invention of telephotography in 1904, which made it possible to send photographs by telegraph, enabled the formation of global visual news culture.[27]

Several historians have challenged this teleological and technocentric account from a media archaeological perspective. As Lisa Gitelman and Geoffrey Pingree have asserted in *New Media* (2003): 'Owing part to the linear progress unthinkingly ascribed to modern technology, media tend to erase their own historical context.'[28] The role of the illustrated newspaper in shaping our current visual culture of the news was erased, or at least ignored, by teleological accounts that give primacy to photographic technology. In order to avoid this pitfall, Jason Hill and Vanessa Schwartz have proposed a contingent history of 'news pictures' as a separate class of images, which does not solely focus on technology but on the discourse, surrounding images of the news.[29] Uncovering these discourse, or 'supporting protocols' as Gitelman describes them, is made difficult by their 'invisibility' in social and cultural practice. In other words, supporting protocols have to be universally accepted in order to work. This makes media 'unique and complicated historical subjects,' of which the 'histories must be social and cultural, not the stories of how one technology leads to another.'[30]

In relation to the history of images of the news, a media archaeological approach points to the fact that we perceive photographs to be 'objective' not only as they are a direct result of specific affordances of photographic technology but also because the 'supporting protocols' tell us that we can trust these images. Similarly, illustrations of the news were perceived as objective (and therefore trustworthy) because nineteenth-century readers generally believed that illustrated newspapers did everything in their power to provide accurate renditions of news events. Brian Maidment has pointed out that it remains difficult for us to understand 'the apparently unworried ease with which Victorians accepted wood engraving as an essentially naturalistic and representational medium.'[31] Yet, from the early 1840s, illustrated newspapers disseminated images of the news on a massive scale *and* developed a discourse of objectivity, based on eyewitness accounts and an elaborate production process, which would be adapted and used for photographs later in the century.[32]

Historiography: in a national context

The world of nineteenth-century periodicals is a *mer à boire*. It is difficult to discover patterns and meaning in the seemingly endless number of titles, publishers, editors, writers, and, in relation to the subject of this book, illustrators and engravers. Historians began using nineteenth-century print media as a source from the 1950s onwards. In *The Victorian Frame of Mind* (1957), Walter Houghton used them to sketch the worldview of Victorians.[33] After this pioneering work, he began an index of all the authors who wrote in British periodicals, resulting in the publication of *The Wellesley Index to Victorian Periodicals* in 1966. A similar enterprise, John North's *The Waterloo Directory of Victorian Periodicals* (1976), records around 125,000 different British titles. In the same period, Michael Wolff founded the *Research Society for Victorian Periodicals* to transcend disciplinary boundaries and discuss projects with a focus on Victorian periodicals.[34]

The first volumes of the official newsletter of the society, the *Victorian Periodicals Review*, hardly saw any discussion of illustrations or illustrated publications: historians mainly used images of illustrated newspapers to support historical narratives based on textual sources. In this regard, their images have served little purpose other than to embellish countless history books concerning the political, economic, and cultural developments of the nineteenth century.[35] In line with the bibliographical interests of Houghton and North mentioned above, articles that do use them as a source mostly consider the work and the artistic style of a single author, while the context and the meaning of the images in illustrated publications remain out of view.[36]

In the 1960s, the rise of social history shifted the attention from the producers of Victorian periodicals to their consumers. Researchers saw the enormous number of titles as evidence of the emergence of the mass public.[37] Because of their impressive circulation figures, illustrated newspapers were especially relevant for this kind of research and historians analysed their images as mirrors of the social relations in the nineteenth century.[38] In contrast, Celina Fox has revealed the blind spots in these mirrors, pointing to the almost complete absence of the lower classes. She describes illustrated newspapers as pieces in the mechanisms of Victorian social control.[39] Similarly, in their contribution to *The Victorian City* (1973), Fox and Wolff have emphasized that these publications only represented a specific part of the urban transformation, offering readers the chance to ignore the more unpleasant sides of the 'urban scene.'[40]

It was not until the 1980s when historians finally became more interested in visual sources. Under the influence of the new cultural history, they started to see representation as a social construct with a unique character in every historical period and conceptualized culture as the sum of all cultural products: a 'mutually intelligible network of signs.'[41] As a result, the separation of high- and low-brow culture as well as the perceived ontological difference between different sign-types faded. Traditional boundaries between history, art history, and literary sciences also became harder to maintain.

In the light of the rise of the new cultural history, several historians began to study the specific nature of the visual representation of illustrated newspapers. Following a broader trend, they focused on how periodicals represented social groups, mainly to explain the rise of nationalism and the production of national identity. Instead of being only interested in how certain groups were represented, scholars started to study the effects these representations had on the reader: how they produced identities or reproduced social categories. Virginia McKendry, for example, used Eric Hobsbawm's concept of the invented tradition to study

8 Introduction

how early representations of Queen Victoria in the *Illustrated London News* 'participated in the creation of the romance between the Queen and her subjects.'[42] However, two other concepts – Edward Said's orientalism and Benedict Anderson's imagined community – have come to dominate the study of the nineteenth-century illustrated press.

In *Orientalism* (1978), Said revealed how the Western world came to see itself as a dynamic, progressive, and rational force in the nineteenth century; meanwhile, it essentialized the other, the 'oriental Other' in Said's case, as static, backward, and irrational.[43] Western nations used representations of the other to justify imperial power relations: 'All cultures tend to make representations of foreign cultures the better to master or in some way control them.'[44] Building on Said's work, Deborah Boyer has shown how British politicians used the visual representations of Burmans in the illustrated press to justify brute colonial military action during the War for the Acquisition of Upper Burma (1885).[45] Julie Codell shines a light on the same phenomenon by noting how the visit of the Zulu king Cetawayo to London challenged representations of him in the illustrated newspapers as a noble or a cruel savage.[46]

Anderson's imagined community has become a principal concept in nationalism studies, surpassing his main adversaries Ernest Gellner and Eric Hobsbawm in the early 1990s.[47] In *Imagined Communities* (1983), he demonstrated that the nation-state is a social construct that depends on forms of mediated contact.[48] Anderson explained this rise of the nation-state in the nineteenth century, underpinned by a widely shared sense of national identity, by pointing out how 'print-capitalism,' the combination of new printing technology and capitalist consumption, enabled mediated contact on a national level and the constant dissemination of nationalist discourse.[49] Because of its emphasis on modern mass print culture, the imagined community proved to be a fruitful conceptual framework to study the production of national identity by illustrated newspapers.

Peter Sinnema is one such historian to use this framework. As the authority on the *Illustrated London News* and the production of identity, his research has focused on the visual and textual representations of the magazine to describe what kind of imagined community it supported.[50] Building on both Said and Anderson, Sinnema has shown that the *Illustrated London News* mainly produced a British identity *ex negativo*; that is to say, its visual and textual representation of others, which in Sinnema's view were mostly 'non-English and non-bourgeois,' resulted in the production of national identity.[51] Jude Piesse has similarly applied Anderson's concept to study how the hugely popular Christmas issues of the *Illustrated London News* and other London weeklies produced national identity in both Britain and its overseas colonies. She argued that the issues offered a 'cohesive and reassuring' narrative that countered the destabilizing effects of large-scale migration on British identity in the mid-nineteenth century.[52]

There have been a large number of studies devoted to the British illustrated newspapers, perhaps due to (as press historian Jean-Pierre Bacot has explained) the general interest in the Victorian era.[53] Conversely, Bacot observed that the few French studies on the illustrated press are mainly bibliographical and descriptive.[54] Drawing on Anderson and Hobsbawm, he regarded the liberal revolutions of 1848 as a turning point in the joint history of the illustrated press and the production of national identity. While British, French, and German publications wilfully placed the events of that year in a European context, they wholeheartedly served the interest of nationalist leaders afterwards. This shift becomes especially evident in their coverage of the Crimean War (1854–1856) and the Franco-Prussian War (1870).[55] Similarly interested in the relationship between war, identity, and the illustrated press, Canadian historian Michèle Martin has studied how British, French, German, and Canadian illustrated newspapers shaped different 'collective national memories' of the Franco-Prussian War.[56]

Although German press historian Hartwig Gebhardt does not explicitly refer to Anderson's concept, his study of the production of national identity by the *Illustrirte Zeitung* uses a similar theoretical framework. Publishers and readers of German publications jointly created an 'image vocabulary': a specific way to visually represent certain subjects that a national audience recognized and accepted. The images in *Illustrirte Zeitung* played an essential role in creating this visual idiom. Just like Anderson, Gebhardt has underscored the importance of massive distribution and the periodicity of the illustrated press for this process.[57] And like Sinnema, he observed that German identity was mainly produced *ex negativo*.[58] Kirsten Belgum's study of the nature of the visual and textual representation of the famous German publication *die Gartenlaube* takes a similar line of inquiry, describing the nature of German nation identity by studying its images.[59]

Theory: the transnational nineteenth-century illustrated press

Media historian Simon Potter has acknowledged the 'wide currency' of Anderson's ideas in his field but noted that, more recently, scholars have become interested in 'analysing the mass media in a transnational context, as an agent of globalization.'[60] Similarly, Marie Cronqvist and Christoph Hilgert have recently alluded to a traditional blind spot in media-history scholarship: the fact that 'the history of media and their contribution to public communication is written from a national point of view.'[61] Consequently, to better understand the nineteenth-century press, historians must escape from the unnecessary and narrow national framework and study newspapers from a transnational perspective.

In recent years, the call for a transnational perspective has resonated in the field of periodical studies. Andrew King, Alexis Easley, and John Morton noted in the introduction to *Routledge Handbook to Nineteenth-Century British Periodicals and Newspapers* (2016) that 'national and geographical limits' are often hard to justify. British periodicals and newspapers were 'influenced in both form and content by those printed in Germany, France, America, and many other countries.'[62] Similarly, in the introduction to *Journalism and the Periodicals Press in Nineteenth-Century Britain* (2017), Joanne Shattock identified the 'transnational connections between the British press and its counterparts in Europe, America and the Empire' as one of the central themes of the book.[63]

Although the introductions and several contributions to these overviews of the field show that most scholars are convinced of the benefits of a transnational perspective, they do not offer a clear definition of the concept.[64] In 2006,

10 *Introduction*

the editors of the *American Historical Review*'s forum on transnational history had already noted: '[Transnational history] is in danger of becoming merely a buzzword among historians, more a label than a practice, more expansive in its meaning than precise in its application, more a fashion of the moment than a durable approach to the serious study of history.'[65]

A precise application of transnational history requires that we distinguish it from other geographies, such as the nation-state and the British Empire, or geographically inspired concepts, like transatlantic journalism and transatlantic print culture.[66] These concepts tend to limit research to constructed geographic borders, while a transnational approach aspires to discover all the meaningful nodes and connections of a network, even if they fall outside traditional geographic categories.[67] For instance, in describing the 'connections between the print culture and periodical networks of mid-nineteenth century London and their counterparts in colonial Melbourne,' Mary Shannon has shown that a transnational approach can be used to shed light on the 'webs of contact and communication that bound the British Empire.'[68] In 'The Virtual Reading Communities of the *London Journal*, the *New York Ledger*, and the *Australian Journal*,' Toni Johnson-Woods noted how, during the mid-nineteenth century, millions of readers read the same serials in these three periodicals, demonstrating that the 'periodical world was truly smaller than the geographical one.'[69] If she had used the British Empire or transatlantic print culture as her key concept, Johnson-Woods would have never discovered this fascinating fact.

This book employs German historian Jürgen Osterhammel's concept of transnational history, because he offers the clearest and most comprehensive definition.[70] Osterhammel views transnational history as different from the supranational, which denotes forms of political organization (such as the European Union or the United Nations) or the international, which signifies economic, political, and cultural connections between groups (such as the First International or the Red Cross), where the borders of the nation-state are an essential part of the relationship.[71] In contrast, transnational history deals with groups and phenomena that develop 'in between' national contexts; it refers to 'a special category of social relations that unfolds in tension with and in contradiction to the assertion of national sovereignties.'[72] This transnational historical approach is, therefore, fundamentally different from a comparative historical approach, which compares the same historical development in two, or more, distinct national contexts. The press takes a central role in Osterhammel's *The Transformation of the World* (2014), his seminal work on the globalization of the world in the nineteenth century. In contrast to Anderson, who sees the newspaper mainly as a national space, Osterhammel noted that newspapers, 'as well as periodicals and magazines, opened communicative spaces of every conceivable dimension.'[73]

Seven years before Conqvist and Hilgert's 2017 article, media historian Marcel Broersma had already applied the concept of transnational history to the study of the press. Broersma argued that national media histories neglect or ignore the fact that medial formats, genres, notions about journalism as a profession, and journalistic practices did not develop autonomously in different national contexts but

Introduction 11

instead were shaped within a transnational space of contact.[74] This observation certainly holds true for the mid-nineteenth-century illustrated press. For example, the *Illustrated London News* profoundly influenced the *Illustrirte Zeitung*, *l'Illustration*, and other European and American titles. The transnational context shaped not only the format of the illustrated newspaper but also the techniques needed to make newsworthy illustrations and even the discourse of objectivity, based on eyewitness accounts of special artists.

In addition to the dissemination of media formats, reproduction techniques, and discourses of objectivity, the visual content of illustrated newspapers was also disseminated within a transnational context. In the mid-nineteenth century, audiences all over the world not only expected an illustration of the news to look a certain way but also, to no small extent, looked at the same images. Why should we describe this emerging visual news culture as 'transnational'? The meaning of these exact same images in different national contexts was similar, but not entirely identical. Textual elements accompanying them, the titles, captions, and articles, shaped the meaning of the same illustrations for different national audiences. As Osterhammel has argued, these various meanings can only be understood if we see the visual culture of the news as a transnational phenomenon, which developed 'in tension with and in contradiction to' different national contexts.[75]

Methodology: working in between print and digital formats

In "The Transnational and the Text-Searchable," Lara Putnam argued that the transnational and digital turn are intimately connected in historical research.[76] On a practical level, digitized versions of sources enable historians to study transnational developments and phenomena without having to travel to the national administrative centres where information is stored in a physical form.[77] More importantly, the ability to explore digitized sources using keyword searches makes it easier to find relevant information without in-depth knowledge of specific national contexts.[78]

Putnam also pointed to several pitfalls that result from the connection between the digital availability of sources and the turn towards transnational history. By depending upon keyword searches, researchers give prevalence to digitized materials; meanwhile, they potentially neglect important but yet-to-be-digitized publications.[79] Laurel Brake has thus urged researchers of nineteenth-century print culture to work between digital and print formats, underlining the notion that digital archives and methods should augment, rather than replace, research in paper archives and traditional research methods.[80] James Mussell similarly argued that we should put print material and digital reproductions 'into dialogue.'[81] Accordingly, this study makes extensive use of not only all sorts of digital archives but also paper versions of several important publications of which no digital versions exist, such as the volumes of *Cassell's Illustrated Family Paper* in the British Library and the French and German versions of the *Illustrated London News* in the Bodleian Library and the Staatsbibliothek zu Berlin.[82]

12 *Introduction*

Putnam contended that the connection between the digital and transnational turn might lead historians to overestimate transnational connections and underestimate the importance of the national context: 'We risk overemphasizing the importance of that which connects, and underestimating the weight of that which is connected.'[83] Before the digital turn, studies mostly concerned themselves with a single well-known illustrated newspaper, which would then be described in depth within a specific national context. This book, following Putnam's argument, attempts to address both the connecting as well as the connected. Hence, a large part of the first chapter is based on an in-depth study of the three most famous European illustrated newspapers, while the remaining chapters refer to around 40 different titles, published in 14 different national contexts, and seek to bring the transnational nature of the mid-nineteenth-century illustrated press into view.

Studying digital sources from a transnational perspective can be challenging. The editorial of the first issue of the *Journal for European Periodical Studies* notes that 'large-scale digitization projects rarely harvest material across national boundaries.'[84] Constance Bantman has rightly added that these projects remain 'overwhelmingly biased towards English language publications.'[85] Digital collections, just like their non-digital counterparts, provide specific kinds of unequal access to the past.[86] However, the hindrances that they throw in our path might be other than what we would suspect. For example, through the use of search engines, it was relatively easy to bring together digitized illustrated newspapers from Denmark, Germany, Poland, Hungary, France, Italy, Spain, and Portugal. However, because of expensive paywalls, I could not make use of Gale's digital collection of the *Illustrated London News*.

The availability of digitized sources also has implications for the methodology of media historical research. Bob Nicholson has argued that keyword searches enable historians to access texts bottom-up, instead of top-down.[87] Relevant information stored in articles is directly available, without having to select relevant titles, issues, and headlines. For this study, several digital databases, such as the British Newspaper Archive, the Dutch digital newspaper archive Delpher, Australian Trove, and French Gallica, were systemically searched with a combination of keywords. This often led to interesting new perspectives. However, as Nicholson has pointed out, this new methodology can also lead to a loss of context. Take for example the description of *Cassell's Illustrated Family Paper* in the *Kerry Examiner and Munster General Observer* quoted above. Besides the fact that it was published in Tralee, I would need to establish whether other contextual factors, such as the political stance of the newspaper, influenced its description of Cassell's illustrated newspaper. More importantly, if the *Kerry Examiner and Munster General Observer* had not been a part of the British Newspaper Archive, I would never have found this review.

This loss of context can only be justified by the quality of new information that a large-scale keyword search-based study of digitized sources can generate. The review of the *Kerry Examiner and Munster General Observer* is valuable because of the specific factual information it conveys. Looking for these kinds of specific facts in digitized sources might be described as the needle-in-a-haystack method. For instance, were I to have used highly contextualized top-down media historical methods, I would have never found the article written by the printer Paul Schmidt in a specialized German trade journal. By searching for the specific word 'cliché' (a metal copy of a wood engraving) in combination with 'l'Illustration' in the large digital collection of Google Books, important information was similarly uncovered.

Digitization not only changes media historical methodology but also fundamentally alters the historical corpus: the newspapers and magazines that are most frequently used in historical research. Studying the impact of the digitization of the *Toronto Star* and the *Globe and Mail* on Canadian historical research, Ian Milligan has shown that citations of these two newspapers in history dissertations 'increased *tenfold* in the wake of digitization, while citations of their un-digitized contemporaries remained steady or fell.'[88] This shift towards digital editions and methodologies was not explicitly made, meaning that Canadian PhD students did not mention the fact that they were using digital versions.[89] The resulting situation is problematic because finding relevant information in digitized versions requires far less immersive research methodologies. In order to avoid this pitfall, I have marked all citations in this book that are the results of a keyword search in a digital version, instead of a systematic top-down study of a paper version (Table 0.2).

Digital archives and digital methods can be used as a starting point for staging new historical questions, organized by other frameworks than the traditional geographic ones, such as the nation-state. Keyword searches in digital archives allow historians to quickly master sources from a plethora of different national contexts. Only a few years ago, it would have been impossible to find, let alone research, all the illustrated newspapers, published in 18 different states, studied for this book. By showcasing the possibilities of digital archives and methods, this book aims to act as a springboard for studies that use the nineteenth-century press to highlight the increasingly transnational nature of the modern world.

The first two chapters of this book attempt to reframe our understanding of the nineteenth-century illustrated press from a transnational perspective. Chapter 1 argues that the three most well-known European illustrated newspapers – the *Illustrated London News*, the *Illustrirte Zeitung*, and *l'Illustration* – attracted diverse audiences beyond the borders of the nation-state in which they were published. The *Illustrated London News* captivated large numbers of readers in the British colonies, the continent, and the United States. The French *l'Illustration* sent more than half of its entire print run abroad, mainly to the French-speaking upper classes of other European countries, such as the Netherlands. The German *Illustrirte Zeitung* targeted readers amongst the scattered ethnic German minorities of the Austro-Hungarian Empire but also reached German immigrant communities in the United States and South America. Instead of being 'national' publications, the three most well-known illustrated newspapers targeted different segments of the global elite and positioned themselves as transnational media corporations.

The second chapter sheds light on the large-scale transnational trade in illustrations of the news in the period 1840–1870. It shows that this exchange did not

14 *Introduction*

come to an abrupt end after 1850 and argues that economic considerations determined this trade. Images flowed from publications that could (due to the quality or quantity of their readership) afford to produce illustrations to titles that (for the opposite reason) had to keep their production costs down. The chapter traces two developments across the period. First of all, the price of illustrated newspapers consistently decreased. Around 1870, multiple titles in a single national context served all the different segments of the expanding reader market. Second, the transnational connections of different illustrated newspapers became increasingly entangled between 1842 and 1870. At the end of the period, a single illustration was often traded multiple times, being bought and sold by several illustrated newspapers, using different techniques of reproduction.

The last two chapters, case studies of the dissemination of images of specific news events, examine different aspects of the transnational trade. Chapter 3 looks at the re-use of *l'Illustration*'s images of the Crimean War in *Cassell's Illustrated Family Paper*. Reaching 500,000 readers at the height of its popularity, this illustrated newspaper was the most important shaper of the image of the Crimean War in Britain. The publication of the same illustrations in the two illustrated newspapers established a transnational community of viewers: different audiences in different national contexts who shared the same image of a certain event. However, the chapter shows how textual elements – titles, captions, and articles – determined the meaning of the French illustrations in the two national contexts. British editors did not hesitate to alter the meaning of French images by changing the textual elements if they thought that the original French interpretation would offend British national sentiments.

The last chapter describes the entanglement of the European and American illustrated press during the Paris Universal Exposition of 1867. Thirty-one illustrated newspapers, appearing in 15 different national contexts, published 1770 images of the exposition. A large-scale analysis of this corpus brings to light how French publications came to dominate the transnational trade in illustrations of the news in the 1860s. The chapter also shows how the trade determined the actual visual mediation of the exposition. Indeed, the image of the exposition in the illustrated press was decidedly less 'French' than the exposition itself.

In 1875 *the Printing Times and Lithographer*, a trade journal for typography, lithography, and paper-making published in London, described the 'ultimate development' of illustrated journalism, a time when 'the whole press will be an illustrated press': 'Then we shall have the artist and the reporter standing side by side, and the event delineated in light and shade as well as in fluent words. Our morning papers will not only drop the same idea simultaneously into a million minds, but present the actual scene before a million eyes.'[90] This future vision of pictorial journalism, written down just before the halftone was invented, demonstrates that it was not photography but the illustrated newspaper and the *cliché* that enabled the formation of a transnational visual news culture. From the early 1840s onwards, images of the news began to speak a language that could be universally understood. Copies of these images were traded in a web that connected publishers in the four corners of the earth. For the first time in history, millions of *readers* started *looking* at the same world.

Title	Publisher	Published	City	Studied
a Ilustração	Feliciano de Castilho	1845	Lissabon	1845
Ábrázolt Folyóirat	Werfer Károly	1848	Košice	1848
o Archivo Pittoresco	António da Silva Túlio	1857–1868	Lissabon	1867
Ballou's Pictorial Drawing-Room Companion	Maturin Murray Ballou	1855	Boston	1855–1857
California Illustrated News	Walter George Mason	1850	San Francisco	1850
el Globo Ilustrado	Chaulié y Ruiz	1866–1867	Madrid	1867
el Museo Universal	Nemesio Fernandez Cuesta	1857–1869	Madrid	1867
el Siglo Ilustrado	R. Labajos	1867–1869	Madrid	1867
España en Paris	Castro y Serrano	1867	Milan	1867
Frank Leslie's Illustrated Newspaper	Frank Leslie	1852–1922	New York	1867
Frank Leslie's Illustrirte Zeitung	Frank Leslie	?	New York	–
Geïllustreerd Nieuws	Albertus Sijthoff	1866–1879	Amsterdam	1866–1870
Geïllustreerde Courant	Koenraad Fuhri	1844	Den Haag	1844
Gleason's Pictorial Drawing-Room Companion	Frederick Gleason	1851–1855	Boston	1851–1855
Harper's Weekly	Harper Brothers	1857–1916	New York	1867
Hollandsche Illustratie	Binger brothers	1863–1919	Amsterdam	1864–1870
el Mondo Illustrato	Giuseppe Pomba	1847–1849, 1860–1861	Turin	1847–1849
Illustrated London News	Hebert Ingram (1842–1860), Lady Ingram (1860–1870)	1842–1971	London	1842–1870
Illustrated London News en Français	Herbert Ingram	1851	London	1851
Illustrated London News. Deutsch	Herbert Ingram	1851	London	1851
Illustrated Midland News	–	1869–1870	–	–
Illustrated Sydney News	Walter George Mason	1853–1872	Sydney	–
Illustrated Times	Henry Vizetelly & David Bogue	1855–1869	London	1867
Illustrated Weekly Times	George Stiff	1843	London	–
Illustratsiya (Иллюстрация)	Kubolnik	1845–1849	St. Petersburg	1845–1849
Illustrerad Tidning	Johan Fredrik Meyer & Per Erik Svedbom	1855–1867	Stockholm	1867
Illustreret Tidende	Otto Herman Delbanco	1859–1924	Copenhagen	1867
Illustrirte Welt	Eduard Hallberger	1853–1878	Stuttgart	1867
Illustrirte Zeitung	Johann Jacob Weber	1843–1944	Leipzig	1843–1870
Illyustratsiya. Vsemirnoye obozreniye (Иллюстрация. Всемирное обозрение)	A. O. Baumann	1858–1863	St. Petersburg	–

(Continued)

Table 0.1 (Continued)

Title	Publisher	Published	City	Studied
Illyustrirovannaya gazeta (Иллюстрированная газета)	A. O. Baumann	1863–1873	St. Petersburg	–
Képesujság	Werfer Károly	1848	Košice	1848
Kłosy	Franciszek Salezy Lewental	1865–1890	Warsaw	1867
l'Emporio Pittoresco	Edoardo Sonzogno	1864–1867	Milan	1867
l'Exposition de Paris	Henry Lenail	1867	Paris	1867
l'Exposition populaire illustrée	M. Montès	1867	Paris	1867
l'Exposition universelle de 1867 illustrée	François Ducuing	1867	Paris	1867
l'Illustration	Édouard Charton	1843–1944	Paris	1843–1870
l'Univers Illustré	Michel Lévy	1858–1900	Paris	1867
l'Universel	Jean-Auguste Marc		Paris	–
l'Universo Illustrato	G. Galimberti	1865–1870	?	1867
la Ilustración	Ángel Fernández de los Ríos	1849–1857	Madrid	1849–1850
la Ilustración Española	Juan Rico y Amat	1845	Madrid	1845
la Presse Illustré	Achille Bourdilliat	1866–1884	Paris	–
le Journal Illustré	Mose Polydore Millaud	1864–1899	Paris	1867
le Monde Illustré	Achille Bourdilliat	1857–1940	Paris	1857–1870
Museo de las Familias	Francisco de Paula Mellado	1843–1870	Madrid	1867
New York Illustrated News	J. Warner Campbell & Co.	1854–1854	New York	
Ny Illustrerad Tidning	Harald Wieselgren	1865–1900	Stockholm	1867
Oberungarische Illustrirte Zeitung	Werfer Károly	1848	Košice	1848
Österreichische Illustrierte Zeitung	John Greis	1851–1854	Vienna	-
Pen and Pencil: An Illustrated Family Paper	Frank Vizetelly & Edward Morin	1855	London	–
Penny Illustrated News	George Stiff	–	London	1867
Penny Illustrated Paper	Lady Ingram	1861–1913	London	1867
Penny Illustrated Weekly News	John Dicks	1861–1869	London	1867
Pictorial Times	Henry Vizetelly and Andrew Spottiswoode (1843–1847), Herbert Ingram (1847–1848)	1843–1848	London	–
South African Illustrated News	Heinrich Egersdörfer	1884–1885	Cape Colony	–
The Graphic	William Luson Thomas	1869–1932	London	–
Tygodnik Ilustrowany	J. Unger	1859–1939	Warsaw	1867
Über Land und Meer	Eduard Hallberger	1858–1923	Stuttgart	1867
Vasárnapi Ujság	Gusztav Heckenast	1854–1921	Pest	1867

Introduction 17

Table 0.2 Abbreviations of keyword searches in digital collections used in this book

Abrv.	Archive	Keywords or publication	Period	Accessed
BERM	Bermuda National Library	'Illustrated London News'	1842–1870	7-7-2014
BNA1	British Newspaper Archive	'Illustrated London News'	1842–1870	17-10-2017
BNA2	British Newspaper Archive	'Electrotype'/'stereotype'	1842–1870	22-5-2015
BNA3	British Newspaper Archive	'Vizetelly'	1842–1895	27-7-2015
BNA4	British Newspaper Archive	'Cassell'	1842–1895	2-3-2016
BNA5	British Newspaper Archive	'Dentu'/'Pierre Petit'	1866–1868	27-1-2017
CDNC	California Digital Newspaper Collection	'Illustrated London News'	1842–1870	13-2-2015
DEL1	Delpher	'Illustrated London News'/'l'Illustration'/'Illustrirte Zeitung'	1842–1870	30-7-2014
DEL2	Delpher	'Hollandsche Illustratie'/'Geïllustreerd Nieuws'	1864–1870	
GAL1	Gallica	'Dentu'/'Pierre Petit'	1866–1868	22-1-2017
GAL2	Gallica	'l'Exposition Universelle'	1866–1868	31-1-2017
GB1	Google Books	'Illustrated London News'	19th C.	15-6-2016
GB2	Google Books	'Illustrirte Zeitung'	19th C.	15-6-2016
GB3	Google Books	'Illustrated London News' AND Boston /'Illustrated London News' AND New York	19th C.	20-6-2016
GB4	Google Books	'cliché'	19th C.	10-6-2015
GB5	Google Books	l'Illustration journal universal	19th C.	15-6-2016
HT1	Hathi Trust. Digital Library	'Illustrated London News' in Hathi Trust's collection of *Punch*	1842–1870	12-4-2016
NYT	New York Times (Proquest Historical Newspapers)	'Illustrated London News'	1842–1870	1-6-2016
PP	PaperPast	'Illustrated London News'	1842–1870	28-7-2014
SING	NewspaperSG	'Illustrated London News'	1842–1870	19-2-2015
TR1	Trove	'Illustrated London News'	1842–1870	4-7-2014
TR2	Trove	'Cassell'	1842–1870	7-3-2016

Notes

1 L. Noir, *Souvenirs d'un simple zouave: Campagnes de Crimée et d'Italie* (1869). Cited in: Figes, *Crimea*, 251.
2 "Débarquement, a Gallipoli, des Zouaves et des highlanders," *l'Illustration* (6 May 1854).
3 **GB5:** P. Schmidt, "Pariser Illustrirte Journale," *Journal für Buchdruckerkunst, Schriftgiesserei und verwandte Fächer* (29 September 1863).

18 *Introduction*

4 "La liste de ses abonnes est la liste des noms les plus distingués dans tous les pays, tous les rangs, tous les genres, *à* tous les titres.": "L'Illustration. Journal Universel. Orné de gravures sur bois sur tous les sujets actuels," *l'Illustration* (6 September 1845).

5 **GB5:** "High life in Persia," *All the Year Round* (3 January 1863).

6 The readership of *l'Illustration* had rapidly expanded as a result of its war coverage. The illustrated newspaper sold 14,121 copies in 1854; a year later, the number of newspapers distributed had risen to 24,150 copies. Marchandiau, *L'Illustration*, 27.

7 **BNA5:** "Cassell's Illustrated Family Paper," *Kerry Examiner and Munster General Observer* (31 January 1854).

8 Ibid.

9 Ibid.

10 Pettegree, *The Invention of News*, 1–17.

11 Janzen Kooistra, "Illustration," 104.

12 "Speaking to the Eye," *Economist* (17 May 1851).

13 Ibid.

14 "Our Address," *Illustrated London News* (14 May 1842).

15 Bryant, "Foreword," 9.

16 Fyfe, "Illustrating the Accident: Railways and the Catastrophic Picturesque in the Illustrated London News"; Sinnema, "Representing the Railway: Train Accidents and Trauma in the 'Illustrated London News'"; Fox, "The Development of Social Reportage in English Periodical Illustration during the 1840s and Early 1850s."

17 Puiseux, *Les figures de la guerre*, 69.

18 Boyer, "Picturing the Other: Images of Burmans in Imperial Britain," 214.

19 These figures are based on 'notices to advertisers' in the *Illustrated London News*, which probably indicates that they are somewhat inflated and should only be used as an approximation of the true circulation of the publication. The last figure that Richard Altick gives in his seminal *The English Common Reader* is 123,000 copies in 1853. 1842. "To Advertisers," *Illustrated London News* (17 September 1855). "The Illustrated London News," *Illustrated London News* (11 August 1857). "To the Trade," *Illustrated London News* (28 November); Altick, *The English Common Reader*, 394.

20 **GB1:** Hubbard, *Hubbard's Newspaper and Bank Directory of the World*, 1945.

21 "Speaking to the eye," *Economist* (17 May 1851).

22 "Le gout des illustrations a pénètre dans les masses il est aujourd'hui répandu partout. On ne veut plus seulement du récit qui parle a l'esprit, on veut l'image qui parle aux yeux. La gravure est devenue le complément indispensable du texte.": "Galvanoplastie," *le Monde Illustré* (5 March 1859).

23 Ibid.

24 Hudson, *Journalism in the United States*, 705; Cited in: Brown, *Beyond the Lines*, 7.

25 Gervais, "Witness to War: The Uses of Photography in the Illustrated Press, 1855–1904," 371; Bardoel and Wijfjes, *Journalistieke Cultuur in Nederland*, 10.

26 Harris, *Cultural Excursions*, 304; Keller, "Early Photojournalism," 180.

27 Paul, *Das visuelle Zeitalter*, 51–4.

28 Gitelman and Pingree, *New Media, 1740–1915*, fig. xiv.

29 Hill and Schwartz, *Getting the Picture*, 3.

30 Gitelman, *Always Already New Media, History, and the Data of Culture*, 7.

31 Maidment, "Illustration," 108.

32 Barnhurst and Nerone, "Civic Picturing vs. Realist Photojournalism"; Gervais, "Witness to War: The Uses of Photography in the Illustrated Press, 1855–1904"; Keller, *The Ultimate Spectacle*; Park, "Picturing the War: Visual Genres in Civil War News."

33 Houghton, *The Victorian Frame of Mind, 1830–1870*.

34 Distad, "The Origins and History of 'Victorian Periodicals Review', 1954–1984," 86–98.

35 The images of the *Illustrated London News* and *l'Illustration* are still part of large commercial image collections today.

Introduction   19

36 See for example: Life, "The Periodical Illustrations of John Everett Millais and Their Literary Interpretation," 50–68.
37 Altick, *The English Common Reader: A Social History of the Mass Reading Public, 1800–1900*.
38 Hibbert, *The Illustrated London News. Social History of Victorian Britain*.
39 Fox, "The Development of Social Reportage in English Periodical Illustration during the 1840s and Early 1850s," 111.
40 Wolff and Fox, "Pictures from Magazines," 565.
41 Gallagher and Greenblatt, *Practicing New Historicism*, 7.
42 McKendry, "The 'Illustrated London News' and the Invention of Tradition," 3.
43 Said, *Orientalism*, 40.
44 Said, *Culture and Imperialism*, 100.
45 Boyer, "Picturing the Other: Images of Burmans in Imperial Britain," 225–6.
46 Codell, "Imperial Differences and Culture Clashes in Victorian Periodicals' Visuals," 410.
47 Blok, Kuitenbrouwer, and Weeda, "Introduction," 3.
48 Anderson, *Imagined Communities*, 26.
49 Ibid., 39–49.
50 Sinnema, *Dynamics of the Pictured Page*, 3.
51 Sinnema, "Reading Nation and Class in the First Decade of the 'Illustrated London News,'" 136.
52 Piesse, "Dreaming across Oceans: Emigration and Nation in the Mid-Victorian Christmas Issue," 38.
53 Bacot, "Le role des magazines illustres dans la construction du nationalisme au XIXe siecle et au debut du XXe siecle," 267.
54 Marchandiau, *L'Illustration*; Watelet, "La presse illustrée en France. 1814–1914."
55 Bacot, "Le role des magazines illustres dans la construction du nationalisme au XIXe siècle et au début du XXe siècle," 273–81.
56 Martin, *Images at War*, 8.
57 Gebhardt, "Auf der Suche nach nationaler Identität," 310–12.
58 Ibid., 318.
59 Most historians do not see *die Gartenlaube* as an illustrated newspaper, but rather as 'family paper' – a specific German type of illustrated magazine. See for example: Bacot, *La presse illustrée au xixe siècle*, 54–5.
60 Potter, "Webs, Networks, and Systems," 623.
61 Cronqvist and Hilgert, "Entangled Media Histories," 130.
62 King, Easley, and Morton, "Introduction," 3.
63 Shattock, "Introduction," 11.
64 Osterhammel, "A Transnational History of Society: Continuity or New Departure?," 29.
65 Bayly et al., "AHR Conversation: On Transnational History," 1441.
66 Smits, "Teaching Transatlanticism," 439.
67 Joel Wiener's discussion of the development of illustrated journalism in a transatlantic context shows the limitations of this approach. For example, he does not mention that *Frank Leslie's Illustrated Newspaper* published a lot of images from French illustrated publications. See: Wiener, *Americanization of the British Press 1830s–1914*, 71–5.
68 Shannon, "Colonial Networks and the Periodical Marketplace," 203.
69 Johnston-Woods, "The Virtual Reading Communities of the London Journal, the New York Ledger and the Australian Journal," 350.
70 Conqvist and Hilgert use the similar concept of entangled history, which came out of several discussions between French and German historians on *histoire croisée* or *Verflechtungsgeschichte*. Cronqvist and Hilgert, "Entangled Media Histories," 53.
71 Osterhammel, "A Transnational History of Society: Continuity or New Departure?," 44–5.
72 Ibid., 45.

20 *Introduction*

73 Osterhammel, *The Transformation of the World*, 26.
74 Broersma, "Transnational Journalism History," 10–12.
75 Osterhammel, "A Transnational History of Society: Continuity or New Departure?," 45.
76 This connection is noticed by many others. See for example: King, Easley, and Morton, "Introduction," 13.
77 Putnam, "The Transnational and the Text-Searchable," 380–1.
78 Ibid., 380.
79 Ibid., 379.
80 Brake, "London Letter: Researching the Historical Press, Now and Here," 247.
81 Mussell, "Digitization," 28.
82 I would like to thank the Research Society for Victorian Periodicals for awarding me a Curran Fellowship, which allowed an extensive research stay at the British Library.
83 Putnam, "The Transnational and the Text-Searchable," 377–8.
84 The Europeana collection, which brings together digital sources from all over Europe, is an important exception to this observation: Remoortel et al., "Joining Forces," 2.
85 Bantman and Silva, "Introduction."
86 Smits, "Problems and Possibilities of Digital Newspaper and Periodical Archives."
87 Nicholson, "The Digital Turn," 66.
88 Milligan, "Illusionary Order"; Cited in: Putnam, "The Transnational and the Text-Searchable," 388.
89 Milligan, "Illusionary Order," 566.
90 **GB1:** "Illustrated Journalism," Printing Times and Lithographer (15 March 1875).

1 Readers all over the world

The audiences of the *Illustrated London News*, *l'Illustration*, and the *Illustrirte Zeitung*, 1842–1870

Introduction

In "Around the World without a Gaze," Peter Sinnema has pointed to the prominent role that newspapers play in the work of Jules Verne (1828–1905). The gentleman traveller Phileas Fogg reads the *Illustrated London News* everywhere he goes during his trip in the novel *Around the World in Eighty Days* (1873).[1] Instead of enjoying some sightseeing in Hong Kong, Fogg 'engrossed himself all evening in *The Times* and *Illustrated London News*.'[2] The irony of Fogg's position cannot escape the reader: 'His journey seems to offer him direct purchase on an Other world, but he prefers to access that world indirectly, through printed and pictorial journalism.'[3] Sinnema argued that the images of the *Illustrated London News* are a form of representational control for Fogg: instead of confronting the inhabitants of the countries he visits directly, he gazes at them through the controlled lens of the illustrated newspaper.

While the *Illustrated London News* certainly fulfils this function in Verne's novel, in reality, others also used the periodical to look back. Underlining the universal comprehensibility of images of the news, the paper contained the following passage in 1859:

> The Chinaman and the Japanese, though unable to read what we write, learn something of the 'barbarians', . . . by contemplation of the pictures that *all the world can understand*, and which they cut out to adorn the cabins of their junks or the walls of their dwellings on shore.[4]

A year later, a correspondent of the *Jersey Independent and Daily Telegraph* exploring China remarked that 'illustrations from the *Illustrated London News*' adorned the walls of barbershops in Tinghae, the capital of the present-day Chinese island of Zhoushan.[5]

This chapter argues that the audiences of illustrated newspapers were far less national than has been previously assumed. It shows that the three most famous mid-nineteenth-century titles – the British *Illustrated London News*, the French *l'Illustration*, and the German *Illustrirte Zeitung* – served diverse audiences, ranging from urban readers to readers in colonies and other nations. These diverse groups of readers are brought into focus by looking at how the illustrated newspapers

22 *Readers all over the world*

described their ideal audiences in different kinds of paratexts, for instance, in the introductions to bounded volumes, new years' greetings, and all sorts of notices informing readers on practical matters, such as the mailing of the publications. In addition, digital archives can be used to research their distribution and reception in specific areas. Two cases – the reception of the three illustrated newspapers in the Australian colonies and the Netherlands – highlight this new methodology.

Historiography and methodology: readership and digital newspaper archives

In the last two decades of the twentieth century, it was widely held that the historical readership of a publication was almost impossible to trace.[6] As a reaction to the empirical research of the 1950s to the 1970s, exemplified by Richard Altick's seminal study *The English Common Reader* (1957), historians focused on 'textual' readers, by critically studying the ways in which text conscripted readers and produced audiences.[7]

Since the late 1990s, several historians and theorists have criticized the focus on the textual reader. In *The Reading Lesson* (1998), Patrick Brantlinger has argued that the gap between the sociology of Altick's common reader and the produced and conscripted textual reader should be bridged to acquire the most realistic picture of actual readers and readings practices.[8] By focusing on 'resisting readers,' several gender historians make the same point. As Hilary Fraser, Stephanie Green, and Judith Johnston would have it in their insightful *Gender and the Victorian Periodical* (2003): 'To neglect the "real" reader is to privilege the ideological positioning of the reader by and in the text, and diminishes our sense of readerly agency, of how the person turning the pages might have resisted, or at least participated in, that positioning.'[9]

This chapter aspires to bridge the gap between the common and textual reader, by focusing on the middle ground where they meet. It arrives at this middle ground in two ways. First, different paratexts, such as introductions of bounded volumes and advertisements, describe the ideal audience of the illustrated newspapers. Also included in this category are all sorts of practical notices concerning, for example, an increase in the price of mailing a periodical. These notices reveal something about 'real' audiences: successful illustrated newspapers operated in a competitive market, and, as a result, their ideal audience – the readers they targeted – must have been attainable. Second, the practical notices concerning the mailing of the periodicals demonstrate that a substantial part of the readership for the three illustrated newspapers lived either abroad or in the colonies.

Digital archives enable research into the distribution and reception of publications in specific geographical contexts. Historians from different fields agree that digital archives offer reliable data for research on the reception of novels. Bob Nicholson, for instance, has pointed out how literary scholars can use digital archives to 'examine how a novel sat within wider cultural discourse.'[10] James Mussell has also argued that we can use digital archives to 'study the construction of authorship, from the different ways that it is signalled across print contexts to the coverage of the emergent author in news, reviews and gossip.'[11] However, these methods have not been applied to more ephemeral publications such as newspapers and magazines. The research of this chapter is consequently based on the premise that media write about other media, especially if they were as successful as the *Illustrated London News*, *l'Illustration*, and the *Illustrirte Zeitung* were in the mid-nineteenth century.

Using keyword searches in digital archives, I studied the distribution of the three illustrated newspapers to map where their different audiences could be found. To begin, I used the British Newspaper Archive to study the distribution of the *Illustrated London News* outside London. Similarly, I looked for references to the British illustrated newspaper in the digital newspaper archives of Australia, Singapore, and Bermuda, the only former British colonies to offer open access to the digitized material of their national libraries. Finally, I studied the availability and reception of all three illustrated newspapers in the Netherlands by looking for references in Delpher: the Dutch digital newspaper archive.

While some countries, like Britain and the Netherlands, boast extensive digital newspaper archives, the digitization of sources is still in its infancy in others. In studying transnational phenomena in digital newspaper archives, we must therefore be aware that they provide unequal access to the past.[12] For example, while the digital newspaper archive Trove can be used to study the reception of the *Illustrated London News* in the Australian colonies, the lack of a similar archive in India obscures a large part of its colonial distribution. Similarly, while the British Newspaper Archive enables a study of the national readership of the British illustrated newspaper, the lack of similar national initiatives when I started my research in 2013 in France and Germany made it much more difficult to chart the national distribution of *l'Illustration* and the *Illustrirte Zeitung*.

Different audiences

This section discusses the different audiences of the three illustrated newspapers. Where – in what geographical areas – can they be located? In this regard, the argument put forward here is that the illustrated newspapers had readers on three geographical levels: the city, the nation, and abroad. In addition, the three illustrated newspapers targeted and found specific audiences, like the many readers of the *Illustrated London News* in the British colonies.

Urban readers

Two of the illustrated newspapers have the name of a city in their title: the *Illustrated London News* and the *Leipziger Illustrirte Zeitung*. When the former completed its second volume in 1843, it prided itself on the fact that it had brought the whole world in front of 'the scrutinizing gaze of the great people of our days – the people which rule the world – the community of London, the new Rome and Athens.'[13] The urban audience was fundamental to the success of the illustrated newspapers.

24 *Readers all over the world*

In their article "The Illustrated Press under siege," Michèle Martin and Christopher Bodnar discussed the 'urban nature of the illustrated press and its production.'[14] Cities provided investors, capital, and a concentration of industries that were essential for the production of illustrations; a central point in communication networks needed for distribution; and most of the 'material' – or news – that the illustrated newspapers covered.[15] Margaret Beetham further noted that cities offered a pool of readers large enough to justify and sustain mass production.[16] Michael Wolff and Celina Fox also emphasized the significance of the urban reader and concluded as follows for the London-based readership of the *Illustrated London News*: 'It is clear enough, not only from their names but also from their contents and from their extraordinary lasting success, that there was a substantial metropolitan readership whose interests were met by these journals [i.e., the *Illustrated London News* and *Punch*].'[17]

In 1842, the *Illustrated London News* published an illustration of its office. A family is looking at the freshly printed pages, displayed in the shop windows, while another man is walking away, already reading it.[18] A year later, another illustration showed the interior of the office. A crowd of newsagents, who distributed the publication in London, anxiously await the publication of the *Illustrated London News*: 'There is our publisher, . . . there is our porter, . . . and last of all, there are the high priests of impatience, the terrible newsmen themselves.'[19] The newsagents are also the central element of an illustration published in 1851: a crowd is storming the office of the *Illustrated London News* while newsagents walk away, carrying large piles of copies (Figure 1.1).[20]

Similar illustrations can be found in *l'Illustration* and the *Illustrirte Zeitung*. On the front page of the 1000th issue of the *Illustrirte Zeitung*, we see a group of people in front of the office of its publisher, Johann Jacob Weber. The illustration shows all sorts of readers – families, businessmen, workers, and children – absorbed in the *Illustrirte Zeitung* (Figure 1.2).[21] We can also see the German counterpart of a newsagent pulling a cart loaded with fresh copies. A frontal view of the office of *l'Illustration*, where parts of the first storey walls are left out, enables a view into the hectic scene inside. On the right side of the image, a crowd is entering the office. They buy their copies on the first floor and hurriedly leave it on the left side of the illustration, almost trampling a man. We can also see a French equivalent of a newsagent, strapping large numbers of issues to his back (Figure 1.3).[22]

It is unclear whether or not the offices of the illustrated newspapers were regularly stormed. In any case, the images point to the double role that the offices played, as places where publications were made as well as sold. Individual buyers and newsagents who distributed copies in other parts of the city picked up the latest issue directly after it was printed. The fact that the illustrated newspapers published images of their busy offices shows not only that they were directly tied to the city but also that they wanted to be perceived in this way: they presented their urban character as an important part of their appeal.

The office of an illustrated newspaper was not the only place in the city where the newspaper manifested itself. Martin and Bodnar have pointed out that

Readers all over the world 25

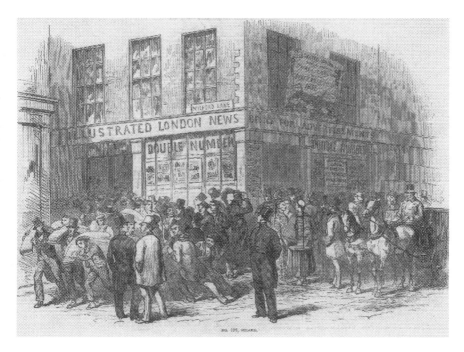

Figure 1.1 A crowd in front of the London office of the *Illustrated London News*, 1851.
'No. 198, Strand,' *Illustrated London News* (24 May 1851). The Hague, Royal
Library of the Netherlands, T 2258 (1851–1).

vendors sold copies on the streets. The famous kiosks of Paris, which (according to them) first appeared around 1854, were a vital part of the urban presence of *l'Illustration*.[23] Already in 1850, an illustration of 'one of the branches of our office . . .,' which seems to have been a predecessor of the kiosks, strategically located near the Palais Royal and the famous Café de la Rotonde in the heart of Paris, appeared in *l'Illustration* (Figure 1.4).[24] In 1857, another illustration of a kiosk – this time also designated as such – was found in the French periodical. The accompanying article described how modern kiosks were illuminated, enabling the sale of *l'Illustration* even at night.[25] Both illustration and text show how fast the 'spectacular reality' of Parisian boulevards, as Vanessa Schwartz described it, was evolving.[26]

The illustrated newspapers presented themselves to the city dweller with all sorts of posters and bills. In 1843, the *Illustrated London News* described its 'immense success bill,' which, 'from mural fronts of London, has tempted other spectators to a field wherein our reapers are gathering the harvest.'[27] These kinds of posters also regularly appear on the pages of *l'Illustration*. Without being mentioned in the accompanying text, we can find them on several illustrations of Parisian streets, hinting at their omnipresence in the city.[28]

Figure 1.2 The office of the *Illustrirte Zeitung* in 1862. 'Die Ausgabe der Illustrirten Zeitung,' *Illustrirte Zeitung* (30 August 1862). Berlin, Staatsbibliothek zu Berlin, 2" Ac 7169.

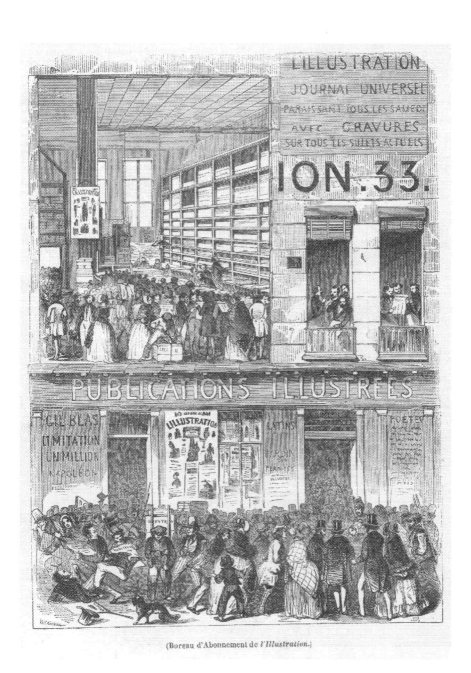

Figure 1.3 Office of *l'Illustration* in 1844. 'Bureau d'abonnement de l'Illustration.' *l'Illustration* (2 March 1844). The Hague, Royal Library of the Netherlands, T 1788 (1844–3).

Figure 1.4 Kiosk of *l'Illustration* in 1850. 'Le pavillon de l'Illustration au Palais-National,' *l'Illustration* (2 March 1844). The Hague, Royal Library of the Netherlands, T 1788 (1850–15-JAN/JUN).

Other types of advertising were also directly linked to the city. Take for example the advertisement campaign accompanying the publication of the first issue of the *Illustrated London News*: 'The above engraving represents the public announcement of the Paper on Friday last. Two hundred men paraded the streets of London to proclaim the advent of this important publication.'[29] A few years later, the article "The curiosities of England I. Advertisements," in *l'Illustration*, described the same campaign. In the French version of events, not two but three hundred 'pole-bearers' followed the procession of the newly elected Lord Mayor of London: a fact never mentioned in the *Illustrated London News*. After the parade, they boarded a decorated steamship that followed the Lord Mayor on the Thames. According to the article, the campaign was very successful: 'A couple of months later, the *Illustrated London News* had 50,000 subscribers.'[30] We also learn that the British publication continued to use aggressive advertising strategies: 'The owners of the *Illustrated London News* have a cart wander

Readers all over the world 29

through all the fashionable neighbourhoods of London, promoting their paper from dusk to dawn.'[31]

In their article, Wolff and Fox noted that *Illustrated London News* also recorded the rapid transformation of London.[32] The enormous engraving of the city that it presented to its readers in 1843 – the 'Colosseum print' – is a good example. In contrast, the more negative social transformation of the city, especially the deplorable situation of the urban poor, was almost entirely absent from its pages.[33] Ann Hultzsch argued that the early *Illustrated London News* provided an immersive but also highly controlled experience of the metropolis.[34] *L'Illustration* depicted the transformation of Paris in a similar way. In 1846, several illustrations of new boulevards appeared in the publication.[35] Just like the *Illustrated London News*, it used the interest in illustrations that showed the transformation of the city to attract new readers. In 1860, the first issue of *Paris Nouveau Illustré* claimed to 'represent the transformation of Paris in both all its details and in its entirety' and was given free to all new subscribers.[36]

The *Illustrated London News* and *l'Illustration* effectively 'integrated themselves,' as Schwartz wrote, into the fast-moving pace of urban life in Paris and London. The connection between the *Illustrirte Zeitung* and its home city of Leipzig was far less pronounced. The newspaper only rarely published illustrations of the city and never referred to its urban audience. This could be explained by the fact that, in 1850, Leipzig had not yet qualified as a modern city. In this regard, Peter Clarke has further pointed out that urban growth in most German states remained 'patchy and localized.'[37] To the city's credit, Leipzig's population rose from around 60,000 inhabitants in 1850 to roughly 106,000 in 1871.[38] In sharp contrast, the population of Paris exploded in the same period: from 1 million in 1850 to 1.8 million in 1872.[39] The same occurred for the population of the *caput mundi* London, rising from around 2.7 million inhabitants in 1851 to the astonishing number of 3.9 million by 1871.[40] The lack of an urban base – consisting of investors, means of production, and most importantly a pool of readers – should be central in explaining the relatively modest success of the *Illustrirte Zeitung*.

National readership

Before turning to the illustrated newspapers themselves, the problematic nature of 'national readership' in the nineteenth century should be examined. In his article, 'When the Provincial Press was the National Press,' Andrews Hobbs has demonstrated that the majority of nineteenth-century newspapers, which we readily describe as national today, were unable to achieve uniform national distribution.[41] Hobbs further argued that our present-day experience colours our view of the nineteenth-century press. For provincial readers, the London press 'did not carry the supremacy by default accorded to it today.'[42] The provincial press, which flourished during the entire nineteenth century, provided most readers outside London with their news.

Could the *Illustrated London News* reach readers all over Britain? Hobbs has stated that the illustrated newspaper was one of the first publications that could

30   *Readers all over the world*

rightly claim to be 'national' in the modern meaning of the word. Most of his criteria – a relatively high and nation-wide circulation, reports on all parts of the country, reports on national institutions, foreign news as it related to Britain, and a national reputation – indeed apply to the *Illustrated London News*. The only problem is that it never explicitly described itself as national.[43]

Nonetheless, two advertising campaigns started by the *Illustrated London News* in the early 1840s make clear that it targeted readers on a national level. First of all, in 1842, the publication distributed around 11,000 copies to all the clergyman of the Church of England, hoping that they would add their flock to 'the flock of the *Illustrated London News*.'[44] A year later, the *Illustrated London News* placed a large number of advertisements in provincial newspapers. At that time, the success of the British illustrated newspaper was far from certain. Although its circulation increased, a competitor was threatening its primacy: the *Pictorial Times*, founded by Henry Vizetelly and printer to the Queen, Andrew Spottiswoode. As we will see in the next chapter, the two publications fought, sometimes literally, for the public's attention.

On the front page of the *Manchester Times* of 16 September 1843, the advertisements for the *Pictorial Times* and the *Illustrated London News* appear together: one underneath the other. Ironically, both warn new subscribers against confusing the two. The ad of the *Pictorial Times* cautioned: 'To prevent disappointment, care should be taken to specify the exact title of the paper – PICTORIAL TIMES.'[45] The advertisement of its competitor stated that its recent success rendered it 'necessary that the public should be on their guard that inferior publications are not substituted for this paper.'[46]

The advertisement of the *Illustrated London News* was specifically produced for the provincial press and provincial readers. It further noted that the 'seed' of the *Illustrated London News* had grown with 'the rapidity of tropical vegetation' and that it could already lay claim to a circulation of 50,000 copies.[47] By enlisting the 'first available talent, both in literature and art,' the editors asserted that 'public opinion [was] in their favour' and they 'recorded [the] encouragement and welcome of the whole provincial press.'[48] The *Illustrated London News* could be ordered at 'all booksellers and Newsmen in town and country' and in this specific case of the 'Manchester agent, Mr. Barton. – office, Ducie Place, Exchange Manchester.'[49]

Using the British Newspaper Archive, I found this specific ad in fifteen different provincial newspapers.[50] The *Illustrated London News* placed many advertisements in the London press and, therefore, it is significant that this specific advertisement did not appear in any of the metropolitan newspapers. Its publication in three Irish newspapers additionally points out that the London head office of the *Illustrated London News* did not coordinate the placing of the ad in all the newspapers. Indeed, modifications in the Irish version of the advertisement reveal that the Irish agent of the *Illustrated London News*, Johnstone & Co., had paid for it.

It is hard to ascertain how many copies of a certain nineteenth-century title were sold. Especially after the abolition of the newspaper stamp, historians have based circulation figures on numbers given by the publications themselves, which makes them unreliable. It is even harder to provide an estimation of the geographical distribution of these copies. Using digital archives, we can find some sources that mention the number of copies of the *Illustrated London News* that were sold outside of London. However, this evidence remains sketchy and can only provide us with a rough estimate.

In 1850, the *Morning Chronicle* published an article from its correspondent in Liverpool, describing the 'amusements and literature of the people' of this town. The correspondent acquired the sales figures of a certain Mr Sheperd, the largest wholesale and retail agent of London-based publications. Sheperd sold 12 dozen, or 144 copies, of the *Illustrated London News* on a weekly basis.[51] The sale figures of the illustrated newspaper and a couple of other 'sixpenny periodicals and newspapers' were also mentioned to contrast them against the main concern of the article: the popularity of 'cheap literature.' Thus, the 144 copies of the *Illustrated London News* appeared negligible in comparison to the 1,800 copies of the *Family Herald*, the 1,560 copies of the *London Journal*, the 600 copies of the *Love Match*, or the 600 copies of *Elza Cook's Journal* sold by Sheperd. Being a respectable businessman, Shepard asked the correspondent of the *Morning Chronicle* to emphasize that 'there was a considerable demand for the indecent and scurrilous publications issued by the Holywell street press in London, but that he invariably refused to supply them to individuals over the counter.' However, 'as a wholesale agent,' he had no other choice but to 'include them with others in executing the orders of the trade.'[52]

In 1863, a small article in *Macniven & Cameron's Paper Trade Review*, reprinted in several British newspapers, mentioned the circulation of the London press in the week after the marriage of the Prince of Wales in 1863. The article shows that the famous railway newsagent, W.H. Smith & Sons, sent 70,000 copies of the *Illustrated London News* to the provinces, which corresponds to roughly 23 per cent of the total print run of 300,000 copies.[53] Although W.H. Smith & Sons was (by far) the largest wholesaler of London-based publications, it is not unlikely that other newsagents also mailed copies of the *Illustrated London News* to the British provinces. Furthermore, some people directly subscribed to the illustrated newspaper, which would increase the dissemination even further.

Clearly, although never explicitly mentioned (and in direct juxtaposition to its name), the *Illustrated London News* can be described as national, due to the fact of its export distribution and advertisements. Can the *Illustrirte Zeitung* and *l'Illustration* be similarly described? Perhaps. To begin, the circulations of the German and French periodicals were much lower than that of the *Illustrated London News*. Between 1842 and 1870, *l'Illustration* never sold more than 30,000 copies, while the *Illustrirte Zeitung* printed 13,000 copies at the most. The German printer Paul Schmidt noted that the *l'Illustration* sent early copies abroad and to the French provinces, while it distributed later editions in Paris.[54] In the 1840s and early 1850s, the French publication made a distinction between readers in Paris, the *départements*, and abroad.[55] The readers in the French provinces paid a surcharge of two Francs a year. In 1855, this distinction between the

32 *Readers all over the world*

metropolis and the provinces disappeared: readers all across France paid 18 Francs for an annual subscription.[56] Interestingly enough, readers in Algeria, colonized by France in 1830, were also considered to be part of this national audience.[57]

Could readers in Paris and the *départements* read the current issue of *l'Illustration* at the same time? Some sources say yes. In 1845, the publication notified a subscriber in Bordeaux that he could expect his copy one day after it was published in Paris, blaming this delay on the French postal system.[58] Although these kinds of messages are scarce, it is clear that *l'Illustration* had a (speedy) national distribution network at its disposal. In 1847 and 1848, the French illustrated newspapers mentioned all the retailers who sold their paper in alphabetical order on its last page.[59] From the 162 businesses, 119 were located in French cities.

Regarding the *Illustrirte Zeitung*, its editors regularly referred to the fact that the newspaper was, above all, a German publication: 'We want to be German, and we will only cover foreign events if they are of consequence for Germany.'[60] However, this focus on national events and readers was much more complicated than the editors led their readers to believe. After all, Germany only became a state after the Franco-Prussian War (1870–1871): until the late 1860s, the borders of Germany were highly contested. Both Prussia and the Austro-Hungarian Empire claimed leadership over a unified German nation-state. Several smaller and still independent German states had to position themselves in this 'German dualism,' as it is often called.[61]

Neither the editors nor the readers of the *Illustrirte Zeitung* had a clear idea of who belonged to the German national audience. In the correspondence column – 'Correspondence with everybody for everybody' – readers frequently posed questions about this subject. In 1844, a reader wondered whether Switzerland should be seen as a part of Germany.[62] The usual answer of the illustrated newspaper was consistent, but also very vague: everybody that *felt* German *was* German and the *Illustrirte Zeitung* was the glue that bound all these different Germans and 'Germanies' together: 'We have succeeded in bringing even the most distant kinsmen into a renewed contact with the mother country and, hereby, we have contributed to a stronger bond between all the lineages and branches of the German tribes.'[63]

The German editors did make a distinction between different geographic areas and states in messages that concerned the mailing of the *Illustrirte Zeitung*. In 1851, the German Customs Union – an alliance of several German states under Prussian control – and the Austro-Hungarian Empire agreed on a single postal tariff. The *Illustrirte Zeitung* frequently informed its readers about the consequences of this new system for its distribution. For a surcharge of one German thaler, it became possible to receive the *Illustrirte Zeitung* at home.[64] Readers in the Austro-Hungarian Empire could receive their copies from the 'K.K. Zeitungsexpedition.'[65] This special branch of the post office could not only be found in the Austrian heartlands but also in cities with a significant German-speaking population in the present-day Czech Republic, Slovakia, Poland, Ukraine, Slovenia and Italy.[66] An article in an Austro-Hungarian journal concerning statistics, noted that, in the first half of 1859, the 'Zeitungsexpedition' in Vienna distributed around 370 copies of the *Illustrirte Zeitung* each week.[67]

The many notices concerning the distribution of the *Illustrirte Zeitung* in the Austro-Hungarian Empire suggest that the majority of its readers could be found here, rather than in the German states controlled by Prussia. In the preface of the fifth volume, the editors felt the need to repudiate the claim that the *Illustrirte Zeitung only* had readers in Austria-Hungary.[68] In 1849, 'Herr R. from L.' wrote that he suspected that its anti-Prussian tone was probably meant to please its 'many readers in Austria.'[69] In the same year, the *Possische Zeitung* accused the *Illustrirte Zeitung* of being pro-Austro-Hungarian. The illustrated newspaper responded in a rather ambiguous way by stating that the author of the article was a 'Prussian and a Liberal.'[70]

The fact that the *Illustrirte Zeitung* had a substantial number of readers in the Austro-Hungarian Empire can also be demonstrated by looking at the frequent clashes between the illustrated newspaper and the censors of the Austro-Hungarian Empire. The 'China of Europe,' as British statesman Benjamin Disraeli (1804–1881) called it in the 1830s, maintained an extensive list of banned books, including works by German poets, such as Goethe and Schiller and philosophers Rousseau and Spinoza.[71] The Imperial government controlled the press and regularly banned or seized newspapers and periodicals. In 1848, a shipment of issues of *Illustrirte Zeitung* was impounded at the border of the Empire because it contained an article about the revolutions from that same year. To be sure, Weber's publication was not on the side of the revolutionaries, but the article offended the Austro-Hungarian censor because it described how the revolution brought German civilization to the brink of the abyss, which he interpreted as a dangerous, defeatist attitude.[72]

Apart from these direct forms of control, Austro-Hungarian readers of the *Illustrirte Zeitung* also paid an additional tax to receive the newspaper. In 1848, the editors wrote to a subscriber that his government regrettably saw it as a 'political journal,' although the newspaper directory of Vienna described it as an 'a-political newspaper.'[73] In the same year, the Austro-Hungarian censor began taxing the *Illustrirte Zeitung* more heavily and started to treat it as a 'foreign' political journal.[74] Unexpectedly, the fact that the illustrated newspaper was designated as a foreign publication proved beneficial when the Austro-Hungarian government introduced even heavier taxation on all newspapers in 1857. The *Illustrirte Zeitung* was fervently opposed to this measure, comparing the new press laws to those of the 'dictator of France,' by which they meant Napoleon III.[75] However, the government continued to designate the *Illustrirte Zeitung* as a 'foreign' political journal, with the fortunate side effect that it would be exempted from the new taxations imposed on 'national' publications.[76]

The troublesome relationship between the *Illustrirte Zeitung* and the Austro-Hungarian Empire seems somewhat strange in light of the fact that many other German states considered the newspaper to be a mouthpiece of its government: these sentiments were not entirely unjustified. For example, in 1867, a year after the German-German War of 1866, in which Prussia clashed with the Austro-Hungarian Empire, Weber, the publisher of the *Illustrirte Zeitung*, received the 'Francis Joseph Order' from the hands of the Emperor himself in recognition of

34   *Readers all over the world*

'the delicate consideration with which [his] artists and writers had treated Austrian subjects in spite of the War of 1866.'[77]

Suspecting the *Illustrirte Zeitung* of being biased towards Austria-Hungary, the other major German power – Prussia – also regularly hampered its distribution. In 1861, the Prussian government introduced a newspaper stamp, taxing all German-language newspapers and periodicals published outside its borders. Readers immediately started to complain, and the *Illustrirte Zeitung* protested against the new measure.[78] According to the *Allgemeine Preußische Zeitung*, this extra tax was warranted since the *Illustrirte Zeitung* had always been anti-Prussian, describing Weber as a 'publisher of anti-Prussian pamphlets.'[79] However, under pressure from the *Illustrirte Zeitung* and other newspapers, including the influential *Allgemeine Zeitung* of Augsburg, the Prussian minister of finance finally retracted the extra tax.[80]

Colonial readers

In the mid-nineteenth century, the British Empire was the only real colonial power. John Darwin has described the period between 1830 and 1870 as a critical phase in the establishment of Britain's 'emergence as a global power in command of a world-system.'[81] It is not entirely coincidental that Darwin's periodization roughly coincides with that of this study. First, as John Mackenzie has argued, the *Illustrated London News* was one of the most important providers of the 'striking imperial and militarist icons of the age.'[82] Second, as Berny Sebe has noted, its combination of texts and images supported Britain's imperialist project in new and appealing ways.[83]

In contrast, Germany, or rather the German states, had never embarked on imperial adventures. Only in 1884, 13 years after its unification, did Germany establish its first colonies: German Cameroon, Togoland, and German New Guinea.[84] However, German publications remained somewhat indifferent to the *Reich*'s imperial exploits. David Ciarlo has observed that the early colonial wars, such as the establishment of German rule in Cameroon (1891–1894), received almost no attention in illustrated newspapers like the *Illustrirte Zeitung*.[85]

The same applied (albeit to a lesser extent) for *l'Illustration*. Historians often make a distinction between the First and the Second French Colonial Empire. The first phase came to a close with the end of the Napoleonic Wars (1814) when France gave up most of its former colonies in the Americas, Africa, and Asia. The second period started with the conquest of Algiers in 1830 but only took off in full force after the establishment of the Third Republic in 1871.[86] In the 1840s and 1850s, *l'Illustration* never specifically directed itself towards colonial readers. Most Frenchmen, including the editors of *l'Illustration*, considered the three *départements d'outre-mer* located in Algeria as provinces of France.[87]

In the 1860s, *l'Illustration* started to display a limited interest in the colonial market. In 1856, tables mentioning the cost of mailing the newspaper abroad did not describe the French colonies as a specific category.[88] Ten years later, two of these lists made a distinction between foreign countries and 'colonies and

Readers all over the world 35

French trading posts.'[89] In contrast to the *Illustrated London News*, which British colonists could receive by paying a small additional sum, a subscription to *l'Illustration* was almost twice as expensive in most of the French colonies than in Paris.[90]

The *Illustrated London News* differed from its French and German counterparts in that it often directly addressed its colonial readers. The editors underlined three reasons for the indispensability of their publication for colonists and their relatives and friends who stayed behind in Britain. Most importantly, the *Illustrated London News* was a link between the colonies and Britain, and its combination of text and images played an essential role in forging this connection. As the introduction to the 1000th issue elucidates:

> To our colonies, this Journal has an interest, which can be claimed by no other. The Australian or the Canadian settled in remote districts, . . . and who has perhaps lost all hope of ever again beholding the land where he was born and where his fathers are buried, looks forward with more pleasure to the arrival of the *Illustrated London News* than to that of any other, whether daily or weekly paper.[91]

The British periodical was the antidote to the homesickness that colonists could feel. Sufferers of this disease were, according to the editors, happy to pay exorbitant prices for their publication: 'We heard a gold-finder declare that in Melbourne he had gladly paid a guinea for a single copy of the "Illustrated London News".'[92] The popularity of the illustrated newspaper among gold diggers in the Australian colonies even led to the publication of an illustration, depicting a provisional 'news-store' in the Ballarat goldfields, which, of course, prominently sold the *Illustrated London News* (Figure 1.5).[93] Making the same point, the article entitled 'Australian Hut' described how Joe, a young Australian sheepherder, dozes off while looking at an advertisement for the British illustrated newspaper:

> Joe had smoked himself into a state of semi-dreaminess, and seated on a log of wood, . . . was contemplating with a most thoughtful visage a large posting-bill – an advertisement of the ILLUSTRATED LONDON NEWS, . . . Doubtless, dreams of greatness, and thoughts of home, were passing through the poor shepherd's mind: he appeared quite lost in thought, and in imagination was far, far away from Australia.[94]

Even a poster of the *Illustrated London News* was enough to take colonists on an imaginary journey to their real home: Britain.

A sizeable colonial audience was also vital for readers in Britain because it ensured that colonists did not lose sight of their mother country.[95] Moreover, it reminded colonists of 'English civilization.' As the publication put it in 1855:

> It will be the constant study of its proprietors, . . . to make the *Illustrated London News* a welcome guest in every family in the realm, and the most

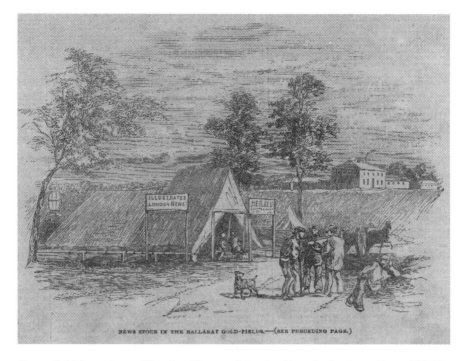

Figure 1.5 News store selling the *Illustrated London News* in the Australian goldfields. "News-store in the Ballarat Gold-Fields," *Illustrated London News* (3 June 1854). The Hague, Royal Library of the Netherlands, T 2258 (1854–1).

dearly prized of all newspapers in those remote dependencies and possessions where Englishmen are building up new Englands, and spreading the name and race, the literature, language, laws, manners, religion, and power of the old country.[96]

The *Illustrated London News* used advertisements in the colonial press to target new subscribers. Between April and October 1845, five colonial newspapers – one in Singapore; two in Sydney, Australia; one in Hamilton Bermuda; and one in Launceston, Tasmania (still called Van Diemen's Land at this point) – all published an advertisement for the *Illustrated London News*, which (besides some minor differences) was almost exactly the same as the one that was used for the provincial press campaign of 1843.[97]

Instead of the claimed 50,000 readers in 1843, two years later, the ad now boasted that the British periodical had a circulation of 70,000 copies. Not only the provincial press but also the 'whole public press of the empire' recommended the *Illustrated London News*.[98] The colonial advertisement referred potential readers to the office of the colonial newspaper that published it and all the newsvendors

Readers all over the world   37

in a specific part of the British Empire. Thus, future readers in Singapore could obtain copies by 'order at the SINGAPORE FREE PRESS, OFFICE, and of all Newsvendors in the East and West Indies, at a small additional charge on the above price.'[99] Inhabitants of the small island of Bermuda could order it at the 'office of the Royal Gazette, Hamilton, Bermuda, and of all Newsvendors in America and the West Indies.'[100]

The head office of the *Illustrated London News* managed the colonial advertising campaign from London. It probably did this in coordination with several colonial newspapers, as the mentioning of the office of the specific colonial newspapers suggests. The proprietors of colonial newspapers profited from publishing the advertisement since they could keep the small additional charge that readers had to pay if they subscribed to the *Illustrated London News* via their office.

Other colonial newspapers re-used the text from the 1845 advertisement campaign of the *Illustrated London News* for other reasons beyond subscriptions and probably placed the ad because the 'small additional charge' could amount to a considerable sum if enough people subscribed via the specific colonial newspaper. In the final months of 1845, the *Australian*, published in Sydney, and the *Hawkesbury Courier* of Windsor, a town in New South Wales, contained the colonial advertisement for the *Illustrated London News*.[101] However, instead of referring potential subscribers to their offices, the advertisement pointed readers to the *Launceston Advertiser*, published in Tasmania, roughly 550 miles away. Similarly, in the final months of 1846, the *Singapore Free Press* published the advertisement and, instead of referring potential subscribers to its office, as it had in 1845, now directed them to the office of the *United Service Gazette* in Madras, India.[102] Readers of the *Courier* of Hobart, Tasmania were similarly asked to write to *United Service Gazette*, almost 5800 miles away.[103]

The importance and size of the colonial readership of the *Illustrated London News* became visible when the British government decided to abolish the newspaper stamp in 1855. In contrast to the repressive European regime, the British government did not exert control over the press in a direct way between 1842 and 1870. However, it made its influence felt through a system commonly referred to as the 'taxes on knowledge.' In the 1840s and early 1850s, this fiscal network, consisting of the newspaper stamp, taxation on advertisements and on paper, pressed heavily on the profits of the British press.[104] A group of reformers, including Charles Knight (1791–1873) the famous publisher from the Society for the Diffusion of Useful Knowledge and the man responsible for the *Penny Magazine*, saw the system as a serious hurdle in the enlightenment of the British middle and lower classes and promoted the term 'taxes on knowledge.'[105] The *Illustrated London News* and its owner Ingram also fought on the front lines of the war against this 'fiscal repression':

> We have no objection to providing the paper and print, the engravings, and all the literary, pictorial, and mechanical outlay necessary to make our Journal more and more worthy of the patronage of its readers; but when the officials

38 *Readers all over the world*

of Somerset House put their hands into our purse to this enormous extent whenever we are inclined to fetch up any area of news, we endeavour, in self-defence, to make such occasions as rare as possible.[106]

The *Illustrated London News* advocated the self-regulatory mechanisms of the free market as opposed to governmental control: 'Let the government leave the size of a newspaper to be settled between those who supply the commodity and those who purchase it.'[107]

'The newspaper stamp abolition bill, which will come into operation on the 30th, promises, or threatens – we hardly know which phrase is the more appropriate of the two – to create a revolution in the newspaper press of this country.'[108] For the editor of the *Illustrated London News*, writing this passage in June 1855, it remained unclear whether the imminent abolition of the newspaper stamp was going to be a blessing or a curse. In fact, he seemed convinced that the end of the hated tax would definitively result in a revolution. What was the effect of this revolution on the colonial audience of the *Illustrated London News*?

As a part of the taxes on knowledge, the stamp prevented the distribution of newspapers and periodicals amongst the lower strata of British society by ensuring that publications remained relatively expensive or even economical inaccessible for the majority of British readers through taxation. In 1836, the British government taxed every printed page of a newspaper one penny.[109] Although the tax limited access for the lower classes, it also made newspapers more accessible to other groups of society. Stamped publications could, as compensation for the tax, freely travel through the postal system.[110] Consequently, the mailing of newspapers was, especially in comparison to letters, extraordinarily cheap. In the early 1840s, posting a letter over a distance of 15 miles cost the sender four pence, while 12 pence had to be paid for a distance of 300 miles.[111] However, the mailing of a stamped newspaper inside the borders of the British Empire was free after the tax of one penny had been paid.

In *Britain's Post Office* (1953), Henry Robison has demonstrated that the newspaper stamp put a severe strain on the postal system: it became almost impossible to process the ever-increasing number of stamped publications.[112] The problem was especially acute for the colonial mail: more than half of its total volume consisted of newspapers.[113] In 1853, the article "Newspaper correspondence across the sea" noted that none of the postbags of the wrecked mail steamer *Orestes* contained letters: only 15,000 newspapers were found.[114] The high number of newspapers in the bags of the *Orestes* was apparently such a remarkable circumstance that even the *Illustrirte Zeitung* described its demise.[115] The newspaper stamp made it lucrative for the *Illustrated London News* and other publications to target readers in the British colonies. After all, the price already included the cost of mailing it. The advertisement campaign started by the *Illustrated London News* in several British colonies in the late 1840s should be seen in this light.

The article "The Newspaper Stamp," published in 1855, gives some interesting statistics about the transmission of stamped newspapers through the post. In 1854, the post office processed 93,000 of the 112,000 stamped newspapers.[116] As mentioned above, Rowland Hill had argued for the abolition of the stamp because

Readers all over the world   39

the post office was losing money fast.[117] Furthermore, the article stated that the tax subsidized the distribution of the *Illustrated London News* and other stamped publications among middle-class readers. William Gladstone (1809–1889), the Chancellor of the Exchequer, made the same point: 'Mr Gladstone objected to the principle of subsidising newspapers at the expense of the community at large, by transmitting them and re-transmitting them at a loss to the Post-office.'[118]

How did the *Illustrated London News* react to the abolition of the obligatory newspaper stamp? First, it complained that cheap newcomers, who could easily copy its successful formula, would threaten its position: 'A flood of cheap newspapers – imitating the titles, style and general appearance, and stealing the news of existing journals.'[119] Second, it feared the negative effect that the rise of cheap 'unstamped' news publications would have on the moral fibre of the British people: 'No calamity we have of late experienced equals the nuisance of the publication of sheets called cheap newspapers, vilely personal and malicious.'[120]

In the first few months of 1855, the abolition of the newspaper stamp seemed to affect a somewhat positive result for the *Illustrated London News*. Members of parliament proposed that the stamp should become optional and this was, according to the editors of the British illustrated newspaper, beneficial for all parties involved:

> Those who desire a cheap press may have it cheapened to the extent of the virtually abolished stamp duty; but without the privilege of transmission and re-transmission by post. Those, to whom the postal privilege is essential, will find that the alteration of the law has produced no considerable change.[121]

However, the leading illustrated newspaper still feared that some of its readers would switch to cheaper competitors. To counter this, it announced a number of changes: the price of the *Illustrated London News* would remain six pence for the unstamped edition, while readers requiring a stamped version paid an extra penny. In return for this increase in price, the *Illustrated London News* promised to publish a free supplement each week. By expanding its content, it hoped to stay ahead of its competitors.[122]

This increase in price seems somewhat illogical. After the abolition of the tax, the *Illustrated London News* would, after all, generate significantly more revenue: no longer did it have to hand over a sixth of its selling price to the government. Moreover, newsagents like W.H. Smith already distributed the *Illustrated London News* for seven pence in total, making most readers in Britain no longer dependent on the relatively slow postal system for its delivery. The proposed price increase points to the fact that the *Illustrated London News* suspected that a substantial number of readers would require a stamped copy of the *Illustrated London News* even after this was no longer obligatory. In other words: a large group of subscribers lived in areas where newsagents and importers had not yet established a commercial distribution network:

> Even this small reduction [of the price], if made, could only apply to the case of those who did not wish to transmit their papers through the post and

40   *Readers all over the world*

would leave a large proportion of their subscribers in the British isles, and the whole of their subscribers on the content of Europe, at the Cape, in India, in China, in Australia, in North and South America, and in every place where the English language is understood, or where British trade, curiosity, or love of adventure is able to penetrate, in exactly the same position as before.[123]

The majority of its subscribers did not appreciate the hidden increase in price. In June 1855, a month before the abolition of the stamp, the *Illustrated London News* finally announced a price cut: 'On a careful consideration of the whole case, and on the wish of the great bulk of our subscribers, we have come to the determination of enlarging the *Illustrated London News* to double its original size and of reducing the price of unstamped copies to Five pence.'[124]

Rowland Hill was far from content with the situation that was supposed to eventuate after the abolition of the stamp. His Royal Mail still had to deliver stamped copies of the *Illustrated London News*, while it lost the revenue created by readers who bought the publication but did not make use of the right to free postal transmission. Therefore, Hill quickly amended his initial proposal. The post office would charge newspapers and periodicals mailed to the colonies or abroad according to their weight, and the newspaper stamp would only be valid in the British Isles.[125] A new stamp, known as the 'Queens Head,' could be used (once only) to mail a publication to the colonies or abroad.

According to the *Illustrated London News*, the proposed measures led to much discontent among its readers. In letters to the editor, newsagents complained not only about the rise in price but also about the considerable delays in delivery that resulted from the introduction of the new system.[126] In an editorial of 21 July 1855, the *Illustrated London News* attacked Hill, who only saw himself as a 'simple letter-carrier' and would rather not deliver newspapers and periodicals at all.[127] Especially colonial subscribers would be the victims of the new measure:

> The consequence has been that very great dissatisfaction had been excited, and that still more will be felt; that many tons of newspapers are lying in the post-office, and will not be forwarded; that our colonists will, to a large extent, be deprived of what is to them a luxury of life, and a necessity of civilisation – the English Newspapers; and that their friends in England will be taxed, without the consent of Parliament, to a serious extent.[128]

After the abolition of the obligatory newspaper stamp in 1855, the cost of mailing newspapers and periodicals depended on their weight: 'packets' that were heavier than four ounces (around 113 grams) had to be stamped twice.[129] The new arrangement was disadvantageous for relatively voluminous publications like the *Illustrated London News*, which often published large supplements, filled with advertisements. To cater to the needs of subscribers in the colonies and abroad, the periodical reluctantly produced a special edition on lower quality paper, the 'thin paper' edition: 'As newspapers sent to most parts of Europe are subject to heavy postage, and charged by weight, copies of the *Illustrated London News*, printed on *thin paper*, may now be had, if specially ordered, for transmission abroad.'[130]

After the abolition of the stamp, newsagents supplying readers in India and Canada complained in letters to the editor about the increasing costs and delays in delivery. The abolition of the stamp would undoubtedly lead to 'indignant remonstrances . . . from every colony.'[131] Newsagents subsequently urged the *Illustrated London News* to inform their colonial readers about the new regulations.[132] Even though the publication complied, complaints from colonial readers poured in: 'The injustice and annoyance to the colonies are . . . to be continued, and the outlying portions of the British empire are still to be hampered with restrictions on the transmission of newspapers to them, from which they have been hitherto very justly exempt.'[133]

Peter Putnis has examined how several London publishers reacted cleverly to the specific demands of the colonial market. Around 1850, newspapers and magazines like the *Home News* and the *European Mail* synchronized their printing with the sailing times of mail steamers leaving for the colonies.[134] The *Illustrated London News* also published special colonial editions. In 1862, it announced a 'Canadian edition,' appearing 'every Tuesday, . . . in time for the Canadian mail.'[135] In 1888, it started a special Australian edition, which contained – besides the regular content – a special Australian supplement.[136]

Case study: the *illustrated London News* in Australia and New Zealand

In 1863 the *Age*, a widely distributed newspaper published in the colonial capital of Sydney, contained an overview of imported British newspapers and magazines.[137] While around 40,400 different copies reached the Australian colonies in 1851, this number had risen to a spectacular 1,330,000 copies by 1862. However, newspapers and magazines not only flowed from Britain to the colonies: the number of colonial publications dispatched from Australia to Britain climbed from 41,537 in 1851 to 650,000 in 1862.[138]

The article also mentioned the specific number of copies received by the book and newspaper trade in Melbourne in the first four months of 1863. From the 95,000 copies sent by each, mostly bi-monthly mail for the whole of Australia, Melbourne dealers imported 24,000 to 25,000 copies. With a total of 4,300 copies, the *Illustrated London News* was the best-selling publication. According to the article, other popular titles included the *Home News* (3,600 copies), *Punch* (2,000 copies), and *Lloyd's Weekly Newspaper* (1,200 copies). The Melbourne trade only received 350 copies of *The Times*.[139]

Advertisements in colonial newspapers reveal that Melbourne was not the only Australian city that received a large number of copies of the *Illustrated London News*. Two Sydney-based wholesalers of British publications – W.R. Piddington and Waugh & Cox – were its most prominent colonial importers. The wholesalers in Sydney regularly placed advertisements that proudly stated the number of copies they received: 'Waugh and Cox have the pleasure to announce

42 *Readers all over the world*

the receipt of One Thousand Copies of the above popular newspaper [*Illustrated London News*].'[140]

Wholesalers distributed the *Illustrated London News* throughout the Australian colonies. Their networks can be partly reconstructed by studying advertisements found in the digitized Australian newspapers of Trove's online archive. During the 1850s, Piddington placed ads for the *Illustrated London News* in the *Sydney Morning Herald*, the leading newspaper of his hometown, but also in several provincial newspapers throughout New South Wales.[141] We can also find his advertisements in newspapers from Melbourne and Brisbane, located in the colonies of Victoria and Queensland respectively.[142] Piddington also offered the *Illustrated London News* in Auckland, New Zealand.[143]

Australian wholesalers probably provided an invaluable service for readers in New Zealand. Immigrants, especially those in the more remote parts of the Empire, often complained that the *Illustrated London News*, to which they had subscribed in Britain, never arrived. In a letter to the editor of the *Lyttelton Times*, 'Materfamilias' describes a visit to a London bookshop before she immigrated:

> I entered a bookseller's shop in London to continue my subscription to the Illustrated London News . . . and begged that for the future they might be 'forwarded to me to Canterbury, New Zealand.' The proprietor arrested his pen, and, looking at me said, 'Madam, it is money thrown away. In all probability, you will never see one paper we might send.'[144]

A year later, a reader of the same newspaper, who lived in Hokitika on the west coast of New Zealand, similarly complained about the imperial post system and noted that the *Illustrated London News*, his illustrated lifeline to the civilized world, never reached him: 'As the West Coast papers contain little but purely local news, [we] obtain a small share of information as to what is going on in the world. In addition to which we are many shillings out of pocket in the cost of postage stamps.'[145] After the correspondent of the *New Zealand Herald* in Harapipi lamented that he received only half of the British publications posted to him, a reader in Tauranga responded: 'All that I can say is that if the people at Harapipi get one half, they are infinitely better off than those at Tauranga, who do not receive one in four posted to them of the *Home News*, *Illustrated London News*, *Fun*, [and] *Punch*.'[146]

Companies such as Piddington and Waugh & Cox catered to the specific needs of subscribers in the more remote parts of the Australian colonies by sending multiple issues of the *Illustrated London News* stitched together. In 1853, the Sydney post office refused to continue handling these packages as 'bundles' of newspapers and not as a book. The cause of this refusal lay in the law, which required them to transmit any newspaper with a stamp for free; however, the post office could charge books and other packages according to their weight. Piddington started an advertising campaign, claiming that the post office failed to recognize the importance of the *Illustrated London News* for colonial life.[147] Different newspapers took the side of either the post office or Piddington and Waugh & Cox.[148]

As the *Sydney Morning Herald* put it: 'As all our contemporaries have had their say upon Mr Piddington's claim to have *The London Illustrated News* circulated through the post as a newspaper, . . . we think it right to express our opinion.'[149]

It is difficult to estimate the number of copies of the *Illustrated London News* that reached the Australian colonies and New Zealand. In 1863, 18 per cent of all 25,000 copies of different publications imported into Melbourne were copies of the *Illustrated London News*. If we use this percentage for the 95,000 newspapers that were, according to the article in the *Age*, imported into all of the Australian colonies, around 17,100 copies reached them by each mail. This number amounts to 8–11 per cent of the total circulation of the *Illustrated London News* at that time.[150]

The British periodical was clearly very popular in Australia and New Zealand; indeed, the publication presented itself quite consciously as the visual link between the colonies and the homeland. However, another reason for its popularity emerges from its reception by the Australian press: immigrants could also see how the British public back home saw them. Through the *Illustrated London News*, to which they ascribed enormous cultural and political influence, the public image of the Australian colonies in Britain could be traced and perhaps even managed.

In 1862, the *Star* had remarked upon some illustrations of the city of Melbourne, which appeared in a recent issue of the *Illustrated London News*: 'No one can overestimate the value of such a means of advertising as that which is offered by an attractive picture in a newspaper with so wide a circulation as the *Illustrated London News*.'[151] The colonial press often underlined the seminal importance of keeping the colonies in the public eye back home as the colonies were (or at least thought to be) greatly dependent on the homeland for their prosperity. In 1861, a letter in the *Argus* even suggested that colonists should pay the *Illustrated London News* to publish information about the relatively high wages of day labourers in Australia; immigration was, after all, the 'only hope for the colony.'[152]

Concerns over how the *Illustrated London News* depicted the colonial world can also be found in the press of neighbouring New Zealand. In 1856, the *Nelson Examiner and New Zealand Chronicle* noted how a certain Mr. Crombie forwarded 'a photographic view of the town of Nelson' to the *Illustrated London News*.[153] The newspaper thanked him for bringing 'before the English public such a correct view of the chief town of the province.'[154] At other times, colonists were very unhappy with the way in which the British periodical represented them. The *Lyttelton Times* complained about the 'wretched wood engraving' that accompanied an article about the harbour of its town: 'It requires the exercise of some faith, and still larger exercise of imagination, to enable the spectator to recognize the scene as the one it is intended to represent.'[155]

International readers

In 1843, an advertisement appeared in *l'Illustration*: 'The Illustrated London News. This magnificent weekly journal, after which l'Illustration is modelled, is

44 *Readers all over the world*

made to excite the curiosity of Englishmen living in France. However, the Illustrated London News is equally interesting for Frenchmen who are studying the English language.'[156] Two years later, 'Messrs. Aubert and Cie, Place de la Bourse, Paris' placed a French ad in the *Illustrated London News*, informing their *clientèle* how they could renew their subscription to the British publication.[157] From 1861 onwards, 'Mr Ludwig Denicke of Leipsic,' regularly notified 'continental subscribers' that he delivered the *Illustrated London News* in 'Germany, Russia, and the eastern portions of Europe.'[158] Mr Denicke also placed German ads for this service in the *Illustrirte Zeitung*.[159]

In this rather interesting interplay between the three newspapers and their advertisements, a flourishing, international audience is revealed. In the following paragraphs, this focus on international readers will be traced in each of the three illustrated newspapers in three particular ways. Firstly, this section examines three special editions of the *Illustrated London News*, published in three languages during the Great Exhibition of 1851. It then turns to the various ways in which all three illustrated newspapers catered to readers abroad. Finally, a case study of their distribution in the Netherlands and its colonies, using the digital newspaper archive Delpher, focuses on their reception in a relatively small European country and its colonies.

The Great Exhibition of 1851 in London was a turning point in the history of the *Illustrated London News*. Geoffrey Cantor has recorded how the periodical thrived as a result of its 'extensive reportage of the Exhibition.'[160] The enormous excitement surrounding it quickly resulted in a doubling of its circulation to 130,000 copies a week and it sold around 200,000 copies of the issue containing illustrations of the opening ceremony of the exhibition.[161] The article, "Speaking to the eye," published in the *Economist* on 17 May 1851 noticed the connection between the exhibition and the illustrated newspaper:

> The Great Exhibition itself, which is a representation to the eye, is a part of the same process. It is performing the office of a large illustrated newspaper . . It wants the facility of spreading that history over the world; and the illustrated paper, without which it is doubtful if it could itself have ever existed, comes to its aid, dispenses the knowledge so scientifically gathered and arranged, and so graphically displayed in Hyde Park over all the nations of the earth.[162]

The illustrated newspaper made the same argument in its final issue of 1851: only the *Illustrated London News* was able to convey the significance of the exhibition to readers all over the world:

> If it called upon those newspapers to bestir themselves, which merely report and describe events by ordinary language in words, it still more urgently called upon such a Journal as the *Illustrated London News*, which a contemporary has called 'the wonder of the 19th century,' to produce not merely a record in language, but in 'pictures' of the treasures of art which were congregated

Readers all over the world 45

together in Hyde Park, and to perpetuate for the instruction of distant readers and posterity, in a manner more thoroughly and effectively than any non-illustrated periodical, however able, might hope to do, the triumphs of art and manufacture effected by the various nations who contributed to the display.[163]

During the exhibition, the publication began to present its illustrations as a universal language: 'The artist speaks a universal language . . . Pictures, then, have a great advantage over words, that they convey immediately much new knowledge to the mind: they are equivalent, . . . to seeing the objects themselves; and they are universally comprehended.'[164]

Why did the *Illustrated London News* stress the universal aspect of its illustrations? During the Great Exhibition, it tried to attract readers abroad on a large scale for the first time. In May 1850, it published a French advertisement, announcing separate editions of the *Illustrated London News* in English, French, and German (Figures 1.6 and 1.7).[165] If we look closely at Figure 1.1 we can see a large sign advertising these foreign editions above the busy head-office office of the illustrated newspaper.

The foreign editions were meant to attract French and German subscribers, writing that 'to some extent, French is a universal language. It is the tongue of the courts, of diplomacy, of educated politeness, everywhere.'[166] Similarly, 'large parts of the continent' spoke German.[167] The international editions could also be bought by the 'hundreds of thousands of people in this country anxious to learn French.'[168]

Bacot has rightly pointed out that no accurate circulation figures for the French edition exist, but it seems to have been a relative success.[169] Thirty-one issues appeared between May and November 1851.[170] The *Illustrated London News en Français* regularly referred to its success, especially in Paris. It published an engraving, showing a crowd storming the office of Aubert & Cie, the French agent of the *Illustrated London News*, which advertised the *Illustrated London News en Français* in its shop windows.[171]

L'Illustration and the *Illustrirte Zeitung* were far from content with the international editions of the *Illustrated London News*. In the introduction to its 16th volume, the *Illustrirte Zeitung* proudly wrote that it secured the favour of German readers despite the competition of its influential British predecessor.[172] Similarly, *l'Illustration* mockingly summed up the benefits of the *Illustrated London News en Français*. The continent could soon enjoy 'this delicate British pleasantry, which tickles the palate like a bottle of gin, and cheers the spirits like a glass of cider.'[173] French readers would be informed that 'captain William Bathurst arrived in Egypt, that Colonel Thompson will come back from the East Indies next month with his wife and daughter, and that Viscount Fielding is getting ready to depart for Rome.'[174] The French edition might have been appealing to the eyes, but it certainly did not speak to the *bon goût* of the French.[175]

In its issue of 4 January 1851, only a day after the publication of the article in *l'Illustration*, the *Illustrated London News* responded to the 'shocking case of unfounded alarm' of 'our small Parisian friend.'[176] Illustrated or not, French and

Figure 1.6 Front page of the German version of the *Illustrated London News* in 1851. 'Unter den Linden und im Hyde-Park,' *Illustrated London News. Deutsch* (21 June 1851). Berlin, Staatsbibliothek zu Berlin, 2" Oo 3919.

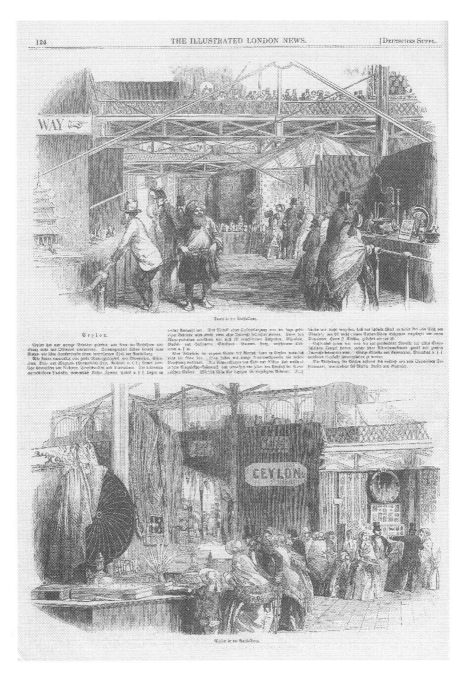

Figure 1.7 Images of the Great Exhibition in the German version of the *Illustrated London News* in 1851. 'Tunis in der Austellung.' *Illustrated London News. Deutsch* (28 June 1851). Berlin, Staatsbibliothek zu Berlin. 2" Oo 3919.

48   *Readers all over the world*

German publications could not convey the significance of the Great Exhibition to their readers:

> It is quite certain that neither the French nor German press can convey to the readers such full details of the Exhibition as we can; and it is equally certain that the *Illustration*, which could not illustrate the warlike doings of the Boulevards of Paris during the revolution or the insurrection, will not be able to illustrate the more peaceful doings in Hyde Park in London during the Exhibition.[177]

The British publication even encouraged *l'Illustration* to compete for the favour of British readers: 'Let it publish in English, and meet us on our own ground.'[178] The newspaper even tauntingly stated that it would even provide free advertising space for the English version of the French periodical.[179]

Despite its condescending tone, the *Illustrated London News* took the criticism of its French counterpart to heart. The next advertisement for the French and German editions explicitly mentioned that 'the elite of the Parisian Press' and 'German authors' would provide the content.[180] French and German readers did not have to fear that the special editions would be literal translations of the English version.

The German and French versions of the *Illustrated London News* stopped publishing after 8 and 31 issues. *L'Illustration* and the *Illustrirte Zeitung* attributed the limited success to the British nature of the international editions. There is some truth to this argument: of the total 335 images published in the French version of the *Illustrated London News*, 115 are related to the exhibition, 161 depict, more or less, typical British subjects, 44 of these deal with the many trips of Queen Victoria for example, and only ten images depict French subjects. The same applies for the German edition: it published 17 images on the exhibition, 13 of which depicted British subjects, while only four had a German theme.

A more plausible reason for the limited success was the fact that the *Illustrated London News* underestimated the stringent control of the press in France and several German states such as Prussia and Sachsen. Moreover, they probably did not know, or care, what its French and German journalists were writing. While the continental competitors of the *Illustrated London News* walked the tight rope of censorship with ease, succeeding in navigating the complicated and unclear rules, the journalists filling the German and French roles of the *Illustrated London News* were unable, or unwilling, to do the same.

The editors of the German *Illustrated London News. Deutsches Supplement* provocatively highlighted the 'freedom' of their publication from the German censors as one of its main selling points. It offered reliable information to readers who 'were limited by the often thrifty and one-sided reports, which German newspapers are allowed to give.'[181] They also advocated freedom – both of speech and industry – which was central to the success of the Great Exhibition and the British Empire: 'Our homeland is engaged in a glorious battle with Great Britain, which should be seen as race of our art and industry, and it can only emerge victorious from this battle, when it emulates England in giving freedom to art and industry.'[182] A French editor noted in an issue of the same date how Britain was the most liberal European country: Republicans were even allowed to advocate the abolition of the monarchy.[183]

In June 1850, the German version was suddenly discontinued after publishing only eight issues. A small message on the last page of the final issue provides the reasons behind the abrupt end: 'The political situation in Germany and the obstacles, which the German governments throw up in the way of the postal transmission of British newspapers, are unable to provide the publication with the firm basis, which is necessary for its success.'[184] In October 1851, a short article in *Illustrated London News en Français* remarked how its agent failed to deliver the three previous issues because the French government had forbidden their circulation.[185] The editorial of the next issue seemed to address the French censor almost directly, arguing that the *Illustrated London News en Français* only set out to unite Britain and France and to be 'an international publication, outside the political sphere, with its calculations, its prejudices, and its hatreds.'[186]

The French censor did not listen, especially not at this time. From August 1851, Napoleon III was planning a coup that would reinstate the French Empire. The suppression of critical newspapers and perceived foreign influences was an essential part of his plan: the *Illustrated London News en Français* remained on the blacklist of the French censor and published its final issue in November 1851. The censor also blacklisted the English version of the *Illustrated London News* in the final days of the coup in December 1851. Consequently, the attempt to conquer the European market with special editions and the universal images of the *Illustrated London News* had failed.

The modest success of the French and German editions of the *Illustrated London News* did not deter it from further ventures on the international market. From 1860 onwards, its agent in Paris sold it in continental France and the French colonies.[187] From 1866 onwards, two Parisian agents, Kirkland of the Rue de Richelieu en 'Messrs. Xavier and Boyveau' of the Rue de la Banque, distributed the *Illustrated London News* not only in France and its colonies, but also in Belgium, Switzerland, Italy, and Spain. Small messages in French – 'Note to our continental subscribers' – regularly informed readers in these countries about price changes and other practical matters.[188] In 1861, the aforementioned Mr Denicke of Leipzig served subscribers in 'Germany, Russia, and the eastern portions of Europe.'[189]

During most of the nineteenth century, the rules and regulations surrounding the ever-increasing national and international mail traffic were in constant flux. Prices changed continually as governments exerted control over the market and private mail companies entered it. The *Illustrated London News* paid ample attention to unexpected increases in costs, caused by the opening of new postal lines. The following notice in the issue of 14 January 1860 informed readers in the 'East Indies, China, Australia, etc.':

In order to pay the cost of transit through Egypt (a cost which has been largely increased, owing, in part to an important improvement in the service)

50 *Readers all over the world*

> newspapers sent via Southampton and Suez, addressed to the East Indies, Ceylon, Mauritius, Hong Kong, China, Australia, or any other country or place eastward of Suez, are now subject to an additional charge of one penny, making the rates as follows . . .[190]

Just after the abolition of the newspaper stamp, the *Illustrated London News* frequently published tables that detailed the mailing costs to over 200 destinations in all the four corners of the world. In 1855, the lists explicitly noted the cost of mailing the illustrated newspaper to the Baltic fleet, the Black Sea fleet, the White Sea fleet, and Scutari: places where large numbers of British soldiers were stationed during the Crimean War.[191] They also mention the specific cost of mailing the *Illustrated London News* to all the British colonies. Even the isolated Falkland Islands could be reached for a surcharge of only one penny per issue. The tables also shed light on *Illustrated London News*'s readership outside the British Empire. For example, 18 different German states are mentioned, suggesting that the British publication had subscribers in all of them. Furthermore, the list mentions several Dutch colonies, such as the Dutch West Indies and Curacao, and three different ways of mailing the newspaper to the Indonesian island of Java: via Holland (two pence), Marseilles (three pence), or Southampton (one penny).

A special 'thin paper' edition of the *Illustrated London News* further substantiates the importance of readers abroad and overseas. Until 1855, the newspaper stamp ensured its free transmission throughout Britain and its colonies, independent of the number of pages or its weight. As a result, the *Illustrated London News* could be printed on high-quality paper, which was relatively heavy. However, after 1855, the weight of a publication determined the postal rates to some colonies and foreign countries. The relatively heavy paper of the *Illustrated London News* subsequently meant relatively high transmission costs; hence, the new thin paper edition kept the newspaper affordable for both colonial and foreign subscribers.[192]

In 1864 and 1865, the *Illustrated London News* provided readers with the international postage rates every week because it often published supplements, making it heavier and thus more expensive to mail.[193] For example, the publication provided different instructions for the 'POSTAGE OF THE ILLUSTRATED LONDON NEWS FOR THIS WEEK (FEB. 6.), consisting of a number and a half-sheet supplement' all over the world. While it was still relatively inexpensive to send it to New Zealand (one penny stamp, normal version), the postal tariffs for Germany made it comparably expensive to receive it in this country (two stamps, thin paper edition).[194]

The United States seems to have been an important foreign market for the *Illustrated London News*. Because the first successful American illustrated newspaper – *Gleason's Pictorial Drawing-Room Companion* – was only started in 1851, the *Illustrated London News* was in high demand in the 1840s and early 1850s. As early as 1843, it alluded to its popularity in Boston and New York by printing an illustration of its 'American agent, Messrs' Redding & Co.' in Boston.[195] The accompanying article notes that the *Illustrated London News* had around 300 subscribers in Boston and New York and that this number was constantly growing.

Readers all over the world 51

An advertisement of Redding & Co., which can be found in the New York *New Mirror* and the Bostonian *Symbol*, further supports the widespread availability of the British illustrated newspaper: 'A weekly publication of London, each number of which is embellished with twenty to fifty of the largest and most splendid wood engravings ever produced in any country. 18½ cents.'[196] However, Redding & Co. was not the only company selling the British periodical in New York. Advertisements in the *New Mirror* show that other companies, such as 'The General Publishing Agency for the United States and Europe' and 'Bungess & Stringer,' also sold it.[197]

In 1845, several British newspapers reprinted an extract from Thomas Horton James' travel report *Rambles in the United States and Canada during the year 1845* (1846), in which he remarks 'you can see the *Punch, Pictorial Times* and *Illustrated London News* in the shop windows almost as abundantly as they are in London. This is not confined to New York but pervades the entire union, as far as New Orleans.'[198] While discussing the failure of the *New York Illustrated News* in 1853, the *New York Times* pointed to the still unrivalled position of the 'original' illustrated newspaper from London.[199]

In his autobiography, the Scottish writer, poet, and journalist Charles Mackay (1814–1889) wrote that the *Illustrated London News* was still considered the most prominent illustrated newspaper in the United States in the late 1850s. At the end of 1857, he travelled to the new world to 'make acquaintance with the people . . . and narrate my impressions in a series of letters to the *Illustrated London News*' and 'deliver a course of lectures . . . in the principal cities.'[200] Hebert Ingram (1811–1860), the publisher of the *Illustrated London News*, hoped that Mackay's trip would increase the 'sale and influence of his great journal.'[201] Upon his arrival in Washington, President James Buchannan (1791–1868) received the correspondent at the White House, demonstrating the influence of the British illustrated newspaper.[202] Mackay also befriended Senator William H. Seward (1801–1872), who hoped to become the Republican candidate in the 1860 presidential race. The senator asked Mackay to insert 'his portrait in the *Illustrated London News*, with a memoir of his life, character, and public services,' which would surely please 'his American friend and supporters.'[203] Although Mackay 'easily accomplished' this, Seward nonetheless lost the nomination to none other than Abraham Lincoln (1809–1865).

The British newspaper was not the only one to enjoy worldwide influence in this manner. In 1845, the *l'Illustration* placed an advertisement with a clear message regarding its own international prestige: 'The list of subscribers is a list of the most distinguished names in all countries, of all ranks, of all types, and of all titles.'[204] In its first issue, the publication already referred readers in Britain to the bookshop of 'J. Thomas, 1. Finch Lane in London.'[205] In the 1840s, the bookshop of Joseph and William Thomas frequently advertised the sale of *l'Illustration* in British newspapers: 'Those who read French will find in this Journal a pictorial history of France.'[206]

Distributing the French publication was not without danger. In 1844, Joseph Thomas was sued by the Society for the Suppression of Vice. In the Mansion House, a witness produced 'a copy of the publication, of which the name was

52 *Readers all over the world*

not mentioned. Like the *London Illustrated News*, or *Pictorial News*, it contained a number of woodcuts, one of them which professed to be the Conversion of St. Paul.' According to the witness, the image was of an 'injurious tendency,' and he had entered the bookshop to confront Thomas with it, who had 'laughed at the complaint.' The fact that Jacques-Julien Dubochet (1789–1868), the publisher of *l'Illustration*, travelled to London to act as a witness for Thomas points to the relative importance of the British market for the French illustrated newspaper. In the end, Peter Laurie, the magistrate preceding over the case, took for granted that 'Mr. Thomas will not sell any more of these caricatures . . . If he do [*sic*] I shall certainly inflict the penalty of 2*l*, which is the utmost fine the law will allow.'[207]

In the late 1840s, the number of foreign retailers of *l'Illustration* increased: the store of J. Issakoff sold it in St. Petersburg, J. Herbert in New Orleans, and Casimir Monier in Madrid.[208] A list of retailers published in 1846 contains 43 businesses that sold *l'Illustration* outside France in countries such as Belgium (Brussels, Antwerp, Charleroi, Namur, Liège, and Ghent), the Netherlands (Amsterdam, Rotterdam, The Hague, Arnhem, and Breda), the German and Italian States, Sweden, Russia, and even the city of Lasi, in present-day Romania. It also mentions retailers in North (New York and New Orleans) and South America (Havana, Cartagena, Caracas).

Two articles written by Paul Schmidt, a German printer who worked for the *l'Illustration* in the early 1860s, provide a rich picture of its foreign readership. In the first article, he explained that the French periodical was dated each Sunday but that the printing actually began three days before, on a Thursday night. He further noted that the first batch of copies had to be completed by Friday morning, because 'at nine o'clock, the copies for England and Holland have to be delivered at the post office.'[209] This already tells us something about the importance of these two markets for *l'Illustration*.

The second article, in which Schmidt describes the main competitors of *l'Illustration*, noted how the four most important French illustrated newspapers – *l'Illustration, le Monde Illustré, le Univers Illustré*, and *le Universel* – printed a total of 86,000 copies (worth 34,050 francs) and added that they sent around 30,000 copies, roughly 35 per cent, abroad.[210] As Schmidt was a printer for *l'Illustration*, he was quite sure about the exact figure for this publication: it sent 12,000 of the total 20,000 copies – almost 55 per cent – abroad.[211]

In an article celebrating the tenth anniversary of the *Illustrirte Zeitung*, the editors stated: 'Five million copies of the *Illustrirte Zeitung* have been distributed over the entire earth. She can be found in Adelaide and Canton but also in San Francisco and New York.'[212] Did the *Illustrirte Zeitung* indeed have the substantial international readership it claimed? Just like *l'Illustration*, the *Illustrirte Zeitung* sometimes mentioned retailers in foreign countries. In 1846, it notified readers in the United States that W. Radde on Broadway, New York, sold copies.[213] However, this network of foreign retailers was less developed than that of its French competitor. Only in several issues published in 1852 can we find the addresses of foreign distribution points: this time in Paris, Strasbourg, London, and New York.[214] The publication mentioned the same addresses in 1862, which suggests that the international distribution network of the *Illustrirte Zeitung* did not expand during this ten-year period.[215] In the second half of the 1860s, the publication listed 26 foreign retailers.[216] Most of the stores located outside of Europe can be found in places with a relatively large number of German migrants. For example, the list mentions retailers in Washington, Cincinnati, Philadelphia, and five different addresses in New York. In South America, we can find stores selling the *Illustrirte Zeitung* in Rio de Janeiro and Valparaiso in Chile, where large numbers of German immigrants lived.[217]

The *Illustrirte Zeitung* often referred to foreign readers in its correspondence column. In 1865, it almost always noted the hometown of letter writers, which provides us with a glimpse of where the readers of the German illustrated newspaper could be found. Of the total 238 letter writers, 141 lived in German-speaking cities. The *Illustrirte Zeitung* answered 21 letters from residents of Berlin and 26 letters from subscribers in Sachsen, the German state where it was published. Supporting previous conclusions about the German readers of the *Illustrirte Zeitung*, 38 letters were written from inside the Austro-Hungarian Empire – 18 from Vienna – but letters also arrived from Agram (Zagreb/Croatia), Laibach (Ljubljana/Slovenia), Triest (Trieste/Italy), Venedig (Venice/Italy), and Pest (Budapest/Romania). The correspondence column also showed that the *Illustrirte Zeitung* had readers in foreign countries: four letters were written from Dutch cities, but letters also arrived from Valparaiso (Chile), Adelaide (Australia), Honolulu (Hawai'i), and Constantinople (Ottoman Empire). The sources mentioned above only provide a sketchy picture of the *Illustrirte Zeitung*'s international audience. In contrast to the somewhat grandiose claims of the publication, they seem to suggest that it was read by small pockets of German-speaking readers outside the heartlands of the Prussian and Austro-Hungarian Empire.

The popularity of the *Illustrated London News* and *l'Illustration* abroad, or at least their perceived influence, can be substantiated by the fact that foreign governments bothered to limit and curtail its circulation. In 1851, an article in the illustrated newspaper itself mentioned how the French post office refused to distribute several influential British publications, including *The Times* and the *Illustrated London News*, during the crisis of 1851.[218] The Dutch *Middelburgsche Courant* observed that the French censor banned the *Illustrated London News* because it contained an illustration depicting Napoleon III 'surrounded by a shredded constitution and bayonets.'[219] In 1867, several Dutch newspapers pointed to an article in the influential French *le Journal des Debats*, describing how the government seized the print runs of several foreign newspapers: it even banned the 'inoffensive' *Illustrated London News* because it published an image of the Parisian ice-skating club.[220] In 1852, both the *Illustrated London News* and *l'Illustration* were impounded at the Madrilenian post office because they contained images of the assassination attempt on Queen Isabelle II.[221]

In his autobiography, Vizetelly wrote that the French government seized the *Illustrated London News* in 1868 after it copied a paragraph from another newspaper that described a plot to assassinate the French emperor. He met with the French censor, hoping to reclaim the 'considerable amount of copies.' The censor

54 *Readers all over the world*

finally agreed, but Vizetelly had to look for the copies in the basement of the 'ministerial hotel' himself:

> I discerned, by the dim light of two or three small lanterns, . . . several little mountains of newspapers – heaps upon heaps of the 'Daily News,' 'Pall Mall Gazette,' . . . the numbers of [the *Illustrated London News*] were only discovered with great difficulty among the paper piles that rose up on either hand.[222]

A similar description can be found in an article concerning the offices of the censors of the Papal States in 1851. In order to limit the amount of English, French, and German newspapers in Rome, the government had instituted an 'enormous rate of postage' of 'a scudo (4s. 3d.).' Besides this tax, two custom agents, 'one a German and the other an Italian,' were charged with detecting 'anti-political and immoral passages' in the foreign publications. As a result, the custom house was filled with 'journals thus tabooed, and whole chests encumber the warehouses filled with papers abandoned by their owners on account of the postage. The *Illustrated London News* . . . was *modestly* taxed at about six shillings per number.'[223]

However, foreign publications, especially illustrated ones, could sometimes benefit from the stringent control exercised over the press in states like France, Prussia, and the Austro-Hungarian Empire. Because censors were concerned with the effects of newspapers and magazines on the masses, they mainly focused on vernacular publications.[224] As a result, the circulation of foreign publications could rise sharply during times of political repression. During the coup of Napoleon III, which reinstated the French Empire in 1851, the prefect of the Pas-de-Calais wrote to the French minister of the interior, remarking that he noticed a sharp increase in the circulation of the *Illustrated London News* in his *département*.[225] Similarly, in the article in which the *Illustrirte Zeitung* defended itself against the allegations of the *Allgemeine Preußische Zeitung*, it noted that the Prussian government exempted both the *Illustrated London News* and *l'Illustration* from paying an extra tax, which had led to an increase in the sale of both publications.[226]

Case study: foreign illustrated newspapers in the Netherlands

The Netherlands provided fertile ground for the illustrated newspapers seeking to expand their readership on the international market due to a number of advantageous conditions. First, the upper classes oriented themselves to foreign cultural zones, and many of them could read French.[227] Second, as Bacot, Martin, and Van Lente have all pointed out, around 1850 many small countries lacked a large enough pool of readers, the essential industries, and the necessary capital to produce their own illustrated newspapers.[228] Third, the Dutch government was relatively unrestrictive when it came to foreign publications entering their country. Finally, the Netherlands was conveniently located between Britain, France, and the German states, which resulted in relatively rapid postal communications.

Despite these advantageous conditions, none of the three major illustrated newspapers explicitly referred to readers in the Netherlands; however, Paul

Schmidt's article confirms that the small European country was a major market for *l'Illustration*. Using the national Dutch digital newspaper archive Delpher, this section demonstrates that the three illustrated newspapers distributed copies in the Netherlands and its colonies and that their owners actively targeted readers in the Dutch market by using advertisements.

Unsurprisingly, the Dutch press usually mentioned the illustrated newspapers when they contained illustrations of Dutch subjects. For example, the liberal *Algemeen Handelsblad* praised *l'Illustration*:

> Of all the foreign illustrated weeklies, which are available in our country, the Parisian *Illustration* is the most widely distributed. This favourable position is not only a result of its beautiful content in general but of its extensive attention to subjects concerning our country, making it a praiseworthy exception in this respect to most foreign magazines.[229]

After this observation, the Dutch newspaper article summarized the illustrations of Dutch subjects that had recently appeared in the French publication: 'The portraits of the King, the Queen and the Prince of Orange, the portrait of Mr de Kock etc. etc.'[230] In 1861, the *Utrechtsche Provinciale en Stads-Courant* mentioned the *Illustrated London News* and *l'Illustration* together after they had published several illustrations of a recent visit of the Royal family to Amsterdam.[231]

At other times, the *Illustrated London News* and *l'Illustration* were the objects of the news themselves. Dutch newspapers, various publications in the Dutch colonies, and even a periodical of Dutch emigrants in the United States had all mentioned the enormous circulation that the British illustrated newspaper achieved during the Great Exhibition of 1851.[232] They also reported on the troublesome relationship between *l'Illustration* and the French censor. In 1851, the *Algemeen Handelsblad* recounted how the censor seized the publication after it could not decipher its weekly rebus.[233] A few years later, several Dutch newspapers reported how the censor had impounded an entire print run of an issue, taking offence to the length of the nose of Napoleon III in one of its illustrations. According to the articles, the censor released the copies after the owners of *l'Illustration* promised that they would portray the 'imperial nose' as having the correct length in the future.[234] The French publication also attracted the attention of the Dutch press when Victor Paulin – the son of one of the founders of *l'Illustration* – sold his majority share in the company to a mysterious Dutch manufacturer after the death of his father in 1859. The 'rich Dutchman,' as several newspapers described him, allegedly paid 1,700,000 francs to Paulin and entrusted the day-to-day running of the publication to Jean-Auguste Marc – the most successful editor of *l'Illustration*.[235]

The Dutch press described the *Illustrated London News* and *l'Illustration* as being widely distributed in the Netherlands, and advertisements in Dutch newspapers confirm this portrayal. In 1851, 'Aubert et Cie,' the French agent of the *Illustrated London News*, regularly advertised for the French edition – the *Illustrated London News en Français* – in the *Algemeen Handelsblad*, the *Nieuwe*

56 Readers all over the world

Rotterdamsche Courant, and the *Nederlandsche Staatscourant*.[236] In 1856, the owners of the *Illustrated London News* placed an advertisement for the regular English edition in the *Algemeen Handelsblad*.[237] The owners of *l'Illustration* also advertised in the *Algemeen Handelsblad* and the *Nieuw Amsterdamsch Handels-en Effectenblad*, albeit in French and not Dutch; even the *Illustrirte Zeitung*, which thus far has been conspicuously absent, advertised in a Dutch newspaper: the *Nieuwe Rotterdamsche Courant*.[238]

In addition to advertisements by the newspapers themselves, several Dutch booksellers also advertised the sale of the three foreign illustrated newspapers. In 1855, the company 'Wed. Krap & Van Duijm' offered to sell the *Illustrated London News* for '35 cents a week.'[239] An advertisement from the same company in the *Nieuwsblad voor den Boekhandel* – a specialized journal for the book and newspaper trade – highlights that the company not only offered individual subscriptions but also acted as a wholesaler, supplying smaller bookshops with copies.[240] Of course, the illustrated newspapers could also be received in the Dutch colonies. Between 1854 and 1856, the competitors 'Van Haren Noman & Kolff' and 'H. M. Van Dorp' in Batavia – the capital of the Dutch Indies at that time – offered annual subscriptions to the *Illustrated London News*, *l'Illustration*, and the *Illustrirte Zeitung*, for 52, 36, and 43 Dutch guilders respectively.[241]

Dutch readers could obtain the foreign illustrated newspapers in two ways. They could receive them at home by writing to the agents of the publications, or they could write to the newspapers' respective offices in London, Paris, and Leipzig. Either way, these individual subscribers had to pay a special tax: all foreign publications had to bear a stamp from the Dutch Inland Revenue.[242] Dutch bookshops imported multiple issues of several French, English, and German publications in packages and thus avoided the extra taxation. An article from 1846 in *l'Illustration* noted that the director of the French postal service was planning to introduce new regulations that taxed all the issues in one packet individually. According to the French editor, this would result in an enormous price increase for their foreign subscribers. This, however, would have serious repercussions for the newspaper as the publication depended on wholesalers like Wed. Krap & Van Duijm, who imported a large number of copies at the same time for its distribution in the Netherlands.[243] An article in the *Leeuwarder Courant* from 1855 refers to this practice, in which customs officers seized packages filled with French newspapers and periodicals at the border, which caused a sharp price increase for these publications in the provincial capital Leeuwarden: 'How high the costs will be, is evident from the fact that the Dutch booksellers sell the widely read *Illustration* for ƒ18, but sent sealed through the post this journal will cost around ƒ28.'[244]

For some, one way around this problem was not to purchase the newspaper at all but to borrow it. Commercial lending libraries all over the Netherlands and its colonies advertised the availability of the three illustrated newspapers in their reading rooms. 'B.H. De Ronden, Utrechtschestraat near the Keizersgracht' in Amsterdam was one of the most fervent advertisers in 1860s, offering membership to his reading room for '50 guilders a year.'[245] The 'reading institution' of 'De Jong Zijlstra' in the small provincial capital of Middelburg offered a shared subscription to just the *Illustrated London News* for '50 cents a quarter.'[246] Reading rooms were also popular in the Dutch colonies, where subscriptions to both Dutch and foreign publications were considerably more expensive. The 'Reading Room of Padang,' located in the colonial capital on the Indonesian island of Sumatra, offered a wide range of publications, including the three illustrated newspapers. Admittance for a day was priced at 50 cents, while a quarterly subscription cost three guilders.[247] Additionally, advertisements reveal that the illustrated newspapers could also be found on the 'reading tables' of pubs and coffee houses in the Netherlands.[248] For example, 'De Brakke Grond,' which is still a well-known pub in the centre of Amsterdam, boasted not only a 'new and elegant POOL table (the best of Amsterdam according to experts)' but also 'The Illustrated London News, L'Illustration, die Illustrirte Zeitung.'[249]

Conclusion

Throughout this chapter, we have seen how the three most well-known illustrated newspapers of the mid-nineteenth century claimed to have had readers all over the world. These statements stand in sharp contrast to most scholarship on the illustrated press, which, being concerned with the production of national identity, assumed that their readership was mostly national. The analysis of these newspapers in this broader context further demonstrates that the transnational distribution of all three illustrated newspapers and the importance of audiences outside the borders of a specific nation-state have been underestimated.

The audiences of the three illustrated newspapers can be located on four geographical levels: the city, the nation, the colony, and abroad. In this regard, the differences between the *Illustrated London News*, on the one hand, and *l'Illustration* and the *Illustrirte Zeitung*, on the other, are striking. The British publication was produced, distributed, and read on a massive scale, while the circulation of its French and German counterparts remained limited. Only the *Illustrated London News* can, for example, be said to have had a truly national readership.

The transnational distribution of all three illustrated newspapers, however, was significant, but it is hard to establish exactly how many copies were sent abroad. Paul Schmidt's article has revealed that *l'Illustration* sent around 50 per cent of its copies abroad in 1863, but it is unclear as to which countries and in what ratio these copies were distributed. Furthermore, we do not know whether the transnational audience of the French illustrated newspaper was as sizeable for the entire period under examination. Similar ambiguities arise for the colonial audience of the *Illustrated London News*. It has become clear that between 8 and 11 per cent of its copies were sent to the Australian colonies in 1863. However, future research has yet to reveal whether the readership in the Australian colonies remained as large during the entire period or whether the different British colonies were equally important.

In 1860, a reading room in the small Dutch colonial town of Padang lured subscribers with the availability of the *Illustrated London News*, *l'Illustration*, and the *Illustrirte Zeitung*, perfectly illustrating the fact that all three periodicals

58 *Readers all over the world*

were distributed throughout the world and contributed to the formation of a transnational visual culture of the news: Dutch colonists were able to share an image of the world with fellow readers in the large capitals of Europe. Four years later, in 1864, readers in Padang could also subscribe to the *Hollandsche Illustratie* (Dutch Illustration): a Dutch publication modelled after the *Illustrated London News*. Contrary to what its name might suggest, this new publication did not provide Dutch readers with a typical Dutch image of the world. As the next chapter shows, the *Hollandsche Illustratie* was filled with images bought from French and German publications, intimating that the transnational trade in images of the news contributed to the formation of a transnational visual news culture.

Notes

1 Sinnema, "Around the World without a Gaze," 144.
2 Ibid.
3 Ibid., 148.
4 "The Illustrated London News," *Illustrated London News* (29 October 1859).
5 **BNA1:** "The British Army in China," *Jersey Independent and Daily Telegraph* (6 July 1860).
6 Colclough, "Readers and Readership: Real or Historical Readership," 530.
7 Altick, *The English Common Reader*, 10.
8 Brantlinger, *The Reading Lesson*, 16.
9 Fraser, Green, and Johnston, *Gender and the Victorian Periodical*, 69.
10 Nicholson, "The Digital Turn," 64.
11 Mussell, *Nineteenth-Century Press in the Digital Age*, 155.
12 Smits, "Problems and Possibilities of Digital Newspaper and Periodical Archives," 139–40.
13 "Our First Anniversary," *Illustrated London News* (27 May 1843).
14 Martin and Bodnar, "The Illustrated Press under Siege," 69–73.
15 Beetham, "Towards a Theory of the Periodical as a Publishing Genre," 19–31; Martin and Bodnar, "The Illustrated Press under Siege," 70; Martin, "Nineteenth Century Wood Engravers at Work," 3–4; Brown, "Reconstructing Representation," 5–38.
16 Beetham, "Towards a Theory of the Periodical as a Publishing Genre," 19–31.
17 Wolff and Fox, "Pictures from Magazines," 560.
18 "Office of the Illustrated London News," *Illustrated London News* (8 October 1842).
19 "A Saturday Scene in Our Publishing-Office," *Illustrated London News* (25 March 1843).
20 "No. 198, Strand," *Illustrated London News* (24 May 1851).
21 "Die Ausgabe der Illustrirten Zeitung," *Illustrirte Zeitung* (30 August 1862).
22 "Bureau d'abonnement de l'Illustration," *l'Illustration* (2 March 1844).
23 Martin and Bodnar, "The Illustrated Press under Siege," 73.
24 "Une des succursales de nos bureaux": "Courier de Paris," *l'Illustration* (20 April 1850).
25 "Les kiosques lumineux," *l'Illustration* (29 August 1857).
26 Schwartz, *Spectacular Realities*, 13–20.
27 "A Saturday Scene in Our Publishing-Office," *Illustrated London News* (25 March 1843).
28 "Une rue souterraine de Paris," *l'Illustration* (24 February 1844); "Ouverture du Musée de l'hôtel de Cluny et du palais des Thermes," *l'Illustration* (23 March 1844).
29 "The 'Illustrated London News' Published Every Saturday: Thirty Engravings: Price sixpence," *Illustrated London News* (14 May 1842).
30 "Quelques mois après, l'Illustrated London News comptait près de 50,000 abonnés": "Curiosités de l'Angleterre. I. Les Annonces," *l'Illustration* (2 February 1850).

31 "Les propriétaires de l'Illustrated London News ont une voiture qui erre du matin au soir dans tous les quartiers fashionables uniquement pour annoncer leur journal.": Ibid.

32 Wolff and Fox, "Pictures from Magazines," 560; Fox, "The Development of Social Reportage in English Periodical Illustration during the 1840s and Early 1850s," 90–2.

33 Wolff and Fox, "Pictures from Magazines," 561.

34 Hultzsch, "The Crowd and the Building," 371.

35 These were later bundled and published separately. Boulevards de Paris, Paris: l'Illustration, 1846.

36 "Qui représentera la transformation de Paris dans tous ses détails et dans son ensemble": "Avis Important," l'Illustration (22 December 1860).

37 Clarke, European Cities and Towns, 226.

38 Schäfer, Bürgertum in der Krise, 27; Green, Fatherlands, 29.

39 Clarke, European Cities and Towns, 226; Chevalier, Labouring Classes and Dangerous Classes in Paris during the First Half of the Nineteenth Century, 182.

40 Clarke, European Cities and Towns, 225.

41 Hobbs, "When the Provincial Press Was the National Press," 20–1.

42 Ibid., 20.

43 Ibid., 22.

44 "A Few Words to the Clergy," Illustrated London News (27 August 1842).

45 **BNA1:** "Sumptuous Present to Its Subscribers by the Pictorial Times," Manchester Times (16 September 1843).

46 **BNA1:** "Published Weekly: Price Sixpence, Stamped, Embellished with Thirty Engravings in Each number, the Illustrated London News," Manchester Times (16 September 1843).

47 Ibid.

48 Ibid.

49 Ibid.

50 **BNA1:** "Published Weekly. Price Sixpence, Stamped, Embellished with Thirty Engravings in Each number, the Illustrated London News," Leeds Mercury (19 August 1843); Derby Mercury (30 August 1843); Sheffield Independent (9 September 1843); Manchester Courier and Lancashire General Advertiser (9 September 1843); Newcastle Courant (22 September 1843); Manchester Times (30 September 1843); Bristol Mercury (30 September 1843); Dublin Evening Post (12 October 1843); Hampshire Telegraph (16 October 1843); Wexford Conservative (28 October 1843); Sligo Champion (4 November 1843); The Hull Packet (17 November 1843); Derby Mercury (22 November 1843); Durham County Advertiser (1 December 1843); North Wales Chronicle (19 December 1843); Coventry Standard (22 December 1843).

51 **BNA1:** "Liverpool (From Our Special Correspondent): The Amusements and Literature of the People: Letter XVI," Morning Chronicle (2 September 1850).

52 Ibid.

53 **BNA1:** "The London Press," Greenock Advertiser (11 April 1863); "Circulation of the London Papers," Paisley Herald and Renfrewshire Advertiser (11 April 1863); "The Prince"s Wedding and the Paper trade," Southern Reporter (16 April 1863); "From Our Aberdeen Correspondent," Dundee Advertiser (24 March 1863); "Marriage of the Prince of Wales: Newspaper Circulation," Elign Courier (17 April 1863).

54 **GB5:** Schmidt, "Pariser Illustrirte Journale: L'Illustration," 22.

55 "Abonnement," l'Illustration (4 March 1843).

56 "Abonnements pour Paris et les départements," l'Illustration (18 August 1855).

57 "Guerre d'Italie," l'Illustration (12 November 1859).

58 "Correspondance," l'Illustration (22 March 1845).

59 "On s'abonnne," l'Illustration (30 January 1847); (6 February 1847); (13 February 1847); (27 February 1847); (6 March 1847); (13 March 1847); (20 March 1847);

60 Readers all over the world

(14 August 1847); (25 September 1847); (25 December 1847); (12 February 1848); (4 March 1848); (11 March 1848).

60 "Wir haben bereits in unserer ersten Erklärung ausgesprochen, dass wir vor allem Deutsch sein wollen und die Angelegenheiten des Auslandes nur insoweit ein Platz einräumen können, als dieselben von Einfluss auf Deutschland sind": "Briefwechsel mit Allen für Alle," *Illustrirte Zeitung* (25 November 1843).

61 Boterman, *Moderne geschiedenis van Duitsland*, 58–9, 105.

62 "Briefwechsel mit Allen für Alle," *Illustrirte Zeitung* (1 January 1844).

63 "Dass es uns gelungen ist, die entfernsten stammverwandten mit dem Mutterlande in neue Verbindung zu setzen, und dazu beigetragen zu haben, um das Band der Deutsche Stamme in allen ihren Abstammungen und Verzweigungen fester zu knüpfen": "Vorwort," *Illustrirte Zeitung* III (1843).

64 "Über den Bezug der Illustrirte Zeitung in den Österreichischen Kronländern," *Illustrirte Zeitung* (18 June 1853).

65 The German word 'expedition' is hard to translate. It is the part of a company that is responsible for the distribution of its goods – 'die Versandabteilung.' In this context, it refers to the part of the post office that is responsible for the local distribution of newspapers. The abbreviation 'K.K.' stands for 'royal and imperial,' a reference to the fact that the Habsburg patriarch was the king of Austria, the king of Hungary, and the emperor of the entire ancient German Empire at the same time. "Illustrirte Zeitung. Mit jährlich über 1000 in den Text gedruckten Abbildungen," *Illustrirte Zeitung* (4 September 1852).

66 Ibid.

67 **GB2:** The article suggests that the *Illustrirte Zeitung* had 370 subscribers in Vienna. However, it could also be possible that 370 copies in total were distributed in the first half of 1859, which would mean that only around 15 subscribers received the paper each week. Whatever may be the case, the relative popularity of the *Illustrirte Zeitung* can be deduced from the fact that only 170 copies of *die Gartenlaube* – a week, or in total – were distributed by the same office. "Das Zeitungswesen in Österreich," *Austria. Wochenschrift fur Volkswirtschaft und Statistik*, vol. 12, no. 1 (1860): 18–19.

68 "Vorwort," *Illustrirte Zeitung* V (1845).

69 "Briefwechsel mit Allen für Alle," *Illustrirte Zeitung* (10 February 1849).

70 "Erklärung," *Illustrirte Zeitung* (24 February 1849).

71 Goldstein, *Political Censorship*, 41.

72 "An unsere Leser," *Illustrirte Zeitung* (1 July 1848).

73 "Briefwechsel mit Allen für Alle," *Illustrirte Zeitung* (26 Augustus 1848).

74 "Briefwechsel mit Allen für Alle," *Illustrirte Zeitung* (3 November 1849).

75 "De Besteuerung der Presse," *Illustrirte Zeitung* (15 August 1857).

76 "An unsere Abonnenten in den K. K. Österreichischen Staaten," *Illustrirte Zeitung* (26 December 1857).

77 **GB2:** "German Illustrated Papers," *The Graphic* (6 December 1890).

78 "Briefwechsel mit Allen für Alle," *Illustrirte Zeitung* (21 December 1861).

79 "Allgemeine Preußische Zeitung," *Illustrirte Zeitung* (11 January 1862).

80 "Ermäßigung der Preußische Zeitungssteuer," *Illustrirte Zeitung* (18 January 1862).

81 Darwin, *The Empire Project*, 57–9.

82 MacKenzie, *Propaganda and Empire*, 20–1; Springhall, "Up Guards and at Them," 51.

83 Sebe, "Justifying "New Imperialism,"" 50.

84 Wesseling, *Verdeel en heers*, 144.

85 Ciarlo, *Advertising Empire*, 170.

86 Aldrich, *Greater France*, 24–6; Wesseling, *Verdeel en heers*, 27.

87 Aldrich, *Greater France*, 94.

88 "Service des postes de France et nouveau prix d'abonnement pur l'étranger," *l'Illustration* (27 December 1856).

Readers all over the world   61

89 "Colonies et établissements Français," *l'Illustration* (19 January 1867); "Tarif des abonnements a l'Illustration," *l'Illustration* (30 January 1869).
90 Ibid.
91 "The Illustrated London News," *Illustrated London News* (29 October 1859).
92 One guinea was worth 21 shillings, or 252 pence. The gold seeker was prepared to pay 42 times the normal price of the Illustrated London News. "News-Store in the Ballarat Gold-Fields," *Illustrated London News* (3 June 1853).
93 Ibid.
94 "Australian Hut," *Illustrated London News* (17 March 1849).
95 "The Illustrated London News," *Illustrated London News* (29 October 1859).
96 "Abolition of the Compulsory Newspaper-Stamp: Permanent Enlargement of the Illustrated London News," *Illustrated London News* (30 June 1855).
97 Many of the newspapers listed below repeatedly published the advertisement. I have only listed the first publication date. "Published Weekly: Price Sixpence, Stamped, Embellished with Thirty Engravings in Each number, the Illustrated London News," *The Singapore Free Press and Mercantile Advertiser* (17 April 1845); *The Sydney Morning Herald* (17 June 1845); *Morning Chronicle* (21 June 1845); *The Royal Gazette* (24 June 1845); *The Cornwall Chronicle* (25 October 1845).
98 **SING:** "Published Weekly: Price Sixpence, Stamped, Embellished with Thirty Engravings in Each number, the Illustrated London News," *The Singapore Free Press and Mercantile Advertiser* (17 April 1845).
99 Ibid.
100 **BERM:** "Published Weekly: Price Sixpence, Stamped, Embellished with Thirty Engravings in Each number, the Illustrated London News," *The Royal Gazette* (24 June 1845).
101 **TR1:** "Published Weekly: Price Sixpence, Stamped, Embellished with Thirty Engravings in Each number, the Illustrated London News," *The Australian* (4 November 1845); *Hawkesbury Courier and Agricultural and General Advertiser* (22 January 1846).
102 **SING:** "Published Weekly: Price Sixpence, Stamped, Embellished with Thirty Engravings in Each number, the Illustrated London News," *The Singapore Free Press and Mercantile Advertiser* (19 November 1846).
103 **TR1:** "Published Weekly: Price Sixpence, Stamped, Embellished with Thirty Engravings in Each number, the Illustrated London News," *The Courier* (30 January 1847).
104 Wood, "Taxes on Knowledge," 454.
105 See for example: Charles Knight, *The Newspaper Stamp and the Duty on Paper Viewed in Their Effects Upon the Diffusion of Knowledge*. London: Charles Knight, 1836.
106 "The Illustrated London News," *Illustrated London News* (30 August 1851).
107 Wood, "Taxes on Knowledge," 454.
108 "The Illustrated London News," *Illustrated London News* (23 June 1855).
109 Robinson, *Britain"s Post Office*, 174.
110 "A Penny Stamp in the Illustrated London News from 1849," *Illustrated London News* (1849).
111 Robinson, *Britain"s Post Office*, 165, 189.
112 Ibid., 174.
113 Ibid., 189.
114 "Newspaper Correspondence across the Sea," *Illustrated London News* (18 June 1853).
115 "Ein transatlantisches Penny Porto," *Illustrirte Zeitung* (17 September 1853).
116 "The Newspaper Stamp," *Illustrated London News* (14 April 1855).
117 Ibid.
118 "Imperial Parliament: The Newspaper Stamp," *Illustrated London News* (28 April 1855).
119 "Abolition of the Compulsory Newspaper-Stamp: Permanent Enlargement of the 'Illustrated London News'," *Illustrated London News* (30 June 1855).
120 "Cheap Newspapers," *Illustrated London News* (3 March 1855).

62 Readers all over the world

121 "The Illustrated London News," *Illustrated London News* (19 May 1855).
122 Ibid.
123 Ibid.
124 "Abolition of the Compulsory Newspaper-Stamp: Permanent Enlargement of the 'Illustrated London News'," *Illustrated London News* (30 June 1855).
125 "The Illustrated London News," *Illustrated London News* (21 July 1855).
126 See: "Newspapers to Canada. To the editor of the Illustrated London News," *Illustrated London News* (30 June 1855); "Newspaper Postage to India: To the Editor of the Illustrated London News," *Illustrated London News* (30 June 1855); "Newspapers to the Colonies," *Illustrated London News* (11 August 1855).
127 "The Illustrated London News," *Illustrated London News* (21 July 1855).
128 Ibid.
129 "The Illustrated London News," *Illustrated London News* (21 July 1855).
130 "Foreign Postage," *Illustrated London News* (2 February 1856).
131 "Newspapers to Canada: To the Editor of the Illustrated London News," *Illustrated London News* (30 June 1855).
132 "Newspaper Postage to India: To the Editor of the Illustrated London News," *Illustrated London News* (30 June 1855).
133 "Newspapers to the Colonies," *Illustrated London News* (11 August 1855).
134 Putnis, "News, Time and Imagined Community in Colonial Australia," 106; Putnis, "The British Transoceanic Steamship Press," 69–70.
135 "To Canadian Subscribers," *Illustrated London News* (18 October 1862); "To Canadian Subscribers," *Illustrated London News* (13 December 1862).
136 Dowling, "Destined Not to Survive," 95.
137 I previously published an extended version of this case study in *Media History*: Smits, "Looking for The Illustrated London News," 80–99.
138 **TR1:** The article from the *Age* is copied in several Australian newspapers: "The English Periodicals and Newspapers," the *Age* (26 May 1863); *Bendigo Adviser* (28 May 1863); *Gippsland Guardian* (12 June 1863); *Portland Guardian and Normamby General Adviser* (29 June 1863); *Border Watch* (10 July 1863).
139 Ibid.
140 "Illustrated London News: Waugh & Cox," The Empire (17 January 1854).
141 **TR1:** Many of the newspapers listed below repeatedly published Piddington''s advertisement. I only list the first publication date. "Illustrated London News," *The Goulburn Herald and County of Argyle Advertiser* (21 August 1852); "Illustrated London News and Punch," *The Maitland Mercury and Hunter River General Advertiser* (29 January 1853); "Illustrated London News," *Bathurst Free Press and Mining Journal* (18 February 1854); "Illustrated London News," *Illawarra Mercury* (10 March 1856); *The Armidale Express and New England General Advertiser* (12 July 1856); "Illustrated London News," *Northern Times* (24 January 1857); "Illustrated London News," *Kiama Examiner* (5 February 1859); "Illustrated London News," *Wagga Wagga Express and Murrumbidgee District Advertiser* (7 May 1859).
142 "Illustrated London News," The Empire (16 January 1852); "Illustrated London News," *The Moreton Bay Courier* (7 August 1852).
143 **PP:** "Illustrated London News," *The New Zealander* (16 April 1851).
144 **PP:** "A Delinquent Letter Carrier: To the Editor of the Lyttelton Times," *Lyttelton Times* (6 February 1864).
145 **PP:** "Newspapers for Hokitika," *Lyttelton Times* (9 November 1865).
146 **PP:** "Harapipi," *New Zealand Herald* (17 April 1868); "Tauranga," *New Zealand Herald* (4 May 1868).
147 **TR1:** "The Sydney Post Office versus the Illustrated London News: To Country Subscribers of the 'Illustrated News'," *The Sydney Morning Herald* (25 October 1851); *The Empire* (27 October 1851); *Bell's Life in Sydney and Sporting Reviewer* (29 October 1851); *The Goulburn Herald and County of Argyle Adviser* (29 October 1851);

Bathurst Free Press and Mining Journal (5 November 1851); *The Moreton Bay Courier* (19 November 1851).

148 **TR1:** "Post-office Grievances," *Bell's Life in Sydney and Sporting Reviewer* (29 October 1853); "Postal Matters Again," *The Empire* (31 October 1853); "The Illustrated London News: To the Editor of the Sydney Morning Herald," *Sydney Morning Herald* (3 November 1853); "The Postal Dispute as to 'the Illustrated London News'," *The Maitland Mercury and the Hunter River General Adviser* (5 November 1853).

149 **TR:** "Sydney, November 2nd 1853," *Sydney Morning Herald* (2 November 1853).

150 It is hard to place a number on the total circulation of the *Illustrated London News*. The special issue concerning the wedding of the Prince of Wales in 1863 sold 300,000 copies, but it is unlikely that this huge number was a regular occurrence. The last regular circulation numbers mentioned by Richard Altick date from 1853 (123,000). I place the regular circulation of the *Illustrated London News* around 150,000 to 200,000 copies, which is an educated guess. Earlier popular special issues of the *Illustrated London News*, such as the one concerning the opening of the Great Exhibition in 1851, resulted in a doubling of its circulation. Altick, *The English Common Reader*, 395.

151 **TR:** "Melbourne," *The Star* (21 December 1861).

152 Ibid.

153 **PP:** "View of Nelson," *Nelson Examiner and New Zealand Chronicle* (19 June 1858).

154 Ibid.

155 **PP:** "View of the Procession and Lyttelton Harbour," *Lyttelton Times* (31 December 1863).

156 "*The Illustrated London News*, ... ce magnifique journal hebdomadaire, qui a servi de modèle à l'Illustration, est fait pour exciter la curiosité des Anglais qui résident en France . . . L'Illustrated London News est intéressant également pour les Français qui étudient la langue anglaise.": "The Illustrated London News," *l'Illustration* (27 May 1843) cited in: Bacot, *La presse illustrée au xix siècle*, 53.

157 "To Correspondents: Notice to French Subscribers," *Illustrated London News* (15 February 1845).

158 This advertisement is regularly repeated. See for example: "To Our Continental Subscribers," *Illustrated London News* (27 July 1861).

159 The Illustrirte Zeitung also advertised in the Illustrated London News. See: "The Illustrated London News," *Illustrirte Zeitung* (13 July 1861); "Leipziger Illustrirte Zeitung," *Illustrated London News* (30 November 1861).

160 Cantor, "Reporting the Great Exhibition," 183.

161 Ibid.

162 The *Illustrated London News* proudly reprinted the article "Speaking to the Eye," *Illustrated London News* (24 May 1851); **GB:** "Speaking to the Eye," *The Economist* (17 May 1851).

163 "The Illustrated London News: Its Supplements and Double Numbers," *Illustrated London News* (27 December 1851).

164 "Speaking to the Eye," *Illustrated London News* (24 May 1851).

165 See for the advertisements: "The Great Exhibition of 1851: The Illustrated London News in Three Languages"; "Grande exposition de 1851. L'Illustrated London News en trois langages"; "The Illustrated London News in drei Sprachen. Die Grosse Kunst- und Gewerbe Ausstellung aller Nationen, in 1851," *Illustrated London News* (4 May 1851).

166 "The 'Illustrated London News' en Français," *Illustrated London News* (17 May 1851).

167 Ibid.

168 Ibid.

169 Bacot, *La presse illustrée au xixe siècle*, 84.

170 Cockerham, "Gautier, Guys, le "Palais de Cristal" et l'Illustrated London News en français de 1851," 969.

64 *Readers all over the world*

171 "Notre Office a Paris, Place de la Bourse," *Illustrated London News en Français* (10 May 1851).

172 "Vorwort," *Illustrirte Zeitung*, vol. 16 (1851).

173 "Cette fine plaisanterie britannique qui chatouille le palais comme une bouteille de gin, et égaie l'esprit comme un verre de cidre.": E. Texier, "Voyage a travers les Journeaux," *l'Illustration* (3 January 1851).

174 "Que tel jour, à telle heure, le capitaine Bathurst est arrivé d'Egypte, que le colonel Thompson reviendra les mois prochain des Grandes-Indes avec sa femme et sa fille, et que le vicomte Fielding se dispose à partir pour Rome.": Ibid.

175 Ibid.

176 "'L'Illustration' and the 'Illustrated London News.' Shocking case of unfounded alarm," *Illustrated London News* (4 January 1851).

177 According to the *Illustrated London News*, *l'Illustration* had bought all the illustrations of the revolution in Paris of 1848 it published. Ibid.

178 Ibid.

179 Ibid.

180 "L'élite de la presse Parisienne"; "Deutsche Schriftsteller": "Prix Six Pence (60 Centimes) le Numero: The Illustrated London News en Français," *Illustrated London News* (27 April 1851); "Sechs Pence (5 Silbergroschen) die Nummer. Die Deutsche Ausgabe der Illustrated London News," *Illustrated London News* (27 April 1851).

181 "Sich auf die oft kargen und einseitigen Berichte beschränken mussten, welche deutschen Zeitungen zu geben erlaubt sind": "An den Redacteur der Deutschen Illustrirten Zeitung," *Illustrated London News. Deutsch* (24 May 1851).

182 "Unser Vaterland, ist in einem ruhmvollen Streit mit Großbritannien begriffen in dem Wettlaufe des Kunstfleißes, und es kann aus diesem Streite nur siegreich hervorgehen, wenn es England auch darin nacheifert, dass es die Fleiße die Freiheit gibt.": "Unsere Zeitung und die Ausstellung im Hyde-Park," *Illustrated London News. Deutsch* (3 May 1851).

183 "La Liberté en Angleterre," *Illustrated London News en Français* (3 May 1851).

184 "Die politischen Verhältnisse Deutschlands und die Verationen, welche die deutsche Regierungen dem Postvertrieb englischer Zeitungen entgegensetzen, geben dem Unternehmen nicht die sichere Grundlage, welche für sein Gedeihen erforderlich scheint": "An unsere Leser," *Illustrated London News. Deutsch* (21 June 1851).

185 "Avis," *Illustrated London News en Français* (25 October 1851).

186 "Il fallait un organe international, en dehors de la politique, de ses calculs, de ses préventions, de ses haines," "Notre Message," *Illustrated London News en Français* (1 November 1851).

187 "France," *Illustrated London News* (14 January 1860).

188 These kinds of notices are regularly published from 1866 onwards. See for example: "Avis a nos Abonnes sur le continent," *Illustrated London News* (16 September 1866); "The Illustrated London News may be bought in Paris," *Illustrated London News* (17 June 1869).

189 This advertisement is also regularly published. See for example: "To Our Continental Subscribers," *Illustrated London News* (27 July 1861).

190 "Postage to the East Indies, China, Australia, etc.," *Illustrated London News* (14 January 1860).

191 "Table of Postage Rates for Stamped and Unstamped Newspapers for the British Colonies and Foreign Colonies," *Illustrated London News* (1 September 1855).

192 "To Correspondents," *Illustrated London News* (2 February 1856).

193 See for example: "Postage of the Illustrated London News for This Week," *Illustrated London News* (6 February 1864).

194 Ibid.

195 "Post-Office, Boston, U.S.," *Illustrated London News* (24 June 1843).

Readers all over the world 65

196 **GB3:** "Redding & Company. No. 8 State Street. Boston: General Agency and Periodical Depot for the United States of American and Foreign Periodicals and Cheap Publications," *The New Mirror* (18 November 1843); "Notices of Literary Works, &c. Foreign Newspapers and Periodicals – Redding & Co.," *The Symbol* (15 December 1843).

197 **GB3:** "Burgess & Stringer: Corner of Broadway and Ann Street. New York. General Agency and Periodical Depot for the United States of American and Foreign Periodicals and Cheap Publications," *The New Mirror* (14 October 1843); "General Publishing Agency for the United States and Europe. at the Sun Office," *The New Mirror* (18 November 1843).

198 **BNA1:** "Literary Extracts (from Rubio's 'Rambles in the United States and Canada'). Cheap Literature in America," *West Kent Guardian* (13 December 1845).

199 **NYT:** "Pictorial Papers," *New York Times* (26 April 1853).

200 Mackay, *Forty Years' Recollections of Life, Literature, and Public Affairs*, 2:375.

201 Ibid.

202 Ibid., 2:379–81.

203 Ibid., 2:392.

204 "La liste de ses abonnes est la liste des noms les plus distingués dans tous les pays. tous les rangs. tous les genres, *à* tous les titres": "L'Illustration. Journal Universel. Orné de gravures sur bois sur tous les sujets actuels," *l'Illustration* (6 September 1845).

205 "On s'abonne," *l'Illustration* (4 March 1843).

206 **BNA6:** "l'Illustration," *The Examiner* (10 June 1843).

207 **BNA6:** "Police Intelligence: Mansion House," *Morning Post* (18 May 1844).

208 "On s'abonne," *l'Illustration* (17 June 1843); "On s'abonne," *l'Illustration* (22 March 1845); "On s'abonne," *l'Illustration* (28 June 1845).

209 "Denn um neun Uhr müssen die Exemplare für England und Holland zur Post.": P. Schmidt, "Pariser Illustrirte Journale," *Journal für Buchdruckerkunst, Schriftgießerei und verwandte Fächer (*29 June 1863).

210 Ibid.

211 Ibid.

212 "Zehn Jahre," *Illustrirte Zeitung* (2 July 1853).

213 "Briefwechsel mit Allen für Alle," *Illustrirte Zeitung* (10 January 1846).

214 "Illustrirte Zeitung. Mit jährlich über 1000 in den Text gedruckten Abbildungen," *Illustrirte Zeitung* (4 September 1852).

215 "Illustrirte Zeitung," *Illustrirte Zeitung* (4 July 1863).

216 "Abonnementsbedinungen," *Illustrirte Zeitung* vol. 53 (1869).

217 Ibid.

218 "The English Press and the French Post-Office," *Illustrated London News* (20 December 1851).

219 "Door eene verscheurde constitutie en bajonetten omgeven.": "Frankrijk," *Middelburgsche Courant* (23 December 1851).

220 "Algemeen Overzicht," *Nieuwe Rotterdamsche Courant* (14 February 1867); "Parijs," *Opregte Haarlemsche Courant* (16 February 1867).

221 **BNA1:** "Spain," *Herts Guardian* (6 March 1852); "Gleanings of the Week," *Bradford Observer* (11 March 1852).

222 Vizettely. *Glances Back through Seventy Years*, Vol. 2, 205–7.

223 **BNA1:** "Foreign Correspondence: Rome," *London Daily News* (27 August 1851).

224 Goldstein, *Political Censorship*, 41–2.

225 Collins, *The Government and the Newspaper Press in France, 1814–1881*, 115.

226 "Allgemeine Preußische Zeitung," *Illustrirte Zeitung* (11 January 1862).

227 De Vries. *Een stad vol lezers*, 343–50; De Vries. "Lezende burgers," 43–4.

228 Bacot. *La presse illustrée au xixe siècle*. 39–41; Martin. *Images at War*, 13; Van Lente. "Illustratietechniek." 269.

66   *Readers all over the world*

229 **DEL1:** "Geen enkel der vreemde geïllustreerde weekbladen is bij ons ten lande zoo algemeen verspreid als de Parijssche Illustration. Deze voorkeur boven zoo vele anderen heeft het zich niet alleen verworven door zijn fraaijen inhoud in het algemeen, maar ook vooral omdat het zoo dikwerf onderwerpen, ons vaderland betreffende, op uitvoerige wijze behandelt en in dit opzigt eene loffelijke uitzondering maakt op de meeste vreemde bladen."; "Binnenlandsche Berigten," *Algemeen Handelsblad* (4 June 1862).

230 Ibid.

231 **DEL1:** "Utrecht," *Utrechtsche Provinciale en Stads-Courant* (29 April 1861).

232 See for the Dutch newspapers: **DEL1:** "Algemene Berigten," *Bredasche Courant* (11 May 1851); *Leydse Courant* (12 Mai 1851); *Groninger Courant* (13 May 1851). See for colonial newspapers: "De wereldtentoonstelling in Londen," *Curaçaosche Courant* (14 June 1851). See for the emigrant newspaper: "Het grootste debiet," *Sheboygan Nieuwsbode* (15 August 1851).

233 **DEL1:** "Parijs, zaterdag 13 december," *Algemeen Handelsblad* (16 December 1851).

234 **DEL1:** "Franse Post," *Algemeen Handelsblad* (4 June 1855); *Rotterdamsche Courant* (4 June 1855); *Provinciale Overijsselsche en Zwolsche Courant* (5 June 1855).

235 **DEL1:** "Buitenland: Frankrijk," *Nieuw Amsterdamsch Handels- en Effectenblad* (29 March 1860); "Buitenlandse Berigten: Frankrijk," *De Tijd* (21 April 1860); "Frankrijk," *Middelburgsche Courant* (21 April 1860); "Frankrijk. Parijs, 19 april," *Leydse Courant* (23 April 1860).

236 **DEL1:** "The Illustrated London News en Français," *Nieuwe Rotterdamsche Courant* (18 April, 26 April, 1 May, 5 May 1851); "The Illustrated London News en Français," *Nederlandsche Staatscourant* (23 April, 25 April, 27 April, 2 May 1851); "The Illustrated London News en Français," *Algemeen Handelsblad* (15 April, 29 April 1851).

237 **DEL1:** "The Illustrated London News. PRIJS VIJF-EN-TWINTIG CENTS," *Algemeen Handelsblad* (15 May, 16 June, 1 July, 15 July 1856).

238 **DEL1:** "L'Illustration," *Algemeen Handelsblad* (8 July 1862); "L'Illustration," *Nieuw Amsterdamsch Handels- en Effectenblad* (19 July 1862); "Illustrirte Zeitung für 1857," *Nieuw Rotterdamsche Courant* (16 February 1857).

239 **DEL1:** "The Illustrated London News, Wed. Krap & Van Duijm," *Nieuw Rotterdamsche Courant* (25 December 1855).

240 **DEL1:** "The Illustrated London News, Wed. Krap & Van Duijm," *Nieuwsblad voor den Boekhandel* (27 December 1855).

241 **DEL1:** "Geïllustreerde tijdschriften. Jaargang 1855. Per mail arriverende," *Javabode* (26 August 1854); "H. M. Van Dorp, Batavia," *Javabode* (26 August 1854).

242 Hemels, *De pers onder het juk van een fiscale druk*, 66.

243 "A nos lecteurs a l'étranger," *l'Illustration* (27 June 1846).

244 "Hoe hoog die kosten alsdan zullen loopen, blijkt enkel daaruit, dat de ook in ons land veel gelezene Illustration door boekhandelaars wordt geleverd voor ƒ18, doch per post en gezegeld verzonden, op ruim ƒ28 zal komen.": **DEL:** "Leeuwarden, 26 april," *Leeuwarder Courant* (27 April 1855).

245 **DEL1:** "Leesbibliotheek van B. H. de Ronden," *Nieuw Amsterdamsch Handels- en Effectenblad* (15 February 1858).

246 **DEL1:** "Lees-inrichting," *Middelburgse Courant* (12 August 1856).

247 **DEL1:** "Leeskamer te Padang," *Pandangsch Nieuws- en Advertentieblad* (26 May 1860).

248 See for example: **DEL:** "Café Neuf," *Algemeen Handelsblad* (26 April 1864); "Café Momus," *Algemeen Handelsblad* (19 February 1871).

249 **DEL1:** "Het nieuwe elegante BILLARD (volgens oordeel van Deskundigen, het fraaiste wat hier ter stede bespeeld wordt)": "Café de Brakke Grond," *Algemeen Handelsblad* (30 October 1863).

2 The transnational trade in illustrations of the news, 1842–1870

Introduction

In *Die deutschen Zeitschriften und die Entstehung der öffentlichen Meinung* (1866), German historian Heinrich Wuttke accurately predicted the future of the press. Most local, and even some national, newspapers would disappear because international conglomerates, controlled by 'telegraph institutes,' would provide the same content to readers all over the world.[1] He had even observed the first signs of this future: 'Illustrated newspapers in London, Paris, and Leipzig traded illustrations and articles so that only one third of their content had to be new.'[2] Wuttke was not the only one to suspect that major illustrated newspapers worked closely together. As Frederic Hudson wrote in *Journalism in the United States* (1873): 'Now the proprietors [of the illustrated newspapers] sell and exchange electrotypes of the most popular pictures. The London *Illustrated News* sends quite a number of its engravings to Paris, Berlin, and Vienna. Some reach New York.'[3]

In contrast to later historians, Wuttke and Hudson underline the transnational nature of nineteenth-century illustrated press. Following this line of inquiry, this chapter describes the trade in illustrations of the news between these publications in the period 1842–1870. It argues that this exchange did not come to an abrupt end around 1850, as some historians have previously claimed, but that its dynamics changed from this moment onwards. Instead of a single source providing illustrations to the rest of Europe, as the British *Penny Magazine* had done in the 1830s and the *Illustrated London News* in the 1840s, different sources in Britain, France, and several German states started to supply publications abroad. Furthermore, from the mid-1850s onwards, the possibility to copy an illustration on a woodblock using a range of photographic techniques not only disrupted the physical trade in *clichés* but also, in its own way, contributed to the emergence of a transnational visual news culture.

After sections on historiography and methodology, the third section of this chapter describes the most important preconditions of the transnational trade in illustrations. Here, it is proposed that several reproduction techniques, such as stereo- and electrotyping and the photographic techniques described above, form the technological basis, while the development of a transnational network of publishers, draughtsmen, and engravers provided the necessary social infrastructure for the trade. A case study on the artist, engraver, and publisher Henry

68 *The transnational trade in illustrations*

Vizetelly shows how these transnational networks are formed around specific influential nodes.

The fourth section describes the transnational trade in illustrations of the news between 1842 and 1870 in three phases. The first period, between 1842 and 1850, is marked by the dominance of the *Illustrated London News*. In the second phase, between 1850 and 1860, images started to flow from the three major European illustrated newspapers to newly established competitors in foreign countries, who often relied on a single foreign source. The founding of several penny illustrated newspapers marks the third phase (1860–1870). Widely distributed penny magazines, like the French *le Journal Illustré*, started to publish old images of the news from several sources and served them to their readers as original illustrations of news events.

Historiography: transnational networks

In contrast to historians studying the illustrated press, scholars of nineteenth-century fashion magazines have readily recognized the transnational nature of their subject. Marianne van Remoortel, for instance, has shown that 'a complex series of transnational exchange practices' shaped European and American fashion magazines.[4] Sharon Marcus further added that 'British fashion after the Napoleonic wars was transatlantic, and British fashion illustration *was* French.'[5] Many historians researching fashion plates similarly emphasize this French origin. In her study, JoAnne Olian estimated that between 1840 and 1870 around 100 European fashion periodicals appeared that 'either [were] French or [used] colour plates imported from France.'[6]

How can the differences between the two fields be explained? Perhaps through two justifications. First, the textual discourses that embedded images in fashion magazines and illustrated newspapers differ. Fashion magazines often prided themselves on the French origin of their illustrations and their 'cosmopolitan' nature.[7] Conversely, most illustrated newspapers emphasized the national character of their visual and textual representation. Second, researchers study fashion magazines and illustrated newspapers in two very different contexts. While scholars have always seen fashion as an intrinsically international phenomenon, Dutch press historian Marcel Broersma has argued that media history is 'institutionally and topically confined primarily to national boundaries.'[8] These boundaries result from the liberal 'normative assumption' that journalism is worth studying because it performs an essential democratic function in the nation-state: the press as the Fourth Estate.[9] This argument also holds true for research concerning illustrated newspapers, which is mostly centred on explaining the role of these publications in the production of national identity and, hence, turns a blind eye to the crucial transnational part of their nature. As a result, these studies readily accept the national textual discourse of the publications because this neatly fits their research questions and hypotheses.

Some historians had already highlighted the transnational nature of the nineteenth-century illustrated press before the concept became *en vogue*. Jean-Pierre Bacot's

The transnational trade in illustrations   69

La presse illustrée au XIXe siècle (2005), Remi Blanchon's *La gravure sur bois au XIXe siècle* (2001), and Eva-Maria Hanebutt-Benz's 'Studien zum Deutschen Holzstich im 19. Jahrhundert' place the development of the illustrated press in a particular country in a broader transnational (referred to by the authors as international) context.[10] Overall, these studies demonstrate that the journalistic form of the illustrated newspaper crossed borders and that actors based in different European countries traded illustrations. However, they also present a clear watershed in the nature of illustrated press around 1850: while illustrated newspapers had been transnational in the first decades of the nineteenth century, they became clearly national after 1850 because they started producing their own illustrations.

In *La presse illustrée au XIXe siècle* (2005), Bacot described the development of the nineteenth-century European illustrated press by classifying it into four generations. The first three generations all had a British origin, while the last sprang up in France.[11] According to Bacot, the first three formats travelled to France, after being developed in Britain. Following this French version, publications all over the world adopted the form.[12] Blanchon has further supported this conclusion by arguing that the nineteenth-century French wood-engraving trade had a British origin.[13] Hanebutt-Benz has added two additional levels to the process of adaptation. German publishers, who adopted the French version of the first three British forms of the illustrated newspaper, were, in their turn, essential for the development of the Northern- and Eastern-European illustrated press.[14]

The founding of the *Penny Magazine* (1832–1848) by Charles Knight in Britain marks the start of Bacot's first generation. Published under the patronage of the Society for the Diffusion of Useful Knowledge, Knight targeted the working and middle class with instructive information.[15] The magazine roughly contained two kinds of content: 'relatively objective factual information' on a wide range of subjects and texts on 'social and moral themes,' describing virtues such as temperance.[16] However, as Patricia Anderson has contended, its most 'distinguishing feature and major selling-point' were the high-quality wood engravings accompanying these articles.[17] The magazine became an instant success, selling around 200,000 copies at its peak.[18]

Noticing the success of the *Penny Magazine*, publishers all over Europe began similar publications. Bacot provided a list of 33 European penny magazines and noted that they copied not only the form of the British example but also its images.[19] In his autobiography, Knight indicated: 'Stereotype casts of its best cuts were supplied by me for the illustration of publications of a similar character, which appeared in eleven different languages and countries.'[20] Many of these publishers, Charton in France, Weber in Sachsen, the Dietrich brothers in Amsterdam, Giuseppe Pomba in Turin, Fernández de los Ríos in Spain, and Alexandre Herculano in Portugal, would start illustrated newspapers in the 1840s, based on the example of the *Illustrated London News*. The dissemination of the form of the *Penny Magazine* and its illustrations in the 1830s thus partly laid the basis for the transnational trade in illustrations of the news.

Bacot further argued that the dissemination of the *Penny Magazine*'s illustrations throughout Europe led to the formation of an 'imaginary European space.'[21]

70 *The transnational trade in illustrations*

This space continued to exist in the early years of the second generation of illustrated newspapers, which began when Ingram founded the *Illustrated London News* in 1842. The French and German adaptations of the British model – *l'Illustration* and the *Illustrirte Zeitung* – and, as this book will demonstrate, other short-lived illustrated newspapers published in the Netherlands, Russia, Portugal, Spain, and Italy still relied heavily on British illustrations in the early 1840s. However, according to Bacot and Hanebutt-Benz, this quickly changed. In the late 1840s, the owners of the *l'Illustration* and the *Illustrirte Zeitung* established art departments to nationalize the production of illustrations.[22]

Shortly after the revolutions in several European countries in 1848, *l'Illustration* announced a new title: *Journées illustrées de la révolution de 1848*. This special edition of the publication would chronicle 'the events of 1848': the revolutionary upheaval in several major European cities. The publication contained illustrations from the *Illustrated London News, l'Illustration*, the *Illustrirte Zeitung*, and *il Mondo Illustrato* and promised to give a complete overview of the events of that troublesome year.[23] According to Bacot, the publishing of this special edition of *l'Illustration* marked 'both the climax and the end of the imaginary European space, developed by the illustrated magazines since 1832.'[24] In this regard, the publication of *Journées illustrées* should be seen as the climax of the imaginary European space because it tried to reach a European audience with illustrations that stemmed from multiple European sources. At the same time, the publication marked the end of the imaginary space because similar enterprises would, according to Bacot, not materialize after it. Hanebutt-Benz came to the same conclusion: after 1850, illustrated newspapers could fill their pages with nationally produced images. The transnational network of publishers, draughtsmen, and engravers that supported the trade in illustrations thus lost its function.[25]

In contrast, German historian Rolf Reichardt viewed the 1848 revolutions as the starting point of an 'increasingly international and interconnected' European press.[26] A network of European publishers used the same images of the revolution, making it one of the first international 'media events.'[27] For example, an image of the *Illustrated London News*, showing a group of rugged revolutionaries in the throne room of the Tuileries Palace, appeared in *l'Illustration*, the *Illustrirte Zeitung*, and *il Mondo Illustrato*.[28] Other European publications, like the Dutch periodical *de Tijd*, used it as a basis for lithographic images of the same event.[29] For the first time in history, the large-scale exchange of *clichés* of the Paris revolution produced a 'transnational *repertoire*': a shared European image of the revolutions.[30]

While penny magazines, just like fashion magazines, did not shy away from emphasizing their transnational nature, the illustrated newspapers of the second generation chose instead to underline the national character of both their visual and their textual content. Both Bacot and Hannebutt-Benz primarily study the three major European illustrated newspapers: the *Illustrated London News, l'Illustration*, and the *Illustrirte Zeitung*. These publications depended less and less on foreign illustrations after 1850. By that time, they established their own engraving departments or were supplied by a large local wood-engraving firm.

The transnational trade in illustrations   71

However, in line with Reichardt's conclusions, this chapter shows that the presented watershed should not be viewed as the end but rather as a new beginning of the transnational trade in illustrations, in which both its dynamics and its focus changed. Instead of one source, as was the case in the penny magazine phase, several sources provided illustrations and distributed them on a transnational level.

Methodology: networks

What kind of sources and what kind of theoretical framework can be used to study the transnational trade in illustrations of the news? Because no single central actor sold images to publications in multiple countries, they had to be sold by many different companies. In other words: numerous actors organized in a network structure sustained the transnational trade in illustrations. In a 2011 theme issue of the *Victorian Periodicals Review* on 'Victorian networks and the periodical press,' Laurel Brake argued that an individual approach to press networks, working outward from an individual case, such as an important journalist, is 'too slow' and does not make use of the opportunities that digital archives and databases increasingly offer researchers.[31] Instead, she proposed several alternative approaches, two of which I apply in this chapter.

The first of these looks at companies or families to bring 'interlocking networks of people, serial titles, and formats' into focus.[32] The third section of this chapter thus discusses the important role of the Vizetelly family (which Brake also mentioned in her article) in the dissemination of the journalistic form of the illustrated newspaper and the resulting transnational trade in illustrations of the news. Second, Brake has suggested placing materials and techniques at the centre of press networks, mentioning the 'bourgeoning industry' of wood engraving as an example.[33] I use this approach to discuss how the dissemination of the modern wood-engraving method by British engravers throughout Europe formed the necessary infrastructure for the transnational trade in news illustrations.

To shed light on the transnational network surrounding the trade in illustrations of the news, I began by constructing a database of British and French engravers, based on bibliographical information provided by 'dictionaries of the engraving trade' of the two countries. I combined this information with biographical data extracted from digital archives, such as Google Books. The database suggests the existence of a tight-knit transnational network of publishers, draughtsmen, and engravers. A limited number of actors, who regularly moved between different national contexts, were crucial for the development of the European illustrated press. Due to the national scope of the dictionaries, the database shows a strong, and expected, bias towards Britain and France. Because of this bias and the over-representation of several actors, I did not use any quantitative methods to analyse the database.

While the illustrated newspapers themselves almost never admitted to using foreign illustrations, other newspapers and periodicals often happily pointed this out. I used the British Newspaper Archive to find more information about the illustrated press in Britain, while I looked for information concerning the prevalence

72 *The transnational trade in illustrations*

of foreign illustrations in Dutch illustrated newspapers in Delpher. In addition to systematic research in digital newspaper archives, I used Google Books to find more information on the transnational trade in illustrations of the news, by searching for specific technologies connected to it. *Cliché*, the French word used in many European languages to describe metal copies of wood engravings, proved to be an exceptionally fruitful keyword. By connecting several illustrated newspapers to legal terms (such as copyright), I found some relevant descriptions of court cases concerning copyright infringement, which also highlighted aspects of the transnational trade in illustrations.

Preconditions of the transnational trade in illustrations

In 1855, the *London Standard* described how the electrotype process gave the world of illustrated newspapers a transnational nature:

> The quickened process of engraving, together with divided work upon blocks, and, most of all, the electro-type, in all its various forms, have combined to render pictorial journalism what it is at the present day, when its international character is emphasized by the interchange of *clichés*.[34]

This section describes the preconditions of the transnational trade in illustrations. First, it explains how illustrated newspapers produced their images, with a particular focus on reproduction techniques, such as stereo- and electrotyping, since they form the technological basis for the transnational trade in news illustrations. Second, this section sheds light on the development of a transnational network of publishers, draughtsmen, and engravers, which provided the necessary social infrastructure for the trade in illustrations.

(Re)producing illustrations of the news

Brian Maidment has remarked that 'despite the centrality of illustrations to the development of Victorian periodicals, there is no recent general history of periodical illustration.'[35] Mason Jackson's *The Pictorial Press* (1883) is still not only the most important primary source on the production of illustrations of the news but also its 'most useful survey.'[36] This section argues that only a few major illustrated newspapers operated in the way that Jackson had described. For the majority of publications, the reproduction of illustrations – a feature glossed over by Jackson – was the essential step in their production process.

Jackson, who was the art director of the *Illustrated London News* for almost 25 years, described the production of an illustration of the news in five stages: sketching, drawing, engraving, electrotyping, and printing. He gave the first part of the process the most attention, presenting the 'special artist' – a sort of visual reporter – as the true hero of the illustrated press:

> Wherever there is any 'moving accident by flood or field' the 'special artist' of the illustrated newspaper is found 'takin' notes.' No event of interest

The artist supplied the sketch 'acquired by long practice a rapid method of working, and can, by a few strokes of his pencil, indicate a passing scene by a kind of pictorial shorthand, which is afterwards translated and extended in the finished drawing.'[38]

'The sketch being completed on paper, the services of the draughtsman on wood come into requisition.'[39] The draughtsman 'translated' the sketch of the special artist into a finished drawing on a woodblock. He or she did this without 'doing violence to the general truth of the representation, and with due consideration for the particular conditions of the moment.'[40] Jackson provided his readers with an excellent example of the translation of a draughtsman. In his book, both the sketch and the final drawing of the 'Surrender of Sedan,' published by the *Illustrated London News* in its issue of 17 September 1870, can be found.[41]

Considering the nature of current affairs, images of the news had to be produced quickly. Major illustrated newspapers consequently maintained a large staff of draughtsmen and engravers who were 'ready at a moment's notice to take up any subject, and, if necessary, work day and night until it is done.'[42] To further speed up production, woodblocks could be taken apart into several pieces, which meant that several engravers could simultaneously work on the same illustration. Jackson admitted that this process 'did not always result in the production of a first-rate work of art as a whole.'[43] Different engravers working on the same block might have had very distinct ways of depicting trees or the waves of a stormy sea. Thus, the superintendent artist – Jackson's job for many years – 'harmonized and dovetailed' the different pieces of the woodblock, retouching the first proof of the engraving and endeavouring 'to blend the differences of colour and texture.'[44]

In their descriptions of the production of images, illustrated newspapers emphasized the same characteristics as Jackson. They too often referred to the heroics of their special artist, which appeared as a professional category after the *Illustrated London News* coined the term during the Crimean War.[45] Describing the personality cult of Giuseppe Garibaldi (1802–1882), Italy's *Pater Patriae*, historian Lucy Riall commented on how these visual reporters became the stars of their coverage during national hero's Italian campaign of 1859.[46] Hence, we find Frank Vizetelly (1830–1883), the special artist of the *Illustrated London News*, narrowly escaping a band of Sicilian bandits, and Edmond Texier, the reporter of *l'Illustration*, sketching dead soldiers on the battlefield near the Italian town of Magenta.[47] In 1867, *l'Illustration* published a full-page illustration, showing its reporter M. Montaud drawing some Cretan insurgents who posed for him on the deck of a steamer (Figure 2.1).[48] However, special artists were not always willing to figure in their own reporting. In 1864, a subscriber asked the *Illustrirte Zeitung* to provide a portrait of its special artist August Beck (1832–1873). The publication promised to ask but doubted if Beck would appreciate the request: the portrait was never published.[49]

Historians of visual culture have noted that a central characteristic of early news photography was the fact that photojournalists were 'highly privileged

Figure 2.1 A special artist of *l'Illustration* in 1867. "M. Montaud, correspondant de l'Illustration, dessinant des volontaires de l'insurection cretoise revenant en Grece, a bord du paquebot autrichien," *l'Illustration* (9 March 1867). The Hague, Royal Library of the Netherlands, T 1788 (1867–1).

witnesses of the event in progress.' From the early twentieth century, large platforms were 'expressly built to give the press photographers an optimal viewpoint: they now act as lieutenants of powerful news organizations and millions of readers.'[50] Contrary to this argument, complaints in the illustrated press about 'sham correspondents' – people pretending to be special artists in order to gain access to news events, all sorts of public gatherings, and theatre shows – demonstrate that the special artists were already privileged witnesses. For example, in 1874, the *Graphic* noted: 'Illustrated newspapers are especially apt to be victimised in this way, for everybody can sketch, or pretend to make marks on a piece of paper, and so these adventurers get a stall at a theatre, or a reserved seat at some public display, under entirely false pretences.'[51]

It might be hard for us to imagine special artists rushing to the scene of an accident or bribing an official to get closer to the news and sketch it 'on the spot,' but this paparazzi-like behaviour, which most historians associate with the photojournalism of the *interbellum*, is frequently described in the nineteenth-century press.[52] For example, when the Queen of Oudh, a princely state in North India, died in 1858, newspapers described how her Parisian hotel was 'besieged by a cloud of interested persons – modellers, photographers, newsmongers [. . .].'[53]

The transnational trade in illustrations   75

However, none of them, including the 'artist of the Illustrated London News,' managed to get a glimpse of the queen. Similarly, after two gunpowder magazines near Woolwich exploded in October 1864, newspapers noted how photographers and 'sketchers of illustrated newspapers' flocked to the scene in droves.[54]

Although large illustrated newspapers certainly employed special artists, they almost certainly overrepresented their role and actual number.[55] The descriptions of the production process neglect to mention that a lot of images were made on the basis of sketches and photographs sent in by amateurs and semi-professionals. In an early biographical sketch of Herbert Ingram, the publisher of the *Illustrated London News*, the *Manchester Guardian*, noted:

> The wide circulation of the paper brings contributions from all parts of the world, by every foreign post. Officers in the army on foreign stations, travellers, merchants, send for its use drawing[s] and sketches, some artistic, some very rough, but all original, of almost every imaginable event, place, and thing.[56]

In the late 1850s, *l'Illustration* received so many photographs that it started its own photographic department, headed by the photographer Numa Blanc (1816–1897).[57]

What happened after the office of an illustrated newspaper received a sketch? In 'The mysteries of *l'Illustration*,' the French illustrated newspaper described the production of its illustrations:

> The artist draws with an ordinary lead pencil on a piece of hard, compact, well-dried and lightly bleached boxwood, the same way as on a sheet of paper. The drawing, judged and accepted, is immediately brought to the general workshop of the engravers, which the attached illustration faithfully shows you. After it arrives, it is engraved, without pause or rest, day and night, because it often has to be completed in less than forty-eight hours.[58]

Two illustrations show the workshop of the engravers both during the day and during the night, emphasizing that the production of images never stopped.[59] Just as in Jackson's book, this article presented the entire production process as a single operation under the control of *l'Illustration*. Similarly, Frank Leslie's two-page illustrated description of the production progress noted:

> Ten or fifteen engravers now seize these fragmentary pieces, and work night and day; not a moment is lost; they silently and industriously pursue their work, and the surfaces of the several blocks are cut away save where they are marked by the image of the artist's pencil, and we have left the surface which makes the impression on our paper known as a wood engraving.[60]

The same elements appear in the article "How the *Illustrirte Zeitung* is made." Two illustrations show the 'ateliers' of the draughtsmen and the engravers of the

76 *The transnational trade in illustrations*

German publication. Contrary to the almost mechanical nature of engraving in the descriptions of Jackson, *l'Illustration* and *Frank Leslie's Illustrirte Zeitung* presented its employees as having a large amount of artistic freedom: 'When he wants to honour his profession, the wood engraver should possess not only a steady hand but also an artistic eye and a notion of the essential nature of the drawing.'[61]

In *The Mass Image* (2008), Gerry Beegan observed that the production process of illustrations was in constant flux in the nineteenth century. The most important development was the decreasing artistic freedom of the engraver. In the 1840s, firms mostly used the 'tint' (or interpretative engraving) method, where individual engravers were free to 'translate' a drawing into an engraving, just as Jackson's draughtsmen were free to translate a sketch into a drawing. As Beegan remarked: 'It was acknowledged that he [the engraver] knew best how to transform the image on the block into a printable matrix.'[62] In the early 1850s, the demand for illustrations rapidly increased as illustrated publications blossomed and visual advertising took off. However, because it took many years to train skilled engravers, they became increasingly scarce and engraving firms could only keep up with the demand by switching to the 'facsimile' method. Engravers using this method only cut the parts of the wood block left blank by the draughtsman. Instead of workshops where masters trained apprentices in an art form, wood-engraving firms increasingly functioned as modern image factories, following an assembly-line system, which depended on 'specialization of the labour force, managerial oversight, splitting up reproduction into many stages, and the adoption of facsimile.'[63]

Beegan has pointed out that it took the *Illustrated London News* until the late 1850s to achieve the level of production described by Jackson; subsequently, this specific way of making illustrations existed for only a couple of years. In the early 1880s, the half-tone revolution, as it is commonly known, enabled the large-scale reproduction of photographs and ended the supremacy of wood engraving as the primary visual medium. Additionally, only several large illustrated newspapers, like the *Illustrated London News* and perhaps *Frank Leslie's Illustrated Newspaper* in New York, could control the entire production from the special artist's sketch to the finished engraving.[64] Other large illustrated newspapers, such as *l'Illustration* and the *Illustrirte Zeitung*, depended on large engraving firms, like ABL in Paris and Eduard Kretzschmar in Leipzig, which also produced illustrations for other illustrated periodicals, books, and advertisements.

If, as we have seen, the production of illustrations largely differed from Jackson's account, why did his description of the production process become so influential? And why did all the illustrated newspapers describe the production of their images in the same way? Several historians have claimed that periodicals used these kinds of descriptions to lend illustrations of the news an authentic quality; for example, Keller has argued that we currently only judge images to be trustworthy if technology produces them without the perceived interference of a human agent.[65] Our visual representations of the news, including photographs and film, derive their genuine quality from the discourse surrounding the technology – the (photo)camera – with which they are made. In contrast to the biased nineteenth-century draughtsman, the camera mediates reality directly to us. Kevin Barnhurst and John Nerone have described this as our assumption that 'photojournalism came out of the camera, fully-armoured, like Athena out of the head of Zeus.'[66]

Keller further argued that this discourse surrounding photographs and film originated in the nineteenth century: 'Contrary to what 20th-century viewers might expect, therefore, it was not camera exposures, but newspaper illustrations which first manifested the novel quality of "authenticity" to the mid-19th-century public.'[67] The objective quality of an illustration of the news did not depend on the affordances of the technology used for its production but on the 'particular mode of its contextualization.'[68] It is precisely this contextualization of an illustration of the news in a textual discourse of authenticity and objectivity that we find in Jackson's description of the production process. The agency of the producers of an illustration of the news – especially that of the special artist – formed the basis for its authentic and objective quality. The changing status of wood engravers demonstrated that this discourse was far from static during the nineteenth century. While Jackson still presented the draughtsman as a vital part of the production process in the 1880s, the wood engraver had, at that time, already been reduced to an almost mechanical tool.

It is important to note that the discourse of authenticity surrounding illustrations of the news was far from generally accepted for the duration of the nineteenth century. The article 'Looking into the middle of next week,' published in the famous satirical magazine *Punch*, is a good example. In this article, the *Illustrated London News* was accused of being the 'author' of the revolutions in Paris of 1848, for how could the publication provide its readers with illustrations 'taken on the spot' of a barricade that was erected by the revolutionaries only two days before the publication came out? Could the *Illustrated London News* predict the future? Was it able to look into the middle of the next week? British readers did not buy illustrated newspapers for their truthfulness but rather for their imagination: 'Illustrations were never meant for history. Whoever expects a "Winner of the Derby" to be a correct likeness? . . . [O]r imagines that a "Grand Battle" or the "Awful explosion of a Powder Mill" was ever sketched on the spot?'[69] The caricature next to the article summarizes the criticism in a visual way, depicting a special artist literally 'taking a barricade on the spot' (Figure 2.2).[70]

Other illustrated newspapers were also regularly accused of publishing 'fantastical images.' In September 1844, the *Morning Post* already noted the absurdity of the 'illustrated system' of the illustrated press. During a visit to the Scottish Highlands, a local newspaper had described how 'her majesty and the Prince had "gone into the field to see the *shearers*."' Ignorant of the fact that shearers are a type of dog, the *Pictorial Times* published an engraving 'representing her Majesty overlooking a body of *sheep-shearers*.'[71] As an often-re-published article of the *Edinburgh Weekly Register* noted, this kind of deceit could only be the tip of the iceberg: 'So much for the vaunted fidelity of those sketches taken on the spot!'[72] Similar accusations pop up in the entire period of this research. In April 1867, *le Figaro* claimed that *l'Illustration* fabricated images of the opening of the

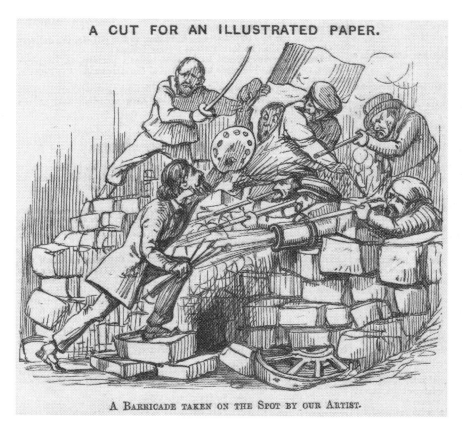

Figure 2.2 A Parisian barricade taken on the spot in 1848. "A Cut for an Illustrated Paper: A Barricade Taken on the Spot by Our Artist," *Punch*, vol. 14 (1848): 45. The Hague, Royal Library of the Netherlands, T 347 (1848–015).

Universal Exposition in Paris. The French illustrated newspaper conceded that many of its competitors published fake images, but it never resorted to falsifications. Only by the 'ingenious application' of the principle of the division of labour to wood engraving could it publish images of the opening ceremony 48 hours after it took place. Moreover, *l'Illustration* emphasized the truthfulness of its illustrations by referring to its production process: the discourse of objectivity in full effect.[73]

Similar to *l'Illustration*, illustrated newspapers often defended themselves and took measures when their 'illustrated system' came under attack. At the end of 1843, the *Dublin Evening Mail* complained about 'the total failure of the portraits' of Daniel O'Connell and the other defendants of the State Trials. The newspaper did not know if this was the fault 'of the artists, the copyists in London, or the engraver,' but the maker of the sketches, a certain mister Jones, was not to blame, 'as we have seen the originals sketches . . . and nothing can be better or more striking than his likeness of the judges, the counsel, and the traversers.'[74] Probably in response to this criticism, the *Illustrated London News* dispatched its chief editor Frederick Bayley (1808–1853) and several artists to Dublin in order to provide its readers with faithful illustrations of the trials in future issues.[75]

Illustrations of the news derived not only their authentic quality but also their commodity value from their contextualization in the production process. The article in *Punch* explicitly points to this: 'And yet these things [the imagined images in the *Illustrated London News*] are indispensable to the success of pictorial papers.'[76] Readers bought the *Illustrated London News* because it promised to provide a truthful mirror of the world, and *this* is the reason why almost all publications described the production of their illustrations in similar terms as Jackson. In practice, however, the majority of nineteenth-century illustrated newspapers did not produce their images in this way. Rather, they copied a large part of their visual material from other illustrated publications. This fact makes it necessary that we see *reproduction* as an essential part of the production process of an illustration of the news in this period.

Around the mid-nineteenth century, publishers used two techniques to copy images: stereotyping and electrotyping. In the 1830s, Charles Knight used the stereotype method to sell copies of the images in his *Penny Magazine* all over Europe. This method involved the covering of the original wood engraving with grease, after which it was brushed with a mixture of 'plaster of Paris,' deriving its name from the large deposit of gypsum, the mineral used for the process, underneath the Montmartre in Paris.[77] When the plaster was dry and the original engraving taken out, a matrix of the illustration appeared, which was its negative image. The stereotyper then poured a mixture of hot iron and antimony into the mould. Once this hardened, he broke the plaster, and an exact copy of the original engraving emerged.[78]

Electrotyping was based on similar principles. In 1860, *le Monde Illustré* described the workshop of M. Coblence in Paris: 'the artist *par excellence* in the field of electrotyping.'[79] A full-page illustration showed all the steps in the production of an electrotype on the basis of a wood engraving.[80] First, a mould, made either of wax or heated gutta-percha (a rubber-like material often used in nineteenth-century industry), was taken of the original wood engraving and covered with a thin layer of 'blacklead': the nineteenth-century name for graphite.[81] The electrotyper placed the mould and a plate of copper in a bath 'filled with a solution of sulphate of copper and sulphuric acid.'[82] A strong electric current, generated by a 'dynamo-electric machine,' caused the copper to decompose and deposit small particles on the layer of graphite, which formed a copper coating, 'producing an exact facsimile of the original engraved block.[83]

The article in *le Monde Illustré* noted that electrotyping was essential for the modern illustrated press because it produced durable plates that were hard enough to endure large print-runs. However, the article also described how the technique

80 *The transnational trade in illustrations*

was of fundamental importance for the emergence of a transnational visual news culture:

> Today, French illustrated publications export a great numbers of their images of the news abroad, and electrotypes are made so fast, that the *clichés* of wood engravings, taken from the hands of the engraver on Wednesday or Thursday, can be sent to London and Berlin on Friday, where they are printed on Saturday, at the same time as Paris prints with the originals.[84]

Electrotyping not only enabled the trade in illustrations of the news, but, as a result of the relative speed of the process, also permitted illustrated newspapers all over Europe to print the same newsworthy illustration on the same day.

Stereo- and electrotyping enabled illustrated newspapers to make an infinite number of copies of their wood engravings. Because these could be bought, sold, and exchanged, they no longer had to produce all the illustrations they published. However, the two techniques still necessitated a form of contact between the original producer of an image and the publisher planning on re-using it. This situation changed when new companies applied photographic techniques to the reproduction of illustrations of the news in the mid-1850s.

In 1866, an article in *Chambers Journal* complained about all the different techniques used by printers to copy illustrations: 'Oh, the graphs and glyphs, the glyptos and typos, the stereos and electros, . . . the lithos and the photos – who can count them all?'[85] The quote illustrates one of Beegan's central arguments: that the dividing line between wood engraving (illustrations) and photography (photographs) as the primary visual medium in the nineteenth-century press is far from clear.[86] In the early 1850s, a new technique was developed, described as photoxylography or xylophotography, that could be used to print an illustration directly onto the woodblock, after which low-paid *facsimile* engravers could quickly cut around the lines. This new technique eliminated the need for draughtsmen in the production process of an illustrated newspaper. In 1859, the *Illustrated London News* noted that photoxylography could be used to turn sketches more rapidly into engravings: 'if [the] sketch be handed over to photographer, he can, in the course of a few minutes, take a photographic copy of the exact dimensions required, which, in very little time longer, can be transferred to the block, and the block be in the hands of the engraver.'[87]

The 'cheap and rapid transference of pictures of all kinds to the wood block,' made possible by photoxylography, eliminated the need for contact between the original producer of an illustration and the publication planning on re-using it. The latter could obtain copies by photographing a printed illustration instead of buying a physical copy, in the form of a *cliché*, from the company that owned the original wood engraving. In this sense, starting in the 1860s, photoxylography enabled the large-scale piracy of illustrations of the news described at the end of this chapter. A description of a photoxylographic technique, developed in 1857 by *monsieur* Lallemand in Paris, already pointed out that it could hugely benefit the cheap illustrated press.[88]

The transnational trade in illustrations 81

It is unclear when and where photoxylography was exactly developed. This partly has to do with the fact that (cheap) illustrated newspapers did not advertise their piracy. Beegan noted that the 'cheapness and speed' of the technique resulted in its widespread use in the 1860s. However, we can find descriptions of the process from the early 1850s. For example, the *Journal of the Photographic Society* noted in 1861 that 'the late Mr. Archer and Mr. William Brown . . . were trying, and did transfer collodion film, by floating it off and getting it on to the wood block; and there were some rough specimens which were submitted to the publishers of the 'Illustrated London News' at that time.'[89] As we will see below, in 1853, *Gleason's Pictorial Drawing Room* was already accused of applying 'a detestable invention for transferring Daguerreotypes to plates for engraving.'[90] In 1857, the *Photographic Notes* wrote that 'one of the best engravers of the Illustrated London News, himself a clever photographer,' had told them that 'Xylo-Photography' would never be 'sufficiently perfected to be of any use.' However, the same article noted that a certain Mr. T Sharp declared that he had, 'for the last six months, regularly supplied one periodical with its illustrations, while he is now actually making arrangements to supply one of the first illustrated papers in the same way.'[91]

The start of a transnational network, 1816–1850

Many historians regard Thomas Bewick (1753–1828) as the 'father of modern wood engraving.'[92] In the last decades of the eighteenth century, he started to use metal engraving tools, such as the burin, instead of the traditional knives, to cut blocks of hard boxwood across the grain. Because of the more delicate lines that metal-engraving tools enabled, Bewick could produce more detailed illustrations and more durable printing blocks. This last feature was especially vital for the development of mass-produced illustrated newspapers. Traditional woodcuts were too delicate to deliver a substantial number of sharp impressions as they wore out quickly with repeated use. Various forms of metal engraving solved this issue as they produced durable matrices; yet, these could not be printed together with type. This is because, in intaglio printmaking (such as metal engraving), the lowered surfaces take the ink, while the raised ones are wiped clean. Type, on the other hand, is printed using a relief printing process, in which ink is only applied to the raised surfaces. Despite its confusing name, wood engraving is a form of relief printing and, as such, can be printed together with type.

Bewick, together with his lesser-known rival Allen Robert Branston (1778–1827), almost singlehandedly revived and modernized wood engraving.[93] Their apprentices and the apprentices of their apprentices distributed the new techniques and made the wood-engraved illustration the visual medium of choice in the nineteenth century. Almost all famous engravers, both those who mainly worked on books and those who worked on periodicals, can be linked to Bewick or Branston. This is valid not only for British engravers but also for their French, German, and even American counterparts.[94] Bewick and Branston are, therefore,

82 *The transnational trade in illustrations*

an excellent starting point for a description of the network of producers of illustrations of the news.

At the start of the nineteenth century, wood engraving was almost entirely forgotten in France.[95] Upon observing the revival and success of the art in Britain, however, the French government and several publishers tried to promote the new technique. After some unsuccessful attempts, the publisher Firmin Didot (1764–1836) persuaded the British engraver Charles Thompson (1791–1843) to immigrate to France in 1816.[96] Several historians have intimated that Thompson, an apprentice of Bewick and Branston, trained several French engravers, including Jean Best (1808–1879), Louis-Henri Brévière (1797–1869), Isidore Leloir (1803–?), and Henri Désiré Porret (1800–1867).[97] However, Blanchon has convincingly demonstrated that only Jean Best could have been a pupil of Thompson.[98] He can, nevertheless, still be seen as the 'father of modern French wood engraving.'[99] Brévière and Porret, while perhaps not directly under his tutelage, did everything to imitate the prolific Thompson and his 'British style.'[100] Thompson also persuaded other British engravers, such as John Andrew, who worked for the *Illustrated London News* in the early 1840s, to join him in Paris. This proved vital for the development of the technique in France.[101]

The biographies of several prominent German engravers further point to this indirect dependency on British wood engravers. Three of them – Kaspar Braun (1807–1877), Carl August Deis (1810–1884), and Johann Rehles – studied wood engraving in the workshop of Louis-Henri Brévière in the late 1830s. Deis would become one of the most prolific draughtsmen and engravers of the *Illustrirte Zeitung*, and Kaspar Braun founded the famous satirical journal the *Fliegende Blätter* in 1845.[102] Wolfgang Weber observed in the biography of his grandfather how two 'Englishmen' living in Leipzig, William Alfred Nicholls and John Allanson, the latter of which was trained by Bewick, engraved most of the early 'original' illustrations of the *Illustrirte Zeitung*.[103]

Several Northern- and Eastern-European countries depended on German engravers for the establishment of their own illustrated newspapers. In 1851, Friedrich Wilhelm Bader was asked to become the head of the engraving department of the short-lived *Österreichische Illustrierte Zeitung*. Bader was a pupil of Deis, who was an apprentice of Brévière, who was inspired by Thompson, who had been a pupil of both Bewick and Branston. Tatsumi Yukiko has similarly demonstrated how four German immigrants, Bauman, Goppe, Marks, and Kornfeld, founded four influential Russian illustrated newspapers and family publications – *Illyustratsiya* (1858–1863), *Vsemirnaia Illyustratsiya* (1869–1898), *Niva* (1870–1917), and *Strekoza* (1875–1918).[104]

We can connect all the early contributors of the *Illustrated London News* to Bewick and Branston. The firm of John Orrin Smith (1799–1843) and William James Linton (1812–1897) engraved a substantial number of the illustrations in its early volumes: Orrin Smith, in turn, was taught by William Harvey (1796–1866), who was the most famous of Bewick's pupils.[105] William James Linton was an apprentice of George Wilmot Bonner (1796–1836), who was discovered by Branston.[106] Ebenezer Landells (1808–1860), who also engraved a substantial

The transnational trade in illustrations 83

number of illustrations in the early volumes of the British publication, was one of Bewick's direct pupils.[107] In regard to Henry Vizetelly, the fourth major engraver of the early volumes of the *Illustrated London News* (and to be discussed in detail in the next section), it suffices to say that he learned wood engraving from Bonner and Orrin Smith and can also be linked to Bewick and Branston.

Besides these men, Frank Leslie (1821–1880), the *nom de plume* of Henry Carter, was one of the most influential early employees of the *Illustrated London News*. Raised to make it big in his family's glove trade, Leslie instead chose a different path for himself and started to send drawings to the famous British illustrated newspaper in the mid-1840s.[108] He was subsequently hired, and, rising quickly through the ranks, he was 'offered the charge of the engraving department on the above-named paper, . . . and here he had an opportunity of increasing his own technical knowledge and becoming acquainted with the best processes of printing then in use.'[109] In 1848, Leslie moved to New York to set up an American version of the *Illustrated London News*.[110] Because he lacked the capital to realize his plan, he began working for several early American illustrated newspapers, including *Gleason's Pictorial* (1851–1853) and the *New York Illustrated News* (1853–1854).[111] A small announcement in *Gleason's Pictorial* shows that Leslie was not the only European-trained engraver to emigrate to the United States: 'A fresh corps of artists and engravers of the first class in their professions – several newly arrived from Europe – are already engaged upon elaborate and beautiful subjects for the paper.'[112]

In 1855, Leslie finally managed to start his own illustrated newspaper: *Frank Leslie's Illustrated Newspaper*. Because of his experience at the *Illustrated London News*, he knew how an illustrated newspaper could be produced, sold, and made profitable.[113] As one of his obituaries described: 'Mr Leslie was the first publisher in America who maintained a full engraving establishment for his own publications alone.'[114] He not only used this engraving department to produce images for his illustrated newspaper but also started several other periodicals – the *Chimney Corner*, the *Boys' and Girls' Weekly, Pleasant Hours*, and the *Lady's Journal* – all based on British examples. He also published *Frank Leslie's Illustrirte Zeitung*: a German version of his newspaper.[115]

Leslie did not sever his ties with the British image industry and continued to import new techniques and skilled engravers. William James Linton, whom he might have met while working for the *Illustrated London News*, and his brother Henry Linton worked for Leslie in the mid-1860s.[116] In 1870, we can find one of Leslie's advertisements in the *London Evening Standard*, which promises 'permanent situations' to 'good wood engravers' who were willing to immigrate to America.[117] They could send proofs of work to an address on Paternoster Row, where he kept a British office.[118]

Another lesser-known *émigré* was Thomas Armstrong (1818–1861). A member of the same generation as Vizetelly and Leslie, he served as an apprentice to an unknown engraver in the late 1830s.[119] Because of his employment at the *Illustrated London News*, it is likely that this was either Orin Smith or Bonner, who trained most of the engravers working for the illustrated newspaper at that time.[120]

84   *The transnational trade in illustrations*

Armstrong contributed to the *Illustrated London News* until 1848, when he left for Paris to witness the revolution. 'Not liking the manners and customs of the French,' as one obituary has it, Armstrong decided to move to Australia.[121] Losing his first wife shortly after his arrival, he packed up his bags and moved to the new American state of California. Instead of becoming a gold digger like everyone else, Armstrong started an illustrated newspaper: the *California Illustrated News* (1851). Several newspapers announcing the new publication stressed his connection to his former British employer: 'The fact of the artist who has undertaken the pictorial department having been long connected with the Illustrated London News, should be sufficient guaranty for his ability [*sic*].'[122] Despite his extensive experience, Armstrong ceased the publication of the *California Illustrated News* after only seven numbers but continued to work for other illustrated periodicals.[123]

Another early employee for the *Illustrated London News*, Walter George Mason (1822–1866), introduced the modern wood-engraving technique and the format of the illustrated newspaper to the Australian colonies. Mason was born in New York, where his father, Abraham John Mason (1794–1858), taught him the art. Mason senior, another of Branston's apprentices, sent Mason junior to London to study wood engraving under Bonner.[124] In the mid-1840s, Walter George worked for the *Illustrated London News* alongside Vizetelly, Carter, and Armstrong. In the early 1850s, he emigrated to Australia, where he started the *Illustrated Sydney News* in 1853.[125]

Just like their British counterparts, the early engravers of *l'Illustration* can be connected to the tradition of Bewick and Branston. ABL, the engraving firm of Andrew, Best, and Leloir, supplied the French illustrated newspaper with most of its illustrations.[126] After the British engraver John Andrew left ABL in 1843, its name changed to Best, Leloir, Hotelin, and Regnier (BLHR). When Leloir either retired or died in 1851, the company became known as Best, Hotelin, and Regnier (BHR).[127]

A range of issues from the 19th and the 20th volume of *l'Illustration* demonstrate the continuing importance of this engraving firm. For this short period, the French illustrated newspaper recorded the names of both the draughtsman and the engraver of its images. In 1852, BHR, or rather the many unknown engravers of its workshop, engraved around 82 per cent of *l'Illustration*'s images.[128] Although we know little about Isidore Regnier (1816–?) and Laurent Hotelin (1821–?), it seems likely that they were apprenticed to the initial founders of the firm, who trained them in Bewick's engraving style.[129] Jacques Adrien Laveille (1818–1862), the second-most prolific engraver of *l'Illustration* in 1852, was also connected to the British tradition. In the early 1830s, he was trained by Porret and lived in London, where he worked under an engraver named Williams.[130]

William Alfred Nicholls and John Allanson, two British engravers living in Leipzig, made most of the early 'original' engravings of the *Illustrirte Zeitung*. Weber was far from content with this situation, probably because the British engravers were relatively expensive.[131] From 1846 onwards, he relied on the services of

The transnational trade in illustrations   85

Eduard Kretzschmar (1806–1858), whom Brockhaus (the printing firm for the *Illustrirte Zeitung*) had sent to Berlin to study wood engraving in the late 1830s.[132] The entry for Kretzschmar in the *Allgemeine Deutsche Biographie* mentions that his workshop made almost all the engravings of the *Illustrirte Zeitung* from 1846.[133] The frontispiece of the 13th volume of the publication depicts Weber and Kretzschmar on the same image.[134] Kretzschmar's 'xylografische anstallt' (wood-engraving firm) expanded rapidly and regularly employed between 30 and 40 engravers. Besides illustrations for the *Illustrirte Zeitung*, the company also produced engravings for other publications, such as the illustrated books published by Brockhaus.[135] When Kretzschmar died in 1858, Weber bought his wood-engraving firm. An article in the *Illustrirte Zeitung* asserted that the company was still able to take on any work previously done by Kretzschmar himself.[136]

Contrary to the contributors of the *Illustrated London News* and *l'Illustration*, we cannot link Kretzschmar directly to British engravers. Hanebutt-Benz, keen to point out the contribution of 'German' engravers, has emphasized this fact.[137] Kretzschmar studied wood engraving as an apprentice of Friederich Unzelmann (1797–1854) in Berlin, who (as far as we know) did not have any contact with British engravers. However, Kretzschmar's cuts look very much like those of his British competitors. Similar to Blanchon's description of Brévière and Porret, the *Allgemeine Deutsche Biographie* indicates that Kretzschmar closely followed 'the English school' of engraving.[138] Because the British engravers John Allanson and William Alfred Nichols made most of the early engravings for the *Illustrirte Zeitung* in their atelier in Leipzig, it is likely that these two men influenced Kretzschmar.

To support her argument for German influence in wood engraving in the nineteenth century, Hanebutt-Benz has highlighted how Kretzschmar and his workshop disseminated the modern wood-engraving technique to several Northern-European countries. In 1859, an apprentice of Kretzschmar, Franz Wilhelm Obermann (1830–1896), became the head of the engraving department of the first Danish illustrated newspaper: the *Illustreret Tidende*. Its founders, Carl Christian Lose (1821–1892) and Otto Herman Delbanco (1821–1890), urged Obermann to emulate the *Illustrirte Zeitung* as much as possible, and, to achieve this, he employed several young German engravers.[139] Furthermore, Obermann encouraged Danish engravers to study the art in Germany. For example, Hans Peter Hansen (1829–1899), who later worked for the *Illustreret Tidende*, was one of Kretzschmar's apprentices in the mid-1850s.[140]

The influence of Kretzmar's engraving school was not limited to Northern Europe. The German engraver Heinrich Egersdörfer (1853–1915) started his career at the *Illustrirte Zeitung*, making sketches for the illustrated newspaper during the Franco-German War of 1870. After living in London for a couple of years, he emigrated to the Cape Colony, where he founded the *South African Illustrated News* (1884–1885).[141] After the publication folded, Egersdörfer travelled to the Australian colonies, where he worked for the *Illustrated Sydney News*, started by fellow *émigré* Walter George Mason in the 1850s. After moving back to the

86 *The transnational trade in illustrations*

Cape Colony, acting as the local correspondent for the London *Graphic*, Egersdörfer returned to London, where he died in 1915.

Case study: Henry Vizetelly's network

After his death on 1 January 1894, several obituaries praised Henry Richard Vizetelly's entrepreneurial spirit: 'One of the most genial and enterprising of journalists, publishers, newspapers owners, and authors is dead.'[142] When he started his last illustrated publication in 1869, the *Oxford Chronicle and Reading Gazette* wrote that 'Mr Vizetelly may justly lay claim as an able pioneer of illustrated journalism.'[143] Henry Vizetelly was not only the most innovative pioneer of the mid-nineteenth-century illustrated press but also a central node in the transnational network that traded illustrations of the news. His voluminous autobiography and articles in the British Newspaper Archive offer an abundance of source material, which makes it possible to follow his career in detail and map his transnational contacts.

Henry Vizetelly was born in 1820 to a family active in journalism and publishing from the late eighteenth century.[144] In 1835, Vizetelly's father apprenticed him to the wood engraver George Wilmot Bonner, whom Henry described as 'second rate.'[145] Two years later, he became a pupil of another famous wood engraver, John Orrin Smith. However, Vizetelly did not like the life of an apprentice. Upon turning 18 in 1838, he purchased his way out of his apprenticeship and started his own company with his brother, 'having acquired the freedom, then necessary for carrying on business within the sacred civic precincts, by so-called servitude.'[146]

In 1837, Henry sold an engraving of the deadly descent of the aeronaut Robert Cocking, who jumped from a hot air balloon to test a parachute he designed, to the *Weekly Chronicle*: possibly his first illustration of a news event.[147] In the early 1840s, the Vizetelly brothers began making 'illustrated supplements' of the news, which they sold to several British newspapers at the same time. One of their first images depicted the wedding of Queen Victoria and Prince Albert in 1840.[148] Another, portraying the christening of the future King Edward VII, the son of Queen Victoria, appeared in January 1842, a couple of months before the first issue of the *Illustrated London News* was released.[149]

According to the commonly accepted foundational story of the *Illustrated London News*, Herbert Ingram approached Vizetelly with his plan for an illustrated newspaper in 1842. Although Vizetelly's exact role remains somewhat unclear, it seems to have been more prominent than Ingram cared to acknowledge. For instance, Vizetelly wrote that he convinced Ingram of the idea that the *Illustrated London News* should publish illustrations of the news, instead of focusing on sensational crime stories. He also claimed to have produced the widely distributed prospectus of the newspaper.[150] The fact that Vizetelly already made illustrated supplements for provincial newspapers in the early 1840s makes these claims plausible.

Henry left the *Illustrated London News* after a couple of months: 'It was not worth my while to be constantly dancing attendance upon him [Ingram]. I severed

The transnational trade in illustrations   87

my connection with the "Illustrated London News," on receipt of a certain sum in lieu of notice.'[151] The relation between Vizetelly and several members of the Ingram family would remain troublesome for the rest of his life. While Henry was the real pioneer of illustrated journalism, the Ingrams did have one clear advantage over him: they were rich and bought every successful title started by Vizetelly.

In 1843, Henry founded his first illustrated newspaper, the *Pictorial Times*, together with Andrew Spottiswoode. The men had high hopes for their venture and used all means necessary to bolster its readership. In November 1843, a 'mock procession' of around 50 people paraded the streets of London, imitating the famous 200 pole-bearers, which the *Illustrated London News* hired to announce its first issue. After stopping in front of the office of its competitor,

> [s]ome of the *Pictorial Times* men were assailed, and as it was presumed that the assailants were connected with the rival paper, the procession adjourned to Spottiswoode's printing office from which 20 or 30 boys were brought out, armed with sticks and other weapons of warfare.[152]

The *Pictorial Times* won the battle, but its owners lost the war. Their publication never turned a profit, and Spottiswoode is said to have lost around 20,000 pounds on the venture.[153] In 1847, Ingram bought the *Pictorial Times* for a small sum and merged it with one of his own: *The Lady's Newspaper*. At the end of 1844, Henry had already left the *Pictorial Times* to 'give greater attention to the largely increasing business which my brother and I were then carrying on, for at this time we were printing illustrated books for all the principal London publishers.'[154]

In the years after the publication of the *Pictorial Times*, Henry continued to produce illustrated news supplements. In 1852, several newspapers referred to the brothers' company when it failed to deliver illustrations of the funeral of the Duke of Wellington on time.[155] The brothers asked to be excused for the late delivery in a letter: 'Sir – We deeply regret the great inconvenience and annoyance you have been subjected to, by the delay that has occurred in the delivery of our Pictorial Supplements, which arose, however, from a variety of circumstances over which we have no control.'[156]

In 1855, the repeal of the newspaper stamp became imminent. This fact, in combination with the high demand for illustrations of the Crimean War at that time, led Henry to make plans for a new cheap illustrated newspaper, which he started together with the publisher David Bogue (1807–1856): 'We decided to call the new paper the "Illustrated Times," settled it should be a trifle smaller in size than the "Illustrated London News," and fixed the price of it at two pence.'[157] The new venture became an instant success, selling almost 200,000 copies of its first issue. To print all these copies in time, 'five or six sets of both engravings and type had to be electrotyped and stereotyped to enable as many sets of the paper to be put to the machine simultaneously.'[158]

In their autobiographies, Henry and his son, Ernest Alfred Vizetelly (1853–1922), mentioned numerous contributors to the early volumes of the *Illustrated*

88 *The transnational trade in illustrations*

Times. Next to several British draughtsmen – Birket Foster, Kenny Meadows, Ansdell, Portch, and Andrews – he also employed French artists, such as Edward Morin, Gustav Doré, and Gustav Janet. These artists contributed to several French illustrated newspapers, including *le Monde Illustré*, *l'Illustration*, *le Journal Illustré*, as well as to the British *Illustrated London News*.[159] The most prolific engravers of the *Illustrated Times* – Henry Linton, Robert Loudon, and the Harrall brothers – also worked for several French publications, especially *le Monde Illustré*, and started to engrave for the *Illustrated London News* when Vizetelly became its continental agent in 1864.[160]

The relatively long connection between several British and French producers of illustrations of the news probably started in the early 1850s, when Edmond Morin (1824–1882) visited the Great Exhibition.[161] The French draughtsman came to London to work for the *Illustrated London News*; here, he met Henry Linton, the younger brother of the famous engraver William James Linton, and moved in with him.[162] In 1855, just before the abolition of the newspaper stamp, Morin and the two Linton brothers started the *Pen and Pencil: An Illustrated Family Paper*, a high-class publication meant to compete with the *Illustrated London News*, with French capital raised by Morin.[163] Despite their talent, the *Pen and Pencil* went bankrupt after publishing only eight issues. Morin was so distraught by the failure that he fell seriously ill.[164] After working for Vizetelly's *Illustrated Times* for two years, he returned to Paris to become the principal draughtsman for a new venture: *le Monde Illustré*.

The foundation of *le Monde Illustré* demonstrates the entangled connections between British and French producers of illustrations of the news, in which Vizetelly, Henry Linton, and Edmond Morin all played an essential role. In 1856, Frank Vizetelly, one of Henry's younger brothers who would later become one of the most famous special artists of the *Illustrated London News*, was sent to Paris to act as the continental representative of the *Illustrated Times*.[165] After a couple of months, he secured the editorship of *le Monde Illustré*, started by the French publisher Achille Bourdilliat (1818–1882).[166] Many British and French employees of the *Illustrated Times* began to work for the publication. Henry Linton engraved the masthead of *le Monde Illustré*, which it would use until the late 1870s; Linton is also mentioned as the sole engraver of its illustrations in the third and fourth volume, although he also appears to have been the chief engraver in the late 1850s and early 1860s.[167] Gustav Doré, Gustav Janet, and Edmond Morin, who were employees of the *Illustrated Times* in the mid-1850s, worked for the French illustrated newspaper until the early 1880s.[168]

Meanwhile, in Britain, Ingram was far from happy with the achievements of the *Illustrated Times*. After several attempts to thwart its success had failed, including the publishing of three cheap illustrated newspapers with similar titles, corporate espionage, and an anti-Semitic smear campaign (Ingram had insinuated that the *Illustrated Times* was supported by 'Rothschild money'), Ingram managed to buy the publication as outright owner.[169] Vizetelly refused Ingram's generous offers at first, but in 1859 he agreed to sell his shares for 4,000 pounds after he came into financial difficulties when publishing the *Welcome Guest*: a periodical

The transnational trade in illustrations   89

intended to compete with Stiff's very successful *London Journal*.[170] In his autobiography, Vizetelly additionally described how he had picked up a 'little gambling habit,' making several unsuccessful and costly trips to the German spa town of Bad Homburg, which could also have been the cause of his financial troubles.[171]

Ingram retained Vizetelly as the chief editor of the *Illustrated Times* after the latter agreed to stay on for five years for the considerable sum of 4,000 pounds.[172] In 1864, the year that his contract would end, he planned on starting a new illustrated newspaper. However, because of his ill health, he decided to accept Mrs Ingram's offer (who now controlled the *Illustrated London News* after her husband's tragic death in 1860) to become the continental representative of the illustrated newspaper in Paris.[173] In this position, Henry would become the essential link between the British and French engraving trade in the 1860s and early 1870s.

On arriving in Paris in the summer of 1865, Vizetelly rented an office in the Rue Richelieu, where many of the French illustrated periodicals had their headquarters.[174] On top of his annual salary of 800 pounds, the British publication gave him the necessary capital to 'purchase electrotypes for the *Illustrated London News*.'[175] Unfortunately, it is unclear how many *clichés* Vizetelly bought and from whom he acquired them, although he did mention that he could spend around 100 pounds or roughly 2,500 francs, a year on them.[176] Schmidt noted that *l'Illustration* made around 40,000 francs a year by selling copies of its engravings, in which the size of a *cliché* determined its price: one square centimetre cost two centimes. From Schmidt's information, one can speculate that Vizetelly could buy around 12.5 square metres of *cliché* a year.[177] In this period, a full-page illustration in the *Illustrated London News* roughly measured 900 square centimetres, which means that Vizetelly could have bought 138 full-page illustrations.[178] These calculations are far from foolproof, but they do show that Vizetelly had the means to buy a considerable number of copies of French images each year.

From his autobiography and his son's own account, it also becomes clear that Henry not only bought and sold *clichés* for the *Illustrated London News* but also traded in copies of engravings outside of his official appointment. Ernest Alfred Vizetelly remarked in *My Adventures in the Commune* (1914): 'He [the Viscount De Bragelonne] turned it into *le Voleur Illustré*, and my father sold him a large number of old wood-blocks and electrotypes of engravings, which he put to use in one or another way.'[179] Henry himself made similar comments on Moïse Polydore Millaud (1813–1871), the founder of *le Journal Illustré*: 'I entered into business relations with him, selling him some thousands of old wood-engravings and electrotypes, which had been published in the "Illustrated Times," and which he unblushingly served up to his readers as engravings of current events.'[180]

As a part of his job, Henry also commissioned sketches, drawings, and finished engravings of European news events for the *Illustrated London News*. Ernest Alfred noted how his spare time

> [w]as spent largely in taking instructions to artists or fetching drawings from them. At one moment I might be at Mont-Martre, and at another in the Quartier Latin, calling on Pelcoq, Antastasi, Janet-Lange, Gustav Janet, Pauquet,

90 *The transnational trade in illustrations*

Thorigny, Gaildrau, Deroy, Bocourt, Darjou, Lix, Moulin, Fichot, Blanchard, or other artist who worked for the *Illustrated London News*.[181]

Ernest Alfred posted sketches to London only occasionally. More frequently he dispatched 'some drawing on wood by rail.'[182] In his autobiography, Henry mentioned the French artists who worked for him in his function as the continental representative of the *Illustrated London News*. He remembered the same names as his son but adds the name of the famous illustrator Vierge.[183] He knew most of these French artists through his friend Gustave Janet, a French engraver, whom he had 'formerly largely employed on the Illustrated Times.'[184] Between 1865 and the mid-1870s, the period that Henry spent in Paris, *le Monde Illustré* employed many of the same artists mentioned by the Vizetellys, as the names under the heading 'artistic team' on the title pages of the French illustrated newspaper reveal.[185]

We should not underestimate the role of French artists in filling the pages of the *Illustrated London News*. Already in 1846, it praised the 'able engravers MM. Best and Leloir' of Paris, who had enabled it to 'present our readers with illustrations of the recent events in Paris. . . . All who are acquainted with the difficulties of the art of engraving will be able to appreciate the amount of exertion and the almost incredible celerity, which have been indispensable to the production of these illustrations within so short a period of the events themselves.'[186] Although Best and Leloir primarily supplied illustrations to *l'Illustration*, the two illustrations to which the notice referred, depicting the assassination attempt on the life of the French King Louis-Philippe on 16 April 1848, only appeared in the *Illustrated London News* (25 April).[187] The connection of Jules Pelcoq with the British publication is another good example. This Belgian artist probably started working for Vizetelly and the *Illustrated London News* around 1867 but became especially valuable after the Prussian army besieged the French capital in 1870. During the Franco-Prussian War (1870–1871), Pelcoq made 'several hundred characteristic sketches, including many of real historical value.'[188] In the early 1870s, he continued to contribute drawings on numerous other European events, such as the World Exhibition in Vienna of 1873. In the mid-1870s, Pelcoq became sick because, according to Vizetelly, of the hardships he endured while sketching for the *Illustrated London News* in 1870. On Vizetelly's instigation, the manager of the illustrated newspaper 'grudgingly presented M. Pelcoq with a thousand francs, considering this paltry sum a becoming acknowledgment of the great services the artist had rendered to the paper.'[189]

In *Paris in Peril* (1882), Henry related how the Belgian artist Pelcoq was quite possibly the most prolific draughtsman of the *Illustrated London News*: he filled 'at this epoch the pages of the *Illustrated London News*.'[190] In his autobiography, he commented that Pelcoq had made 'some thousands of drawings for the paper.'[191] Vizetelly was not the only one to notice that French artists contributed a significant proportion of the illustrations in the *Illustrated London News*. An article with the appropriate title, "Our art is not our own to give," published in the *Tomahawk*, 'a Saturday journal of satire,' remarked upon Pelcoq's prominent role:

The transnational trade in illustrations   91

Now, we are not going to quarrel with the proprietors for employing a cheap foreigner in preference to native talent, but if they prefer a French artist, why choose M. Jules Pelcoq, . . . who is evidently completely unfit for illustrating a periodical which, up to the present time, has some right to its reputation.[192]

The significant role of French artists after Vizetelly moved to Paris suggests that the *Illustrated London News* deliberately shifted a part of its production to a low-wage country.

In 1896, the famous British journalist George Sala wrote about Henry Vizetelly:

I knew him intimately during very many years of his busy, industrious, and not very fortunate life. He ought to have made a large fortune, since he was not only a man of considerable literary attainments and of long journalistic experience, but he was also the possessor of the keenest business faculty imaginable.[193]

The qualification 'not very fortunate' especially applied to the last years of Vizetelly's professional and personal life. Indeed, the second volume of his autobiography ends rather abruptly after he wrote: 'My eldest son and my second wife both unhappily died in 1874, and I quitted France a few years afterwards when my engagement with the "Illustrated London News" was terminated by a friendly arrangement.'[194]

After staying in Berlin for a couple of years in the late 1870s, Henry started publishing cheap English translations of French novels in London. This part of his life has received the most scholarly attention.[195] In the 1880s, Vizetelly & Company, which Henry started with his son Ernest Alfred, published around 250 titles, 140 of which were British translations of original French works.[196] The catalogue of the company included 14 works by Émile Zola and the first British edition of Gustave Flaubert's *Madame Bovary*, translated by Eleanor Marx (the daughter of Karl).[197] In 1888, a British court charged Henry with obscene libel for publishing three translations of Zola: *Nana, Piping Hot,* and *The Soil.*[198] After a lengthy trial, a judge condemned him to three months in prison, during which his publishing house went bankrupt. Henry died a few months later on 1 January 1894. The *London Daily News*'s description of his funeral is exemplary for this last tragic phase of his life: 'Owing to the severe weather, the ground being thickly covered with snow, there were only a few friends present.'[199]

Three phases of the transnational trade in illustrations of the news

In terms of the changing relationships between different actors in different national contexts, we can divide the transnational trade in illustrations of the news into three phases. The dominance of the *Illustrated London News* marks the first period, between 1842 and 1850. From 1843 onwards, famous imitators, like *l'Illustration*

92 *The transnational trade in illustrations*

and the *Illustrirte Zeitung*, and more short-lived ventures in smaller European countries copied both the form of the British example and its images. In the second phase (1850–1860), the three most important European illustrated newspapers could all produce large numbers of images, and these started to flow from the major European publications to newly established competitors in foreign countries, who often relied on a single foreign source. The founding of several penny illustrated newspapers marks the third phase (1860–1870). Publications of this generation, such as the French *le Journal Illustré*, published old images of the news from several sources and served them to their readers as original illustrations of news events. In the same decade, some publications started applying photoxylographic techniques on an unprecedented scale. This form of piracy fundamentally altered the shape and dynamics of the transnational trade in illustrations of the news.

The first phase: from London, to Paris, to St. Petersburg

In the winter of 1849, the Prussian geographer and naturalist Alexander von Humboldt found himself in an awkward situation. A guest brought the latest issue of the *Illustrirte Zeitung* to a *soirée* of Frederick William IV (1795–1861), the king of Prussia. A contour map of the entire earth impressed the king; nevertheless, it would be the cause of Humboldt's embarrassment. In a letter to his friend, geographer Heinrich Berghaus (1797–1884), he described the situation:

> When I got the map and had looked somewhat better at it, I could only roar with laughter. The king asked me why I laughed so loud. Because, I answered, this map is old and probably copied from a Parisian *cliché*. . . . It was clear that the king resented my remarks.[200]

Berghaus promised his friend to write a letter to the *Illustrirte Zeitung* asking for rectification, also remarking on German illustrated newspapers in general:

> It is deplorable that these periodicals, like the *Illustrirte Zeitung*, are in the hands of ignoramuses. I am speaking in general about these illustrated publications, which took root in our country after French and English examples, and are not meant as mediums of instruction for the reader, but solely as a high-risk investment of the entrepreneur.[201]

In the early 1840s, these kinds of embarrassing situations must have happened quite often. While most readers of illustrated newspapers in France and the German states would have been impressed by the 'original' illustrations of the news that they presented, people with a trained eye, such as Humboldt and Berghaus, would have easily spotted the large-scale re-use of old and foreign engravings.

After the *Illustrated London News* published its first issue in May 1842, the French *l'Illustration* (March 1843) and the German *Illustrirte Zeitung* (July 1843) quickly followed its example. In the early 1840s, the re-use of illustrations in *l'Illustration* and the *Illustrirte Zeitung* is evident. To its credit, the French illustrated newspaper often acknowledged its source. In July 1847, a small disclaimer next to an illustration of the 'Dangerous descent of M. Gypson's balloon' noted: 'We borrow from our London confrère, the *Illustrated London News*, an engraving and the following letter, which he published in his latest issue of 10 July.'[202] *L'Illustration* copied illustrations not only from its British counterpart but also from other titles owned by Ingram, including the *Lady's Newspaper*.[203] British illustrations travelled relatively fast from London to Paris. According to the disclaimer, *l'Illustration* printed the 'Dangerous descent of M. Gypson's balloon' a week after it appeared in the pages of its 'British brother.'[204]

Already in 1843, the *Nottingham Review* noted that the *Illustrirte Zeitung* possessed 'even less originality' than *l'Illustration*: 'it copies the great majority of its designs from those [the illustrated newspapers] of London and Paris.'[205] In the first ten years of its existence, producing original illustrations proved to be difficult for the *Illustrirte Zeitung*. In 1846, the *Journal für Buchdruckerkunst* wrote that the German illustrated newspaper still heavily depended on the *Illustrated London News* and *l'Illustration* for 'the delivery of a large number of *clichés*.' If the illustrated newspaper wanted to 'establish itself as a German company,' it had to 'emancipate itself from [these] English and French publications.'[206] In 1853, even the *Illustrirte Zeitung* had to confess that, in the first years of its existence, its illustrations were often foreign copies: 'When we began our paper, we necessarily had to stand on the shoulders of the English and the French, without whose progress and help we would have been unable to fill a single issue.'[207] Indeed, leafing through the early volumes of the *Illustrirte Zeitung*, the practice of publishing foreign engravings becomes clear. Without mentioning its source, the German publication used many illustrations from *l'Illustration* and some from the *Illustrated London News*. A series of articles concerning the reform of national postal services in Europe is a good example. The *Illustrirte Zeitung* published the only original article in the series – on the German states – without an illustration in its issue of 5 April 1848.[208] The second article, concerning the British Post, appeared a few weeks later. This time, the German periodical copied both the text – in a German translation – and the illustrations from the *Illustrated London News*.[209] The third article, describing the general post office in Paris, was copied word for word from *l'Illustration*.[210]

Only a few months after the *Illustrirte Zeitung* published its first issue, the *Zeitung für die elegante Welt* (1801–1859), a German literary journal, commented on its engravings: 'The larger woodcuts are to a large extent taken from the English and the French "Illustration".'[211] Similarly, a short-lived feud between the *Illustrirte Zeitung* and the famous satirical journal the *Fliegende Blätter* (1845–1944) in 1847 demonstrates that Weber's use of *clichés* did not go unnoticed in the German states. After the satirical journal published a caricature, depicting the *Illustrirte Zeitung* as an old woman looking through the garbage for a joke about the *Fliegende Blätter*, the *Illustrirte Zeitung* reacted by depicting the editors of the satirical journal in a pile of dirt.[212] The *Fliegende Blätter* aimed its next caricature right at the heart of the illustrated newspaper. We see a young girl, the French maid Marianne, feeding an old woman: the *Illustrirte Zeitung* wearing a dress made of newspaper articles. The caption leaves nothing to the imagination: 'How the *Leipziger Illustrirte Zeitung* is dressed in cheap clothes by the Parisian *Illustration* and is being fed the left-overs of the rich French *cuisine*, so that she is prevented from starving to death' (Figure 2.3).[213]

Figure 2.3 Skizzen aus dem Leber. einer Frühverblühten (1847). "Skizzen aus dem Leben einer Frühverblühten." *Fliegende Blätter*, vol. 5, no. 107 (1847). Berlin, Staatsbibliothek zu Berlin, 4" Yy 111.

The transnational trade in illustrations   95

Aside from the *l'Illustration* and the *Illustrirte Zeitung*, publishers in several other European countries with smaller national reader markets started illustrated newspapers in the 1840s, modelled after the *Illustrated London News*. Because most of these titles only published a limited number of issues, they have not received a great deal of attention from historians. In relation to the subject of this book, they are relevant because they copied both the form of the *Illustrated London News* and the illustrations of the three major European illustrated newspapers.

The first imitator of the *Illustrated London News*, published in a relatively modest reader market, was the Dutch *Geïllustreerde Courant* (1844), which I discuss in detail in the fourth section of this chapter.[214] For now, it suffices to note that the Dutch publication relied on illustrations from the *Illustrated London News*, *l'Illustration*, and the *Illustrirte Zeitung*. A year later, in 1845, the Russian publisher Nestor Kukolnik (1809–1868) began another imitator of the British publication: Иллюстрация (*Illyustratsiya*). It appeared just before Tsar Nicholas I of Russia (1796–1855) cracked down heavily on the press, fearing that the widespread revolts throughout Europe in 1848 would spill over into Russia.[215] However, even before this crackdown, the Russian censor kept a strict eye on the *Illyustratsiya*. On the bottom of the last page of each issue, we can find the date and the names of the specific censors that approved its publication. For example, its first issue of 31 March 1845 was allowed to 'go to print, St. Petersburg, 25 March 1845. Censors: J. Okakan and A. Nkkitenko.'[216]

A contemporary article about the Russian illustrated newspaper in the German *Archiv für Wissenschaftliche Kunde von Russland* (1841–1867) noted that similar ventures in Britain, France, and Germany, which gave 'themselves the task of sweetening the hardship of reading for the audience with simultaneously presented eye candy,' had inspired the *Illyustratsiya*.[217] Kukolnik tried to provide his readers with illustrations of Russian subjects, made by Russian artists and engravers, but he mostly failed to achieve this goal. Only a quarter of the images published in *Illyustratsiya* were original, which is to say that Russian artists made them.[218] The German magazine pointed out that these original images 'blatantly failed' to compete with the foreign second-hand illustrations in any way.[219]

In the first volume of *Illyustratsiya*, we find illustrations from the three major European illustrated newspapers. In November of 1844, a massive flood hit the Italian city of Florence. Almost three months later, the *Illustrated London News* published an image of the destroyed Ponte de Perro, a corruption of the Italian *Ponte di Ferro*, named after the metal used for the construction of the suspension bridge.[220] A copy of this image appeared six months later in the Russian periodical.[221] *Illyustratsiya* also published an illustration of Queen Victoria leaving Windsor castle, made by the British engraver William Henry Prior (1812–1882), the father of famous war correspondent for the *Illustrated London News*, Melton Prior (1845–1910), from *l'Illustration*.[222] The Russian illustrated newspaper had the best contacts with the *Illustrirte Zeitung*. An illustration of a new hotel in Hamburg, made by the British engravers of the *Illustrirte Zeitung* Nichols and Allanson, was re-published four months after it appeared in Germany.[223]

96 *The transnational trade in illustrations*

Just before Kukolnik began the *Illyustratsiya*, the Spanish publisher Juan Rico y Amat (1821–1870) founded *la Ilustración Española* (1843–1844) in Madrid.[224] The title and year of publication both suggest that the form of the *Illustrated London News* had inspired him. However, the periodical only lasted a couple of months, and not a single surviving issue was to be found in the European archives.[225] Four years later, in 1849, another publisher from Madrid, Ángel Fernández de los Ríos (1821–1880), who also owned *el Semanario pintoresco español* (1836–1857), the Spanish version of the *Penny Magazine*, founded *la Ilustración* (1849–1857). The first article of the first issue reveals how he based his publication on the examples of the *Illustrated London News*, *l'Illustration*, and the *Illustrirte Zeitung*.[226] Fernández de los Ríos wanted to introduce Spain to the British invention of illustrated journalism: the regular visual representation of news events.[227]

In his article on *la Ilustración*, Ángeles Quesada Novás concluded that the re-use of both images and texts from foreign publications seems to be the most important theme throughout the history of the Spanish illustrated newspaper.[228] Although we can find some illustrations made by Spanish artists in its first volume, British, French, and German copies fill the majority of the pages.[229] *La Ilustración* managed to re-publish some images relatively quickly. In 1849, an image depicting the assassination attempt on the life of Queen Victoria appeared in the Spanish publication only two weeks after the *Illustrated London News* published it.[230] However, this was not always the case, and, sometimes, Fernández de los Ríos used older images. An illustration showing the Parisian cemetery Père Lachaise, signed by the French engraving firm BLHR, was published in *l'Illustration*: five years later, it appeared in the Spanish publication.[231]

It is often impossible to establish the extent to which an illustrated newspaper depended on foreign material. However, in the case of *la Ilustración*, we know the exact ratio between original and second-hand illustrations for the period 1849–1854. According to an article published in 1856, a total of 15,086 images appeared in *la Ilustración*: Spanish artists made 6,121 (40 per cent) of them, while Fernández de los Ríos bought the other 8,965 illustrations (60 per cent) from France, Britain, and Germany.[232] The article demonstrates that re-published images were significantly cheaper than the ones made in Spain: Spanish engravers charged around 41 francs, while a *cliché* would cost 30 francs.[233] A couple of weeks later, the *Illustrirte Zeitung* published a modified version of the Spanish article, mainly to point out that it supplied a large number of the second-hand illustrations in *la Ilustración*, although the exact number is not revealed.[234]

In April 1844, the Portuguese novelist and historian Alexandre Herculano (1810–1877) and the writer and journalist António Augusto Teixeira de Vasconcelos (1816–1878) founded *a Illustração. Journal Universal* (1844–1845). Just like the publishers of *l'Illustration* and the *Illustrirte Zeitung*, Herculano was also responsible for the Portuguese version of the British *Penny Magazine: O Panorama* (1837–1868). He copied British press formulas, noting in the first issue of *a Illustração* that only the 'support of the public' could help him 'reach the degree of perfection and completeness' of the *Illustrated London News*.[235]

The transnational trade in illustrations 97

Although Herculano and Teixeira de Vasconcelos referred to the *Illustrated London News* in the first article of their periodical, its illustrations were mainly French *clichés* bought from *l'Illustration*. An image of Saint Isaac's Square in St. Petersburg is a good example of this.[236] The masthead for *a Illustração*, a view of Lisbon from the river Tagus, is one of the few original illustrations, which further reveals the twin influences of both French and British illustrated papers, being an 'imitation of the *Illustration* of Paris, and the *Illustrated London News* of Britain.'[237] The Portuguese illustrated newspaper stopped publishing in September 1846, only two years after its establishment.

In 1847, the Piedmontese publisher Giuseppe Pomba (1795–1876) founded the first Italian illustrated newspaper: *il Mondo Illustrato* (1847–1849, 1860–1861). Just like his counterparts in other countries, Pomba initiated his career by publishing *il Teatro Universale* (1834–1848), an Italian version of the *Penny Magazine*. In their article on censorship of the visual arts in nineteenth-century Italy, Antonello Negri and Marta Sironi have noted that his illustrated newspaper was the 'first important attempt to publish a periodical intended to offer space to Italian writers and artists united in promoting a process of modernization and national unity.'[238] Indeed, *il Mondo Illustrato* hoped to provide a link between the several Italian states: 'Who has not heard people wailing for not knowing in Naples what happens in Turin; in Rome what is painted in and sculpted in Milan or in Venice?'[239] The article "To the Italian public," which can be found several times in its first volume, even records the exact distribution of the 3,338 copies Pomba sent to the different Italian states. For example, booksellers in the Sardinian states sold almost 900 copies, while only 121 copies were distributed in the Duchies of Modena, Luca and Parma.[240]

In line with the nationalist aspirations of its publisher, *il Mondo Illustrato* contained many illustrations made by Italian artists of Italian events. A certain 'Chiappori' made an image of a mass demonstration at the Victor Emmanuel square in Turin, after Rome, Florence, and Turin signed a declaration in favour of an Italian customs union.[241] These images and the nationalist tone of many of its articles resulted in bans for Pomba's publication in the Kingdom of Lombardy-Venetia, the Papal States, and the Kingdom of the Two Sicilies.[242]

Il Mondo Illustrato also contained copies of British and French images. For example, *l'Illustration*'s image of Windsor Castle can be found in the Italian periodical.[243] The article "To the Italian public" contains a detailed overview of the production costs of *il Mondo Illustrato*, providing a rare glimpse in the day-to-day operations of a nineteenth-century illustrated newspaper. This overview demonstrates that Pomba spent 8,000 lira, or roughly 315 pounds, on 'engravings and *clichés* purchased from English and French newspapers.'[244] Although we do not know the exact ratio between Italian and foreign illustrations, the Italian images seem to have been much more expensive to produce. *Il Mondo Illustrato* paid 'drawers on paper and wood in Turin' (11,918 lira), 'engravers in Turin' (26,624,00 lira), and provided them with 'boxwood for engraving, its preparation, tools and other expenses of the engraving workshop' (2,378,83 lira).[245]

98   *The transnational trade in illustrations*

In 1848 the Hungarian printer Werfer Károly, also known by his German name Carl Werfer, published two illustrated newspapers. In January 1848, he founded the *Ábrázolt Folyóirat* (Illustrated Magazine), which changed its name to Képesujság (Illustrated News) after three months and then, after another five months, to *Mulattató Képesujság* (General Interest Illustrated News), and in April of the same year, he also started a German publication: the *Oberungarische Illustrirte Zeitung*.[246] Living in the provincial town Košice (Kassa in Hungarian and Kaschau in German), presently located in eastern Slovakia, but then part of the Austro-Hungarian Empire, Werfer started his illustrated newspapers in a period of political turmoil. After news of the Parisian revolution of 1848 reached Lajos Kossuth (1802–1894), nationalist hero and all-round nineteenth-century celebrity, he wrote a speech asking Archduke Franz Joseph (1830–1916) to grant far-reaching autonomy to the Kingdom of Hungary. An initial uprising on 15 March 1848, followed by several mass demonstrations in Buda and Pest, resulted in the acceptance of a liberal Twelve Points plan, which, among other things, demanded immediate freedom of press. Many publishers in the Austro-Hungarian Empire made use of this political *momentum*: the number of newspapers that discussed 'political affairs' jumped from 19 to 306, now uninhibited by the strict imperial censors.[247] In Košice, Werfer changed the a-political 'Illustrated Magazine,' which was heavily censored, into the political 'Illustrated Newspaper.' At the same time, he also started the *Oberungarische Illustrirte Zeitung*. An advertisement for this publication, titled 'The press is free!,' noted: 'The barbaric scissor of close-minded censors will no long put constraints on the most honourable part of men: his thoughts.'[248]

Werfer hoped that his illustrated newspapers would contribute to the formation of independent, or at least an autonomous, Hungary. In an advertisement he apologized for the fact that the *Oberungarische Illustrirte Zeitung* was written in German: 'Patriots might accuse us of *Antinationalisirung*, because we publish a German newspaper. We can merely reply that we can only tell our German brothers in German that they should learn Hungarian.'[249] Similar to this language problem, Werfer largely failed to procure Hungarian illustrations of Hungarian news. After printing two illustrations of the 1848 revolutions engraved by Hungarian artists, 'The people's assembly of Kassa fly the national flag on the town hall' and 'The people of Pest submit the Twelve Point Plan to the City Council,' the majority of the images in both his illustrated newspapers were copied from foreign publications.[250] Dezsényi Béla showed that a mere 37 of the total 233 illustrations published in *Képesujság* were made by Hungarian artists: *l'Illustration* was the most important source for the rest of the images.[251] However, Werfer's publications also contained images that were first published in the *Illustrated London News*, which the French illustrated newspaper had probably resold. For example, on 12 May 1848 the *Oberungarische Illustrirte Zeitung* published an image of the Chartist demonstration on the Kennington-Common.[252] The illustration was originally published in the *Illustrated London News* (15 April) but also appeared in *l'Illustration* (22 April).[253]

Similar to its start, the end of the *Képesujság* was closely tied to the developments of the Hungarian Revolution of 1848.[254] The countryside around Košice

The transnational trade in illustrations   99

became a theatre of the civil war that followed the 1848 revolutions: Austrian forces defeated the Hungarian army on 8 December 1848 and 4 January 1849 and marched into the city on 15 February 1849. After publishing the last issue of the *Képesujság* on 9 December, Werfer joined Hungarian nationalist forces in the East-Hungarian city of Debrecen.[255]

The second phase: new competitors

Bacot and Hanebutt-Benz have both argued that the illustrations of *l'Illustration* and the *Illustrirte Zeitung* became national around 1850. However, in 1870, the *Gentleman's Magazine* still remarked upon the transnational trade in images of the news: 'Borrowed cuts appear in European papers. In England, France and Germany there is a system of purchase or exchange of illustrations.'[256] Major European illustrated newspapers did not stop publishing foreign *clichés* after 1850. In fact, new competitors in Britain, France, and Germany, like the *Illustrated Times* and *Cassell's Illustrated Family Paper* in Britain and *l'Univers Illustré* in France, started to appear; consequently, to compete with the original illustrated newspapers, these new publications relied on large numbers of *clichés*, mostly purchased from a single foreign source. However, some of the new players, like the influential *le Monde Illustré*, quickly started to produce high-quality illustrations and sell these on the international market.

In 1859, the French trade journal *Chronique du journal général de l'imprimerie et de la librairie* described a lawsuit that the publisher Ernest Bourdin filed against the owners of *l'Univers Illustré* (1858–1912): a competitor of *l'Illustration* that had begun in 1858. Bourdin claimed that the French illustrated newspaper illegally copied two illustrations, which 'one of our foremost draughtsmen, M. Raffet' made for him.[257] In defence of his client, the lawyer of *l'Univers Illustré* explained how the transnational trade in illustrations functioned:

> Following from reciprocal agreements between the major illustrated publications of England and Germany, *l'Univers Illustré* had the right to reproduce engravings found in these publications at its convenience, . . . just as they – in their turn – could republish engravings, using the electrotype process, which initially appeared in the French paper.[258]

L'Univers Illustré was not guilty of an infringement of Bourdin's copyright because it had purchased the engravings from two of its European partners. According to the newspaper's lawyer, the first appeared in the *Illustrated London News* and the second in the *Illustrirte Zeitung*.[259] If anyone was guilty of copyright infringement, it must have been these two publications. The judge found this defence credible and ruled in favour of the *l'Univers Illustré*.

In 1861, the same trade journal described a similar case, again involving *l'Univers Illustré*. This time a certain Mr Marchal, the 'owner and author' of an illustration of the Chinese city of Peking, which appeared in *l'Illustration*'s issue of 4 September 1858, sued the illustrated newspaper.[260] According to Marchal,

100 *The transnational trade in illustrations*

l'Univers Illustré published a bad copy of this illustration in its issue of 3 January 1861. Michel Lévy (1821–1875), the publisher of the periodical, explained how:

> *L'Univers Illustré* had made an arrangement with the two largest illustrated newspapers of Germany and England, under which it could reproduce engravings that had appeared in these newspapers for a certain fee, and conversely these newspapers across the Rhine and the Canal had the right to reproduce illustrations from *l'Univers Illustré*.[261]

However, the French illustrated newspaper had not bought the 'view of Peking' from one of its foreign partners. Lévy remembered that the *Illustrirte Zeitung* published an illustration of the same subject: 'Was this a copy of M. Marchal's drawing? The director of the *l'Univers Illustré* did not know.'[262] He only knew that he instructed a 'talented artist' to make a new 'view of Peking,' based on the illustration in the *Illustrirte Zeitung* and the sketch of an army officer who recently visited China as a member of a military expedition. The two ways in which Lévy defended himself seem to contradict each other: he claims that an artist exclusively made the illustration of Peking for his publication, but if it *was* a copy of Marchal's drawing, he blamed the *Illustrirte Zeitung* for copying it.

L'Univers Illustré started its career relatively late in comparison to the other major European illustrated newspapers. Therefore, it may come as somewhat of a surprise that it could partake in the transnational exchange of illustrations that existed since the early 1840s. How can this be explained? While *l'Univers Illustré* was relatively young, its owner was a major European publisher. In 1863, Paul Schmidt noted:

> The extensive business relations of Mr Lévy provide him with as many clichés, which are unknown in France, as he likes; this makes him a formidable opponent, which is also amply shown by the 25,000 subscribers of his newspaper.[263]

Lévy founded *l'Univers Illustré* on the idea that it was much cheaper to buy foreign engravings than produce original ones. The lawyer of the French illustrated newspaper underlined this point at the end of his plea: 'It is this artistic and international association, which enables us to sell each issue for only three sous.'[264]

In 1872, the Dutch newspaper *de Nederlandsche Spectator* wrote: 'Nowadays, the international trade in illustrations is increasing. French publications copy English cuts, and English publications those from France.'[265] The flow of illustrations from the large illustrated newspapers to cheaper publications abroad described here is hard to trace. Just like the major illustrated newspapers, cheaper imitators did not advertise the fact that they relied heavily on foreign *clichés*. However, illustrations of the three major illustrated newspapers – the *Illustrirte Zeitung, l'Illustration* and the *Illustrated London News* – and new players, like the influential *le Monde Illustré*, did end up in foreign publications between 1850 and 1860.

The transnational trade in illustrations 101

The *Illustrirte Zeitung* was the first illustrated newspaper that advertised the sale of its illustrations. Already in 1845, an advertisement offered '*clichés* from wood engravings in the *Illustrirte Zeitung* and the other illustrated publications of my house.'[266] The copies cost '3⅓ Thaler for one column, 6⅔ Thaler for two columns and 10 Thaler for three columns, independent of their height.'[267] Between 1843 and 1870, this kind of advertisement regularly appeared in the German publication, and the price of the *clichés* stayed roughly the same. From the early 1850s, the advertisements emphasized that the *Illustrirte Zeitung* could deliver *clichés* 'in four to six days.'[268] This addition was mainly meant to appeal to illustrated *news*papers because they needed illustrations of news events as quickly as possible.

Did Weber manage to sell the illustrations of the *Illustrirte Zeitung* to other publications? A passage in the 1000th issue of the *Illustrirte Zeitung* refers to the large-scale re-use of its images in Europe:

> In this regard it suffices to remember that a substantial part of the literature published since then not only borrowed the principles with which the Illustrirte Zeitung was started but also endowed their works with clichés from its enormous stock of images; this relationship of dependency exists between the Leipziger Illustrirte Zeitung and illustrated newspapers published at the same time in France, England, Italy, Spain, Denmark and Russia; all these publications refer – by their larger or smaller resemblance to the Illustrirte Zeitung – to their German predecessor and regularly publish a greater or lesser portion of its illustrations.[269]

In this quote, Weber points to both the transnational network of major illustrated newspapers and to smaller publications that entirely depended on the *Illustrirte Zeitung* for their illustrations. The final section of this chapter shows how a small Dutch publication, the *Geïllustreerde Nieuws*, bought all its illustrations from the *Illustrirte Zeitung*.

In comparison to the *Illustrirte Zeitung*, *l'Illustration* only rarely referred to the fact that it sold illustrations. Paul Schmidt wrote about the sale of *clichés* by the French journal: '*L'Illustration* provides *clichés* from its woodcuts for two centimes per square centimetre and *galvanos* for three centimes, and sells them for roughly 40,000 Fr. a year in total.'[270] Knowing that the *l'Illustration* had a print run of 27,000 copies in 1863, that a single issue sold for 75 centimes, and a yearly subscription cost 36 Francs, the trade in *clichés* yielded an income equal to the sale of 53,000 single copies, or 1,100 yearly subscriptions. However, as we will see below, the publication also sold the 'exclusive right' to buy its illustrations to publishers in other countries. It is unclear if Schmidt added these substantial sums to his calculation.

In 1855, a small notice appeared on the front page of *l'Illustration*: 'Regarding international treaties, the editors reserve the right of reproduction and translation abroad.'[271] To what international treaties did the notice refer? On 2 February 1856, articles appeared in several provincial British newspapers, discussing the

102　*The transnational trade in illustrations*

court case of *Cassell v. Stiff*.[272] John Cassell (1817–1865) was the publisher of *Cassell's Illustrated Family Paper* (1853–1867), which mainly published illustrated *feuilletons* but, as we will see in the next chapter, became popular with its engravings of the Crimean War (1853–1856). In the mid-1840s, George Stiff worked as the foreman for the engravers of the *Illustrated London News*; thereafter, he started the *Illustrated Weekly Times*, a short-lived competitor of the famous illustrated newspaper. The *London Journal*, which Stiff began in 1845, became a tremendous success in the mid-1850s, selling around 500,000 copies a week.[273]

Cassell sued Stiff to restrain him from 'publishing certain numbers of his journal, containing views of the Paris exhibition, on the ground that they were copied from sketches in the French paper, *L'Illustration. Journal Universelle*, to which the plaintiff claimed having the exclusive right.'[274] Stiff defended himself by stating that he copied the illustrations of the exhibition in the *London Journal* 'from photographs publicly offered for sale in Paris and that none of the sketches in question were copied by him from the French paper referred to.'[275] According to the newspaper articles, the judge believed Stiff's claims and did not grant Cassell an injunction.

The case was more complicated than its description in the press suggests, however. In June 1855, Cassell bought the British copyright of *l'Illustration* from Armand le Chevalier and Jean-Baptiste-Alexandre Paulin – the publishers of the French publication at that time.[276] This kind of arrangement became possible because Britain and France signed a treaty that protected copyright in both countries in 1852.[277] Two conditions had to be met in order for the court to recognize the copyright of a French publication in Britain. Chevalier and Paulin had to state their intention of reserving their copyright abroad: 'Le Chevalier and Paulin published this newspaper in France, and on the title page of it they had caused to be printed a message, reserving their right to reproduce it in this country.'[278] This first condition explains the message that appeared on the cover of *l'Illustration* in 1855. The owner of the copyright also had to register it at the Company of Stationers in London: the trade guild of British printers, bookbinders, booksellers, and publishers. The description of the case notes how Chevalier and Paulin travelled to London to register the copyright and deposit the latest issue of *l'Illustration* at the office of the guild.[279]

The judge dismissed the case because Cassell and the publishers of *l'Illustration* failed to meet all the criteria of the bilateral copyright treaty. According to the verdict, the agreement stated that French newspapers or any other periodically published works that were 'not intended to be completed in any definite number of parts' had to be registered at their commencement or three months after the signing of the treaty in 1852. As *l'Illustration* was started in 1843, and Chevalier and Paulin only claimed their copyright in 1855, three years after the bilateral agreement came into effect, they could not register its copyright in Britain.

Although Cassell could not claim the British copyright of *l'Illustration*, he could make an exclusive arrangement with the French publishers. An article in the *Art Journal* (1850–1880) about the case noted that Cassell paid Chevalier and Paulin 12,500 francs annually, or around 500 pounds, for the exclusive right

The transnational trade in illustrations 103

to publish the illustrations of *l'Illustration* in Britain.[280] The 'sale of copyright' basically entailed that the French publishers promised to deal exclusively with Cassell. The British publisher probably still paid his French partners for every *cliché*.[281]

Just like Lévy in France, Cassell's success, both of his books and periodicals, was largely based on his contacts with foreign publishers, authors, artists, and engravers. A contemporary biography of Cassell noted how he often travelled overnight to Paris to 'see a number of friends and transact business with artists and engravers.'[282] Another biographer of Cassell remarked that he often travelled 'to France, where he was well known, and where he was thus enabled to effect a very considerable business in the exchange and purchase of illustrations for his various works.'[283] After Cassell died in 1865, his wife recalled how several of his French friends, like Jean Best from the engraving firm that supplied *l'Illustration*, the Hachette family, and Michel Lévy (the owner of *l'Univers Illustré*), came to pay their final respects at his funeral in London.[284]

Cassell was one of the first British publishers to use French *clichés* on a large scale, but he would not be the last. However, material demonstrating other instances of this practice is far from conclusive. For example, short articles published in several provincial newspapers in 1859 describe the engravings of the *Illustrated News of the World*, a short-lived competitor of the *Illustrated London News*, as 'thoroughly French.'[285] The earlier quoted article in the *Gentleman's Magazine* also observed an arrangement between the *Illustrated Midland News* (1868–1871), which was an attempt to publish a provincial illustrated newspaper and 'a leading paper in Paris.'[286] The owners of the *Illustrated Midland News* 'shared the expense of producing certain pictures, which . . . on being engraved were electrotyped, and became the English copyright of the English paper.'[287]

The article in the *Gentleman's Magazine* also made the following remark: 'Nearly all the pictures in the *Illustrated Times* are French electrotypes. It is the duty of an agent in Paris to select these each week, and send them over to London.'[288] This agent was, of course, Henry Vizetelly. However, the *Illustrated Times* did not always rely on foreign *clichés*. On 5 April 1856, a small message appeared directly under its title: 'The right of translation and reproducing illustrations is reserved.'[289] The message, which is similar to the one on the front page of *l'Illustration*, appeared right after the court case of *Cassell vs. Stiff* was reported in the news and indicates that Vizetelly sold, or planned on selling, illustrations and articles abroad. The appearance of the message also coincides with the new position of Frank Vizetelly, who was sent to Paris by his father to act as the continental representative of the publication.[290]

It is hard to find information concerning the sale of illustrations from the *Illustrated London News* to foreign publications. A somewhat unlikely source, a report written in 1882 by special agent 'C.C. Adams, in charge of the Second District' of the American Treasury Department, reveals how much money the British illustrated newspaper wanted in exchange for copies of its engravings. A special agent named Starring acquired this information because the Treasury Department suspected that the *Illustrated London News* undervalued 'electrotype

104 *The transnational trade in illustrations*

and stereotype plates,' meaning that it did not declare their real worth to American customs to avoid paying high import duties.[291] According to Agent Adams, the costs were: 'Double page, £10; single page, £5; half page, £2 10s., and intermediate sizes in proportion, none, however small, less than 5s.'[292] In addition, the British periodical only furnished *clichés* 'to known dealers in the trade' that met all four conditions: first, that the publication desiring the *clichés* sent a copy of its most recent issue to the *Illustrated London News*; second, that it guaranteed that the copies would not be resold; third, that an interval of one month elapsed between the publication of the illustrations in the British newspaper and the buyer's publication; and last, that the *Illustrated London News* could refuse requests at all times without giving an explanation.[293]

In contrast to the *Illustrirte Zeitung*, the *Illustrated London News* never advertised the sale of engravings, but it often complained that its illustrations were 'pirated' by imitators all over the world. In 1854, it regularly printed a message on its second page: 'Proprietors of publications who have copied the Engravings, etc. from the *Illustrated London News*, are hereby cautioned that, if such acts of piracy are continued, persons committing the same will be prosecuted.'[294] In its 1,000th issue, an editor noted that the United States had 'three if not four illustrated journals, some of which have not only imitated our general design, but borrow weekly our best illustrations without the least acknowledgment of the source whence they derive them.'[295] Several continental illustrated newspapers were guilty of the same crime: 'Spain, Russia, and Germany have each their illustrated weekly newspaper, which do us the honour of copying our illustrations, sometimes with and quite as often without acknowledgement.'[296]

At the end of the 1850s, next to the famous illustrated newspapers started in the early 1840s, *le Monde Illustré* also began selling illustrations of the news to foreign publications. In an 1859 article on electrotyping it boasted: 'There are two sorts of illustrated publications: the ones that publish new engravings, specifically made for them, that seize and fixate the news in its rapid flight . . . ' and those that 'offer their subscribers only old plates, already published abroad, already known by many and bought for a low price by people who are not so much looking for quality, but for a bargain . . . .'[297] Of course, *le Monde Illustré* belonged to the first category. Because it produced high-quality images, illustrated newspapers in 'England, Italy or Spain' found an 'immense advantage in buying *clichés* of engravings, which were originally published by the most popular [*en vogue*] publication.'[298] *Le Monde Illustré* saw no good reason to deny these foreign illustrated newspapers the right to buy its marvellous illustrations. However, it could never part with the original wood engravings, which it considered to be the 'archive of its achievements.' Therefore, the invention of the electrotype was a godsend. As Chapter 4 will show, in the 1860s, *le Monde Illustré* quickly became one of the most prominent suppliers of images of the news in the world.

The third phase: illustrated penny papers

The third generation of illustrated newspapers – the penny papers – started in London. As with the abolition of the newspaper stamp in 1855, the repeal of the

The transnational trade in illustrations 105

paper duty in 1861, the last of the hated taxes on knowledge, marked a new round of competition for publishers of illustrated newspapers. In 1861, three new publications appeared, which were all sold for one penny: the *Penny Illustrated Paper*, the *Penny Illustrated News*, and the *Penny Illustrated Weekly News*. Two usual suspects started the first two publications: the Ingram family founded the *Penny Illustrated Paper* and their old competitor, George Stiff, the *Penny Illustrated News*. John Dicks set up the *Penny Illustrated Weekly News*. Although he was reasonably new to illustrated *news*papers, Dick's portfolio included periodicals that carried illustrated fiction, such as the *Bow Bells* magazine and the famous 'penny dreadful' *Reynolds's Miscellany*.[299]

The three new publications all targeted a massive audience. After noting that 'a new era is opened to us by the Repeal of the Paper Duties,' the *Penny Illustrated Newspaper* stated that it wanted to be an 'illustrated paper for the million[s].' It hoped 'to study the masses, to understand them, to sympathize with them, to co-operate in a labour of love in whatever may interest them.'[300] The *Penny Illustrated Weekly News* similarly praised the masses: 'It is the million[s], the great bulk of the middle and working classes, who, above all, require a truthful record of events in the striking form of pictorial illustration, as well as verbal description.'[301]

In order to remain cheap, the penny illustrated newspapers filled their pages with re-used illustrations. Their established publishers could use images that previously appeared in their other, often more expensive, titles. Because of this advantage, several British newspapers were sure that the *Penny Illustrated Paper* would become a success. The *Dundee Courier* wrote: 'And as there are tons of old woodcuts lying in the *Illustrated London News* cellars, all of which are with a little alteration now being used over again, there is no reason why the *Penny Illustrated Paper* should not succeed.'[302] Wolff and Fox noted how the *Penny Illustrated Paper* also made use of old illustrations of the *Illustrated Times*, which the Ingram family bought from Henry Vizetelly in 1859.[303]

The British press did not see the re-use of engravings or the use of foreign *clichés* by the illustrated penny papers as a problem. However, these practices could lead to embarrassing situations. As the American journal the *Literary World* remarked in 1871:

> Occasionally this dispersion of *clichés*, especially if they are portraits, leads to ludicrous results. We have known them do very different duty to that for which they were originally intended. It is often true of portraits as those of whom they represented – that one in its times plays many parts.[304]

Four years later the same periodical caught the *Pictorial World* – a short-lived British illustrated penny paper – making such a mistake. It used an image of a church in France for a story about the death of Charles Kingsley, an evangelical priest of the Church of England. These kinds of mistakes were bound to happen: 'It is to be feared illustrated periodicals often blunder in this way, especially when they have *clichés* from France and Germany, with no accompanying letter-press.'[305]

106   *The transnational trade in illustrations*

The journalistic format of the illustrated penny paper originated in Britain, but it became especially influential in France. According to Bacot, the third generation took off with the founding of *le Journal Illustré* in 1864. However, he forgets *l'Universel*, founded in 1862 by the proprietors of *l'Illustration*: 'A journal of the same size, with the same number of woodcuts, as the *Illustration*, sold for 5 sous per copy. Its woodcuts, which are taken from the *l'Illustration*, only get new captions.'[306] Just like the *Penny Illustrated Paper*, the owners of *l'Illustration* used *l'Universel* to re-publish second-hand illustrations and became fairly successful, selling around 11,000 copies in 1862.[307]

Not only was *le Journal Illustré* not the first French illustrated penny paper, neither could it boast the highest number of readers: *la Presse Illustré* (1866–1884) had 2,000 subscribers more than *le Journal Illustré* in that year. Just like the *Penny Illustrated Paper* and the *Penny Illustrated News* in Britain, Achille Bourdilliat, the owner of *le Monde Illustré*, started *la Presse Illustré*, and the publication is yet another clear example of how illustrated penny papers used old illustrations to fill their pages. Bacot has shown that *la Presse Illustré* used a single image several times: it only altered the captions. Furthermore, *le Monde Illustré*, another of Bourdilliat's enterprises, previously contained many of its illustrations.[308]

In 1864, Moïse Polydore Millaud (1831–1870), the publisher of *le Petit Journal*, founded *le Journal Illustré*: the most famous French illustrated penny paper, reaching around 105,000 subscribers in 1866.[309] According to Martin, its primary objective was 'clearly to be affordable to as many people as possible, while keeping a high standard for its engravings.'[310] Selling at only ten centimes, it was certainly affordable, especially compared to more expensive journals like *l'Illustration*, which sold at 75 centimes. However, the 'high standard' of its engravings, and especially their originality, can be questioned. In this regard, an article on the history of the French illustrated press since the foundation of *l'Illustration* in 1843 noted that some French illustrated newspapers, like *l'Illustration* and *le Monde Illustré*, were much too costly, while the inexpensive ones, like *le Journal Illustré*, lacked quality. This lack of quality was mainly due to the large-scale borrowing and stealing of illustrations:

> One hardly ever sees more than reproductions, both in the illustrations and the text. Photogravure and the borrowing of illustrations – the borrowing being free most of the times, because the mentioning of the source at the bottom of the engraving constitutes free publicity for the original publication – are the two main levers of cheap [illustrated] publications.'[311]

Le Journal Illustré was always meant to be an international undertaking. Echoing the universal rhetoric of the *Illustrated London News*, it noted in its first issue: 'Engraving speaks all languages. It is understood by all nationalities.'[312] The newspaper also listed the prices of several international sister publications in European countries and noted that the 'best Italian, German and Dutch' writers would provide the articles in these journals. Furthermore, Russian, Spanish, and

The transnational trade in illustrations   107

Arabian versions of the journal would quickly become available. Bacot further observed that *le Journal Illustré* referred quite often to the fact that it specifically made a particular illustration for one of its foreign versions.[313]

Bacot laments the fact that many illustrated newspapers from the nineteenth century, especially the cheap ones with massive circulations or the foreign versions of publications like *le Journal Illustré*, have been forgotten. There is, indeed, almost no information available about publications like *l'Universel* or *la Presse Illustrée*. Concerning the foreign versions of *le Journal Illustré*, it should, however, be noted that these are often not forgotten but rather 'nationalized' by historians. In this regard, the following case study of Dutch illustrated newspapers demonstrates that the *Hollandsche Illustratie*, as one example, began as the Dutch version of *le Journal Illustré*, before it was subsumed by scholars into national history.

Case study: foreign illustrations in Dutch illustrated newspapers, 1830–1870

The first Dutch illustrated publications appeared shortly after the *Penny Magazine*.[314] In 1834, the Dietrich brothers, two successful publishers and booksellers from Amsterdam, started the *Nederlandsch Magazijn* (1834–1838). The *Nederlandsch Magazijn* published illustrations from the original British *Penny Magazine* and the *Pfennig-Magazin* from Leipzig. Therefore, it also contained French images of *le Magasin Pittoresque* since the *Pfennig-Magazin* used these as well. In his standard work on the history of different illustration techniques in the Netherlands, David van Lente noted that the quality of these foreign illustrations contributed significantly to the success of the Dutch publication.[315]

The success of the *Nederlandsch Magazijn* and the adaptations of the *Penny Magazine* in other European countries prompted several influential citizens in the Dutch city of The Hague to found *De Nederlandsche Maatschappij van Schoone Kunsten* (Dutch society of Fine Arts). The society set out to promote wood and metal engraving in the Netherlands and even financed a Dutch engraving and lithograph school. Wood engraving in the country remained underdeveloped, however, and the school had to import paper, wood for engravings, and printing ink from Brussels and Paris.[316]

Henry Brown, the school's first director, also had to be imported. His life exemplifies the importance of British engravers for the spread of wood engraving in Europe. After John Allanson taught him the art of wood engraving in London, Brown immigrated to Paris to work for the French penny magazine *le Musée des familles* in 1834.[317] In 1837, he became the director of the newly established wood-engraving school in Brussels, where he instructed many Belgian engravers. After working as the director of the Dutch engraving school for only a year, he moved back to Belgium in 1841, where he became a professor at the Royal Academy of Art in Antwerp.[318]

The school in The Hague had to finance itself, and students paid their tuition by selling drawings and engravings. Thus, in order to create a market for their art,

108 *The transnational trade in illustrations*

they started the *Kunstkronijk* (1840–1909): an art magazine that published more than 800 wood engravings and 96 lithographs in the first four years of its existence. While the *Kunstkronijk* thrived, the engraving school quickly found itself in financial difficulties. In 1843, an entrepreneurial publisher from the city of Haarlem, Koenraad Fuhri (1814–1858) saved both the school and the art magazine.[319]

In the same year that he bought the *Kunstkronijk*, Fuhri started an imitation of the *Illustrated London News*, called the *Geïllustreerde Courant* (Illustrated Gazette). Students of the engraving school supplied the first Dutch illustrated newspaper with several images of Dutch subjects.[320] On the front page of its third issue, we can find a large portrait of Willem II (1791–1849), the king of the Netherlands.[321] Other more or less typical Dutch subjects, like steam-powered pumping stations, the town of Scheveningen, and railway stations on the line between Amsterdam and Haarlem, also appeared on its pages.[322]

The *Geïllustreerde Courant* copied the majority of its images from the *Illustrated London News*, *l'Illustration*, and the *Illustrirte Zeitung*. For example, it purchased the illustration on the front page of its second issue, which showed the main hall of the industrial exhibition in Paris, taken from *l'Illustration*, and a portrait of Emperor Nicholas I of Russia from the *Illustrirte Zeitung*.[323] Nonetheless, the short-lived illustrated newspaper only referred to one of these sources in its final issue: an article on the American presidential elections noted that 'an American correspondent in New York of the daily paper the *Illustrated London News*' made the images accompanying it.[324] A couple of weeks earlier, in its issue of 7 December 1844, the *Illustrated London News* had indeed published the same image.[325] The *Geïllustreerde Courant* re-published many other illustrations of the *Illustrated London News* without mentioning the British publication. Several images depicting the London post office, which also appeared in the *Illustrirte Zeitung*, can be found in the *Geïllustreerde Courant*.[326]

Van Lente has noted that, in the mid-1860s, the publication of illustrated newspapers in the Netherlands entered a new phase.[327] Adopting the model of the penny illustrated newspaper, a new generation of Dutch publishers realized that they could make use of the abundant supply of illustrations made abroad. Albertus Sijthoff (1829–1913) was one of the most important exponents of this development. Fuhri, the pioneer of the Dutch illustrated press, went bankrupt in 1856, after which he immigrated to the United States. Before he left the Netherlands, he sold the copyright of the *Kunstkronijk* and all of its illustrations to Sijthoff, who was a former pupil. One of Sijthoff's publications, the *Geïllustreerde Nieuws* (Illustrated News), provides an example of the use of foreign illustrations, which can be researched rather well as the library at the University of Leiden has preserved a part of Sijthoff's company records and his correspondence.

Sijthoff started the *Geïllustreerde Nieuws* in 1866. His timing was perfect. Dutch readers were interested in images of the Austro-Prussian War, which had just begun, and with the *Geïllustreerde Nieuws*, Sijthoff tapped into this demand: his periodical reported extensively on the war, and it could do so because it contained copies of images made by the German *Illustrirte Zeitung*. The fact that it never published a programme underlines that Sijthoff began the *Geïllustreerde*

Nieuws to sell German illustrations of the war to a Dutch audience. Its first issue starts *in media res*, directly describing the events of the war in 1866.

In his history of Sijthoff's business, Dutch historian Rimmer van der Meulen gives a detailed account of the contact between it and F. A. Brockhaus, the publishing company in Leipzig, which printed and distributed the *Illustrirte Zeitung*.[328] A letter of 13 June 1866 from the German company sums up the specifics of their deal. Weber, the publisher of the *Illustrirte Zeitung*, accepted Sijthoff's offer of 500 thalers, roughly 75 pounds, per quarter for the Dutch copyright of the *Illustrirte Zeitung*: 'During this arrangement, Herr. J. J. Weber is obliged to refrain from selling his illustrations [to other parties] in Holland.'[329] Brockhaus' tender also included the costs for the printing of the German illustrations on his presses in Leipzig, which meant that Sijthoff did not buy *clichés* of images but partly printed pages. After Brockhaus shipped the printed pages to Leiden, Sijthoff could print Dutch text on the blank spaces. As Marianne van Remoortel has pointed out in her study, Sijthoff probably used a similar arrangement to publish his fashion magazine the *Gracieuse*, which printed Dutch articles next to the images of the famous German magazine *der Bazar*.[330]

The German printer also provided Sijthoff with a detailed outline of the costs involved: the printing of 2,000 copies would cost around ten thalers, the paper around two thalers, and the packaging one thaler. Van der Meulen has noted that the *Geïllustreerde Nieuws* was reasonably popular during the war of 1866, selling all the 2,000 copies that Brockhaus provided. And yet, after the war, public interest quickly faded, leaving it with only 500 subscribers by 1869. Luckily for Sijthoff, the Franco-Prussian War revived interest in the *Geïllustreerde Nieuws*. In 1871, it sold around 2,500 copies. Eventually, the apparent limited Dutch interest in the more peaceful development of Germany after its unification in 1871 was to be the end of Sijthoff's venture, and, due to a deteriorating number of subscribers, he ceased publication in 1879.[331]

The letter from Brockhaus publishers to Sijthoff provides a unique overview of the expenditure of an illustrated newspaper and the revenue it needed to be profitable. How much money did the Dutch publisher stand to make if he sold all 2,000 copies of the *Geïllustreerde Nieuws*? A subscription to the newspaper cost 2,175 Dutch guilders per quarter, which meant that a subscriber paid 16.7 Dutch cents for a single copy. If Sijthoff sold all 2,000 copies, he made 334 Dutch guilders.[332] After subtraction of the 91.70 guilders he paid to Brockhaus, 242.3 guilders remained to cover the Dutch production costs and more than enough profit. Furthermore, Sijthoff did not need an elaborate organization for all of this: he could do without an editorial staff, printers of illustrations, special artists, and so on. The risk involved in the undertaking was relatively limited and the return relatively high.

We can connect the success of the *Geïllustreerde Nieuws* to the interest of the Dutch public in German affairs. While the newspaper never directly admitted that it used only German illustrations, its sales figures suggest that Dutch readers understood that it contained 'German' news. In 1866, a commentator in the famous Dutch literary journal *de Gids* already thanked Sijthoff for the German

110   *The transnational trade in illustrations*

images in the *Geïllustreerde Nieuws*: 'We have to be grateful to Mr Sijthoff for his efforts to already somewhat "Germanize" our people because the annexation of our country by the North German Empire is seen to be imminent by many.'[333] Dutch schoolchildren could already familiarize themselves with the 'great men and the great deeds of the Prussian Empire.'[334]

The review in *de Gids* noted that the quality of the illustrations in the *Geïllustreerde Nieuws* was good, especially when they were compared to those of the *Hollandsche Illustratie* (Dutch Illustration), which barely deserved a place among the 'incunable specimens of wood engraving exhibited in the town hall of Haarlem.'[335] The *Hollandsche Illustratie* (1864–1919) was the sole competitor of the *Geïllustreerde Nieuws*. In the last two decades of the nineteenth century, it was the only Dutch publication that could be qualified as an illustrated *news*paper.

The 'Gebroeders van Es' of Amsterdam published the first 26 issues of the *Hollandsche Illustratie*, after which the 'Gebroeders Binger,' based in the same city, bought it.[336] In contrast to Sijthoff's publication, two articles in the first volume clearly stated the aims of the *Hollandsche Illustratie*. Similar to announcements in the *Illustrated London News*, *l'Illustration*, and *Illustrirte Zeitung*, the articles underlined the benefits of a publication that combines text and illustrations, asserting that every Dutch reader could find something enjoyable in the *Hollandsche Illustratie*. The articles also stressed the lack thus far of a Dutch illustrated newspaper.[337] However, the supposed Dutch nature of the *Hollandsche Illustratie* is highly questionable.

What was the origin of the illustrations in the *Hollandsche Illustratie*? Joan Hemels and Rene Vegt have commented that, in its first year, the publication gave a Parisian address, Rue Richelieu 112, as the location of its head office.[338] From this, the scholars concluded that *l'Illustration*, which had its office in the same street, was probably the source of the illustrations printed in the *Hollandsche Illustratie*. However, the French source was not *l'Illustration*, but *le Journal Illustré*. How can this claim be demonstrated? First, there is the question of the Parisian address of the office of the *Hollandsche Illustratie*. In 1864, *l'Illustration* was not located at Rue Richelieu 112, but Rue Richelieu 60, as we can read on the front pages of the publication in this period.[339] Nonetheless, a relatively new and internationally orientated illustrated newspaper *could* be found at Rue Richelieu 112. *Le Journal Illustré* prominently printed the address of its office in the centre of its front page.[340] Furthermore, as we saw earlier, this publication claimed that it published a Dutch version.

To further research the origins of the illustrations in the *Hollandsche Illustratie*, I identified as many draughtsmen and engravers as possible of its images in the years 1864 to 1870. A substantial number of illustrations were signed. Of the total 1,678 illustrations that appeared in the Dutch publication between 1864 and 1870, we can attribute 443 to a specific draughtsman or a specific engraver. The remaining 1,235 images could not be identified: either they were not signed or the signatures were illegible or scratched out. Illustrated newspapers such as the *Hollandsche Illustratie* scratched out the signatures of foreign producers to hide the fact that they used *clichés*. An example of this practice can be found in the illustration 'Les courses d'Epson en Angleterre' (The Epsom racetrack in Britain), which originally appeared in *l'Illustration* in 1845.[341] A small box, located at the top left of the illustration, proudly mentions its source: 'The Epsom Derby. May 1845. British engraving of the *Illustrated London News*.[342] Twenty-four years later, in 1869, the *Hollandsche Illustratie* published the same image but did not mention that it had bought the image from *l'Illustration*, and the box containing the reference to the *Illustrated London News* was left empty.[343]

The majority of the illustrations in the *Hollandsche Illustratie* stem from *le Journal Illustré*, which filled its pages with all kinds of illustrations, old and new, that the owners had bought, borrowed, or pirated from multiple sources. It is highly likely that *l'Illustration* sold the illustration of the Epsom Derby to *le Journal Illustré* and that this publication resold it to the *Hollandsche Illustratie*. Somewhere in this chain, probably at *le Journal Illustré*, the reference to the *Illustrated London News* was removed. While *l'Illustration* was still proud of the British origin of the illustration, the *Hollandsche Illustratie* understandably did everything to hide the fact that they used a 24-year-old illustration that had already been published in three other newspapers to illustrate the Epsom Derby of 1869.

At this point, it is of some relevance to explore the engravers of these illustrations in more depth. Henry Linton, who signed the largest number of the identified illustrations published in the *Hollandsche Illustratie*, worked for two illustrated newspapers in the 1860s: the British *Illustrated Times* and the French *le Monde Illustré*, both of which were connected to Henry Vizetelly and his British and French friends. From this fact, we can assume that the *Hollandsche Illustratie* most likely contained many illustrations that were originally published in these two publications.

However, engravers who did not work for the *Illustrated Times* or *le Monde Illustré* also signed a substantial number of illustrations. For example, Verdeill, Jayher, and Roevens primarily worked for the *l'Illustration*. Furthermore, several German images also appeared in the *Hollandsche Illustratie*. From 1866 to 1870, 53 illustrations signed by 'EHXA' were published in the periodical. The abbreviation stands for 'Eduard Hallberger Xylografische Anstallt' (Eduard Hallberger's Wood Engraving firm). Eduard Hallberger (1822–1880) was a publisher of several illustrated periodicals and books from the German city of Stuttgart. He founded the *Illustrirte Welt* (1853–1911), an illustrated newspaper, and the hugely successful *Über Land und Meer* (1858–1923).

In regard to this last engraver, it is somewhat problematic to use the adjective 'German' to describe Hallberger's illustrations that appeared in the *Hollandsche Illustratie*. In 1862, an article in the French magazine *le Tour du Monde* (1860–1914) made a reference to the *Illustrirte Welt* and *Über Land und Meer*: 'Most of their illustrations are *clichés* of the *Magasin Pittoresque*, *l'Illustration*, *le Monde Illustré*, the *Journal pour Tous*, *le Tour du Monde* or the *Illustrated London News*.'[344] The illustration 'De theems-dam en het onderaarsche London' (The Thames embankment and subterranean London) is a clear example of this.[345] Eduard Hallberger's engraving firm signed the image, but the same illustration

112 *The transnational trade in illustrations*

first appeared in the *Illustrated London News* in June 1867.[346] Hallberger's *Über Land und Meer* published the illustration a year later, in May 1868 (Figure 2.4).[347] How, then, did this particular illustration travel from the *Illustrated London News* to the *Hollandsche Illustratie*?

Hallberger could have bought a *cliché* of the illustration from the *Illustrated London News*; however, this would not explain the initials 'EHXA' on the version of the *Hollandsche Illustratie*. It is more likely that the German newspaper made 'German' copies of illustrations in the *Illustrated London News*. From the mid-1850s, photoxylographic techniques could be used to print an image of an illustration directly on a woodblock, after which the nameless workmen of 'EHXA' would engrave it.[348] The illustration of the Thames embankment in the *Hollandsche Illustratie* was, therefore, a *cliché* of a German copy of a British engraving.

The complicated provenance of the illustration does not end there, however. The *Hollandsche Illustratie* did not buy the illustrations signed by 'EHXA' directly from Eduard Hallberger in Stuttgart. *Le Journal Illustré* also contained engravings that German publications originally published. In 1868, the Dutch periodical contained the illustration 'Remembering the German war of 1866,' which *le Journal Illustré* had previously published in its issue of 22 July 1866 under the title 'The War – a German composition sent to *le Journal Illustré* by our correspondent.'[349] The signature 'XA E. Hallberger' in the lower left corner

Figure 2.4 The Thames embankment and subterranean London (1868). 'Section of the Thames Embankment,' *Illustrated London News* (22 June 1867). The Hague, Royal Library of the Netherlands, T 2258 (1867–1).

The transnational trade in illustrations   113

of the engraving reveals that *Über Land und Meer* had published it originally. The image can be found in the issue of June 1866 with yet another caption: 'Germania cover your head!'[350]

The diverse origins of the illustrations published in the Dutch *Hollandsche Illustratie* point to the transnational entanglement of several European illustrated newspapers in the mid-1860s. The Dutch publication got all its illustrations from *le Journal Illustré*. However, this French title published second-hand, and sometimes very old, images from multiple titles, including the French *l'Illustration* and *le Monde Illustré*, the British *Illustrated Times*, and the German *Über Land und Meer*. Additionally, this last title contained images from multiple sources, including *l'Illustration, le Monde Illustré*, and the *Illustrated London News*. These connections explain the publication of the image of Thames embankment in the *Hollandsche Illustratie*, and it also makes it possible that some illustrations, which *le Monde Illustré* published initially, reached the Dutch title. The French periodical first sold them to *Über Land und Meer*, which sold them to *le Journal*, which, in its turn, sold them to the Dutch publication.

Just like the *Geïllustreerde Nieuws*, contemporaries reprimanded the *Hollandsche Illustratie* for using foreign material. Critics especially pointed to the discrepancy between the proud adjective 'Dutch' in the title of the publication and its complete reliance on *clichés*. Already in June 1864, the Dutch satirical magazine *Asmodée* pointed out that the illustrations from the *Hollandsche Illustratie* were not only of French origin but also poorly printed. The article ended with a warning to everyone 'who values his money and good taste': 'Do not buy the *Hollandsche Illustratie*: it is a rag of a paper.'[351]

After the Gebroeders Binger bought the publication from the Gebroeders van Es in 1865, they reaffirmed that the *Hollandsche Illustratie* would start to honour its name and no longer be 'a bastard daughter of France.'[352] Its 'Dutch spirit' would no longer be hampered by 'illustrations that only Frenchmen can understand.'[353] Several Dutch newspapers reacted positively to the new national course of the *Hollandsche Illustratie*. The leading *Algemeen Handelsblad* wrote on 24 July 1865: 'The *Hollandsche Illustratie* deserves the approval and support of our fellow countrymen.'[354] The question immediately arises, however, as to whether it had deserved this praise. It is true that the Gebroeders Binger *did* give the text of their publication a national character; for example, they enlisted the services of Nicolaas Beets (1814–1903), a famous Dutch author. Nevertheless, its illustrations continued to be predominantly French and, to a lesser degree, German. Gerhard Thomas Mohrman sharply alluded to this in his pamphlet *Hollandsche Illustratie? Neen, Fransche kwakzalverij!* (1865) (*Dutch Illustration? No, French quackery!*). Mohrman, a publisher himself, seemed to have understood the business model of the Gebroeders Binger all too well.[355]

Piracy: European illustrations in America

In the mid-1850s, it became possible to use photoxylographic techniques to pirate (to use the contemporary phrase) illustrations. Because of the lack of international copyright regulations, American publishers pirated British illustrations on

114   *The transnational trade in illustrations*

a massive scale. The new possibilities changed the dynamics of the transatlantic trade in illustrations. During the 1840s and the early 1850s, British illustrations of the news could not be copied without redrawing them. In an article about its American agent, the *Illustrated London News* wrote: 'Our own Journal . . . is got up in such an expensive form that the Yankees cannot reprint it, and the American artist would not attempt to copy our fine engravings: we are, therefore, our own cure against a reprint.'[356] This meant that if American publications wanted to print illustrations of the *Illustrated London News*, they had to be *clichés*. In 1843, the *New World* (1840–1845) announced that its next volume would contain a 'romance by Henry Cockton . . . entitled THE SISTERS, which will be reprinted from the *Illustrated London News*, with all of the beautiful embellishments.'[357] The same volume of the *New World* contained several articles with illustrations from the *Illustrated London News* under the title 'From our foreign files.'[358]

There is evidence that American illustrated newspapers, such as the Bostonian *Gleason's Pictorial Drawing-Room Companion* and its successor *Ballou's Pictorial Drawing-Room Companion*, already began pirating European illustrations of the news in the mid-1850s. In 1853, George Derby (1823–1861), under the pen name John Phoenix, wrote several satirical articles for the *San Diego Herald*. One of them was written with 'the most intense delight' after Derby had learned of the failure of the *New York Illustrated News*: 'we hope that it will never be revived, and that Gleason will also fail as soon as he conveniently can, and that his trashy Pictorial will perish with him.'[359] Derby mocked the high pretence of the American illustrated press, which claimed that it contained original illustrations, which were always made 'regardless of expense.' In fact, *Gleason's Pictorial*, 'it should have been Gleasons Pickpocket,' used a 'detestable invention for transferring daguerreotypes to plates for engraving, having come into notice about this time.'[360] In other words, Derby accused the Bostonian illustrated newspaper of using photographic techniques to pirate illustrations. Underlining his point, Derby added a fake issue of an illustrated newspaper, the *Phoenix's Pictorial and Second Story Front Room Companion*, to his article. Using common printer's stock cuts, he mocked the re-use of the same illustration for multiple news stories. For example, the same small *vignette* of a house, printed five times, illustrated the mansion of 'John Phoenix, San Diego,' 'the house in which Shakespeare was born,' 'the residence of Sir Walter Scott,' and 'The Capitol at Washington.'[361]

The successor of *Gleason's Pictorial*, the similarly named *Ballou's Pictorial*, frequently contained copies of images taken from different European illustrated newspapers. For example, during the Crimean War, it printed images from the *Illustrated London News*, the *Illustrated Times*, and *l'Illustration*.[362] Were these images printed from electrotypes? Or was Derby right in asserting that *Ballou's* used a photoxylographic technique? In August 1854, a year after Derby published his article, the American illustrated newspaper published an article describing 'nothing short of an application of the daguerreotype or photographic process to engraving upon steel . . . we are promised views of nature drawn and engraved by herself.'[363] While this new technique still had to be developed, the same article noted that Messrs Southworth & Hawes had already perfected 'the daguerreotype

The transnational trade in illustrations   115

process upon a prepared plate, and the lines thus delineated were then engraved with the burin, thereby securing a fidelity and accuracy that the best trained eye and hand could never attain.'[364] *Ballou's* closely collaborated with the daguerreotype firm of Southworth & Hawes, frequently printing portraits based on their work, so it is entirely possible that the publication also used this new photoxylographic technique to pirate the European illustrated press.

In the 1860s, *Frank Leslie's Illustrated Newspaper* and *Harper's Weekly* – the two largest American illustrated newspapers – started to pirate European illustrations on a massive scale. In 1865, the British *Pall Mall Gazette* still noted with some pride that *Harper's Weekly* re-published an illustration of the *Illustrated London News*.[365] By 1867, anger replaced this initial pride. In that year, the *Worcester Journal* wrote: 'The proprietors of the *Illustrated London News, Punch*, and other English illustrated publications, should memorialize the Senate for the protection against the Yankee robbers, who reproduce their work as original drawings.'[366] Three years later, the *Manchester Evening News* remarked:

> Even the pictorial weeklies are now pirated in Boston and New York, and we have the *Graphic* and the *Illustrated London News* regularly issued under the titles of the *Every Saturday* and *Harper's Weekly* . . . by far the greater part of their artistic wares comes from abroad.[367]

In 1870, an article in the British *Gentleman's Magazine* – which was itself pirated by the American publication *Littell's Living Age* – discussed the questionable practices of American illustrated newspapers.[368] The illustrations of the *Graphic* (1869–1932), a newly founded British illustrated newspaper known for the quality of its engravings, were especially popular: '*Harper's Weekly* has reproduced nearly all the *Graphic* pictures.'[369] The article points out that *Harper's* did not buy *clichés* of British publications, which it presented as the normal way by which illustrations were traded in Europe:

> Pressmen in this country would at once believe that the *Graphic* had made an arrangement with *Harper's* for the purchase of electrotypes from the Strand; but this is not so. *Harper's* photographs the *Graphic* upon wood-blocks, engraves and prints them as its own.[370]

In fact, almost 'all the illustrated papers in America' pirated illustrations from European publications in this way.[371]

According to an article in the *Gentleman's Magazine, Frank Leslie's Illustrated Newspaper*, the most important competitor of *Harper's Weekly*, was 'less guilty' of piracy because it explicitly referred to the source of the illustrations. In a later issue, the *Gentleman's Magazine* published a letter from Frank Leslie himself, explaining the practice:

> We do take, and reduce by photography, the most important pictures of foreign illustrated periodicals, . . . and we avow the fact by heading these

116 *The transnational trade in illustrations*

pictures 'Spirit of the European Illustrated Press.' We take these pictures on the same principle that the European newspapers copy out from American newspapers such American intelligence and criticism on current affairs as, it is supposed by them, may interest their readers, and *vice versa*.[372]

Leslie's letter shows that American publications not only used photoxylography to keep their production cost down: by the late 1860s, the Harper brothers and Frank Leslie were influential publishers and printers with relatively deep pockets, who could afford 'American' illustrations. Publications like *Frank Leslie's* published pirated illustrations not only because they were cheap but also because they could be produced relatively fast.

Contrary to the American interest in European illustrations, European readers did not seem to have been equally fascinated by American affairs. American publications never complained of being copied in Europe, and we do not find sections titled 'Spirit of the American illustrated press' in any of the major European illustrated newspapers. This one-way stream of images suggests that, in the period of this research, the transatlantic visual culture was much more oriented towards Europe than the other way around. Frank Leslie's obituary in his own *Popular Monthly* supports this argument: 'In brief, Frank Leslie's *Illustrated Newspaper* is the only national newspaper ever published in America, not limiting itself to the reproduction of European engravings, but illustrating the current history of American events, so that it supplies a pictorial record of the times we live in.'[373] The emphasis on 'American events' seems to point out that being interested in these events was still rather special in the mid-nineteenth century.

Conclusion

The first part of this chapter described two important preconditions for the transnational trade in illustrations of the news. First of all, we saw how two reproduction techniques, stereo- and electrotyping, enabled illustrated newspapers to make an infinite number of copies of their wood engravings. Because they could be bought, sold, and exchanged, publications no longer had to produce all the illustrations they published. These techniques were also of fundamental importance for many illustrated newspapers in smaller European countries, which depended on the cheap copies of foreign publications to fill their pages. Second, we have seen how the expansion of British engravers between 1816 and 1850, who disseminated the new modern wood-engraving technique of Thomas Bewick around the world, created the basis for the transnational trade in illustrations. In the early 1830s, the actors in this network bought and sold the images of the British and French penny magazines, and in the early 1840s, the same thing would happen with the illustrations of the three major European illustrated newspapers: the *Illustrated London News*, *l'Illustration*, and the *Illustrirte Zeitung*.

After the foundation of the *Illustrated London News* in 1842, publishers all over Europe recognized its innovative nature. Next to the well-known and successful French and German adaptions, publications in other countries, like the Dutch

The transnational trade in illustrations 117

Geïllustreerde Courant, the Russian *Illyustratsiya*, and Portuguese *a Illustração*, also copied the form of the British periodical. However, these titles also copied the British, French, and German images of the news. The exploration into these adaptions has revealed that an intricate transnational web of illustrated newspapers exchanged visual material on a large scale in the 1840s.

The network of the 1840s marks the first phase in the transnational trade of images of the news; however, in contrast to claims made by previous studies, this transnational trade did not disappear or become national after 1850. In the second phase (1850–1860), the three most important European illustrated newspapers could all produce large numbers of images, and these images started to flow from the major European publications to newly found competitors in foreign countries, who often relied on a single foreign source. The French publication *l'Univers Illustré* used images of the *Illustrated London News* and the *Illustrirte Zeitung*; likewise, *le Monde Illustré* published copies from the *Illustrated Times* and British *Cassell's Illustrated Family Paper* became the most popular illustrated periodical during the Crimean War by publishing the French images from *l'Illustration*.

The founding of several penny illustrated newspapers marks the third phase (1860–1870). Publications of this generation, such as the French *le Journal Illustré*, re-published old images to illustrate new news events. Periodicals of this generation were often linked to another illustrated newspaper, which, by publishing a cheap version, hoped to serve different strata of the reader market: as we saw, the Ingram family started the *Penny Illustrated Paper*; *l'Universel* can be connected to the publishers of *l'Illustration*; and *la Press Illustré* to Achille Bourdilliat, the owner of *le Monde Illustré*.

In addition to uncovering these connections, this chapter demonstrates the benefits of a transnational approach in press and media history. Because they were relatively unsuccessful or considered to be vulgar by historians, many of the titles mentioned in this chapter do not take a prominent place in national histories. However, publications such as the Russian *Illyustratsiya* tell us a great deal about the fundamental transnational nature of the illustrated press in the mid-nineteenth century. Moreover, this chapter reveals how a transnational approach can broaden scholarly perspectives. As the case study in this chapter established, historians have overlooked the transnational nature of many illustrated newspapers, like the *Hollandsche Illustratie*, because they only studied it in a national context.

Notes

1 A fascinating observation in a period that saw the formalization of cartel agreements between Reuters, Wolff, and Havas, three important news agencies, which effectively divided the world into three zones of influence. Putnis, "Reuters in Australia," 69.
2 "Vorläufer waren die 'illustrieren Zeitungen' in London, Paris und Leipzig, die ihre Zeichnungen und Aufsätze sich gegenseitig zu Verfügung stellten, so das jede nur zu einem Drittel neu sein notwendig hatte.": Wuttke, *Die deutschen Zeitschriften*, 150.
3 Hudson, *Journalism in the United States*, 709.
4 Remoortel, "Woman Editors," 270. For the international ambitions and connections of Dutch women's periodicals, see: Jensen, *Bij uitsluiting voor de vrouwelijke sekse geschikt*, 183–31.

118   *The transnational trade in illustrations*

5 Marcus, "Reflections on Victorian Fashion Plates," 11.
6 Olian, Full-Colour Victorian Fashions, V.
7 Boardman, "A Material Girl," 97.
8 Broersma, "Transnational Journalism History," 10.
9 Ibid.
10 In this chapter, I consciously avoid the term "international" because, as Broersma argues, it is still centred on the "national" level as the main category of analysis. Bacot, *La presse illustrée au xixe siècle*, 10–15; Blanchon, *La gravure sur bois au XIXe siècle*, 6; Hanebutt-Benz, "Studien Zum Deutschen Holzstich Im 19. Jahrhundert," 656.
11 Bacot, *La presse illustrée au xixe siècle*, 10–15.
12 Ibid.
13 See for example his chapter on the arrival of the British engraver Thompson in Paris. Blanchon, *La gravure sur bois au XIXe siècle*, 47–62.
14 Hanebutt-Benz, "Studien Zum Deutschen Holzstich Im 19. Jahrhundert," 781.
15 Weller, "Preserving Knowledge through Popular Victorian Periodicals," 202.
16 Anderson, *The Printed Image*, 54.
17 Ibid.
18 Bacot, *La presse illustrée au xixe siècle*, 28–9.
19 See: "Tableau 1. Les premiers magazines illustrés de connaissances utiles dans le monde (1831–1845).": Ibid., 211.
20 Knight, *Passages of a Working Life during Half a Century*, vol. 2, 223.
21 Bacot, *La presse illustrée au xixe siècle*, 59.
22 Blanchon, *La gravure sur bois au XIXe siècle*, 63–71.
23 "Journées illustrées de la Révolution de 1848," *l'Illustration* (12 August 1848).
24 "Marque également l'acmé et la fin de l'espace imaginaire européen développe par les magazines illustres depuis 1832.": Bacot, *La presse illustrée au xixe siècle*, 59.
25 Hanebutt-Benz, "Studien Zum Deutschen Holzstich Im 19. Jahrhundert," 786.
26 Reichardt, "Das grosste Ereignis der Zeit," 32.
27 Ibid.
28 Ibid., 27.
29 Ibid.
30 Ibid., 32.
31 Brake, "Time's Turbulence," 116.
32 Ibid., 119.
33 Ibid., 120.
34 **BNA1:** "New Books: The Pictorial Press," *London Standard* (26 May 1855).
35 Maidment, "Illustration," 106.
36 See for example: Tucker, "'Famished for News Pictures,'" 216; Martin, *Images at War*, 46.
37 Jackson, *The Pictorial Press*, 328.
38 Ibid., 317.
39 Ibid.
40 The word "draughtsman" suggests that women were entirely absent in the production of illustrations. However, Catherine Flood demonstrates that women were often employed to draw images on wood. Flood, "Contrary to the Habits of Their Sex?," 107; For the quote, see: Jackson, *The Pictorial Press*, 319.
41 British illustrated newspapers often exhibited the sketches on which their illustrations were based. In 1870 for example, several provincial newspapers noted that a travelling exhibition displayed the original sketches that were used for the illustrations of the Franco-Prussian War of 1870. **BNA1:** "Newcastle Fine Art Gallery," *Newcastle Courant* (30 December 1870).
42 Jackson, *The Pictorial Press*, 317.
43 Ibid., 321.

The transnational trade in illustrations   119

44 Ibid.
45 Janzen Kooistra, "Illustration," 104.
46 Riall, *Garibaldi*, 255.
47 Ibid.; "Un dessinatueur de l'Illustration sur le champ de bataille de Magenta," *l'Illustration* (18 June 1859).
48 M. Montaud, "correspondant de l'Illustration, dessinant des volontaires de l'insurection cretoise revenant en Grece, a bord du paquebot autrichien," *l'Illustration* (9 March 1867).
49 "Briefwechsel mit alle für alle," *Illustrirte Zeitung* (16 April 1864).
50 Keller, "Early Photojournalism," 184.
51 **BNA1**: "Sham Correspondents," *The Graphic* (14 February 1874).
52 Gervais and Morel, *The Making of Visual News*, 51.
53 **BNA1**: "The Late Queen of Oude," *Elign Courant, and Morayshire Advertiser* (19 February 1858).
54 **BNA1**: "The Scene after the Explosion," *Dunfermline Saturday Press* (8 October 1864).
55 **GB1**: "How Illustrated Newspapers Are Made," *Frank Leslie's Illustrated Newspaper* (2 August 1856).
56 **BNA1**: "The Career of an English Letter-Press Printer (From the Manchester Guardian)," *Westmoreland Gazette* (19 March 1853).
57 "Photgraphie centrale de l'Illustration," *l'Illustration* (22 January 1859).
58 "L'artiste dessine avec un crayon ordinaire de mine de plomb, sur un morceau de buis bien sec, bien uni, légèrement blanchi, comme sur une feuille de papier. Le dessin, jugé et accepté, est immédiatement porté à l'atelier général de graveurs, dont le dessin ci-joint vous offre l'image fidèle. Des qu'il arrive, on le grave, sans trêve ni repos, jour et nuit car souvent il doit être achevé en moins de quarante-huit heures.": "Les Mystères de l'Illustration," *l'Illustration* (2 March 1844).
59 "Atelier des Graveurs de l'Illustration pendant le jour," *l'Illustration* (2 March 1844); "Atelier des Graveurs de l'Illustration pendant la nuit," *l'Illustration* (2 March 1844).
60 "How Illustrated Newspapers Are Made," *Frank Leslie's Illustrated Newspaper* (2 August 1856).
61 Der Xylograph, "wenn er seinem Beruf Ehre machen soll, muss nicht bloß eine geschickte Hand, sondern auch ein künstlerisch gebildetes Auge und Verständnis für das Wesen der Zeichnung haben": "Wie die Illustrirte Zeitung entsteht," *Illustrirte Zeitung* (30 August 1862).
62 Beegan, *The Mass Image*, 56.
63 This change had a profound effect on the social status of the wood engraver. Martin even considers engravers to be one of the first "proletarian classes of the mass media industry." Ibid., 59; Martin, "Nineteenth Century Wood Engravers at Work," 133.
64 Brown, *Beyond the Lines*, 34–40.
65 Keller, *The Ultimate Spectacle*, 73.
66 Barnhurst and Nerone, "Civic Picturing vs. Realist Photojournalism," 60.
67 Keller, *The Ultimate Spectacle*, 73.
68 Ibid.
69 **HT1**: "Looking into the Middle of the Week," *Punch*, vol. 19 (1848): 39.
70 **HT1**: "A Cut for an Illustrated Paper: A Barricade Taken on the Spot by Our Artist," *Punch*, vol. 14 (1848): 45.
71 **BNA1**: "Cockney's in Scotland," *Morning Post* (28 September 1844).
72 **BNA1**: "English Notion of Shearing (from the Edinburgh Weekly Register)," *Statesman and Dublin Christian Record* (8 October 1844).
73 "Comment se fait L'Illustration," *l'Illustration* (13 April 1867).
74 **BNA1**: "The London Illustrated Newspapers and the Portrait of the Irish 'Conspirators'," *Dublin Evening Mail* (6 December 1843).
75 **BNA1**: "News," *Dublin Monitor* (12 January 1844).

120 *The transnational trade in illustrations*

76 Ibid.

77 Martin, *Images at War*, 57.

78 Ibid.

79 **GAL:** "l'artiste par excellence dans l'art de l'electrotypie": Emile Bourdelin, "L'electrotypie ou la Galvanoplastie. Appliquée a la reproduction du texte et des gravures sur bois," *le Monde Illustré* (7 January 1860).

80 **GAL:** "Ateliers d'electrotypie," *le Monde Illustré* (7 January 1860).

81 **GAL:** Emile Bourdelin, "L'electrotypie ou la Galvanoplastie. Appliquée a la reproduction du texte et des gravures sur bois," *le Monde Illustré* (7 January 1860).

82 Jackson, *The Pictorial Press*, 325.

83 Ibid.

84 **GAL:** "Aujourd'hui, les publications illustrées françaises expédient à l'étranger un grand nombre de leurs dessins d'actualités, et l'opération électrotypique se fait avec une telle rapidité que les clichés des bois, sortis le mercredi ou le jeudi des mains des graveurs, peuvent être expédiés le vendredi pour Londres et Berlin, où on les tiré le samedi en même temps qu'à Paris on imprime avec les originaux.": Emile Bourdelin, "L'electrotypie ou la Galvanoplastie. Appliquée a la reproduction du texte et des gravures sur bois," *le Monde Illustré* (7 January 1860).

85 **BNA2:** "Different Kinds of Printing: From Chambers Journal," *the Manchester Courier and Lancashire General Advertiser* (10 February 1866).

86 Beegan, *The Mass Image*, 8.

87 "Photography Applied to Engraving on Wood (Xylophotography)," *Illustrated London News* (8 January 1859).

88 **GB2:** Krüger, *Vademecum des praktischen Photographen*, 241.

89 **GB1:** "Photographic Society of London: Ordinary General Meeting," *Journal of the Photographic Society* (15 January 1861).

90 George Derby, under the nom de plume John Phoenix, wrote the article "illustrated newspapers" in 1853. It was re-published in this collection from 1856. **GB3:** Derby, *Phoenixiana, or, Sketches and Burlesques*, 117.

91 **GB1:** "Photo-Xylography," *Photographic Notes* (15 November 1857).

92 Gregory and Stevenson, *The Routledge Companion to Britain in the Eighteenth Century*, 316.

93 We know a great deal about the life of Thomas Bewick, which probably has to do with the fact that he, just like Henry Vizetelly, wrote an autobiography: *A Memoir of Thomas Bewick*. I have based this paragraph on the excellent chapter of Blanchon: Blanchon, *La gravure sur bois au XIXe siècle*, 22–7.

94 Hanebutt-Benz makes the same point while discussing the German situation. Blanchon, *La gravure sur bois au XIXe siècle*, 6; Hanebutt-Benz, "Studien Zum Deutschen Holzstich Im 19. Jahrhundert," 656.

95 Blanchon, *La gravure sur bois au XIXe siècle*, 6.

96 Ibid., 45.

97 Gusman, *La gravure sur bois en France au XIXe siècle*, 144; Hanebutt-Benz, "Studien Zum Deutschen Holzstich Im 19. Jahrhundert," 656.

98 Blanchon, *La gravure sur bois au XIXe siècle*, 52.

99 Ibid., 58.

100 Ibid., 74, 77.

101 Ibid., 72; Hanebutt-Benz, "Studien Zum Deutschen Holzstich Im 19. Jahrhundert," 656.

102 Hanebutt-Benz, "Studien Zum Deutschen Holzstich Im 19. Jahrhundert," 733.

103 Later in this chapter, it will become clear that in the early 1840s, Weber bought most of the illustrations for his newspaper from *l'Illustration* and the *Illustrated London News*. Weber, *Johann Jakob Weber*, 40.

104 Yukiko, "Russian Illustrated Journals," 164.

105 **GBX:** Lewer, "John Orrin Smith, Engraver," *the Essex Review*, vol. 31, no. 122 (1922): 57.

The transnational trade in illustrations 121

106 Smith, *Radical Artisan*, 3, 13.
107 Engen, *Dictionary of Victorian Wood Engravers*, 147.
108 GBX: Holloway, *Famous American Fortunes and the Men Who Have Made Them*, 322.
109 Ibid., 323.
110 Brown, *Beyond the Lines*, 18.
111 Leslie made a beautiful image of Gleason's production process. Ibid.
112 "For the New Year," *Gleason's Pictorial Drawing Room Companion* (2 December 1854).
113 Brown, *Beyond the Lines*, 18.
114 GBX: Kimball, "Frank Leslie," *Frank Leslie's Popular Monthly*, vol. 9, no. 3 (1880): 260.
115 Ibid., 259.
116 Engen, *Dictionary of Victorian Wood Engravers*, 44.
117 **BNA1:** "To Wood Engravers Wishing to Emigrate to America," *London Evening Standard* (22 August 1870).
118 Ibid.
119 **GBX:** Lekish, *Embracing Scenes about Lake Tahoe & Donner*, 3.
120 **GBX:** "Thomas Armstrong," *Hurchings' California Magazine*, vol. 5, no. 10 (1861): 434.
121 Ibid.
122 **CDNC1:** "The California Illustrated News," *Daily Alta California* (28 August 1850).
123 "Thomas Armstrong," *Hurchings' California Magazine*, vol. 5, no. 10 (1861): 435.
124 **TR1:** "Wood Engraver: Artist of Old Sydney," *Sydney Morning Herald* (30 January 1937).
125 Downling, "Destined Not to Survive," 92.
126 The preface to the second volume of *l'Illustration*, which designates the firm as "our engravers," makes this clear: "Preface," *l'Illustration*, vol. 2 (1843). Also Jobling and Crowley note that ABL contributed around 25 per cent of all the illustrations in the first two volumes of the French newspaper. Jobling and Crowley, *Graphic Design*, 36, note 12.
127 Blanchon, *La gravure sur bois au XIXe siècle*, 232.
128 Ibid., 80.
129 Ibid., 245.
130 Ibid., 231.
131 Weber, *Johann Jakob Weber*, 40.
132 Clauß, "Kretzschmar," 140.
133 Ibid.
134 "Frontispiece," *Illustrirte Zeitung*, vol. 26 (1849).
135 Clauß, "Kretzschmar," 140.
136 "P.P," *Illustrirte Zeitung* (4 September 1858).
137 Hanebutt-Benz, "Studien Zum Deutschen Holzstich Im 19. Jahrhundert," 799.
138 Clauß, "Kretzschmar," 140.
139 Hanebutt-Benz, "Studien Zum Deutschen Holzstich Im 19. Jahrhundert," 783.
140 Nyrop, "Hans Peter Hansen," 633.
141 Botha, "The South African Illustrated News as Source for the Cultural Historian," 39; Rosenthal, *Heinrich Egersdörfer*, 18.
142 **BNA3:** "Death of Mr. Henry Vizetelly," *Lancashire Evening Post* (3 January 1894).
143 **BNA3:** "Progress of Illustrated Journalism," *Oxford Chronicle and Reading Gazette* (2 September 1869).
144 Merkle, "Vizetelly & Company as (Ex)Change Agent," 88.
145 Vizetelly, *Glances Back through Seventy Years*, 1893, I:109.
146 Ibid., I:198.
147 Ibid., I:130–1.
148 From the British Newspaper Archive it becomes clear that at least the *Royal Cornwall Gazette* and the *Northern Wig* bought the supplement. **BNA3:** "The Royal Marriage,"

122 *The transnational trade in illustrations*

Northern Wig (18 February 1840); "The Royal Marriage," *Royal Cornwall Gazette* (14 February 1840).

149 "Christening festivities," *Western Times* (29 January 1842).

150 Vizetelly, *Glances Back through Seventy Years*, 1893, I:220–5.

151 Ibid., I:222.

152 **BNA3:** "London letter," *Leicestershire Mercury* (18 November 1843).

153 **BNA3:** "The Career of an English Letter-Press Printer (From the Manchester Guardian)," *Westmoreland Gazette* (19 March 1853).

154 Vizetelly, *Glances Back through Seventy Years*, 1893, I:281.

155 **BNA3:** "Our Promised Pictorial Supplement," *Belfast News-Letter* (24 November 1852); "Our Promised Pictorial Supplement of the Duke's Funeral," *North Wales Chronicle* (26 November 1852); "Local and Provincial," *Manchester Courier and Lancashire Advertiser* (27 November 1852); "Illustrations of the Duke's Funeral," *Leeds Intelligencer* (27 November 1852).

156 **BNA3:** "Our promised Pictorial Supplement," *Belfast News-Letter* (29 November 1852).

157 Vizetelly, *Glances Back through Seventy Years*, 1893, I:384.

158 Ibid., I:396.

159 Ibid., I:390; Vizetelly, *My Days of Adventure*, 5.

160 Vizetelly, *My Days of Adventure*, 5.

161 GB: Beraldi, *Les graveurs du XIXe siècle*, 126–9.

162 GB: ibid., 127.

163 Williamson, "Illustrated Journalism in England: Its Development. – II," 340.

164 "Morin fut si impressionné de cet échec qu'il en tomba gravement malade.": **GB:** Beraldi, *Les graveurs du XIXe siècle*, 127.

165 Vizetelly, *Glances Back through Seventy Years*, 1893, II:85.

166 Ibid.

167 These are the only volumes of the 1850s, 1860s, and 1870s that mention the name of the engraver in their index. "Table Alphabétique des Gravures," *le Monde Illustré*, vol. 3 (1858): 419–20; "Table Alphabétique des Gravures," *le Monde Illustré*, vol. 4 (1858): 419–20.

168 This becomes clear from the lists of artistic employees, which are published on the title pages of the bounded volumes of *le Monde Illustré*.

169 Vizetelly, *Glances Back through Seventy Years*, 1893, I:424–5.; **BNA3:** "Notes from Our London Correspondent," *Yorkshire Gazette* (29 September 1855).

170 Vizetelly started the *Welcome Guest* because he was impressed by the enormous success of Stiff's *London Journal*. In his autobiography he admits to have been mainly impressed by the £24.000 that Ingram paid Stiff for his journal in 1857. Vizetelly, *Glances Back through Seventy Years*, 1893, II:60.

171 Ibid., II:27–9.

172 Ibid., II:60.

173 Ibid., II:118.

174 Ibid., II:123.

175 Ibid., II:120.

176 Ibid.

177 2500 francs = 250,000 centimes / 2 [price per square centimetre cliché] = 125,000 square centimetre of cliché / 10000 = 12.5 square metre of cliché.

178 One full page in the *Illustrated London News* measured 14 × 10 inches, or 35.5 × 25.4 centimetres. This roughly equals 900 square centimetres. Vizetelly could buy 125,000 square centimetres a year (see previous note). Divided by 900, 138 full pages remain.

179 Vizetelly, *My Days of Adventure*, 190–1.

180 Vizetelly, *Glances Back through Seventy Years*, 1893, II:338.

181 Vizetelly, *My Adventures*, 17.

182 Ibid.

The transnational trade in illustrations 123

183 Vizetelly, *Glances Back through Seventy Years*, 1893, II:338–44.
184 Ibid., II:338.
185 "Partie Artistique," *le Monde Illustré*, vol. 16–30 (1865–1872).
186 "To Correspondents," Illustrated London News (25 April 1846).
187 "Lecomte Shooting at King Louis Philipe," *Illustrated London News* (25 April 1846); "Arrest of Lecomte by Millet, a Groom of the Royal Household," *Illustrated London News* (25 April 1846).
188 Ibid.
189 Ibid.
190 Vizetelly, *Paris in Peril*, I:242.
191 Vizetelly, *Glances Back through Seventy Years*, 1893, II:340.
192 "Our Art Is Not Our Own to Give," *the Tomahawk* (1 June 1867).
193 Sala, *The Life and Adventure*, I:270.
194 Vizetelly, *Glances Back through Seventy Years*, 1893, II:431.
195 See for example: Korey and Fisher, *Vizetelly & Compan(Ies)*; Merkle, "Vizetelly & Company as (Ex)Change Agent."
196 Merkle, "Vizetelly & Company as (Ex)Change Agent," 89.
197 Ibid., 96.
198 Ibid., 98.
199 **BNA3**: "Funeral of Mr. Henry Vizetelly," *London Daily News* (6 January 1894).
200 **GB4**: "Als es an mich kam und ich es etwas naher angesehen hatte, musste ich laut auflachen. Der König fragte, warum ich so herzhaft lache? Weil, habe ich geantwortet das Bild ein alte Karte ist, wahrscheinlicher ein Pariser cliché [. . .]. Der König hat mir meine Bemerkung übel genommen.": Berghaus, *Briefwechsel Alexander von Humboldt mit Heinrich Berghaus*, vol. 3, 102.
201 **GB4**: "Traurig ist es das Blätter, welche diese Illustrirte Zeitung, auf den großen Hausen berechnet sind, sich in die Händen von Ignoranten befinden. [. . .] ich spreche im Allgemeinen von dieser periodischen Illustrations-Literatur, die sich als Nachbildung der französischen und englischen bei uns eingenistet hat, nicht als Belehrungsmedium der Leser, sondern als Geldspekulation der Unternehmer." Berghaus, *Briefwechsel Alexander von Humboldt's mit Heinrich Berghaus*, vol. 3, 104.
202 "Nous empruntons à notre confrère de Londres, l'Illustrated London News, la gravure et la lettre suivante, qu'il a publiée dans son dernier numéro en date du 10 Julie.": "Descente périlleuse du ballon de M. Gypson, a Londres, le 6 Juliet 1847," *l 'Illustration* (17 July 1847).
203 "La Saint-Valentin en Angleterre (14 fevrier)," *l'Illustration* (17 February 1849).
204 "Descente périlleuse du ballon de M. Gypson, a Londres, le 6 Juliet 1847," *l 'Illustration* (17 July 1847).
205 **BNA1**: "Review: Pictorial Times," *Nottingham Review* (22 December 1843).
206 **GB**: "Das Institut der Illustrirten Zeitung zu Leipzig," *Journal für Buchdruckerkunst* (15 January 1846).
207 "Als wir mit unsere Zeitung begannen, sahen wir uns genötigt, uns auf die Schultern der Engländer und Franzosen zu stellen, ohne deren Vorgang und Aushülfe wir außer stand gewesen sein wurden auch nur eine einzige vollständige Nummer herzustellen": "Zehn Jahre," *Illustrirte Zeitung* (2 July 1853).
208 "Das europäische Postwesen," *Illustrirte Zeitung* (5 April 1845).
209 "Das europäische Postwesen II. Das Postwesen in England," *Illustrirte Zeitung* (14 June 1845); "Saturday Night at the General Post-Office, Newspaper Department," *Illustrated London News* (1 March 1845).
210 "Das europäische Postwesen III. Frankreich," *Illustrirte Zeitung* (19 July 1845); "De l'administration des Poste et de la Reforme postale," *l'Illustration* (27 April 1844).
211 **GB5**: "Die größeren Holzschnitte [sind] auch großentheils der englischen und der französischen 'Illustration' entnommen.": "Leipzig," *Zeitung für die elegante Welt* (5 July 1843).

124 *The transnational trade in illustrations*

212 "Skizzen aus dem Leben einer Frühverblühten. Nro. 1.," *Fliegende Blätter*, vol. 106 (1847): 79; "Eine Überraschung," *Illustrirte Zeitung* (4 September 1847).

213 "Wie die Leipziger Illustrirte Zeitung von der Pariser Illustration um ein billiges bekleidet und mit dem Überresten der französischen reichen Küche gefüttert wird, damit sie nicht verhungert.": "Skizzen aus dem Leben einer Frühverblühten. Nro. 2.," *Fliegende Blätter*, vol. 107 (1847): 88.

214 I have tried to find all the European imitators of the *Illustrated London News* in the 1840s. Although I found several of them, it is unclear if more early adaptions of the British publication exist.

215 Betz and Nedd, "Irony, Derision, and Magical Wit," 12.

216 "Печатать позволяется," *Illyustratsiya* (25 March 1845).

217 **GB2:** "Die Aufgabe gestellt haben, dem Publikum die Mühseligkeiten der Lektüre durch die zugleich dargebotene Augenweide zu versüßen": "Russische Illustrirte Zeitung," *Archiv für wissenschaftliche Kunde von Russland*.

218 "Dieses letztere ist auch wirklich in so reichlichem Maße geschehen, dass von den bisher gelieferten Illustrationen kaum der vierte Theil auf Originalität Anspruch machen können.": Ibid.

219 "Eklatante Weise missglückt": Ibid.

220 "Florence, from the Ponte de Perro, after the late inundations," *Illustrated London News* (4 January 1845).

221 "Мостъ Перро во Флиренціи," *Illyustratsiya* (14 June 1845).

222 "Виндзорскій ааиокъ," *Illyustratsiya* (30 June 1845); "Châteaux Windsor," *l'Illustration* (19 October 1844).

223 "Hotel St. Petersburg am Jungfernstieg," *Illustrirte Zeitung* (10 May 1845); "Пербургскэя гоститшца въ Гамбурге [The Hotel in Hamburg]," *Illyustratsiya* (8 september 1845).

224 Hartzenbusch, *Apuntes para un catálogo de periódicos madrileños desde el año 1661 al 1870*, 98.

225 Ibid.

226 Quesada, "La Ilustración. Periódico Universal (1849–1857). Panorámica General," 242.

227 Ibid.

228 Ibid., 250.

229 Ibid., 242.

230 "The Outrage," *Illustrated London News* (22 May 1849); "Atentado contra la reina Victoria," *Ilustración* (9 June 1849).

231 "Vue générale du Père Lachaise," *l'Illustration* (2 November 1844)"; "Paris – Cementario del Padre Lachaisse," *La Ilustración* (3 November 1849).

232 Note 7, cited in: Novás, "La Ilustración. Periódico Universal," 242.

233 "Das Etablissement der 'Illustracion' in Madrid," *Illustrirte Zeitung* (15 November 1856).

234 Ibid.

235 "A Illustração," *a Illustração* (April 1845).

236 "Place Saint-Isaac, a Saint-Pétersbourg," *l'Illustration* (24 August 1844); "Praça de Santo Isaac, S. Petersburgo," *a Ilustração* (1 January 1846).

237 Ibid.

238 Negri and Sironi, "Censorship of the Visual Arts in Italy 1815–1915," 203.

239 "To the Readers", *il Mondo Illustrato* (2 January 1847). Cited in: Ibid.

240 "Al public Italiano," *il Mondo Illustrato* (13 November 1847).

241 "Veduta della piazza Vittorio Emanuele in Torino, il giorno 3 Novembre," *il Mondo Illustrato* (13 November 1847).

242 Negri and Sironi, "Censorship of the Visual Arts in Italy 1815–1915," 203.

243 "Castello di Windsor," *il Mondo Illustrato* (26 June 1847).

244 "Al public Italiano," *il Mondo Illustrato* (13 November 1847).

The transnational trade in illustrations 125

245 Ibid.
246 I would like to thank my colleague Pal Kelemen for pointing me to Werfer and the *Képesujság*, his comments and help with understanding the Hungarian sources.
247 Sperber, *The European Revolutions*, 1848–1851, 154.
248 **GB:** "Die barbarische Scheere engherziger Censoren wird nicht mehr das Edelste des Menschen, die Gedanken, beschnizeln.": "Die Presse ist frei!" *Der Ungar. Zeitschriftliches Organ für magyarische Interessen* (2 April 1848).
249 **GB:** "Vielleicht werden uns die Patrioten den Vorwurf der Antinationalisirung machen, wenn wir eine teutsche [*sic*] Zeitung erscheinen lassen. Wir können ihnen nur erwidern, dass wir unseren deutschen Mitbrüdern nur in teutschen Sprache sagen können, dass, sie ungarisch lernen sollen.": "Die Presse ist frei!" *Der Ungar. Zeitschriftliches Organ für magyarische Interessen* (2 April 1848).
250 "Kassa népgyülése kitűzi városházán a nemzeti lobogót," *Képesujság* (25 March 1848); "Pest lakossága 12 pontból álló kérelmet nyújt be a városi két tanácsna," *Képesujság* (25 March 1848).
251 Dezsényi Béla, "Az első magyar képes hetilap A kassai "Ábrázolt Folyóirat" története," 29.
252 "Die Chartischen bringen ihre petition auf enem Triumphbogen nach London," *Oberungarische Illustrirte Zeitung* (12 May 1848).
253 "The meeting on Kennington-Common – From a Dagueurreotype," *Illustrated London News* (15 April 1848); "Manifestation chartiste a Kennington-Common," *l'Illustration* (22 April 1848).
254 Werfer had already stopped publishing *Oberungarische Illustrirte Zeitung* after the issue of 30 June 1848. The reasons for this are unclear but may involve an insufficient number of subscribers.
255 Dezsényi Béla, "Az első magyar képes hetilap A kassai "Ábrázolt Folyóirat" története," 26.
256 "Illustrated Newspapers," *the Gentleman's Magazine*, new series, vol. 4 (1870): 462.
257 **GB4:** "Chronique Judiciaire," *Chronique du journal général de l'imprimerie et de la librairie* (12 March 1859).
258 **GB4:** "Il a expliqué comment, par suite de traits réciproques aves les principaux recueils illustrés de l'Angleterre et de l'Allemagne, l'Univers Illustré a le droit de reproduire toutes les gravures à sa convenance qui se trouvent dans ces recueils, de même qu'a leur tour ils peuvent reproduire, par la galvanoplastique, les gravures originales publiées dans le journal français.": Ibid.
259 Ibid.
260 **GB4:** "Jurisprudence. Une vue de Pékin," *Chronique du journal général de l'imprimerie et de la librairie* (22 November 1861).
261 **GB4:** "L'Univers illustre avait passé avec les deux plus grands journaux illustres de l'Allemagne et de l'Angleterre des traits aux termes desquels, moyennant une certaine rétribution, il peut reproduire les gravures qui ont paru dans ces journaux, et réciproquement ces journaux d'outre-Rhin et d'outre-Manche ont le droit d'emprunter à l'Univers illustre ses dessins.": Ibid.
262 "Etait-ce une copie du dessin de M. Marchal? le directeur de l'Univers Illustré n'en savait rien.": Ibid.
263 **GB4:** "Die ausgebreiteten Geschäftsverbindungen des Herrn Lévy verschaffen ihm so viele in Frankreich unbekannte Clichés, als er nur wollte, darum wurde er ein gefährlicher Gegner, was hinreichend seine 25,000 Abonnenten bezeugen.": P. Schmidt, "Pariser Illustrirte Journale," *Journal für Buchdruckerkunst, Schriftgießerei und verwandte Fächer* (29 June 1863).
264 **GB4:** "C'est à cette espèce d'association artistique et internationale que nous devons de pouvoir vendre chaque numéro trois sous.": "Chronique Judiciaire," *Chronique du journal général de l'imprimerie et de la librairie* (12 March 1859).

126 *The transnational trade in illustrations*

265 **GB4:** "Er bestaat ten aanzien der illustratie tegenwoordig een toenemend internationaal verkeer. De franschen tijdschriften nemen engelsche etsen over, de engelsche bladen den franschen.": "Berigten en mededelingen," *de Nederlandse Spectator* (1872): 161.

266 "Anzeige [1027]. Clichés von Holzschnitten," *Illustrirte Zeitung* (13 September 1845).

267 Ibid.

268 "Illustrirte Zeitung. Mit jährlich über 1000 in den Text gedruckten Abbildungen," *Illustrirte Zeitung* (4 September 1852).

269 "Es genüge in dieser Beziehung nur daran zu erinnern, dass ein sehr großer Theile der seither erschienenen Literatur nicht nur die Grundsätze nach denen sie verfährt, von der Illustrirte Zeitung entlehnte, sondern sich auch aus den massenhaften Bildervoräthen des Etablissements die Clichés entnahm, mit denen sie ihre Werke ausstattete, ein Abhängigkeitsverhältnis, welches auch zwischen der Leipziger Illustrirte Zeitung und den gleichzeitig erscheinenden Illustrirten Zeitungen in anderen europäischen Ländern, in Frankreich, England, Italien, Spanien, Danmark und Russland besteht, die alle durch ein mehr oder minder große Ähnlichkeit mit der Illustrirten Zeitung auf ihre deutsche Vorgängerin hinweisen, und von dieser regelmassig einen größeren oder geringeren Theile ihrer Illustrationen entnehmen.": "Nummer Tausend," *Illustrirte Zeitung* (30 August 1862).

270 **GB4:** "L'Illustration gibt Clichés von ihren Holzschnitten zu 2 Centimen den Quadratzentimeter, und Galvanos zu 3 Centimen, und verkauft deren ungefähr für 40,000 Fr. das Jahr.": P. Schmidt, "Pariser Illustrirte Journale. L'Illustration," *Journal für Buchdruckerkunst, Schriftgiesserei und verwandte Fächer* (17 June 1863).

271 "Vu les traites internationaux, les éditeurs se réservent le droit de reproduction et de traduction à l'étranger": "Frontpage," *l'Illustration* (4 August 1855).

272 **BNA4:** In the British Newspaper Archive the article "Newspaper copyright – Cassell v. Stiff" can be found in the *Herts Guardian, Agricultural Journal*, and *General Advertiser and the Wells Journal* of 2 February 1856. It is highly likely that other provincial newspapers also carried the message because the words of the article are entirely the same. This means that the article was probably delivered to the two provincial papers by a news service or copied from a London newspaper. "Newspaper copyright – Cassell v. Stiff," *Herts Guardian, Agricultural Journal, and General Advertiser* (2 February 1856); "Newspaper copyright – Cassell v. Stiff," *Wells Journal* (2 February 1856).

273 Ingram, the owner of the *Illustrated London News*, bought the *London Journal* in 1857 but sold it back to Stiff in 1859 after he had unsuccessfully tried to rebrand the newspaper. "Obituary. George Stiff," *the Bookseller* (1 December 1874).

274 **BNA4**: "Newspaper copyright – Cassell v. Stiff," *Herts Guardian, Agricultural Journal, and General Advertiser* (2 February 1856).

275 Ibid.

276 GB: Kay and Johnson, *Reports of Cases*, II:279.

277 Seville, *The Internationalisation of Copyright Law*, 51–2. Deazley, R. (2008) "Commentary on *International Copyright Act* 1852," in *Primary Sources on Copyright (1450–1900)*, eds L. Bently & M. Kretschmer, www.copyrighthistory.org

278 Kay and Johnson, *Reports of Cases*, II:279.

279 Ibid.

280 **GB:** "Copyright in Engravings," *the Art Journal* (1 March 1856). For the conversion of francs to pounds, I used: J.J. Kreenen, *Beschrijving van Alle Landen, Staten En Rijken Der Aarde* (Zwolle: Van Hoogstraten & Gorter, 1867), 82.

281 Ibid.

282 Pike, *John Cassell*, 108.

283 **GBX:** Curwen, *A History of Booksellers*, 272.

284 Pike, *John Cassell*, 126–7.

The transnational trade in illustrations   127

285 **BNA2:** "Illustrated News of the World," *Newcastle Guardian and Tyne Mercury* (6 August 1859).
286 **GBX:** "Illustrated Newspapers," *the Gentleman's Magazine*, new series, vol. 4 (1870): 462.
287 Ibid.
288 Ibid.
289 "Illustrated Times," *Illustrated Times* (5 April 1856).
290 Vizetelly, *Glances Back through Seventy Years*, 1893, II:83.
291 **GB4:** Adams, "Underevaluation. 4. – Electrotype and Stereotype Plates," 14.
292 Ibid., 15.
293 Ibid.
294 "Piracies. – Notice," *Illustrated London News* (15 July 1854).
295 "The Illustrated London News," *Illustrated London News* (29 October 1859).
296 Ibid.
297 **GAL:** "Il y a deux sortes de publications illustrées: celles qui donnent des gravures inédites, spécialement faites pour elles, retraçant exactement les scènes du jour, saisissant et fixant les actualités dans leur vol rapide, photographiant pour ainsi dire les évènements; puis, celles qui n'offrent a leurs abonnes que d'anciennes planches déjà publiées a l'étranger, connue pour la plupart et achetées a bas prix, pour être livrées a prix réduit a l'acheteur qui cherche moins la qualité que le bon marché dans le choix de ses lectures.": "Galvanoplastie," *le Monde Illustré* (5 March 1859).
298 " . . . une publication qui serait faite dans un pays voisin, en Angleterre, en Italie ou en Espagne, trouve un immense avantage a acheter les cliches des gravures données d'abord par la feuille en vogue, qui reflète dans ses scènes les plus frappants la marche des évènements": "Galvanoplastie," *le Monde Illustré* (5 March 1859).
299 Barnham, "John Dicks."
300 "Topics of the Week," *Penny Illustrated Paper* (12 October 1861).
301 "To Our Readers," *Penny Illustrated Weekly News* (12 October 1861).
302 **BNAX:** "The London Press," *Dundee Courier* (29 October 1861).
303 Wolff and Fox, "Pictures from Magazines," 563.
304 **GB4:** "Literary Table Talk," *the Literary World* (15 September 1871).
305 **GB4:** "Literary Table Talk," *the Literary World* (1 October 1875).
306 **GB4:** "Ein Journal von derselben Große, derselben Zahl der Holzschnitte als die Illustration, zum dem Preise von 5 Sous die Nummer. Alles sind alte Holzschnitte, der Illustration entnommen, welche man nur eine zeitgemäße Unterschrift gibt.": P. Schmidt, "Pariser Illustrirte Journale," *Journal für Buchdruckerkunst, Schriftgiesserei und verwandte Fächer* (29 June 1863).
307 Ibid.
308 Bacot, *La presse illustrée au xixe siècle*, 123.
309 Jobling and Crowley, *Graphic Design*, 20.
310 Martin, *Images at War*, 28.
311 **GB4:** "Ici, le procède règne en maitre; on ne vit guère, en fait d'illustration comme de texte, que de reproductions. Photogravure et location de cliches, location le plus souvent gratuite, la spécification de l'origine au bas de la gravure constituant pour l éditeur une réclame, sont les deux grands leviers de la publication bon marche.": François Thiébaut-Sisson, "La Presse Francaise Illustré," *la Nouvelle Revue*, vol. 10, no. 53 (1888): 646.
312 Cited in: Jobling and Crowley, Graphic Design, 25.
313 Bacot, *La presse illustrée au xixe siècle*, 124–6.
314 Claassen, "Het Nederlandsch Magazijn, Het Nederlandsch Museum En De Honigbij," 135.
315 Van Lente, "Illustratietechniek," 265.
316 Ibid.
317 Blanchon, *La gravure sur bois au XIXe siècle*, 118.

128　*The transnational trade in illustrations*

318 Ibid.
319 Van Lente, "Illustratietechniek," 265.
320 "De redactie aan het publiek," *Geïllustreerde Courant* (6 July 1844).
321 "Willem II, Koning der Nederlanden," *Geïllustreerde Courant* (20 July 1844).
322 "Droogmaking van het Haarlemmer-Meer," *Geïllustreerde Courant* (24 August 1844); "Scheveningen," *Geïllustreerde Courant* (31 August 1844); "Stations-gebouw te Haarlem," *Geïllustreerde Courant* (28 September 1844); "Stations-gebouw te Amsterdam," *Geïllustreerde Courant* (28 September 1844).
323 "Exposition de l'Industrie – Vue générale de la salle des Machines," *l'Illustration* (18 May 1844); "Zaal der Tentoonstelling te Parijs," *Geïllustreerde Courant* (14 July 1844); "Nikolaus I, kaiser von Russland," *Illustrirte Zeitung* (13 July 1844); "Nicolaus I, keizer van Rusland," *Geïllustreerde Courant* (5 October 1844).
324 "De korrespondent te New York van het dagblad de London Illustrated News": "Verkiezing van den president," *Geïllustreerde Courant* (28 December1844).
325 "Exterior of a Polling Booth, New York," *Illustrated London News* (7 December 1844); "Verkiezingen in Noord-Amerika," *Geïllustreerde Courant* (28 December 1844).
326 "Over het postwezen," *Geïllustreerde Courant* (28 September 1844).
327 Van Lente, "Illustratietechniek", 268–9.
328 Meulen, *Een veertigjarige uitgeversloopbaan*, 69–71.
329 Note that Sijthoff paid £200 a year less for the copyright of the *Illustrirte Zeitung* than Cassell had paid for the British copyright of *l'Illustration*. "[. . .] Herr J. J. Weber sich verpflichtet, wahrend der Dauer dieses Verhältnisse keine Clichés nach Holland zu verkaufen": Ibid., 70.
330 Research of Van Remoortel shows that Sijthoff probably used a similar arrangement to publish his fashion magazine *De Gracieuse*, which was based on the famous German magazine *Der Bazar*. Remoortel, "Woman Editors," 282.
331 Meulen, *Een veertigjarige uitgeversloopbaan*, 71.
332 Hemels and Vegt, *Het geïllustreerde tijdschrift in Nederland*, I:172.
333 **GB4:** "Voor 't overige mag men welligt den Heer Sijthoff, met het oog op de inlijving van ons land in den grooten noordduitschen keizerstaat, welke door sommigen als zeker te gemoet gezien wordt, dankbaar zijn voor deze poging om ons volk al vast wat te germaniseren.": "Bibliografisch Album. Geïllustreerd Nieuws," *de Gids* 30 (September 1866): 560.
334 "En wij worden behoorlijk op de hoogte gebragt van de kennis aan de groote mannen en de groote daden der Pruisen.": Ibid.
335 According to the *Oxford English Dictionary* of 1933, "incunable" refers to "the earliest stages or first traces in the development of anything." In this case, the word seems to refer to the sixteenth-century wood engravings, which were exhibited in Haarlem. "Onder de incunabelen der houtsnijkunst op het Stadhuis te Haarlem.": "Bibliografisch Album. Geïllustreerd Nieuws," *de Gids* 30 (September 1866): 560.
336 Hemels and Vegt, *Het geïllustreerde tijdschrift in Nederland*, I:220.
337 "Een praatjes," Hollandsche Illustratie, vol. 1, no. 1 (1864): 1–6; "Een woord tot het publiek," *Hollandsche Illustratie* (new series), vol. 1, no. 1 (1864): 2.
338 Hemels and Vegt, *Het geïllustreerde tijdschrift in Nederland*, I:220.
339 **GBX:** See the Covers of *l'Illustration* (2 January 1864) and *le Monde Illustré* (2 January 1864).
340 **GBX:** See the cover of the first issue of *le Journal Illustré* (3 April 1864).
341 "Les courses d'Epson en Angleterre," *l'Illustration* (7 June 1845).
342 "Course D'Epsom. Mai 1845. Gravure anglaise de l'Illustrated London News": Ibid.
343 "De wedrennen te Epsom in Engeland," *Hollandsche Illustratie*, vol. 5, no. 51 (1868–1869): 404.
344 **GB4:** "La plupart de leur dessins sont des cliches du Magasin Pittoresque, de l'Illustration, du Monde Illustre, du Journal pour Tous, du Tour de Monde et

The transnational trade in illustrations 129

de l'Illustrated London News.": M. Duruy, "De Paris a Bucharest, Causeries Geographiques," *le Tour du Monde*, vol. 5, no. 117 (1862): 199.

345 "De theems-dam en het onderaarsche London," *Hollandsche Illustratie*, vol. 5, no. 3 (1868/1869).

346 "Section of the Thames *Embankment*," *Illustrated London News* (22 June 1867).

347 "Der Themsedamm. Das unterirdische London," *Über Land und Meer*, vol. 20, no. 32 (May 1868): 512.

348 A copy of the image, made by using the photographic technique, appeared in the American *Frank Leslie's Illustrated Newspaper*: "Section of the Thames Embankment," *Frank Leslie's Illustrated Newspaper* (27 July 1867).

349 The image also appeared in the *el Siglo Ilustrado*, the Spanish version of *le Journal Illustré*: "Ter herinnering aan den duitschen krijg van 1866," *Hollandsche Illustratie*, vol. 5, no. 7 (1868–1869): "La Guerre – Composition Allemande envoyée au journal illustré par notre correspondent," *le Journal Illustré* (22 July 1866); "La Guerra," *el Siglo Ilustrado* (18 November 1867).

350 This kind of textual rebranding of the same illustration by different illustrated papers will be the object of the third chapter. "Germania verhüll dein Haupt," *Über Land und Meer*, vol. 16, no. 38 (June 1866): 601.

351 "Wie zijn geld lief heeft en zijn goeden smaak niet wil bederven, koope de hollandsche illustratie niet, want met een woord: 't is een lor in folio": Hemels and Vegt, Het geïllustreerde tijdschrift in Nederland, Vol. 1, 81.

352 "En geen bastaarddochter van Frankrijk meer zijn zal.": "Een woord tot het publiek," *Hollandsche Illustratie*, vol. 1, no. 1 (1864/1865): 2.

353 "De Holllandsche geest zal niet meer stuiten op uitsluitend voor Frankrijk verstaanbare platen": Ibid.

354 **DEL2:** "Binnenland, Zondag 23 Julij," *Algemeen Handelsblad* (24 July 1865).

355 Mohrman, *Hollandsche Illustratie?*; Neen, *Fransche Kwakzalverij*, 1.

356 "Post-office, Boston, U.S.," *Illustrated London News* (26 July 1843).

357 **GB3:** "Prospectus of the New World," *the New World* (15 July 1843).

358 **GB3:** See for example: "From the Illustrated London News. Angling. The Salomon," *the New World* (8 July 1843).

359 GB: "Illustrated Newspapers," San Diego Herald (1 October 1853). Reprinted in: Derby, *Phoenixiana, or, Sketches and Burlesques*, 16–24.

360 Ibid., 17.

361 Ibid., 20.

362 For example, from *l'Illustration*: "Entrenched Tirailleurs before Sebastopol," *Ballou's Pictorial Drawing-Room Companion* (13 January 1855); "Tirailleurs retranchés. – D'après un croquis de M. Dulong," *l'Illustration* (18 November 1854). From the *Illustrated London News*: "Fort of Fidieh-Tabiassi – View of the Town and Plain of Schumla," *Ballou's Pictorial Drawing-Room Companion* (8 April 1853); "Fort of Fidieh-Tabiassi – View of the Town an Plain of Schumla," *Illustrated London News* (4 March 1854). From the *Illustrated Times*: "The Council of War," *Ballou's Pictorial Drawing-Room Companion* (15 December 1855); "The Council of War," *Illustrated Times* (6 October 1855).

363 "The Daguerreotype," *Ballou's Pictorial* (19 August 1854).

364 Ibid.

365 **BNA2:** "The Arts, Literature &c," *Pall Mall Gazette* (30 June 1865).

366 **BNA2:** "Protection," *Worcester Journal* (9 March 1867).

367 **BNA2:** "The Literature of the United States," *Manchester Evening News* (18 February 1870).

368 **GB1:** "Illustrated Newspapers," *the Gentleman's Magazine*, new series, vol. 4 (1870): 452–70; "Illustrated Newspapers: From the Gentleman's Magazine," *Littell's Living Age* (23 April 1870).

130   *The transnational trade in illustrations*

369 **GB1:** "Illustrated Newspapers," *the Gentleman's Magazine*, new series, vol. 4 (1870): 452–70, 461.
370 Ibid., 461–2.
371 Ibid., 462.
372 Ibid., 754.
373 **GBX:** R. Kimball, "Frank Leslie," *Frank Leslie's Popular Monthly*, vol. 9, no. 3 (1880): 259.

3 Foreign images of war

L'Illustration's images of the Crimean War in Cassell's Illustrated Family Paper

Introduction

In the introduction to this book, I described how readers all over the world saw *l'Illustration*'s images of the Crimean War. While publications in Germany, Spain, and the United States reprinted only a few of these French illustrations, *Cassell's Illustrated Family Paper* in Britain relied almost entirely on them, purchasing 295 of its 361 war illustrations from *l'Illustration* and translating many of its articles word for word.

The re-publication of the French images in John Cassell's publication is significant in the light of its enormous audience and corresponding influence. Its circulation quickly rose from around 150,000 copies after its launch in 1853 to an astonishing 500,000 copies by the end of 1854. Consequently, this transnational trade in illustrations of the news resulted in more British people seeing the war images created by Henri Durand-Brager (the famous special artist of the French publication) than those of Constantin Guys, the artistic correspondent of the *Illustrated London News*, which printed an average of 130,000 copies during the Crimean War. Similarly, more people read the translated French articles in *Cassell's Illustrated Family Paper* than the reports of the legendary war correspondent William Howard Russell in *The Times*, which had a circulation of around 50,000 copies.

This chapter demonstrates that a transnational perspective is needed to fully understand the role of the illustrated press during the war and the visual representation of the Crimean War in general. The publication of the same images in several illustrated newspapers established a transnational community of viewers: different audiences in different national contexts who shared the same image of a certain event. While texts could cross national borders, mostly in the form of translated articles, their translation always entailed a certain nationalization of the information. In contrast, images could not be translated: if images crossed a language border, for example, by being published in two illustrated newspapers, the image – in some form, at least – remained the same, regardless of audience.

The reality of the transnational trade in illustrations of the news, however, was somewhat different to the straightforward situation sketched above. First of all, while it is impossible to translate images, they could be adjusted, as this chapter will prove. For example, *Cassell's Illustrated Family Paper* removed the

132 *Foreign images of war*

signatures of French producers to hide their foreign origin. More importantly, by altering textual elements, such as captions, Cassell could change the original meaning of the French illustrations.

The illustrated newspaper is a good example of what the visual culture theorist William James Thomas Mitchell has described as a composite work: a medium that consists of several forms of discourse (verbal, visual, and audial) at the same time. Hence, if historians set out to interpret the meaning of composite works, they should not separate the images in illustrated newspapers from their texts, such as captions and articles. By researching the image-text relationships in the two illustrated newspapers, this chapter shows that the British publication copied most of the original French images *and* many of its texts. In particular, *Cassell's Illustrated Family Paper* translated captions and articles, often word for word, and its editors imitated the French emphasis on eyewitness accounts and objective reporting. However, the British editors did not hesitate to alter the meaning of French images by changing the textual elements if they thought that the original French interpretation would offend British national (and nationalist) sentiments. Thus, by interpreting these images within their textual context, two points of interest come to the fore: first, that copied French images and articles could be easily integrated into British public discourse about the Crimean War. This shows that both countries had become part of a transnational visual culture of the news. Second, however, small changes and additions to the textual elements in *Cassell's Illustrated Family Paper Newspaper* reveal that some transnational elements had to be nationalized to suit specific audiences.

This chapter consists of six sections: the first four provide the necessary background and thus address historiography, methodology, a historical overview of the Crimean War, and an introduction to *Cassell's Illustrated Family Paper*. The last two sections set out to analyse *l'Illustration*'s images of the Crimean War in the context of their publication in a French and a British illustrated newspaper. The fifth section concentrates on the original corpus: the images of the Crimean War published in *l'Illustration*. Three questions are central to this analysis: Who made the images? What kind of subjects do they depict? And, referring back to Mitchell's composite work theory, how do visual and textual elements relate to each other? The final section looks at the re-publication of the French images in *Cassell's Illustrated Family Paper*. Did the British publication acknowledge the authors of the original images? Was the publication interested in the same subjects? Were the original captions and articles translated, or were new texts created?

Historiography: the Crimean War and visual reportage

Many historians consider the Crimean War as a watershed in the shared history of war and the (mass) media, describing it as the first 'real' media war: a conflict that could be experienced 'through cultural documentation not only after the fact but as events were transpiring.'[1] Because of new communication technologies such as the telegraph, the time it took for newspaper correspondents to send

Foreign images of war   133

reports to their editors in London had diminished considerably. At the start of the war, it still took 10 to 14 days to send a message from the Eastern-European battlefields to the British capital. By the end of the war, there was a telegraph line as far as the Crimean peninsula, reducing the time needed to reach the city to just a couple of hours.[2] The contrast with the previous major European conflict, the Napoleonic Wars of 1803–1815, is striking. News of Napoleon's defeat at Waterloo had taken two days to reach Paris and three to reach London.[3] During the same conflict, news from the Eastern-European front was 'underway' for nearly two months before the London press could print it.[4]

In the mid-1850s, news not only travelled faster but also became important in the political process. The reporting of several London newspapers about the war gave rise to a new set of relations between the military and the home front.[5] Public opinion expressed and, in some ways dictated by influential newspapers, began to influence political decision-making.[6] A good example is the inadequate housing, clothing, and medical care that British soldiers endured during the winter of 1854–1855. The reporting of several metropolitan newspapers about the lack of provisions resulted in public outrage, leading to the fall of the Aberdeen government in January 1855.[7] Surprisingly, the strand of historiography that deals with the influence of newspapers in politics (concerning the Crimean War) has focused on a select number of titles to the exclusion of several widely disseminated illustrated newspapers, especially *Cassell's Illustrated Family Paper*, even though it reached a far larger audience. Addressing this phenomenon, Hobbs' description of the dominance of *The Times* and its star reporter William Howard Russell (1820–1907), in nineteenth-century scholarship, as 'deleterious' certainly holds true for research concerning its shaping of the home front during the Crimean War.[8]

The Crimean War is also considered to be the first media war because of the perceived new role of photography in visualizing the conflict. Almost all books on the history of photojournalism start with a chapter on the Crimean War and Roger Fenton, 'the first photojournalist,' who took around 315 pictures near the eastern battlefields. Tellingly, a chapter in Paul's *Bilder des Krieges Krieg der Bilder* (2004) on the visualization of war in the nineteenth century is titled 'The beginning of the photographic shaping of the image of war.'[9] Similarly, in an introduction to a collection of articles concerning media and the Crimean War, the editors stated:

> First and foremost, the Crimean War was the first war to be photographically recorded. Using the new technology of photography, it became possible for the first time for contemporaries to receive pictorial evidence of the war far away from the actual front.[10]

Several authors, however, reject the claim that photography had already played a significant role during the Crimean War. Robert Desmond has pointed out not only that most photographers arrived relatively late in the Crimea – Roger Fenton got there in March 1855 – but also that 'because of the technical limitations then

134 *Foreign images of war*

attached to photography, the views were static, reflected little of the realities of the war, and were seen by few persons.'[11] Similarly, Thierry Gervais has argued that the purpose of Fenton's expedition – he was sent to the Crimea by a Mancunian art dealer to take photos that could serve as the basis for lithographs – as well as the very limited dissemination of his images make it an untenable position to see him as the first photojournalist.[12]

A more fundamental critique of these kinds of teleological accounts comes from Keller. In the 1850s, it was still difficult to print photographs on a large scale in newspapers and magazines, making photography a 'fledgling, technically deficient medium hard-pressed to gain a foothold.'[13] Keller described how a battle between different visual media was at its height at this time. His book contains chapters on history painting, lithography, shows, photography, and the illustrated press, in which the differences between these media are emphasized. For example, the images of the illustrated newspapers were by far the most widely disseminated. At the same time, Keller also discerned a common trend: eyewitness observation gained 'an ascendancy over interpretative historical accounts on the visual level no less than on the verbal.'[14] Reporting, in both its visual and textual forms, increasingly focused on notions of objectivity. Keller agrees with several authors that illustrated newspapers displayed this 'novel quality of authenticity' well before the press started to reproduce photographs in the final two decades of the nineteenth century.[15] This particular authenticity was not based on a discourse surrounding the technical capabilities of the medium of wood engraving, as would be the case for photography, but stemmed from the 'particular mode of its contextualization in the press.'[16] In other words, the relationship between image and text in the illustrated newspaper – the central concern of this chapter – gave the illustrations of the Crimean War their new objective and authentic quality.

Keller's book offers a sharp critique of teleological accounts of the visual coverage of war and expands our view by pointing to the competition between different visual media. However, his visual culture studies approach also limits his interpretation in some ways. His chapter on the illustrated press, for instance, is centred on a single special artist: Constantin Guys. This focus is understandable. In *The Painter of Modern Life* (1863), modernist writer *par excellence* Charles Baudelaire had described his close friend Guys as the archetypical *flâneur*: a modern city dweller who is exceptionally attuned to the new ways of seeing modernity. Not surprisingly, Baudelaire's praise has made Guys a favourite subject of proponents of visual culture studies.[17]

Keller's focus on Guys, who worked exclusively for the *Illustrated London News*, leads him to overestimate the importance of both Guys and his employer. Quoting the famous satirical journal *Punch*, he wrote that it almost seemed as though the British government had 'declared war with Russia expressly for the benefit of the *Illustrated London News*, and nobody else, . . . inasmuch as that paper is evidently deriving the greatest advantage from its prosecution.'[18] This statement seems to hold true for the entire British illustrated press. Keller's focus on the *Illustrated London News* has resulted in an underestimation of the enormous appetite of the British public for *all* illustrations of the news during the

Foreign images of war 135

mid-1850s. While the 130,000 copies of the *Illustrated London News* are impressive, the combined circulation of the illustrated press (around one million copies) and the differences in price – ranging from one to six pennies – demonstrate the influence that these publications had in all walks of life. These circulation figures become even more significant if we consider that *The Times*, which was the largest daily newspaper of the period, with a circulation of 50,000 copies, only reached an audience equalling 10 per cent of the readership that *Cassell's Illustrated Family Paper* enjoyed.[19]

Keller's focus on Guys has naturally led him to interpret the visual representation of the Crimean War from a national perspective: he is mainly concerned with the images in the *Illustrated London News* and the French painter's British employer. Therefore, Henri Durand-Brager, the special artist of *l'Illustration* who was at least as important in shaping the image of the Crimean War in Britain, escaped his notice. However, studies that do recognize Durand-Brager's role, such as Puiseux's *Les Figures de la Guerre* (1997) and Marchandiau's *L'Illustration* (1987), are similarly limited by their national focus: in this case on Durand-Brager and *l'Illustration*, neglecting the transnational dissemination of his images in Britain.[20] By focusing on the entire visual corpus of *l'Illustration* and *Cassell's Illustrated Family Paper* together, a more comprehensive – and hence transnational – perspective can be achieved regarding the role of the illustrated press during the war and the image of the Crimean War in general.

Methodology

Two databases containing entries for illustrations of the Eastern front of the Crimean War in *l'Illustration* and *Cassell's Illustrated Family Paper* form the basis for this chapter. To keep the size of the databases manageable, I have only studied images and articles related to the Crimean front and not the second front in the Baltic Sea. I used the entries in the two databases, which included the title, date, page number, and names of producers (if available), to establish whether illustrations appeared in both publications. In order to allow a comparison of the nature of the visual representation of the Crimean War in the two illustrated newspapers, the primary subject and (if possible) the nationality of the subject of the illustration were added to the initial entries.

Significantly, this chapter studies not only the illustrations but also the textual elements that accompanied them. In *Iconology* (1986), Mitchell has noted that, in a composite work, texts and images cannot be separated on a fundamental level: 'The differences between sign-types are matters of use, habit, and convention. The boundary line between texts and images, pictures and paragraphs, is drawn by a history of practical differences in the use of different sorts of symbolic marks, not by a metaphysical divide.'[21] Based on this premise, he concluded that the designation 'visual medium,' often used to describe illustrated newspapers and also photography, film, and television, is 'highly inexact and misleading.'[22] All media, which are commonly seen to be either purely textual, visual, or audial, encompass at least one other form of representation.

136 *Foreign images of war*

Because we cannot separate the sign-types of texts and images on a fundamental level, it is impossible to describe the meaning of a composite work by studying these two forms of discourse separately. In composite works, textual and visual forms of discourse always relate to each other. However, Mitchell warns against simply comparing, or juxtaposing, the textual or visual elements of a composite work to explain their respective meanings:

> The most important lesson one learns from composite works, like . . . illustrated newspapers, is that comparison itself is not a necessary procedure in the study of image-text relations. The subject matter is, rather, the whole ensemble of relations between media, and relation can be many other things besides similarity, resemblance, and analogy. Difference is just as important as similarity.[23]

Using the illustrated newspaper as an example, Mitchell has noted how, in most cases, the relationship between image and text involves 'the clear subordination and suturing of one medium to the other, often with a straightforward division of labour.'[24] The functioning of this most common set of relations becomes clearer in his discussion of the photographic essay: 'The normal structure of this kind of imagetext involves the straightforward discursive or narrative suturing of the verbal and the visual: texts explain, narrate, describe, label, speak for (or to) the photographs; photographs illustrate, exemplify, clarify, ground, and document the text.'[25]

This chapter focuses on the French and British captions that accompany the illustrations to study whether they describe and explain them in the same way. In the sixth section of this chapter, it will become clear that *Cassell's Illustrated Family Paper* not only bought *l'Illustration*'s images but also translated many of its captions and articles. It follows that most of the re-published images retained their original meaning. The appropriation of *l'Illustration*'s famous special artist Henri Durand-Brager will further show that *Cassell's Illustrated Family Paper* also adopted the French publication's discourse, which was mostly textual, on objective reporting. However, as several examples will reveal, by changing some captions and articles, the British publication fundamentally altered the original meaning of some French illustrations. This occurred especially when a British audience might have otherwise found the French illustrations and captions offensive.

The Crimean War

In his book *Crimea* (2010), Orlando Figes described three main causes of the Crimean War: religious tensions centred on access to several holy sites in the Ottoman Empire, the declining power of the Sublime Porte (the central Ottoman government, headed by the Sultan), and the territorial ambitions of the Russian empire.[26] He pointed out that the Christian identity of Russia strongly informed its imperial ambitions and resulted in a desire to Christianize Ottoman lands. Similarly, references to the Christian identity of the Russian Empire and the Muslim

Foreign images of war 137

faith of the Porte tempered the willingness of Britain and France to interfere on behalf of the Ottoman Empire. As *Cassell's Illustrated Family Paper* somewhat blatantly stated in an article accompanying a portrait of Tsar Nicolas: 'For the Turk, as a Turk, we have no sympathy; but all the sympathy in the world have we for the cause of justice, freedom, civilisation, and Christianity, which is put in imminent danger by the misdeeds of the great northern aggressor.'[27]

The immediate cause of the war was of a religious nature. In 1850, French Emperor Napoleon III, seeking to strengthen Catholic support for his regime, demanded the same privileged access to holy sites in the Ottoman Empire for Catholics, which the (Russian) Orthodox Christians already enjoyed.[28] After the Sultan agreed, Tsar Nicolas I responded by proclaiming a protectorate over all Orthodox Christians living in the Ottoman Empire. When the Sultan rejected this claim, Russian troops occupied the Danubian principalities (Moldavia and Wallachia, located in present-day Romania) in the summer of 1853, which, until then, functioned as a buffer zone between the two powers.[29] Under the leadership of General Omar Pacha (1806–1871), an Ottoman general who started his career in the Austro-Hungarian army, Ottoman troops managed to fend off the invading forces and stopped them at the town of Silistra, located on the present-day border between Romania and Bulgaria. Russian soldiers also invaded the Ottoman Empire in the northeast of present-day Turkey, near the town of Kars. An attempt to reinforce the Turkish forces there led to the destruction of an Ottoman naval fleet in the harbour of the Turkish city of Sinop on 30 November 1853, at the cost of 4,200 lives.[30]

The events at the end of 1853 triggered angry responses in the French and British press.[31] The destruction of the Turkish fleet in the harbour of Sinop, which according to *The Times* dispelled 'the hopes we have been led to entertain of pacification,' especially heightened the pressure on the British and French governments to intervene.[32] Acceding to this pressure, they demanded that the Russian troops leave the Danubian principalities and, after the Russian Tsar refused to comply, declared war at the end of March 1854.

In the spring and summer of 1854, the allies increased their military presence around the Crimean peninsula, sending troops to Gallipoli and Scutari, south of Istanbul, and later to Varna, a town on the Black Sea coast of present-day Bulgaria.[33] In this stage, a second front opened up in the Baltic Sea, where the allied fleet threatened the Kronstadt fort, which defended the harbour of St. Petersburg.[34] In the autumn of 1854, the allied forces, concentrated around Varna, relocated to the Crimean peninsula to strike a blow at the Russian Black Sea fleet, stationed at Sevastopol. Several historians have noted that the allied troops did not necessarily have to advance on Sevastopol. After receiving an ultimatum from the Austro-Hungarian Empire, the Russian Tsar pulled his troops from the Danubian principalities, neutralizing the original *casus belli*. However, public pressure and geopolitical considerations led the allied governments to a show of force: they needed a decisive victory over the Russian armies to save face.

After the landing of allied troops near Eupatoria, in Kalamita Bay on 14 September 1854, the allies and the Russian Empire fought a series of relatively traditional battles. On 20 September 1854, allied forces defeated the Russian commander

138   *Foreign images of war*

Menshikov (1787–1869) at the Battle of the Alma. After this victory, the French commander Canrobert (1809–1895) and the British general Lord Raglan (1788–1855) decided against an immediate assault on Sevastopol and prepared a siege of the town, positioning their troops near the cities of Kamiesh and Balaklava. In the Battle of Balaklava on 25 October, in which the famous 'Charge of the Light Brigade' occurred, the Russian general Liprandi (1796–1864) attacked the base of the British forces to break the siege. While they lost the battle, the Russian commanders realized that the allied siege lines were thin and could not be sufficiently manned, which led to the last encounter before the siege of Sevastopol: the Battle of Inkermann (5 November 1854). Although outnumbered, French and British troops managed to hold their ground. As a result, the Russian commanders stopped trying to defeat the allies in the field and retreated to Sevastopol.

During the winter of 1854–1855, the war was marked by the heavy bombardment of Sevastopol and the terrible conditions in the town, the defending forts, and the allied trenches. The winter was lethal for troops on all sides, but the British press documented the tragic faith of the ill-equipped British army exceptionally well. At the start of spring, almost the entire original British expedition force had been wiped out.[35] After a relatively successful bombardment and several attacks on the Russian positions by the allies at the start of September 1855, the Russians finally abandoned Sevastopol, crossing its harbour on a pontoon bridge.

Contrary to the expectations of the allies, even after they conquered Sevastopol, the Russians were not especially eager to sign a peace treaty. It would take a threat of a massive assault on Kronstadt, the fort defending St. Petersburg in the Black Sea, to bring them to the negotiating table. On 30 March 1856, a peace treaty was finally signed in Paris. Warships could no longer use the Turkish Straits, the negotiators designated the Black Sea as neutral terrain, and neither the Russian nor the allied armies could station troops in the region. The treaty also gave the Danubian principalities a limited amount of independence, foreshadowing the establishment of the Romanian nation in 1867. At the end of the war, approximately 95,000 Turkish soldiers, 95,000 French soldiers, 21,000 British soldiers, and 400,000 Russian troops had lost their lives. Tragically, most allied soldiers – around 60,000 Frenchmen and 16,000 British troops – did not die on the battlefield, but of disease.[36]

Cassell's Illustrated Family Paper

To understand the re-publishing of *l'Illustration*'s images of the Crimean War in *Cassell's Illustrated Family Paper*, it is important to have an idea of the character of this publication. Despite its enormous popularity in the mid-1850s, Cassell's publication has received a limited amount of scholarly attention, which can be explained by the general disdain of nineteenth-century cultural elites and some present-day historians for mass, or popular, culture.[37] By using digital newspaper archives, this section explores how the publication achieved its popularity by providing first-rate French engravings of the Crimean War for a modest price.

Foreign images of war   139

Cassell's publication has received some attention from scholars interested in its popular fiction, focusing on its aim to elevate middle-class readers.[38] However, while the second, or new, series of *Cassell's Illustrated Family Paper*, begun in 1857, certainly focused on fiction, counting famous writers, such as Joseph Conrad (1857–1921) and Conan Doyle (1859–1930), among its contributors, the three volumes of the first series (December 1853–December 1856) mainly reported on one news event: the Crimean War. Around 50 per cent of all the illustrations in the first three volumes concerned the war, while many other images relate to the subject. However, these first three volumes, which made Cassell's publication highly popular, have never been studied.

In a review of the first issue, the small *Enniskillen Chronicle and Erne Packet* wondered whether *Cassell's Illustrated Family Paper* had 'intended to record current events?'[39] As subsequent issues appeared, it quickly became apparent that images of the news were indeed the most important feature of the publication. A month later, the Irish *Downpatrick Recorder* favourably compared Cassell's paper to a rival with 'high pretensions,' of course, referring to the *Illustrated London News*.[40] In a similar vein, the *Wiltshire Independent* noted that *Cassell's Illustrated Family Paper* was especially suitable for the countless readers who could 'not afford to take its more impressing relative the *Illustrated London News*.'[41]

In 1853 and 1854, the newspaper stamp still prohibited the printing of news by unstamped publications. King has remarked that the *London Journal*, one of Cassell's competitors, did not print images of the news because of the tax.[42] Surprisingly, *Cassell's Illustrated Family Paper* was allowed to ignore these regulations. In 1854, the London *Morning Post* pointed out: '[It is] prohibited by the commissioners of the Inland Revenue from inserting current news; but it contains comments upon the news of the day almost as fresh and authentic as the news itself, while the illustrations are spirited in design and carefully engraved.'[43] Indeed, *Cassell's* seemed to have the advantage over its competitors: when Henry Vizetelly's *Illustrated Times* tried to ignore the stamp a couple of weeks before its abolition in 1855, the publication had to pay a fine of 11,000 pounds to the Inland Revenue. Furthermore, Ingram, the owner of the *Illustrated London News*, did everything in his power to frustrate the initial success of the *Illustrated Times* but seems to have left Cassell's publication alone.

The general disinterest, or even disdain, for the penny press by the bourgeois press and its influential and well-connected owners might explain the lack of commotion surrounding the publication of news illustrations in Cassell's paper. In 1854, 'W.W.,' the anonymous London literary correspondent of the *Aberdeen Journal*, noted how the penny press was 'decidedly making way in the world.'[44] The aggregate print run of the three foremost penny papers – the *London Journal*, the *Family Herald*, and *Cassell's Illustrated Family Paper* – amounted to almost one million copies, leading W.W. to estimate that around five to six million people read at least one of these publications. Therefore, he was

> [o]bliged to admit that – little account as is generally taken of it by the educated classes, and by those who generally tread principally in the higher

140 *Foreign images of war*

walks of literature, – the penny press of this country constitutes a power in the state which is by no means to be thought lightly of, and exercises a vast influence, for good or evil, over a large portion of the community that can be said to be directly affected by any engine whatsoever.[45]

The penny press 'moulded the minds and formed the tastes and opinions' of a sizeable audience.[46] Even the Church 'found fewer followers assembled on the Sabbath' within its walls as a result.[47]

The article in the *Aberdeen Journal* hints that the London-based press did not write about *Cassell's Illustrated Family Paper* because its audience, the relatively limited number of upper-class readers, did not know, or care, about its existence. My research in digitized newspapers supports this claim. The paragraph in the *Morning Post* is the only relevant reference to Cassell's publication in a metropolitan newspaper that was uncovered by a keyword search in the British Newspapers Archive, British Library Newspapers, and the Times Archive. However, as the contemporary journalist Thomas Frost observed in his autobiography, *Cassell's Illustrated Family Paper* was at the same time '[f]amiliar in the mouth as household words. It met the eye at every turn; on every dead wall and hoarding; in the advertisement pages of every publication.'[48] The reviews and advertisements in provincial newspapers, which catered to readers of more modest means, reflect this popularity and can shed light on the readership of the publication.

Almost every review of, and advertisement for, *Cassell's Illustrated Family Paper* mentions its low price. One of the first ads, published in 37 different newspapers between 9 and 17 December 1853, gives the following short description: 'Eight pages, same size as "Illustrated London News", Price One Penny.'[49] After more than 150,000 copies of the first issue were sold, a second advertisement, which appeared in 42 different newspapers between 23 and 31 December, calls the family paper 'the greatest achievement in the history of cheap literature.'[50] Furthermore, several reviewers praised its remarkable low price. The *Halifax Courier* asked its readers to buy a copy and solve the question of 'how such a publication can be sold for a penny.'[51] Similarly, the reviewer of the *Leeds Times* described Cassell's publication as 'a miracle of cheapness.'[52]

The price of *Cassell's Illustrated Family Paper* reflects its intended lower-class audience. The introduction to the correspondence column of the paper, 'our editorial table,' which started to appear regularly from July 1855, further supports this argument.[53] An editor thanked a certain H. Rawlinson for recommending the newspaper to his friends and asked other readers to follow his example:

> What *workman* is there who could not induce one or two workmates to take our journal? What *lady reader* cannot, in the various circles in which she moves, name . . . *Cassell's Illustrated Family Paper*? Or what *youth* is there who . . . will not rejoice to be able to add one new subscriber?[54]

Indeed, this quote reveals that an audience consisting of all the members of working-class families would help to maintain the publication's status as a 'wonder of the age' and 'one of the greatest engines for the promotion of education and a love of fine art.'[55]

Reviewers also frequently invoked Cassell's ambition to uplift the readers of his paper. In 1857, the *Leicester Chronicle* hoped that the publication would 'be seen in the household of every working man.'[56] The *Belfast Mercury* noted that all classes could read the family paper, but it especially hoped it would reach 'the industrial class.'[57] Anderson's study of the correspondence columns of *Cassell's Illustrated Family Paper*, the *Family Herald*, and the *London Journal* supports these findings. The vast majority of the letters to the editor were concerned with a 'program of self-improvement.'[58] The pseudonyms used to write to the paper, such as apprentice, mechanic, and labourer, show that there is 'no reason to doubt the contemporary view that these miscellanies had a substantial working-class following.'[59] Besides the social class of its readers, the geographical dissemination of *Cassell's Illustrated Family Paper* can be sketched by referring to advertisements and reviews. Newspapers all over Britain printed the first two aforementioned advertisements, which suggest a widespread national distribution.[60] Furthermore, the first ad explicitly mentions the possibility to receive monthly instalments of the publication, which was more convenient and cheaper for people 'living in remote areas.'[61]

An advertisement in the *Jersey Independent and Daily Telegraph* and an article in the religiously orientated *Coleraine Chronicle* shed more detailed light on the extraordinary dissemination of *Cassell's Illustrated Family Paper*. In 1855, J. Metivier, Cassell's agent in Jersey, noted how the publication reached a circulation of 'above 700 copies' on the small island.[62] Similarly, the newspaper of the small northern-Irish town of Coleraine mentioned that Cassell's publication had sold 'more than 100 copies' a week during the war.[63]

Cassell's Illustrated Family Paper was not only read in Britain. John Cassell was a great admirer of the United States and visited the country in 1852 and 1860.[64] During his first trip, he possibly met C. McKee, the manager of the 'Foreign News Agency,' a company located in the Sun Building, New York. Whether this was the case or not, it is clear that this company advertised the sale of *Cassell's Illustrated Family Paper* – 'a remarkable periodical' – in the United States in 1856. Four advertisements on the first page of the *New York Tribune* of 4 April 1856 praised Cassell's publication for its cheap price and noted that its two million readers – it was widely believed that every copy had multiple readers – made it the most widely read illustrated weekly in the world, comparing its print run of 250,000 copies with the 150,000 copies of the *Illustrated London News*, the 90,000 copies of the *Illustrated Times*, the 100,000 copies of *Ballou's Pictorial* from Boston, and the meagre 15,000 copies of *Frank Leslie's Illustrated Newspaper*.[65]

Cassell's publication also reached the booming Australian colonies. The successful bookseller and publisher George Robertson (1825–1898) offered it in Melbourne.[66] Between May and July 1855, another company, Slater, Williams, and Hodgson, regularly placed advertisements in the *Age* and the *Argus*, the two largest newspapers of the town, when they received new issues of Cassell's publication. Ads in several Tasmanian newspapers in 1855 and 1856 show that the

142   *Foreign images of war*

paper was also available here.[67] Finally, an advertisement in the *Mount Alexander Mail*, the newspaper of Castlemaine, a city located in the heart of the Australian goldfields, makes clear that *Cassell's Illustrated Family Paper* also reached this flourishing part of the colony.[68]

In 1870, an article in *the Gentleman's Magazine* noted: 'The illustrated papers in the colonies are mostly too far away from contemporary publications to obtain the assistance of *clichés*; but for all that the illustrated mania is spreading even in the colonies.'[69] Contrary to his observation, Cassell sold not only copies of his paper in the Australian colonies but also *clichés* of its illustrations. Before Slater, Williams, and Hodgson started to offer the British version of the paper in April 1855, they advertised the sale of *Cassell's Illustrated Family Paper and Melbourne Advertiser*. In his article about the Australian illustrated press, Peter Dowling has noted that 11 issues of this publication saw the light in 1854.[70] However, advertisements in the *Argus* suggest that Slater, Williams, and Hodgson published at least 20 issues.[71] It is almost certain that this Australian version contained some of *l'Illustration*'s images of the Crimean War. The advertisement announcing its 12th issue promised portraits of the Russian princes *Woronzow* and Gortschakoff.[72] Nine months earlier, the illustrations appeared together in *Cassell's Illustrated Family Paper* on 18 March 1854, and almost a full year earlier in *l'Illustration* – in the issue of 31 December 1853.[73] The same occurred for two portraits of the French Marshall Saint Arnaud and the British commander Lord Raglan, which appeared in *l'Illustration*'s issue of 18 March 1854, in *Cassell's Illustrated Family Paper*'s issue of 29 April 1854 and were announced to appear in the 20th issue of the Australian version in January 1855.[74]

Were the readers of *Cassell's Illustrated Family Paper* aware of the French origin of its illustrations? The coverage in the British press makes clear that many reviewers at least questioned how Cassell could afford such high-quality wood engravings. In December 1853, the *Salisbury and Winchester Journal* commented that its readers would probably be 'as much puzzled' as it was to know 'how Mr Cassell intends to maintain a staff of writers, illustrators, compositors, and paper makers out of profits which at present must be *nil*.'[75] In its review, published on the same day, the *Hereford Times*, referring to the price of Cassell's publication, noted that the 'excellent engravings' alone were worth 'twice the money.'[76]

Cassell's Illustrated Family Paper never openly referred to the French origin of its illustrations. Rather, they remained coy on the subject; for example, the editor asked readers to calculate the amount of money spent on each issue: 'Employing as we do the highest literary talent, as well as the first artists and engravers of the day, a statement of our weekly outlay would be deemed fabulous.'[77] A couple of weeks later, the editor made a similar point in his response to a letter by 'F.B.G.' The editor was not 'disposed to tell you what this or that particular engraving costs' but noted that some engravings had cost between 50 and 60 pounds.[78] Describing the production process of a major illustrated newspaper, like the *Illustrated London News*, the editor explained how a special artist first had to visit 'the *locale* of the subject,' how then a draughtsman had to transfer this sketch onto wood, and how, finally, the engraver also had to be paid for his services.

Foreign images of war 143

As we will see later in this chapter, Cassell published some original illustrations in his paper, but these were dwarfed by the number of those purchased from *l'Illustration*. The answer to 'F.B.G' indicates that many readers did not believe the misleading statements about the illustrations in the family paper: 'People may well wonder, and exclaim, as they often do: "Really, we cannot understand how ever John Cassell can produce such a journal for a penny!"'[79] As we have seen in Chapter 2, the court case of *Cassell v. Stiff* in January 1856 made explicitly clear that most of the illustrations came from *l'Illustration*. Moreover, the article by 'W.W.' in the *Aberdeen Journal* suggests that well-informed pressmen were already aware of this fact as early as 1854: 'They are none of them especially engraved for Mr Cassell, but are all reproduced from blocks which were in the first instance cut for, and used by, American and French newspapers, and particularly the Parisian *L'Illustration*.'[80]

From November 1858 onwards, the new series of *Cassell's Illustrated Family Paper* stopped publishing illustrations of the news; instead, it focused on popular fiction and no longer used *l'Illustration*'s images. This change in editorial policy is surprising. As we have seen above, two years earlier, its editor-in-chief John Tillotson still attributed its success entirely to the French illustrations of the Crimean War. After *Cassell's Illustrated Family Paper* ceased publishing images of the news, it rapidly lost 200,000 of its readers, as an article in the *Morning Post* recorded.[81] What caused the sudden change in strategy? Did the French images become too expensive? Although sources are hard to find, this question deserves further attention from scholars.

The original corpus

Based on a database of *l'Illustration*'s images of the Crimean War, this section will address three questions: Who made the illustrations? What do they depict? And how do textual elements, such as captions and articles, describe or explain them? An answer to these questions allows for an adequate comparison between the original corpus and the part that *Cassell's Illustrated Family Paper* re-published. Did John Cassell systematically avoid buying images of certain subjects? Did he only purchase illustrations of British soldiers? Was he specifically interested in certain producers?

Prolific draughtsmen and a daring special artist

Who made the illustrations of the Crimean War in *l'Illustration*? The caption underneath an image often mentioned the artistic correspondent who sent in a sketch. The draughtsman responsible for the reworking of a sketch into an image usually signed his (as far as we know all of *l'Illustration*'s draughtsman in this period were men) work in the lower-left or lower-right corner of the illustration. Furthermore, in the mid-1850s, the 'table générale,' or index, to each volume listed all the images for which a specific draughtsman was responsible.

In the period between 1853 and 1857, *l'Illustration* published 678 illustrations concerning the Eastern theatre of the Crimean War. Fifty-six of these images

144 *Foreign images of war*

cannot be attributed to an artistic correspondent, a draughtsman, or both. In most cases, this suggests that *l'Illustration* used an old engraving, which it had published previously. When new illustrations were not yet finished, or if there was simply nothing new to report, illustrated newspapers often re-published old images to satisfy the appetite of the public for content relating to the war. The portraits of 'General Gortschakoff' (Pyotr Gorchakov, 1790–1868) and Prince Woronzoff (Mikhail Semyonovich Vorontsov, 1782–1856) published on *l'Illustration*'s front page on 31 December 1853 are good examples. Besides the fact that both portraits were not signed, the general and the prince appear much too young in their illustrations: in 1853, they were 53 and 70 years old, respectively. The exceptionally brief description of the portraits also suggests that they were re-used page-fillers: 'We have nothing, in particular, to say about these high-ranking men.'[82]

A draughtsman signed most of the French illustrations (around 83 per cent), which indicates that *l'Illustration* commissioned them during the war. Table 3.1 shows that three draughtsmen made the majority of *l'Illustration*'s images of the conflict. Jules Worms (1832–1924) was by far the most prolific. He was responsible for approximately 25 per cent of all the French illustrations. Unfortunately, we know almost nothing about Worms apart from a few details. Charles Philipon, a contributor to the pioneering satirical journal *Charivari*, taught him the art of wood engraving, and he worked for *l'Illustration* between 1853 and 1867.[83] He later became a successful painter, exhibiting romantic pieces at the Paris Salon throughout the 1860s and 1870s.[84] A similar history can be outlined for Pharamond Blanchard (1805–1873), who made 95 illustrations in the corpus. After contributing many drawings to *l'Illustration* between 1846 and 1873, he became a historical and landscape painter.[85]

Sketches formed the basis for around 40 per cent of all the illustrations of the Crimean War in *l'Illustration*. However, at the beginning of the war, the French illustrated newspaper had never employed special artists. Rather, it received drawings from artistic correspondents who, sometimes on a quite regular basis, sent sketches to its head office. In her chapter on the visual representation of the

Table 3.1 Most common draughtsmen of illustrations concerning the Crimean War in *l'Illustration*, 1853–1858

Draughtsman	Number of illustrations
Jules Worms	176
Pharamond Blanchard	95
Jules Gaildrau	84
Ange Luis Janet (Janet-Lange)	43
Louis Le Breton	31
Valentin Foulquier	28
Thomas Henry Nicholson	14
M.E. Forest	12
Avril Frères (maps)	10

Crimean War, Puiseux has noted that *l'Illustration* corresponded with 20 to 30 artistic correspondents on, or near, the Crimean battlefields.[86] While she stated that the publication especially sent some of these men to the east, I have not found any evidence to support this. As the case of Henri Durand-Brager will show, it is more likely that all the artistic contributors travelled to the eastern battlefield as soldiers, diplomats, or civilians and that most of them were irregular contributors, who were not employed by the illustrated newspaper.

L'Illustration credits 56 different artistic correspondents for their sketches of the Crimean War. Most of these correspondents, 38 to be exact, contributed only a single sketch. Of the five most prolific artistic correspondents – Durand-Brager (164), M. Dulong (29), M. Brindesi (12), F. Quesnoy (9), and M. Letuaire (9) – only Durand-Brager seems to have functioned as a special artist, that is to say, a regular contributor of sketches and a paid employee of *l'Illustration*.

L'Illustration did not pay the vast majority of its artistic correspondents, nor can they be described as professional journalists. For example, Pierre Letuaire (1798–1885) was not a journalist but a painter, who contributed sketches from Toulon: a large French naval base. Illustrations based on his sketches show not only troops leaving for the war but also wounded troops and Russian prisoners returning from the battlefield. Strategically located in the important port city, Letuaire contributed work not only to *l'Illustration* but also to other illustrated newspapers, such as *le Monde Illustré*.[87]

The subjects of the sketches from another contributor, M. Dulong, suggest that he was connected to the French military and only contributed sketches when it suited him. His first contribution shows horses being loaded in a French military ship sailing for Constantinople.[88] A month later, several of his sketches show how the Sultan received the French emperor, Napoleon III, in this same city.[89] Two images published in October 1854 place him with the landing of French troops at Kalamita Bay.[90] After sketching several major battles, one of his last contributions, published in the issue of 9 December 1854, shows Russian prisoners in Constantinople, which suggests that Dulong had also returned to the capital of the Ottoman Empire.[91]

Finally, just like Pierre Letuaire, the Italian-born Giovanni Jean Brindesi (1826–1888) contributed sketches to further his career as a painter and illustrator. It is unclear what Brindesi was doing in Constantinople before the start of the war or how he ended up there, but several of his sketches in *l'Illustration* indicate that he was well connected. He was present at balls given by French and the Austrian ambassadors to the Porte and seems to have been (literally) close to the Sultan when the third division of the French army marched in front of him.[92] Two years after his sketches appeared in *l'Illustration*, Brindesi published several books containing illustrations of Ottoman dress and daily life in Constantinople. The first of these books, *Anciens costumes turc de Constantinople* (1856), appeared directly after the war.[93]

Jean-Baptiste Henri Durand-Brager (1814–1879) contributed by far the most sketches to *l'Illustration*. His illustrations were seen not only by the French readers of *l'Illustration* but also by the extensive readership of *Cassell's Illustrated*

146 *Foreign images of war*

Family Paper in Britain, German subscribers to the *Illustrirte Zeitung*, the American audience of *Ballou's Pictorial Drawing-Room*, and the Spanish readers of *la Ilustracion*. Durand-Brager is the perfect embodiment of Keller's description of the integration of visual media in the 1850s. He sketched the war but also painted and photographed it. Below, we will learn how Durand-Brager, a marine painter employed by the French army, became a special artist of a major illustrated newspaper. Moreover, we will also see how his initial employer – the French navy – continued to influence his later work.

Several historians note that *l'Illustration* sent Durand-Brager in particular to the Crimea.[94] However, an article written by Victor Paulin, the editor of the illustrated newspaper, printed next to Durand-Brager's first batch of sketches, describes him as being attached to a reconnaissance mission of the French navy under the leadership of Admiral Ferdinand-Alphonse Hamelin.[95] While Paulin praised his talents – 'It would have been impossible to choose a better-skilled draughtsman and a better-practised hand' – he does not describe him as a special artist of *l'Illustration*.[96] Durand-Brager is still clearly seen as an artistic correspondent, an irregular contributor of sketches rather than a special artist: a paid correspondent who reports the war with both pencil and pen.

Published letters from Durand-Brager to Paulin reveal his strong alliance to the French navy.[97] He ends a report on the start of the siege of Sevastopol with the following: 'I would like to have a practised pen to be able to portray all the services of the navy. . . . I hope that some writer, more accustomed to this genre of writing than me, will appreciate the immensity of their services.'[98] He concludes his letter of introduction to the readers of the illustrated newspaper in a similar way: 'I am pleased to announce that his Excellency the Minister of the Navy kindly encouraged my job, taking this publication under his dignified and benevolent patronage.'[99] However, the letter also refers to the objective discourse surrounding the relatively new profession of the special artist.[100] Durand-Brager promised Paulin to 'bring before the eyes of your readers' the camps, the tents, and the trenches and sketch 'every type of soldier' of the French army and its allies.[101] In line with the objective language surrounding pictorial reportage, he described his style as being 'without literary pretension' and stated that he will 'simply tell as much as possible.'[102] In one of his earlier letters, he had already emphasized the nature of his sketches: 'All of this is history and not fantasy.'[103]

After *l'Illustration* published his portrait, Durand-Brager's transformation from marine painter to a special artist was complete (Figure 3.1).[104] In this portrait, we can see him standing in a trench, while he is busy sketching a scene. The binoculars, positioned in front of him, underline his status as an eyewitness reporter. A rifle, standing next to him on the ground; his semi-military uniform; and the soldier standing next to him can all be construed as revealing his attachment to the French military. As Keller and Riall have observed, images of special artists sketching battlefields, often made by themselves, confirmed the discourse of objectivity surrounding their work. They presented themselves as eyewitnesses who were uniquely able to place the events of the war before the eyes of the readers.[105]

Figure 3.1 Henri Durand-Brager (1856). 'Durand-Brager.' *l'Illustration* (9 February 1856). The Hague, Royal Library of the Netherlands, T 1788 (1856–27).

148   *Foreign images of war*

Durand-Brager's work for *l'Illustration* was not limited to the genre of pictorial reportage. His earliest contributions, images of Russian fortifications used for strategic purposes by the general staff, are a product of his work for the army. His contract with the illustrated newspaper also mentioned a series titled 'Types and faces of the Orient,' which promised to show the daily life of French soldiers on board transport ships and in the camps. These images do not refer to any specific event, and Durand-Brager intended them as 'souvenirs' of the war. It is probably because of these kinds of illustrations that the French minister of the Navy praised his 'national and patriotic style,' which so aptly represented 'the painstaking efforts, the noble work, and the success of our marines and soldiers.'[106]

The different genres employed by Durand-Brager are not the only reason why he is a good example of Keller's notion of the integration of different visual media. After the war, he made a series of 21 oil paintings concerning the war, commissioned by Napoleon III. In her thesis on paintings of the Crimean War, Annie Bardon has mentioned that Durand-Brager based at least 15 of these paintings on illustrations in *l'Illustration*.[107] Despite the patronage of the French government both during and after the war, Durand-Brager not only made paintings that showed the victorious allied forces. In 1857, the Russian Tsar commissioned him to paint *Le Combat de Sinope*, detailing the destruction of the Turkish fleet in 1853: the *casus belli* for Britain and France.[108]

In addition to illustrations and paintings, Durand-Brager also made photographs. Bardon has noted that he took a total of 48 pictures, divided into three series concerning the battle of Kinburn, Sevastopol after its occupation, and the French camp in Kamiesh.[109] It remains unclear for what purpose Durand-Brager took the photos. He never exhibited them, as Fenton had done, nor did he use them for his paintings or illustrations in *l'Illustration*.[110] Some researchers, like Bernard Marbot, have claimed that the sparse use of photographs by Durand-Brager can be explained by the fact that he probably did not take them but only signed them. As was common in the early days of photography, Durand-Brager worked together with a technician, a certain *monsieur* Lassimone. Marbot therefore suggests that Durand-Brager provided Lassimone with access to the battlefields and naval expeditions, while the latter did most of the actual work.[111]

Views, troops, and ships: the subjects of *l'Illustration*'s Crimean War images

What kind of subjects can we find in *l'Illustration*'s coverage of the Crimean War? As Table 3.2 shows, images that fall under the category 'troops' are the most common. They show unknown soldiers in all sorts of activities: embarking or disembarking ships, marching, in their camps, and on the battlefield. Only 68 illustrations in this category depict actual battles. Of course, the categories 'portraits' and 'types' also depict soldiers. However, in contrast to the unnamed soldiers of the 'troops' category, portraits depict a specific soldier, mostly military commanders. Several images of lower officers, often depicted in the process of

Foreign images of war 149

Table 3.2 Subjects of the original and re-published images of *l'Illustration* concerning the Crimean War

Subject	Number in l'Illustration	Percentage in l'Illustration	Number in Cassell's	Percentage in Cassell's
Troops	230	34%	133	45%
Views	189	28%	92	31%
Types	56	8%	0	0%
Ships	51	7.5%	13	4.5%
Portraits	38	5.5%	26	9%
Diplomatic	33	5%	10	3.5%
Anthropological	19	3%	5	1.5%
Maps	15	2%	4	1.5%
Other	47	7%	12	4%
Total	678	100%	295	100%

dying a heroic death, form a notable exception to this rule. The illustration of Second Lieutenant Pousin saving his captain's life is a good example.[112]

The category 'types' becomes common after Durand-Brager started sending in sketches for the 'Types and Faces of the Orient' series from March 1855. His images portray 'typical' soldiers, or common events in the life of soldiers, and do not refer to a specific person or event. Good examples of this category include 'the logical thinker' and 'the enthusiast.' The images 'in the cold,' 'in the snow,' and 'in the rain' depict soldiers dealing with the typical conditions of camp life (Figure 3.2).[113]

Images in the second category, 'views,' show buildings, towns, and fortifications but do not depict any human interaction. However, the textual elements accompanying these images often provide a context. The first few illustrations based on sketches of Durand-Brager exemplify this well: we see several coastal towns and fortifications, yet, without the accompanying textual elements, it would be entirely unclear why these images were relevant.[114] Reading the accompanying captions and articles, we learn that the towns were situated on the Black Sea coast and that Durand-Brager sketched them for reconnaissance purposes.[115]

The category 'ships' is in many ways similar to the category 'troops' but concerns the actions (including battles) of ships. We can attribute the relatively high number of images that depict the action of ships to the fact that Durand-Brager was attached to the French navy and spent the majority of the war on board a ship. The final two categories – diplomatic and ethnographical – represent the actions of different actors. The category 'diplomatic' contains images that show diplomats, several peace conferences, and diplomatic events taking place during the war and mostly in Constantinople, such as the ball given by the Austrian ambassador.[116] The category 'ethnographical' concerns images of the ethnic groups living in the theatre of war, such as the 'Costumes of a woman in Sinop' or the 'Karaite Jews of the Crimea.'[117] This kind of visual description of ethnic groups was popular in the mid-nineteenth century, as the success of the famous travel magazine *le Tour*

Figure 3.2 In the rain (1856). 'Par la pluie,' *l'Illustration* (24 May 1856). The Hague, Royal Library of the Netherlands, T 1788 (1856–27).

du Monde and similar publications demonstrate. *L'Illustration* could re-publish these illustrations from previously published travel accounts, providing an easy and cheap way to satisfy the appetite of their readers for any visual material concerning the Crimean War. Many of the illustrations that were not signed by either a draughtsman or an artistic correspondent fall within this category.

In his letter to the readers of *l'Illustration*, Durand-Brager promised to sketch all the different types of troops from the French army and navy, including the soldiers of the 'noble allies' of France. Although it is often impossible to assign a specific nationality to the images in the category 'views,' captions underneath images in the categories 'troops,' 'ships,' and 'portraits' often make clear which country the depicted soldiers were fighting for. Aside from the small number of images of Piedmontese soldiers, Swiss and German mercenaries, and Greek militias, most illustrations show troops from France, Britain, the Ottoman Empire, or Russia.[118] As Table 3.3 shows, the majority of images deal with the actions of French troops. Soldiers of France's allies – Britain and the Ottoman Empire – are roughly equally represented. Finally, there is a considerable number of images that show joint French and British troop actions.

Explaining images with captions and articles

Captions strongly influence the interpretation of illustrations by readers. They tell readers not only *what* they are supposed to see – the event, object, or person – but also *how* they should interpret the scene. Captions frequently point to the degree to which an image fits the discourse of objectivity promoted by *l'Illustration*. Take, for example, the illustration of a soldier with a cat on his shoulder, published on 18 November 1854.[119] Its caption, 'A zouave with his cat,' steers the

Table 3.3 The main nationalities shown on images in the original and the re-published corpus

Nationality	Number in l'Illustration	Percentage in l'Illustration	Number in Cassell's	Percentage in Cassell's
French	164	48%	54	34%
French and British	21	6%	19	12%
French, British and Russian	2	1%	1	0.5%
French and Ottoman	2	1%	1	0.5%
French and Russian	4	1%	2	1%
British	29	6.5%	27	17%
British and Ottoman	1	0.5%	0	0%
British and Russian	2	1%	0	0%
Ottoman	36	10.5%	12	7.5%
Russian	42	12%	35	22%
Russian and Ottoman	3	2%	1	0.5%
Other	4	2%	1	0.5%
Unknown	32	9%	2	1%
Total	342	100%	159	100%

152   *Foreign images of war*

reader towards interpreting the image as saying something about the character of *all* Zouaves. If the caption had read 'Jean Dupont, of the first zouave regiment, with his cat Felix, just before the Battle of Inkerman (5 November), sketched by our special artist Henri Durand-Brager,' the image would have had a different and more specific meaning. These kinds of specific captions are an important part of the discourse of objectivity because they support the unique nature of the depicted event: objective images, or language, never urge readers to see something universal but present singular facts. Furthermore, because readers could – in theory – check their veracity, images with specific captions seem more objective. To return to the previous example, friends of Jean Dupont could compare his portrait to the actual person.

Most captions accompanying *l'Illustration*'s images of the war point to a specific action, or location, related to the war. The image, 'Attack of a Turkish fleet by Russian ships in the harbour of Sinope,' published on 24 December 1853, is one such example.[120] Despite the fact that the image refers to a specific event – the Battle of Sinop – the caption does not mention the date of 30 November 1853. The article accompanying the illustration only describes the town of Sinop but does not refer to the battle.[121] Like many similar images with this kind of caption, the illustration of the battle in the harbour of Sinop was meant to provide readers with a visual background story of a certain event, which would have been already familiar to the readers of *l'Illustration*, because they would have read about it in other publications.

Captions that mention both a specific date and place especially fit the discourse of objectivity that *l'Illustration* promoted. The image 'Entry of the Franco-British squadron in the Avacha Bay, August 29, 1854 – after [a sketch] by Viscount René de Kerret, aboard the frigate *Forte*' is a perfect example.[122] Its caption not only mentions a specific place and date but also notes the eyewitness who made the sketch as well as the circumstances that enabled him to do so. The same applies for the image 'Review of the 3rd Division of the Eastern Army, passing before S. M. the Sultan, 17 June 1854, between the Maltepe hospital and the Rami Tchiflik barracks – from sketches by J. Brindesi.'[123] The caption notes the event, the specific place (between the hospital and the barracks), the date (17 June 1854), and the eyewitness (J. Brindesi). It also reveals something about the production process, noting that the draughtsman used *several* of Brindesi's sketches for the image.

The third category of captions describes images that fall within the 'type' category. Instead of pointing to a specific news event, these illustrations present general ideas or even universal truths. This category also includes images of an allegorical nature. The image 'After the battle of Inkerman – Fraternisation of the two armies' is a good case in point.[124] The image shows British and French troops standing over the corpse of a Russian soldier. Its caption promotes a general, and highly political, meaning: after they have won a major battle, the former foes – Britain and France – could finally become allies. A similar effect can be seen in the image entitled 'The peace.' On the left side of the image, we see French soldiers and a battlefield. In the middle of the illustration, an angel appears above a

Foreign images of war 153

gravestone surrounded by clouds. On the right side, we see the inhabitants of the Crimea, waving to the angel. In the upper-right corner, the battlefield has changed into fertile farmland (Figure 3.3).[125] The image conveys the idea that the sacrifice of French soldiers enabled peace and prosperity on the Crimean peninsula.

French illustrations in *Cassell's Illustrated Family Paper*

In one of the final articles concerning the Crimean War, *Cassell's Illustrated Family Paper* reflected on its coverage of the conflict: 'Thanks to our correspondents, literary and artistic, we have, throughout the war, been able to present to our readers a constantly varying panorama of the scenes in the East.'[126] It brought all the aspects of the war before the eyes of the reader: 'fortresses and harbours, plans of attack, encamping troops in the rain, in the snow, in the frost, types of the varied nations and tribes that have taken part in the struggle.'[127] Publishing 361 images relating to it, *Cassell's* had indeed covered the war extensively. However, most of this coverage was not original: it had purchased 295 illustrations from the *l'Illustration* and translated many of its articles. Many questions arise as a consequence of this: Which part of the French corpus did the British publication use? Did the French and British readers consequently share an image of the Crimean

Figure 3.3 The peace (1856). 'La paix.' *l'Illustration* (16 February 1856). The Hague. Royal Library of the Netherlands. T 1788 (1856–27).

154   *Foreign images of war*

War? Did the re-publication of the French illustrations and articles in a British context change their meaning?

"Our artist"

Most illustrated newspapers – with the *l'Illustration* as a notable exception – did not mention the names of their draughtsmen. In line with this general trend, *Cassell's Illustrated Family Paper* did not publish the signatures of the French artists. After all, their names might lead readers to suspect that the British illustrated newspaper was, in fact, not very 'British' at all. The signatures of French draughtsmen and engravers only appear on a few of the re-published images. In most cases, *Cassell's Illustrated Family Paper* removed the lower corners of the *cliché*, where the producers signed their work. If this was not possible, the publication blurred the signatures or, as the image 'Carrying the wounded Russians to the St. George's, Bucharest' shows, scratched them out.[128]

While *Cassell's Illustrated Family Paper* never acknowledged the role played by draughtsmen in the production process, it did increasingly reflect on the role played by artistic-contributor-turned-special-artist Henri Durand-Brager. The British publication published 56 illustrations made from his sketches. As the war raged on, *Cassell's Illustrated Family Paper* presented the French marine painter not only as *a* special artist but also as *our* special artist.

Similar to the French publication, *Cassell's Illustrated Family Paper* mentioned Durand-Brager for the first time, without actually naming him, in an article accompanying his sketches of Russian fortresses on the Black Sea coast: 'Instructions were given to a distinguished marine painter, who combines precision of detail with a general effectiveness of composition, to accompany the expedition with the purpose of taking sketches of the scenes presented to view.'[129] Although *Cassell's Illustrated Family Paper* continued to publish his sketches, it took until March 1855 before it mentioned Durand-Brager again. The article "The Crimea – Panorama of Sebastopol" described 'one of the most interesting features of the present war': never was a war 'so badly conducted, and so well reported.'[130] Especially the accuracy of 'sketches made on the spot of those actual conflicts' by special artists transformed how readers could experience the conflict.[131] Again, this article referred to Durand-Brager, without naming him, as 'an artist in the Crimea, to whose pencil we have already been considerably indebted.'[132]

The introduction of the special artist as a character in his own reporting is an essential part of the discourse of objectivity promoted by the nineteenth-century illustrated press. *Cassell's Illustrated Family Paper* had realized this in the second half of 1855. In August of that year, an article describing the destruction of the Russian harbour town of Kertch attributed the 'animated sketch' of this event to Durand-Brager for the first time.[133] Roughly a month later, in the issue of 20 October, a caption noted that 'a drawing by Durand-Brager' formed the basis for an illustration.[134] In November 1855, an article accompanying several illustrations of the siege of Sevastopol consisted largely of a translated letter written by the French artist: '"As your readers," he [Durand-Brager] says, "can examine for themselves the details of the whole, it is not necessary to enter into any very minute description".'[135]

In the final months of 1855, *Cassell's Illustrated Family Paper* frequently referred to Durand-Brager as a special artist in its captions and translated his letters for the accompanying articles.[136] Some months later, the British publication re-published his portrait under the title "our artist" (Figure 3.1):

> We have much pleasure, after having made use of his valuable communications from the commencement of the war, after having enriched our ILLUSTRATED FAMILY PAPER with plans, views, and scenes, . . . in presenting the artist to whose energy and zeal we owe so much – Durand-Brager himself.[137]

Not surprisingly, *Cassell's Illustrated Family Paper* removed the signatures of Jules Worms and Best, Hotelin et Cie, the draughtsman, and the engraving firm responsible for the illustration.[138]

The article next to the portrait is an almost word-for-word translation of *l'Illustration*'s description, but the British publication also changed significant parts of Durand-Brager's biography. For example, the French text notes: 'His reputation, already noticeable before the war, has now turned into real popularity.'[139] In a very similar vein, *Cassell's Illustrated Family Paper* writes: 'His mission to the Crimea made him famous – famous with the pencil as Russell with the pen; that reputation will now be still further enhanced.'[140] While these kinds of additions are telling, the untranslated parts of the original article are equally revealing. The French article cited three letters from the French minister of the navy praising the special artist, but the British publication only wrote that he received 'the congratulations of the Government for the services he has rendered to the fleets.'[141] It is unclear to which government the quote refers, while the use of the plural 'fleets' suggests that Durand-Brager was on the payroll of both the French and the British navy.

The increased number of references to Durand-Brager in *Cassell's Illustrated Family Paper* suggests that readers reacted positively to the discourse of objectivity surrounding special artists. This is further confirmed by the fact that the British publication went even further than *l'Illustration* in linking Durand-Brager to its coverage of the conflict. In May 1856, when the war was drawing to a close, it published the article "Coming Home":

> Our correspondent, seeing that his days are numbered in the Crimea, that he must henceforth employ his pencil on other topics, sends us a sketch of himself – a reminiscence of how he spent the last Christmas day.[142]

The accompanying illustration, titled "Our Correspondent," supposedly shows Durand-Brager celebrating Christmas alone in his tent in the Crimea.[143] However, *l'Illustration*, which had published the same illustration a couple of months earlier, never used it in this way. In fact, Durand-Brager did not make the original illustration, and the accompanying article did not mention him at all. In reality,

156 *Foreign images of war*

the image, with the caption, 'A battalion commander in his *intérieur*. Furniture of Sevastopol. Wallpaper and cloth by the house of Godillot, of Paris,' did not depict Durand-Brager on Christmas day but rather how a French officer 'survived' the harsh conditions of the Crimean winter in relative comfort.[144]

French subjects in a British publication?

Cassell's Illustrated Family Paper published roughly 50 per cent – 295 of the 678 original images – of *l'Illustration*'s war illustrations. In all likelihood, John Cassell could probably choose which French images he bought. Table 3.2 compares the subjects of the images in the French corpus with those in the re-published corpus of *Cassell's Illustrated Family Paper*. The main differences are easy to spot: Cassell published relatively more portraits and more images of troops and fewer illustrations that fall within the categories 'views' and 'ships.' Interestingly, the British publication did not re-publish any of Durand-Brager's 'types.' How can these differences be explained?

Cassell's Illustrated Family Paper could only print illustrations after they appeared in *l'Illustration*, which meant that it published them at least one week, but more often two or three weeks, after the French paper. This delay might explain why Cassell bought considerably more portraits and images of troops. In contrast to illustrations that depict actual events, portraits and generic images of troops retained their news value longer. We can explain the fact that Cassell did not buy any of Durand-Brager's types by referring to the subject matter of these illustrations: the British public might not appreciate the 'souvenirs,' as Durand-Brager called them, of the daily life of French soldiers. Roughly 50 per cent of the images in the categories 'ships' and 'troops' depict French forces, and Cassell preferably published images depicting British soldiers. He bought nearly all *l'Illustration*'s images – 27 of the total 29 – that only showed British troops. Furthermore, he also purchased 19 of the 21 images that represented both French and British troops. These numbers imply that Cassell bought images that he thought his British readers would like.

The image of the Crimean War presented in *Cassell's Illustrated Family Paper* did not consist entirely of illustrations acquired from *l'Illustration*. Sixty-six of the 361 images relating to Crimean theatre of the war had come from another source. The majority of these illustrations depict the actions of British troops. By buying material from sources other than *l'Illustration*, Cassell hoped to imbue his illustrated newspaper with a more British character. Thomas Henry Nicholson (d. 1870) made a substantial number of these images of British troops, 11 to be exact.[145] Although some of his illustrations also appeared in *l'Illustration*, the ones he made for *Cassell's Illustrated Family Paper*, such as 'The Death of Captain Vicars,' 'The heroic and gallant exploit of Lance Corporal Quinn,' and 'The four-footed hero attacking the Russian officer,' predominantly show the heroic acts and deaths of British officers.[146] Several other illustrations that were not made by Nicholson depict the same theme: 'Hewett firing the Lancaster gun on the advancing Russians,' 'Colonel Windham with Daniel Mahoney ad Cornellis entering the Redan,' 'The Earl of Cardigan leading on the light cavalry,' and 'Sergeant Davies defending the colours' are good examples of this theme.[147] Although it does not show a heroic act in the military sense of the word, the portrait of Florence Nightingale (who came to prominence while serving as a manager of nurses trained by her during the Crimean War), published in Cassell's paper of 10 February 1855, is another good example.[148]

Cassell could not have purchased these kinds of heroic images from *l'Illustration*, since the French publication only highlighted the acts of French soldiers, like the illustration showing the death of Second Lieutenant Poussin.[149] Referring to Keller's notion of the integration of different visual media, these illustrations should remind us that illustrated newspapers not only published objective visual reportages but also incorporated highly nationalist imagery, closely resembling battle, or history, painting.

Changing meanings: British textual elements accompanying French illustrations

Although most of *l'Illustration*'s images retained their original meaning in their re-published form, *Cassel's Illustrated Newspaper* deliberately altered the meaning of some of them by changing their captions or by writing new articles to accompany them. In some cases, the British editors did not translate the original textual elements because they were likely to harm the national sentiments of British readers. At other times, *Cassell's Illustrated Family Paper* used French images of one specific event to illustrate another, thinking that this would be more appealing to a British audience.

The journalist and radical writer Thomas Frost (1821–1908), who worked for John Cassell's publishing firm in 1854, wrote how its illustrations were equal 'to those which embellished the illustrated newspapers published at six times the price' (referring to the *Illustrated London News*) because they 'were printed from electrotypes procured from the office of l'Illustration.'[150] Frost also recalled how John Tillotson, the editor-in-chief of the family paper, asked him to write an article on the Crimean War:

> 'You know what sort of thing we want,' he continued, 'The popular clap-trap about British valour, and a compliment to the Emperor, you know. It has all been said before, but we must say something about recent events, for our war illustrations are exceedingly popular, and that is the key that our accomplishments must be played in.'[151]

Towards the end of 1854, Cassell fired Frost and two of his colleagues because the firm became 'involved in pecuniary difficulties.'[152] In another version of his memoirs, Frost wrote that the joint editorial staff of *Cassell's Family Newspaper* and *Magazine of Art* only consisted of 11 employees.[153] Thus, Cassell sustained a successful illustrated newspaper with an impressive circulation with just a few staff members. This demonstrates that his choice to not only copy the French

158 *Foreign images of war*

illustrations but also use the original French captions and articles was, to no small extent, economically motivated.

By changing the original French captions and articles in minor and more significant ways, Frost and his colleagues altered the meaning of many of *l'Illustration*'s images. Having said that, they also translated many captions and articles almost word for word. Take, for example, the portraits and biographical sketches of several political and military leaders, published in both the French and British illustrated newspapers. The first paragraph of the biographical sketch accompanying the portrait of the French 'Admiral Hamelin' (Durand-Brager's commanding officer in the navy) in *l'Illustration* declared: '*Hamelin (Ferdinand-Alphonse), commandant en chef de l'escadre française dans la Dardanelles, est né a Pont-l'Evêque (Calvados), le 2 septembre 1796. Il entra au service en qualité de marin à l'âge de dix ans.*'[154] A few months later, *Cassell's* re-published Hamelin's portrait, alongside which the first paragraph stated: 'Ferdinand Alphonse Hamelin, Commander in Chief of the French fleet in the Dardanelles, was born at Pont l'Eveque (Calvados) the 2nd of September 1796. He entered the naval service at ten years old.'[155]

The biographical sketch of 'Abdul Medjid, Sultan of Turkey' starts with a somewhat complex French sentence: '*Le 1er juillet 1839, le chameau noir qui va s'agenouillant de porte en porte, c'est-à-dire la mort, s'arrêta devant le kiosque de Tchamlidja.*'[156] Roughly one month later, *Cassell's Illustrated Family Paper* begins its sketch of the Sultan's life with the same words: 'On the first of July, 1839, "the Black Camel, which kneels at every door" – that is death – stopped before the kiosk of Tchamlidja.'[157] Other biographical sketches, such as the ones of Marshall Saint Arnaud and the Russian emperor Nicolas, are also literal translations. Only the biographical sketch of Lord Raglan, the commander of the British troops in the Crimea, differs from the French version, probably because the original article criticized the often incompetent and unquestioned leadership of the aristocracy in the British army, which shows that *Cassell's* editors altered textual elements when they were likely to offend British nationalist sentiments.[158]

L'Illustration often used captions and articles to surround its images with a discourse of objectivity. Just as it was eager to present Durand-Brager as its own special artist, *Cassell's Illustrated Family Paper* also mimicked the objective captions accompanying the French illustrations. The issue of 3 June 1854, for example, contained two images – 'Presentation of the Algerian Flag to the emperor of the French, 16th April 1854' and 'Grand review on the champ de mars by the emperor of the French, in honour of his royal highness the duke of Cambridge and the English officers, on the 12th of April, 1854' – which appeared side by side in *l'Illustration*'s issue of 22 April 1854.[159] *Cassell's* first caption only describes Napoleon III's presence at the ceremony. The original caption – '*Présentation a LL. MM. du drapeau offert part la population algérienne aux troupes d'Afrique partant pour la guerre d'Orient, le 16 avril 1854*' – not only tells us a great deal more about the event (the flag in question was not the flag of Algeria but the battle flag of Algerian auxiliary troops fighting for the French empire) but also notes the presence of both the emperor *and* the empress of France: 'LL. MM' stands

Foreign images of war 159

for 'their majesties.'[160] We can indeed find Empress Eugénie de Montijo (1826–1920) on the illustration (Figure 3.4). Changing a caption, however slightly, could also have been a deliberate effort to nationalize a French image. The original title of the second illustration in *Cassell's Illustrated Family Paper* of 3 June 154 had been '*Grande revue passé au champ de Mars, en présence du Duc de Cambridge, le 12 avril 1854.*'[161] Here, *Cassell's* editors changed 'in the presence of' into 'in honour of his Royal Highness' to appeal to a British audience.

In contrast to the previous examples, changing captions and writing new articles could also alter the meaning of illustrations in more significant ways. In its issue of 8 April 1854, *l'Illustration* published the image 'Reading, by the Minister of State in the Senate, of the message announcing the state of war with Russia, on 27 March 1854.'[162] In the previous issue, the French illustrated newspaper described how the French Senate and the British House of Lords received the declaration of war against the Russian Empire.[163] All the members of the Senate reacted with 'unanimous consent and energetic applause' after the interior minister made the announcement.[164] Almost a year later, *Cassell's Illustrated Family Paper* used the same illustration, published with the caption 'Meeting of the French legislative assembly: News from the East,' to illustrate the differences between British and French political systems.[165] It presented the French legislators as being 'mad with excitement' and motivated by a hunger for revenge: 'She [France] has not merely her interest to protect, she has also her reverses to revenge – to efface, . . . the memory of 1812.'[166] The description implies not only that Britain's motives were more honourable, pragmatic, and rational but also that France could, or was even likely to, turn on its present ally. After all, which defeat would have been more harmful to the French national ego: the defeat of the French forces in Russia in 1812 or Napoleon's final defeat at Waterloo by the Duke of Wellington in 1815?

Cassell's Illustrated Family Paper frequently altered captions and articles when the French descriptions were offensive to British nationalist sentiments. The image 'Fantasy uniforms of English officers at Scutari,' published by *l'Illustration* on 17 June 1854, reflects this notion well (Figure 3.5).[167] The image is part of a longer report about the British camp by M. Dulong, who, in a letter published next to the images, wrote: 'You will find, like me, that the officers [are dressed with a] carelessness to which our eyes are not accustomed and which differs completely from the uniform . . . of the French officer.'[168] A month later, *Cassell's Illustrated Family Paper* published the same illustration but changed its caption to 'Easy costume of English officers at Scutari.'[169] It also published Dulong's letter but changed the part about the uniforms: 'You will see the officers have rather more free-and-easy air about them than accords with very strict notions of military discipline.'[170]

In the previous two examples, the British textual elements interpret the events of the original illustrations in a new way, but the basic facts stay the same. However, *Cassell's Illustrated Family Paper* sometimes changed even these factual elements. In September 1854, *l'Illustration* published an article that is one of the best examples of objective reporting in the French publication. In this article, Pharamond Blanchard described and sketched the life of Russian prisoners of war on the small Île-d'Aix in the southeast of France: a naval base where

Figure 3.4 The French emperor and empress and the Algerian flag (1854). 'Présentation a LL. MM. du drapeau offert part la population algérienne aux troupes d'Afrique partant pour la guerre d'Orient, le 16 avril 1854,' *l'Illustration* (22 April 1854). The Hague, Royal Library of the Netherlands, T 1788 (1854–23).

Figure 3.5 Imaginative uniforms of English officers at Scutari (1854). 'Tenue de fantaisie des officiers anglais a Scutari,' *l'Illustration* (17 June 1854). The Hague, Royal Library of the Netherlands, T 1788 (1854–23).

Napoleon spent his last days on French soil in 1815. With his article, Blanchard hoped to debunk some popular myths about the prisoners, which the Parisian press eagerly spread. Despite stories about exotic and even barbaric Cossacks, Blanchard discovered that most prisoners were, in fact, Polish Catholics.[171] It was easy to find six of them to serve as models for one of his sketches: 'a couple of pinches of tobacco put me in the good graces of mister Chouta, Chachan, Schmeleski, Kawalewski, etc.'[172] Besides this group portrait and two engravings showing the arrival of the Russian prisoners on the island, Blanchard also sketched the women of the Polish soldiers.[173] He expected them to wear 'exotic costumes,' such as the ones used in the famous *Opéra comique* in Paris, but found that they were 'simply dressed in English textiles.'[174] Three of the women, 'Olga, Mina, and Avroura,' posed 'with gaiety' for the special artist: only their names added 'a bit of local colour.'[175]

The differences in the use of Blanchard's images between *l'Illustration* and *Cassell's Illustrated Family Paper* are striking. Instead of a French island, the British publication reports that we see Russian prisoners now arriving in Sheerness. The British and French navies indeed shipped Russian soldiers, taken prisoner at the Battle of Bomarsund, to both the Île-d'Aix and Sheerness, but the French images only show those in France. The British publication even altered one of the images to make its textual reportage more credible. On the original illustration, 'Transport of Russian prisoners of the Bomarsund garrison to the Île-d'Aix,' we see several small rowing boats, flying large French flags (Figure 3.6).[176] In its re-published form, 'Disembarkation of Russian prisoners at Sheerness,' the boats

162 *Foreign images of war*

Figure 3.6 Disembarkation of Russian prisoners at the Île d'Aix (1854). 'Transport des prisonniers russes de la garnison de Bomarsund a l'ile d'Aix,' *l'Illustration* (30 September 1854). The Hague, Royal Library of the Netherlands, T 1788 (1854–24).

fly the British flag instead.[177] It is clear that Cassell's editors altered not only the textual elements but also the image itself. Because it was hard to change electrotyped copies of the original illustration in this detailed manner, it seems likely that Cassell had ordered a British version of the original image especially from *l'Illustration*.

Besides the altered illustration, Blanchard's nuanced and objective description differs from the populist tone of the article in the British publication. The French reporter took great care to portray the Polish soldiers and their wives as simple, decent Catholics. He undoubtedly hoped that the two group portraits would humanize them. The British article, however, did the opposite and remarked upon 'the fierce appearance [of] the Cossacks of the Don' and the 'Mongolian countenance' of many of the ordinary soldiers and concluded by implying not only Britain's benevolence but also its supremacy: 'Our readers may rest assured that there are thousands in Russia who would gladly exchange conditions with [the prisoners of war].'[178]

Conclusion

Cassell's Illustrated Family Paper was the most important shaper of the image of the Crimean War in Britain. In general, historians have largely overlooked the role of the British illustrated press during this conflict; more specifically, they have underestimated the influence of Cassell's publication in this field. At the height of its popularity, it reached 500,000 readers, who mostly came from a very different social background than the average reader of the *Illustrated London News* or *The Times*. The image of the war that *Cassell's Illustrated Family Paper* presented to these readers is highly relevant, if only for the reason that it was these readers who decided whether their sons should volunteer to fight and die on the battlefields of the Crimean peninsula.

This case study supports the main argument of this book that images of illustrated newspapers were transnational products. As we have seen in the previous chapter, some contemporary critiques, like the Dutch printer Mohrmann, claimed that a particular 'national character' marked illustrations, making French images 'incomprehensible' for ordinary Dutch readers. The massive readership and popularity of Cassell's publication firmly contradict these kinds of statements. Moreover, the British publisher could pass off the French illustrations as his own, even in the politically charged atmosphere of the Crimean War and when nationalist sentiments were running hot.

The dissemination of *l'Illustration*'s images in the French and British publication produced a community of lookers: audiences in France and Britain who shared the same image of the Crimean War. In the mid-1850s, images in illustrated newspapers spoke a 'universal language,' as the *Illustrated London News* famously put it in 1851. However, as this chapter has shown, images should not be separated from the captions and articles that accompanied them. While the editors of *Cassell's Illustrated Family Paper* spent a fair amount of time translating articles from *l'Illustration*, they also altered the meaning of some images by changing captions – sometimes by mistake and sometimes deliberately – and writing new articles. When the French combination of image and text was thought to be offensive to a British audience, *Cassell's* editors nationalized the image by selective translation and adding new, often fictional, descriptions. While small alterations in the captions were frequent, outright deception (as was the case of the Russian prisoners of war in Sheerness) was relatively rare: the basic facts from *l'Illustration*'s reports were mostly copied verbatim by the British publication.

Not only the French images but also *l'Illustration*'s discourse of objectivity had a transnational nature. While the French illustrated newspaper based its medial form and its emphasis on eyewitnesses and objective reporting on the example of the *Illustrated London News*, *Cassell's Illustrated Family Paper* introduced a large part of the British public to this discourse of objectivity and visibility by centring the discourse on the special artist, as *l'Illustration* developed it. Cassell's paper increasingly copied the French publication's emphasis on objective reporting: its appropriation of Durand-Brager as 'our artist' is the critical element in this process. Ideas concerning objectivity and visuality, but also more concrete concepts like objective reporting, eyewitness accounts, and the *persona* of the journalist, took shape within the transnational network of producers of illustrated newspapers.

164 *Foreign images of war*

Ultimately, illustrations of the news not only crossed national borders, they were also able to transcend differences in social class. While Parisian elites mainly read *l'Illustration*, *Cassell's Illustrated Family Paper* explicitly targeted and reached a less affluent, but far broader, audience in Britain. Of course, differences between the captions and articles of both publications also play a role here. Indeed, as this chapter has shown, the way in which they altered the meaning of the images to suit the perceived social-cultural background of readers of the French and British publication deserves further scholarly attention.

Notes

1 Markovits, *The Crimean War in British Imagination*, 3; Maag, *Pyta, and Windisch, Der Krimkrieg als erster europäischer Medienkrieg*, 7; Paul, *Bilder Des Krieges*, 62.
2 Desmond, *The Information Process*, 181–2.
3 Cathcart, *The News from Waterloo*, 175.
4 Desmond, *The Information Process*, 181–2.
5 Paul, *Bilder Des Krieges*, 59.
6 Figes, *Crimea*, 304–11; Markovits, "Rushing into Print," 562–6.
7 Figes, *Crimea*, 310; Markovits, *The Crimean War in British Imagination*, 9.
8 Hobbs, "Deleterious Dominance," 472.
9 "Die Anfange der fotografischen Modellierung des Kriegsbildes": Paul, *Bilder Des Krieges*, 59–85.
10 "Vor allem aber ist er der erste photographisch dokumentierte Krieg. Mit der neuen Technologie der Photographie schien sich den Zeitgenossen zum ersten Mail die Möglichkeit zu eröffnen authentische Bildzeugnisse von dem Kriegsgesehen fernab der Heimatfront zu erhalten.": Maag, Pyta, and Windisch, *Der Krimkrieg als erster europäischer Medienkrieg*, 7.
11 Desmond, *The Information Process*, 181.
12 Gervais, "Witness to War," 372; Keller, *The Ultimate Spectacle*, 123–6.
13 Keller, *The Ultimate Spectacle*, 34.
14 Ibid., 29.
15 Ibid., 71.
16 Ibid.
17 Baudelaire's essay on his friend Guys is considered to be one of the fundamental primary texts of nineteenth-century visual culture studies. See for example: Schwartz and Przyblyski, *The Nineteenth-Century Visual Culture Reader*, 35.
18 Keller, *The Ultimate Spectacle*, 10.
19 See for circulation of the Times: Fenton, *Palmerston and the Times*, 133.
20 Puiseux, *Les figures de la guerre*, 64–5; Marchandiau, *L'Illustration*, 27–8.
21 Mitchell, *Iconology*, 69.
22 Mitchell, "There Are No Visual Media," 257.
23 Mitchell, *Picture Theory*, 89.
24 Ibid., 91.
25 Ibid., 83.
26 Figes, *Crimea*, XXI.
27 "Nicholas, Emperor of Russia," *Cassell's Illustrated Family Paper* (6 May 1854).
28 Keller, *The Ultimate Spectacle*, 13.
29 Figes, *Crimea*, 14.
30 Ibid., 142.
31 Ibid., 144–52.
32 Cited in: Ibid., 144.
33 Markovits, *The Crimean War in British Imagination*, 8.

Foreign images of war 165

34 This chapter does not consider this second front, but, as will become clear in the sixth section of this chapter, images of *l'Illustration* depicting events in the Baltic Sea were used by *Cassell's Illustrated Newspaper* to illustrate the Crimean side of the conflict.

35 Keller, *The Ultimate Spectacle*, 15.

36 For Turkish, French, and British death see: Cummins, *The War Chronicles*, 100; For the Russian casualties see: Gouttman, *La guerre de Crimée*, 479.

37 In *The London Journal* (2004), one of the few monographs dealing with a publication similar to *Cassell's Illustrated Newspaper*, King noted that nineteenth-century "periodicals with truly large circulations are not . . . studied nearly so much [as their high-end contemporaries] because they survive in very low numbers. . . . [T]heir very scarcity today confirms their low prestige." King, *The London Journal*, 16.

38 Anderson, *The Printed Image*, 88; Altholz, *The Religious Press*, 48; Armetta, "Cassell's (Illustrated) Family Paper," 101; Delafield, *Serialization and the Novel in Mid-Victorian Magazines*, 86–91.

39 **BNA4:** "Cassell's Illustrated Family Paper," *Enniskillen Chronicle and Erne Packet* (15 December 1853).

40 **BNA4:** "Cassell's Illustrated Family Paper," *Downpatrick Recorder* (28 January 1854).

41 **BNA4** "Review: Cassell's Illustrated Family Paper," *Wiltshire Independent* (13 July 1854).

42 King, *The London Journal*, 189.

43 **BNA4:** "Cassell's Illustrated Family Paper," *Morning Post* (8 March 1854).

44 **BNA4:** W.W, "Literature and Art: London, May 15, 1854," *Aberdeen Journal* (24 May 1854).

45 Ibid.

46 Ibid.

47 Ibid.

48 Frost, *Forty Years' Recollections: Literary and Political*, 226.

49 **BNA4:** "Eight Pages," *Belfast Mercury* (9 December 1854); *Saunders's News-Letter* (9 December 1854) *Kelso Chronicle* (9 December 1854); *Shrewsbury Chronicle* (9 December 1854); *Berkshire Chronicle* (10 December 1854); *Northampton Mercury* (10 December 1854); *Hertford Mercury and Reformer* (10 December 1854); *Worcester Journal* (10 December 1854); *Leeds Times* (10 December 1854); *Wexford Independent* (10 December 1854); *Bolton Chronicle* (10 December 1854); *Halifax Courier* (10 December 1854); *Downpatrick Recorder* (10 December 1854); *Limerick and Clara Examiner* (10 December 1854); *Galway Mercury, and Connaught Weekly Advertiser* (10 December 1854); *York Herald* (10 December 1854); *Southern Reporter and Cork Commercial Courier* (10 December 1854); *Westmeath Independent* (10 December 1854); *Huddersfield and Holmfirth Examiner* (10 December 1854); *Banner of Ulster* (10 December 1854); *Northern Standard* (10 December 1854); *Liverpool Mail* (10 December 1854); *Belfast Commercial Chronicle* (10 December 1854); *Exeter and Plymouth Gazette* (10 December 1854); *Aris's Birmingham Gazette* (12 December 1854); *Sussex Advertiser* (14 December 1854); *Aberdeen Journal* (14 December 1854); *Kings Country Chronicle* (14 December 1854); *Bradford Observer* (15 December 1854); *Enniskillen Chronicle and Erne Packet* (15 December 1854); *Stamford Mercury* (16 December 1854); *Waterford News* (16 December 1854); *Elgin Courier* (16 December 1854); *Elgin Courant, and Morayshire Advertiser* (16 December 1854); *Ulster Gazette* (17 December 1854); *Silurian, Cardiff, Merthyr, and Brecon Mercury, and South Wales General Advertiser* (17 December 1854).

50 **BNA4:** "The Greatest Achievement in the History of Cheap Literature," *Carlisle Journal* (23 December 1853).

51 **BNA4:** "Cassell's Illustrated Family Paper," *Halifax Courier* (24 December 1853).

52 **BNA4:** "Cassell's Illustrated Family Paper," *Leeds Times* (24 December 1853).

166　*Foreign images of war*

53　In this issue the publication announced that it would start to regularly answer some of the many letters that it received: "Our editorial table," *Cassell's Illustrated Family Paper* (14 July 1855).

54　"Our editorial table," *Cassell's Illustrated Family Paper* (1 September 1855).

55　Ibid.

56　**BNA4:** "Cassell's Illustrated Family Paper," *Leicester Chronicle* (12 December 1857).

57　**BNA4:** "New Series (Review)," *Belfast Mercury* (27 October 1857).

58　Anderson, *The Printed Image*, 143.

59　Ibid., 148.

60　See note 49.

61　**BNA4:** See for example: "Eight Pages," *Belfast Mercury* (9 December 1854).

62　**BNA4:** "The Week's Number of Cassell's Illustrated Family Paper," *Jersey Independent and Daily Telegraph* (29 December 1855).

63　**BNA4:** "The Religious Revival," *Coleraine Chronicle* (30 July 1859).

64　On his first visit, John Cassell acquired the rights to Harriet Beecher Stowe's *Uncle Tom's Cabin* (1852). He sold 100,000 copies of the first print in Britain. Holden Pike, *John Cassell* (London: Cassell and Company, 1894), 91, 109.

65　**GBX:** "A Remarkable Periodical"; "Inspect the Figures!"; "Dick Tarleton"; "Two Million Readers," *New-York Daily Tribune* (4 April 1856).

66　**TR2:** "Literary Intelligence," *the Argus* (28 October 1854).

67　**TR2:** "Periodicals to Commence, January, 1856," *Colonial Times* (23 August 1855).

68　**TR2:** "Cassells, Cassells, Cassells," *Mount Alexander Mail* (1 July 1856).

69　**GB1:** "Illustrated Newspapers," *the Gentleman's Magazine*, new series vol. 4 (1870): 452–70, 461.

70　Dowling, "Destined Not to Survive," 87.

71　**TR2:** The last advertisement I found announces the publication of issue number 20: "Cassell's Illustrated Family Paper and Melbourne Advertiser," *the Argus* (3 February 1855).

72　**TR2:** "Cassell's Illustrated Family Paper and Melbourne Advertiser," *the Argus* (9 December 1854).

73　"Prince Woronzow," *Cassell's Illustrated Family Paper* (18 March 1854); "Prince Gortschakoff," *Cassell's Illustrated Family Paper* (18 March 1854); "Le Prince Michel Woronzoff," *l'Illustration* (31 December 1853); "le général Gortschakoff," *l'Illustration* (31 December 1853).

74　"Le maréchal Le Roy de Saint-Arnaud, commandant en chef de l'armée française d'Orient," *l'Illustration* (18 March 1854); "Lord Raglan, général en chef des troupes anglaises de l'armée d'Orient," *l'Illustration* (18 March 1854); "Marshall Arnaud, Commander in Chief of the French Army in the East," *Cassell's Illustrated Family Paper* (29 April 1854); "Lord Raglan, Commander in Chief of the English Army in the East," *Cassell's Illustrated Family Paper* (29 April 1854). The publication of the two portraits in *Cassell's Illustrated Family Paper* and *Melbourne Advertiser* was announced on 19 January 1855: "Cassell's Illustrated Family Paper and Melbourne Advertiser," *the Argus* (19 January 1855).

75　**BNA4:** "Cassell's Illustrated Family Paper," *Salisbury and Winchester Journal* (24 December 1853).

76　**BNA4:** "Cassell's Illustrated Family Paper," *Hereford Times* (24 December 1853).

77　"Our editorial table," *Cassell's Illustrated Family Paper* (1 September 1855).

78　"Our editorial table," *Cassell's Illustrated Family Paper* (15 September 1855).

79　Ibid.

80　**BNA4:** W.W, "Literature and Art: London, May 15, 1854," *Aberdeen Journal* (24 May 1854).

81　**BNA4:** "Popular Literature," *Morning Post* (13 October 1858).

82　"Nous n'avons rien à dire de particulier de ces deux personnages très-haut placés.": A. Paulin, "Histoire de la semaine," *l'Illustration* (31 December 1853).

Foreign images of war   167

83 Worms, Jules. In Allgemeines Künstlerlexikon. 2017. Berlin, Boston: K. G. Saur. Retrieved 10 January 2018, from www.degruyter.com/view/AKL/_00162481
84 The careers of Worms and Blanchard support an important point made by Keller about the visual representation of the Crimean War: in the mid-nineteenth century, different visual media, like history painting and illustration, clearly crossed over and competed with each other. Ibid.
85 Treydel, Renate. Blanchard, Pharamond. In Allgemeines Künstlerlexikon. 2017. Berlin, Boston: K. G. Saur. Retrieved 10 January 2018, from www.degruyter.com/view/AKL/_10128084
86 Puiseux, *Les figures de la guerre*, 64.
87 Felbinger, Udo. Létuaire, Pierre. In Allgemeines Künstlerlexikon. 2017. Berlin, Boston: K. G. Saur. Retrieved 10 January 2018, from www.degruyter.com/view/AKL/_00089065
88 "Installation des chevaux du corps d'expédition d'Orient, à bord du Rolland, a Toulon," *l'Illustration* (29 April 1854).
89 "Reschid-Pacha offrant les pipes et le café au prince et à sa suite"; "Réception du prince Napoléon par le Sultan, le 1er mai 1854"; "Incendie à Constantinople, le 4 mai 1854"; "Le prince Napoléon recevant le Sultan dans son palais"; "Le sultan se rendant, en barque, au palais de Tefterdar-Bournou, résidence de prince Napoléon," *l'Illustration* (27 May 1854).
90 "Reconnaissance de la vile d'Eupatoria – d'après un croquis de M. Dulong"; "La golfe de Kalamita – d'après un croquis de M. Dulong," *l'Illustration* (7 October 1854).
91 "Prisonniers russes faits à la bataille d'Inkermann, et conduits à Constantinople," *l'Illustration* (9 December 1854).
92 "Bal donné par le général Baraguey-d'Hilliers, ambassadeur de France a Constantinople," *l'Illustration* (4 March 1854); "Bal donné par l'ambassadeur d'Autriche a Constantinople, le 6 février 1854," *l'Illustration* (11 March 1854); "Revue de la 3e division de l'armée d'Orient, passée par S. M. Le sultan, le 17 juin 1854, entre l'hôpital de Maltepe et la caserne de Rami-Tchiflik – d'après les dessins de M. J. Brindesi," *l'Illustration* (1 July 1854).
93 Ritter, Catrin. Brindesi, Giovanni. In Allgemeines Künstlerlexikon. 2017. Berlin, Boston: K. G. Saur. Retrieved 10 January 2018, from www.degruyter.com/view/AKL/_10141745
94 Marchandiau, *L'Illustration*, 26; Puiseux, *Les figures de la guerre*, 64–5.
95 Paulin, "Expédition du Cacique et du Samson," *l'Illustration* (22 April 1854).
96 "Es était impossible de choisir une dessinateur plus habile et d'un main plus exercée": Ibid.
97 Puiseux, *Les figures de la guerre*, 68; Keller, *The Ultimate Spectacle*, 74.
98 "Je voudrais avoir une plume assez exercée pour être en état de vous dépeindre tous les services que rend ici la marine. . . . J'espère que quelque écrivain, plus habitué qui moi à ce genre d'écrits, saura faire apprécier l'immensité de ces services.": Durand-Brager, "Sebastopol," *l'Illustration* (16 December 1854).
99 "J'ai le plaisir de vous annoncer que Son Excellence le ministre de la marine a bien voulu encourager mon travail, en prenant cette publication sous son digne et bienveillant patronage.": Durand-Brager, "Alma, Inkerman. Types et physiomonies de l'armée d'Orient," *l'Illustration* (3 March 1855).
100 Puiseux, *Les figures de la guerre*, 67.
101 "Pour mettre sous les yeux de votre lecteurs": Durand-Brager, "Alma, Inkerman. Types et physiomonies de l'armée d'Orient," *l'Illustration* (3 March 1855).
102 Ibid.
103 "Théâtre de la guerre en Crimée," *l'Illustration* (27 January 1855).
104 "Durand-Brager," *l'Illustration* (9 February 1856).
105 Keller, *The Ultimate Spectacle*, 74; Riall, *Garibaldi*, 255.
106 Cited in: Paulin, "Durand-Brager," *l'Illustration* (9 February 1856).

168   *Foreign images of war*

107 Bardon, "Militarmalerei Im Second Empire," 84.
108 Stolpe, Elmar. Durand-Brager, Henri. In Allgemeines Künstlerlexikon. 2017. Berlin, Boston: K. G. Saur. Retrieved 10 January 2018, from www.degruyter.com/view/AKL/_10198399
109 Bardon, "Militarmalerei Im Second Empire," 84–5.
110 In contrast to Bardon, Weston Naef states that some of Durand-Brager's paintings, like Panorama of Kamiesh, which was exhibited at the 1857 Paris Salon, must have relied on photographs in order to supply the details. Naef, "Beginnings of Photography," 58; Bardon, "Militarmalerei Im Second Empire," 84–5.
111 Marbot, "Durand-Brager," 59.
112 "Le sous-lieutenant Poussin, tué a l'attaque du bastion central, en enlevant son capitaine blesse," *l'Illustration* (27 October 1855).
113 "Le raisonneur"; "La carte a payer"; "l'enthousiaste"; "Par la froid"; "Par la neige"; "Par la pluie," *l'Illustration* (24 May 1856).
114 "Expédition du littoral de la mer Noire – Redout-Kaleh"; "Soukoum-Kaleh"; "Batoum"; "Fort de Touaps"; "Fort de Sotcha"; "Incendie du fort de Soubishik," *l'Illustration* (22 April 1854).
115 Paulin, "Expedition du Cacique et du Samson," *l'Illustration* (22 April 1854).
116 "Bal donné par le général Baraguey-d'Hilliers, ambassadeur de France à Constantinople," *l'Illustration* (4 March 1854).
117 "Costumes des femmes a Sinope," *l'Illustration* (7 January 1854); "Juifs karaïtes de Crimée," *l'Illustration* (29 December 1855).
118 "Officiers et soldats du bataillon grec à Balaklava," *l'Illustration* (18 November 1854); "Soldat du contingent de l'armée tunisienne," *l'Illustration* (30 June 1855); "Uniformes des légions suisse et allemande formée en Angleterre pour la guerre de Crimée," *l'Illustration* (15 September 1855).
119 "Zouave avec son chat," *l'Illustration* (18 November 1854).
120 "Attaque d'une flottille turque par les bâtiments russes, dans le port de Sinope," *l'Illustration* (24 December 1853).
121 "Sinope," *l'Illustration* (24 December 1853).
122 "Entrée de l' Escadre Franco- Anglaise dans la Baie d'Avacha, le 29 Août 1854. – d'après Le vicomte René de Kerret, a bord de la frégate amirale La Forte," *l'Illustration* (2 December 1854).
123 "Revue de la 3e division de l'armée d'Orient, passée par S. M. Le sultan, le 17 juin 1854, entre l'hôpital de Maltepe et la caserne de Rami-Tchiflik – d'après les dessins de M. J. Brindesi," *l'Illustration* (1 July 1854).
124 "Après la bataille d'Inkermann – Fraternisation des deux armées," *l'Illustration* (2 December 1854).
125 "La paix," *l'Illustration* (16 February 1856).
126 "Crimean Sketches: The Zouaves," *Cassell's Illustrated Family Paper* (28 June 1856).
127 Ibid.
128 "Carrying the Wounded Russians to the St. George's, Bucharest," *Cassell's Illustrated Family Paper* (11 March 1854).
129 "The Shores of the Black Sea," *Cassell's Illustrated Family Paper* (8 July 1854).
130 "The Crimea: Panorama of Sebastopol," *Cassell's Illustrated Family Paper* (10 March 1855).
131 Ibid.
132 Ibid.
133 "Kertch," *Cassell's Illustrated Family Paper* (11 August 1855).
134 "Bombardment of Sebastopol: Battery of English Mortars, to the Left of the Ravine of Karaballia, at the Front of the Height Used for Purposes of Observation, from a Drawing by Durand Brager," *Cassell's Illustrated Family Paper* (20 October 1855).
135 "Sebastopol," *Cassell's Illustrated Family Paper* (17 November 1855).
136 The captions of five illustrations mention Durand-Brager as the special artist: "Bombardment of Sebastopol: Battery of English Mortars, to the Left If the Ravine of

Foreign images of war 169

Karaballia, at the Front of the Height Used for Purposes of Observation, from a Drawing by Durand Brager," *Cassell's Illustrated Family Paper* (20 October 1855); "A Panoramic View of the South Side of Sebastopol, from a Drawing by Durand Brager," *Cassell's Illustrated Family Paper* (17 November 1855); "The English Attack on the Redan: From a Sketch Made on the Spot by Durand Brager," *Cassell's Illustrated Family Paper* (17 November 1855); "Head-Quarters of Omar Pacha at Scukoum Kale (From a Sketch by Durand Brager)," *Cassell's Illustrated Family Paper* (12 January 1856); "Interior of the Casemates of the Garden Battery, Sebastopol: From a Drawing by Durand Brager," *Cassell's Illustrated Family Paper* (16 February 1856).

137 "Our Artist," *Cassell's Illustrated Family Paper* (22 March 1856).
138 "Durand Brager, Artistic Correspondent in the Crimea," *Cassell's Illustrated Family Paper* (22 March 1856).
139 "Sa réputation, déjà notable avant la guerre, est devenue aujourd'hui une véritable popularité.": "Durand-Brager," *l'Illustration* (9 February 1856).
140 "Our Artist," *Cassell's Illustrated Family Paper* (22 March 1856).
141 Ibid.
142 "Coming Home," *Cassell's Illustrated Family Paper* (31 May 1856).
143 "Our Correspondent," *Cassell's Illustrated Family Paper* (31 May 1856).
144 "Un chef de bataillon dans son intérieur. Meubles de Sébastopol. Tenture et étoffes de la maison Godillot, de Paris," *l'Illustration* (26 January 1856).
145 Some historians describe Nicholson as the "principal artist" for *Cassell's Illustrated Newspaper* between 1853 and 1857. Because Nicholson was only responsible for a small part of the images in the British publication – 20 to be exact – this designation hardly seems appropriate. Furthermore, his images not only appeared in the British publication: *l'Illustration* also published 14 of them. The publication date of these images suggests that Nicholson sold them to both publications and that they jointly commissioned them. Vaughan and Vaughan, *Shakespeare's Caliban*, 239.
146 "The Death of Captain Vicars," *Cassell's Illustrated Family Paper* (2 June 1855); "The Heroic and Gallant Exploit of Lance Corporal Quinn," *Cassell's Illustrated Family Paper* (4 August 1855); "The Four-Footed Hero Attacking the Russian Officer," *Cassell's Illustrated Family Paper* (15 December 1855).
147 "Hewett firing the Lancaster gun on the advancing Russians," *Cassell's Illustrated Family Paper* (13 January 1855); "Colonel Windham with Daniel Mahoney ad Cornellis entering the Redan," *Cassell's Illustrated Family Paper* (24 November 1855); "The Earl of Cardigan Leading on the Light Cavalry: The Last Charge at Balaklava," *Cassell's Illustrated Family Paper* (6 January 1855); "Incidents in the War: Sergeant Davies Defending the Colours," *Cassell's Illustrated Family Paper* (27 January 1855).
148 "Miss Florence Nightingale," *Cassell's Illustrated Family Paper* (10 February 1855).
149 "Le lieutenant-colonel Edouard Vaissier, tué le 17 mars devant la tour Malakoff," *l'Illustration* (24 April 1855); "Le sous-lieutenant Poussin, tué a l'attaque du bastion central, en enlevant son capitaine blessé," *l'Illustration* (27 October 1855).
150 Frost, *Forty Years' Recollections: Literary and Political*, 228.
151 Ibid., 231–2.
152 Ibid., 237–8.
153 Frost, *Reminiscences of a Country Journalist.*, 114.
154 "M. L'admiral Hamelin, chef d'escadre française dans les Dardanelles," *l'Illustration* (29 October 1853).
155 "Admiral Hamelin," *Cassell's Illustrated Family Paper* (18 February 1854).
156 "Le sultan Abdul-Medjid," *l'Illustration* (25 March 1854).
157 "Abdul Medjid, Sultan of Turkey," *Cassell's Illustrated Family Paper* (6 May 1854).
158 "Marshall Arnaud, Commander in Chief of the French Army in the East," *Cassell's Illustrated Family Paper* (29 April 1854); "Le maréchal Le Roy de Saint-Arnaud, commandant en chef de l'armée française d'Orient," *l'Illustration* (18 March 1854); "Nicholas, Emperor of Russia," *Cassell's Illustrated Family Paper* (6 May 1854); "L'empereur Nicolas," *l'Illustration* (25 March 1854); "Lord Raglan, général en chef

170 *Foreign images of war*

des troupes anglaises de l'armée d'Orient," *l'Illustration* (18 March 1854); "Lord Raglan, Commander in Chief of the English army in the east," *Cassell's Illustrated Family Paper* (29 April 1854).

159 "Presentation of the Algerian Flag to the Emperor of the French, 16th April 1854"; "Grand Review on the Champ de Mars by the Emperor of the French, in Honour of His Royal Highness the Duke of Cambridge and the English Officers, on the 12th of April, 1854," *Cassell's Illustrated Family Paper* (3 June 1854).

160 "Présentation a LL. MM. du drapeau offert part la population algérienne aux troupes d'Afrique partant pour la guerre d'Orient, le 16 avril 1854," *l'Illustration* (22 March 1854).

161 "Grande revue passé au champ de Mars, en présence du Duc de Cambridge, le 12 avril 1854," *l'Illustration* (22 April 1854).

162 "Lecture, par M. le ministre d'Etat, au Sénat, du message annonçant l'état de guerre avec la Russie, les 27 mars 1854," *l'Illustration* (8 April 1854).

163 "Histoire de la Semaine," *l'Illustration* (1 April 1854).

164 "Assentiment unanime et d'énergiques applaudissements": "Histoire de la Semaine," *l'Illustration* (1 April 1854).

165 "Meeting of the French Legislative Assembly: News from the East," *Cassell's Illustrated Family Paper* (3 February 1855).

166 Ibid.

167 "Tenue de fantaisie des officiers anglais a Scutari," *l'Illustration* (17 June 1854).

168 "Vous trouverez, comme moi, que messieurs les officiers on un laisser-aller auquel nos yeux ne sont point accoutumés. Cela diffère entièrement de la tenue sévère, ficelée, comme on dit, et boutonnée jusqu'au menton de l'officier français.": "Tenue de fantaisie des officiers anglais à Scutari," *l'Illustration* (16 June 1854).

169 "Easy Costume of English Officers at Scutari," *Cassell's Illustrated Family Paper* (22 July 1854).

170 "Camp of the English at Scutari," *Cassell's Illustrated Family Paper* (22 July 1854).

171 Ibid.

172 Ibid.

173 "Femmes russes prisonniers a l'ile d'Aix," *l'Illustration* (30 September 1854).

174 "Sont tous bonnement habillées en percale peinte anglaise": Blanchard, "Le prisonniers de Bomarsund à l'ile d'Aix," *l'Illustration* (30 September 1854).

175 "Il n'y a que leurs noms qui aient un peu de couleur locale.": Ibid.

176 "Transport des prisonniers russes de la garnison de Bomarsund a l'ile d'Aix," *l'Illustration* (30 September 1854).

177 "Disembarkation of Russian Prisoners at Sheerness," *Cassell's Illustrated Family Paper* (4 November 1854).

178 Ibid.

4 Images of the world

The transnational trade in illustrations and the visual representation of the Universal Exposition of 1867

Introduction

> Where is Algeria? Between France and the Netherlands. Where shall we meet tomorrow? In Algeria for sure. Later in Brazil. It is very close. In between, we will have lunch in Russia, for the taste of caviar. If we stay until tonight, we will have tea with the Chinese. These are the things we hear all day among the thousands of travellers who have come to make their tour of the world in a park of forty hectares.[1]

In *Les curiosités de l'exposition universelle de 1867* (1867) the French author, journalist, and poet Théophile Gautier (1811–1872) wrote down his impressions of the Paris Universal Exposition of 1867. The subtitle of the book, 'followed by an overview of the means of transportation, the price of entry, etc. containing six plans,' indicates that Gautier hoped to profit from the 11–15 million visitors who would come to *champs de mars* between April and October 1867.[2]

The French writer frequently emphasized the confusion that visitors were likely to feel at the exposition: it was easy to get lost on the streets of the 'universal city.'[3] Preconceived notions amplified these feelings. Because of the extensive attention the exposition received in the French and foreign press, many visitors had already formed a picture in their mind. The illustrated newspapers, which were able to show the attractions of the *champs de mars* to their readers, were especially guilty of presenting it incoherently:

> Do you remember seeing, on the front pages of certain illustrated journals, a strange collection of all the monuments of the four principal points, mixed willy-nilly like the different floors of an amphitheatre; at the top, the domes, columns, minarets, lighthouses, and bell-towers; below, the ancient temples, European buildings, Chinese kiosks, Indian pagodas, fountains, statues, a whole fantastic, incoherent world, where the different architectural styles of all peoples are randomly grouped together by the whim of the artist?[4]

Another guidebook, published just before the opening of the exposition, described the same sentiment: 'All the newspapers, big and small, illustrated or without

172   *Images of the world*

images, have promised marvels and wonders. Let us modestly hope that half of these are realised.'[5] After the first issue of *l'Exposition Universelle* appeared (an illustrated newspaper devoted to the 1867 exposition), the correspondent of the British *Morning Advertiser* expressed similar doubts: 'If it [the exposition] ever approaches the beauties displayed in its illustrations, it will be the most splendid spot whichever adorned the earth.'[6]

In *Fleeting Cities* (2010), Alexander Geppert has argued that most historians base their research concerning nineteenth-century world exhibitions (Britain), universal expositions (France), or world fairs (United States) on sources relating to the organizers of these events. His research on five *fin-de-siècle* exhibitions is, however, based on a much wider field of inquiry and demonstrates how five groups of actors shaped the exhibitions and their meaning: exhibition initiators; exhibition organizers; domestic and foreign participants; professional observers, such as journalists; and, finally, national and international audiences.[7] Concerning the last group, Geppert has noted that it should include audiences that 'participated in the events via the mass media.'[8] This chapter therefore focuses on how a specific part of the nineteenth-century mass media, the illustrated press, mediated the Paris exposition of 1867 to its readers and shows how a study of the dissemination of images of the event sheds new light on both the illustrated press and nineteenth-century world exhibitions.

The visual representation of the exposition of 1867 in illustrated newspapers is a perfect case study to demonstrate the central argument of this thesis: the existence of a transnational visual culture of the news in the mid-nineteenth century. Because it generated an enormous amount of interest all over the world, publications eagerly tried to provide their readers with images of it. Based on a study of 31 illustrated newspapers published in 15 different European countries and the United States, this chapter explores how certain images of the exposition, being copied and sold, were disseminated on a massive scale. By doing so, this chapter provides a nearly complete overview of the transnational trade in illustrations of the news in its heyday.

While at least 11 million people bought a ticket, millions more experienced the 1867 exposition in a mediated form by reading about it in the press. Illustrated newspapers underlined that readers could visit the exposition on their pages. Writing only a few days after the official opening, the *Illustrated London News* noted: 'To many who are unable to visit the original, our illustrations, we trust, will help to make up their loss, and will give them an accurate, even if it must be but a faint, idea of the International Exhibition at Paris, and of its most noteworthy contents.'[9] This chapter shows that the transnational trade in illustrations structured the experience for many of these readers. By dividing the images of 31 titles into 12 different categories and by looking to what country they refer, it will become clear that the readers of illustrated newspapers saw a different exposition than the people who travelled to Paris. Several smaller nations with modest exhibitions became very visible on the pages of the illustrated newspapers, while large industrial countries with extensive exhibitions, such as the organizing country of France, attracted comparably less attention.

Images of the world   173

After sections on historiography, methodology, and an introduction to the Paris exposition of 1867, the first part of this chapter describes the transnational trade in illustrations of the news in 1867. The connections between different European and American illustrated newspapers took on many shapes and forms. They range from a very close relationship between two publications (a foreign edition) to a very indirect connection between multiple titles (the use of photoxylographic techniques to pirate illustrations). The second part of this chapter studies the visual representation of the exposition of 1867 in the illustrated press in two sections. The first section establishes the general characteristics of the visual corpus of the five largest suppliers of images of the 1867 exposition by dividing their images into 12 different categories and examining which nations they refer to. The second section investigates which element of this corpus was copied by the remaining 26 smaller illustrated newspapers.

Historiography

Like Gautier, authors of guidebooks for the exposition of 1867 hoped that their books would give readers an overview of the exhibition grounds. Historians studying nineteenth-century world exhibitions share the central concern of these guidebooks: many of them try to distil the order, the central idea, or the meaning of one, or several, exhibitions. As a result, they conceptualize expositions as 'fleeting magnifying glasses,' offering immediate insight into the structure or specific characteristic of the societies, which they were meant to represent.[10] Geppert is justifiably critical of this approach, which takes exhibitions 'at their word' and sees them as perfect, uncontested end products of the unambiguous intentions of their authors.[11]

Geppert has neglected to analyse where the conceptualization of the exhibitions as 'fleeting magnifying glasses' originated. In my view, this mostly has to do with the way in which scholars used different kinds of sources. For example, Wolfram Kaiser pointed out how organizing committees and exhibitors tried to present a coherent narrative during the exposition. However, many contemporary commentators and visitors found that these mass events 'did not convey order or give orientation, but could instead be a very disturbing, disintegrating experience.'[12] In other words: exhibitions often did not have the intended effect. Therefore, it is important to study which factors influenced their mediation and reception by different audiences. In this regard, the transnational trade in illustrations of the news takes a primary role; arguably, it was this trade that was responsible for structuring the nature of the visual representation of the exposition by the illustrated press.

Many studies concerning world exhibitions use the images of illustrated newspapers to illustrate or embellish historical narratives derived from other sources, which means that they neglect to contextualize the illustrated newspaper as a source in itself. Instead, scholars studying these images assume them to be neutral and objective visual representations of the exhibitions.[13] Not surprisingly, this is exactly how the illustrated newspapers presented their coverage. The *Illustrated*

174 *Images of the world*

London News noted: 'The Paris Exhibition will hold up for a little while a mirror to mankind, reflecting all the prominent types of the race in their most civilized mood.'[14] The British publication likewise presented itself as the mirror of this mirror, giving an objective and complete visual account of the exposition.

By looking at the origin of images in the illustrated press, this chapter will demonstrate that the visual coverage of the 1867 exposition in the illustrated press was neither objective nor neutral. Most importantly, the visual coverage of the exposition was not structured by a clearly defined programme but by the transnational trade in illustrations: publications could not choose which part of the mirror they mirrored but depended on the supply of visual material from a limited number of mostly French producers of illustrations. This factor has to be taken into account if we want to describe the nature of the experience of readers who visited the exposition on the pages of the illustrated press.

Several scholars note the focus of many studies concerning nineteenth-century world exhibitions on the production of national identity.[15] For example, Paul Greenhalgh has used Hobsbawm's concept of 'invented tradition' to discuss how the exhibitions penetrated 'higher levels of cultural production with nationalist dogma'; Peter Hoffenberg discerned that Hobsbawm's concept can shed new light on the 'debate about the foundations, structures, and functions of "the ideology of The New Imperialism".'[16] However, Benedict Anderson's notion of the 'imagined community' remains the dominant conceptual lens through which historians study exhibitions.[17]

This kind of research can be problematic because it tends to see the national pavilions and exhibitions as uncontested expressions of ideas about national identity. In *Displaying the Orient* (1992), Zeynep Çelik has pointed to the power relations that structured these representations of identity. Citing Walter Benjamin's idea of the phantasmagorical nature of nineteenth-century cities, she wrote: 'The architectural representation of cultures at world's fairs was double-sided, making a claim to scientific authority and accuracy while nourishing fantasy and illusion.'[18] Building on Çelik's ideas, the fifth section of this chapter argues that we cannot consider every pavilion at the 1867 exposition as an expression of self-defined identity.

Methodology

In many ways, the methodology of this chapter is similar to that of the previous one. For this chapter, I examined 31 illustrated newspapers published in 15 different countries to see whether they contained illustrations of the Universal Exposition of 1867 (Table 4.1). Images depicting the exposition were recorded in a database, noting their title, caption, publication date, subject, and authors. The computer program Gephi was used to visualize the connections between them (Figure 4.1). Gephi not only provides researchers with the opportunity to make complex networks visible but can also analyse connections with the help of an algorithm.[19] Illustrated newspapers that produced a large number of original images take a central place in the network visualization, while publications that only reproduced a limited number of images from a single source can be found on its fringes.

The size of the corpus points to the close connection between the digital and transnational turn in historical research.[20] The digital availability of sources often makes research from a transnational perspective feasible: digitized versions of many of the publications, especially those published in Eastern Europe, were found online. However, the digital availability of sources might also lead to a bias for a specific country. For example, 5 of the 31 titles were published in Madrid. I found these illustrated newspapers via the Biblioteca Digital Hispánica: the digital portal of the National Library of Spain, which provides easy access to both popular and somewhat more obscure nineteenth-century periodicals. It is unclear how much of the corpus of this chapter depends on differences in the development of online infrastructure by several European national libraries.

As Laurel Brake has aptly pointed out, the online accessibility of certain nineteenth-century newspapers and periodicals can result in the fact that historians easily overlook relevant publications that have not been digitized.[21] She thus urges researchers to 'work between' online and offline sources, contextualizing the one with the other. While I studied the paper versions of several publications for this chapter, it remains unclear as to whether I could have found more relevant titles in European archives. For example, I found references to a Russian and an Italian title, the *Illiustrirovannaia Gazeta* and *il Giornale Illustrato*, but I could not find the relevant issues of these publications online or in the European libraries I visited.

Besides illustrations of the park, the palace, and the pavilions, illustrated newspapers sometimes published images of the actual exhibited products and works of art. However, I did not include illustrations of this last category in the database. The main reason for this is that contemporaries mostly separated the two groups of images. In 1851, the *Illustrated London News* asked its readers for sketches of items exhibited in the Crystal Palace that could be reworked into illustrations.[22] This relatively cheap way of generating content significantly contributed to the popularity of the British publication, which doubled its circulation during the Great Exhibition. Several large illustrated newspapers continued this practice in 1855 (Paris) and 1862 (London). However, in 1867, the organizing committee decided to monetize this lucrative practice and sell the exclusive right to publish visual images of exhibited items to the French publisher Pierre Dentu. Publishers in other countries, such as Samuel Carter Hall (1800–1889) of the British *Art Journal* (1839–1912), bought the right to publish images of exhibited items in their own country. The fifth section of this chapter will discuss the implications of Dentu's monopoly for illustrated newspapers. For now, it suffices to note that most 'regular' illustrated newspapers were banned from publishing illustrations of exhibitions items although they were allowed to publish images of the exhibition grounds.

176   *Images of the world*

Table 4.1 Original and copied illustrations concerning the 1867 exposition in 31 European and American illustrated newspapers

Title	Published	Dates	Total	Originals	Copies
Illustrated Times	London	1855–1869	64	0	64
Illustrated London News	London	1842–1971	88	88	0
Illustreret Tidende	Copenhagen	1859–1924	15	1	14
l'Illustration	Paris	1843–1944	85	85	0
le Journal Illustré	Paris	1864–1899	23	15	8
le Monde Illustré	Paris	1857–1940	159	159	0
l'Exposition universelle de 1867 illustré	Paris	1867	480	480	0
l'Univers Illustré	Paris	1858–1912	124	76	48
l'Exposition de Paris	Paris	1867	12	12	0
l'Exposition Populair Illustré	Paris	1867	108	82	26
Über Land und Meer	Stuttgart	1858–1923	52	35	17
Illustrirte Welt	Stuttgart	1853–1878	18	10	8
Illustrirte Zeitung	Leipzig	1843–1944	46	46	0
Vasárnapi Ujság	Pest	1854–1921	9	0	9
l'Emporio Pittoresco	Milan	1864–1867	13	0	13
l'Universo Illustrato	Milan	1865–1870	43	1	42
Tygodnik Ilustrowany	Warsaw	1859–1939	4	0	4
Kłosy	Warsaw	1865–1890	20	0	20
Archivo Pittoresqo	Lissabon	1857–1868	7	0	7
Familia	Pest	1965–1944	1	0	1
il Globo Ilustrado	Milan	1867	51	0	51
el Museo Universal	Madrid	1857–1869	38	3	35
Museo de las Familias	Madrid	1843–1870	8	0	8
el Siglo Illustrado	Madrid	1867–1869	12	0	12
España a París	Milan	1867	67	0	67
Illustrerad Tidning	Stockholm	1855–1867	34	0	34
Ny Illustrerad Tidning	Stockholm	1865–1900	17	5	12
Geïllustreerd Nieuws	Amsterdam	1866–1879	44	0	44
Hollandsche Illustratie	Amsterdam	1863–1919	29	0	29
Frank Leslie's Illustrated Newspaper	New York	1852–1922	92	4	88
Harpers' Weekly	New York	1857–1916	7	1	6
		Total	1770	1103	667

The Universal Exposition of 1867

Many contemporary guidebooks begin by emphasizing the size of the *champs de mars*: the grounds where the 'new tournament of modern civilization' was held.[23] It occupied 146,588 square metres, or roughly 14 hectares.[24] The periphery of the exhibition palace, located in the middle of the grounds, measured one and a half kilometres.[25] The palace itself consisted of seven concentric galleries that divided the exhibition into several themes. The first gallery showed 'works of arts' of all participating nations, and the organizers devoted the second gallery to the liberal arts. After galleries displaying furniture (3), clothing (4), and raw materials (5), the sixth and largest gallery, the machine room, housed all sorts of new technology.[26] In the seventh ring, on the outside of the palace, visitors could

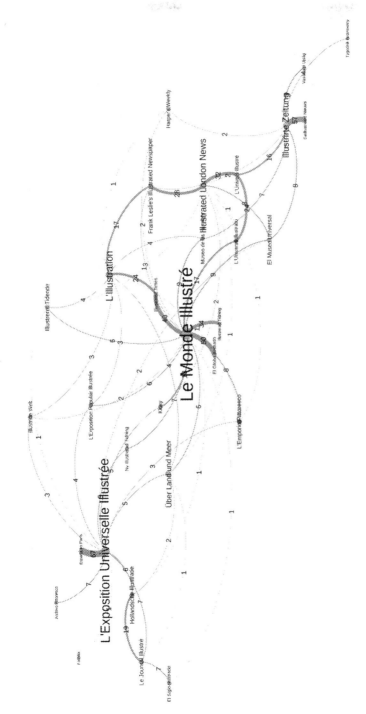

Figure 4.1 Network visualization: the transnational trade in illustrations of the 1867 exposition.

178 *Images of the world*

find all sorts of restaurants: 'Cafés of all nations, *brasseries*, Dutch, Belgian, and English taverns, Spanish posadas, kitchens, laboratories, pastries, confectioneries, etc.'[27] Sixteen transverse segments, named after countries and continents, divided the concentric galleries. By walking from the seventh gallery to the centre of the palace, a visitor would see all the different exhibitions of one nation, while a walk in one of the concentric galleries allowed a comparison of several nations on a single theme.[28]

Several historians have noted that the Paris Exposition of 1867 was the first world exhibition to include entertainment elements. In this regard, Greenhalgh has described how the French organizers realized 'the importance of entertainment as crowd-puller' and fully integrated it 'into the conceptual fabric of the exhibition tradition' after 1867.[29] Similarly, Kaiser has commented on how the fun-fair side of the exposition of 1867 was probably an essential part of the visitor experience.[30] The last part of the sixth section of this chapter reveals that illustrated newspapers were keen on acquiring images of these restaurants and bars, making entertainment a central part of their visual mediation of the exposition. Entertainment features also figure prominently in contemporary guidebooks. Describing the Dutch café, Gautier was impressed by the headdress of its waitresses, which he pronounced as achieving a very 'picturesque effect.'[31] Less subtle in his description, Henry Vizetelly writing for the *Illustrated London News*, observed: 'Its main attractions seem to be not its schnapps and other strong drinks, . . . but its young Dutch *fraus*. . . . One of them . . . is considered a sort of beauty, and is sighed over all day long by stout, middle-aged men, who loiter near her with *bocks* of beer before them.'[32]

The main innovation of the Paris exposition was the fact that it broke with the notion of a single exhibition palace.[33] The organizing committee invited all 50 participating nations and several large private companies to build small pavilions in the park surrounding the exhibition palace, causing it to resemble an 'enormous pleasure garden,' where all sorts of architectural styles were mixed.[34] In his guidebook, Gautier divided the park into four quarters, each named after a country or region. While the 'French quarter' only housed pavilions built by the French government and French companies, the 'Belgian quarter' also housed the Dutch fine-arts pavilion. Several 'Germanic countries,' including the Austro-Hungarian Empire, were located in the 'German quarter,' and in the 'Oriental quarter,' visitors could find the 'Egyptian stables,' the palace of the Bey of Tunisia, not to mention the 'Japanese house.'[35]

Previous research has largely overlooked the presence of several private companies at the 1867 exposition. Operating on a transnational level, they made use of the occasion to generate interest for their products. The French ironmaster Creusot, closely aligned with the regime of Napoleon III, showcased a locomotive commissioned by the British Great Eastern Railway Company.[36] The pavilion of the Dutch Coster Company demonstrated the process of polishing diamonds.[37] Heinrich Drasche (1811–1880), the largest brick manufacturer of the Austro-Hungarian Empire, exhibited statues of terracotta in his pavilion.[38] Under the pretext of being a part of the Egyptian exhibition, Ferdinand de Lesseps (1805–1894), the developer of the Suez Canal, used his 'temple of the isthmus of Suez' to attract new investors for his company.[39] Other firms, such as the technology company Siemens and the weapons manufacturer Krupp, exhibited their products in the national sections of the palace, in this case, of the Prussian state.

Aside from adding entertainment and allowing national pavilions, the French exhibition tradition differed in other ways from the British one. For example, in contrast to the relatively minor role played by the British government in 1851, Napoleon III's regime bankrolled the first three French expositions (1855, 1867, 1878). The French emperor hoped that these would help him introduce and enforce free trade policies and streamline his country 'into a progressive industrial state,' modelled after Britain.[40] To these contemporary motivations, Kaiser adds that the emperor actively legitimized his colonial exploits at the expositions and used them to bolster France's 'international prestige' and cultivate foreign alliances.[41]

Most importantly, Napoleon III hoped that the French expositions affirmed to the world that his second empire had 're-established order, introduced a stable form of government, and guaranteed economic progress and prosperity.'[42] In light of this, the influence of prominent Saint-Simonians, such as the commissioner general of the 1867 exposition Frédéric Le Play (1806–1882), is understandable. Saint-Simonian political ideology – anti-revolutionary and anti-socialist in its scope – promoted paternalist policies enacted by the state and large private companies, meant to foster social stability between the upper and the rapidly expanding working classes.[43] It presented French society as a 'beautifully tuned machine' where workers and their employers, content with their respective places in the social order, lived in harmony.[44] A special section of the 1867 exposition, aptly titled *la paix sociale* (social peace), showcased affordable social housing, exhibited cheap consumer goods, and presented information on the exemplary social programmes of French employers such as Creusot, which were often supported, in some way or another, by the French state.[45]

The transnational network

In August 1867, the French publisher François Ducuing (1817–1875) sued his small-time rival M. Montès for copyright infringement. The title of Montès' *l'Exposition Populaire Illustrée* was conspicuously similar to Ducuing's *l'Exposition Universelle de 1867 Illustrée*. An article in *l'Univers* describes how Ducuing alleged that this was harmful because 'every day [it led to] misunderstanding and confusion. All the time, readers are likely to mistake *l'Exposition Populaire* for the publication of Ducuing, which they intended to buy.'[46] The article also remarked that the interest of the public not only spawned many new publications but had also 'given free range to all sorts of reproductions of the pen and of the pencil.'[47] This section deals with these reproductions of the pencil, the transnational trade in images during the 1867 exposition, and describes the connections between all the 31 illustrated newspapers studied for this chapter.

180   *Images of the world*

Through French eyes

In 1867 the 31 illustrated newspapers published a total of 1770 images of the exposition (Table 4.1). I designated 1,103 of them as 'original,' meaning that the publication in question was the first to publish it. Next to these originals, 495 images were copies: images previously published by another illustrated newspaper. Eighty images were copied by hand: smaller illustrated newspapers commissioned artists and engravers to redraw and re-engrave original images of other publications. The network visualization makes these three different methods of reproduction visible (Figure 4.1). The origin of the remaining 16 images is vague. Although it seems likely that they were copies, as they were all published in illustrated newspapers that relied on foreign visual material, I could not find the original image in one of the other publications.

The figures mentioned above suggest that most illustrated newspapers published original images. However, only ten publications produced more than ten original images. Table 4.2 shows that five of these regularly sold copies of images to smaller illustrated newspapers. Ducuing's *l'Exposition Universelle* stands out because it produced 480 originals illustrations. However, this does not mean that his magazine was the most influential shaper of the image of the exposition. Table 4.2 shows that *le Monde Illustré* was the most central node of the network. It produced 159 original images, which appeared 235 times in 16 smaller illustrated newspapers; in comparison, Ducuing's illustrations appeared only 116 times in 8 smaller illustrated newspapers. The role of the *Illustrirte Zeitung* is similarly central to that of *le Monde Illustré*. The German publication only produced 46 original illustrations; nevertheless, these images appeared 95 times in 8 smaller illustrated newspapers. Finally, the images of the *Illustrated London News* and *l'Illustration* were copied 72 and 61 times, respectively.

In the run-up to the Universal Exposition of 1867, all sorts of Parisian publishers tried to profit by establishing special illustrated publications. Two of them, *l'Exposition de Paris* and *l'Illustrateur de l'Exposition Universelle*, both sold for 30 centimes and only published nine and four issues respectively. The aforementioned *l'Exposition Populaire* sold on the streets of Paris for ten centimes and published 69 issues and 54 images of the exposition. Ducuing's *l'Exposition*

Table 4.2 Illustrated newspapers of which images were copied in other publications

Title	Original illustrations	Copies in other illustrated newspapers
le Monde Illustré	159	235
l'Exposition Universelle de 1867 Illustré	480	116
Illustrirte Zeitung	46	95
Illustrated London News	88	72
l'Illustration	85	61
le Journal Illustré	15	26
l'Univers Illustré	76	24
Über Land und Meer	35	3

Universelle, which sold for 50 centimes, published 60 issues. However, in comparisons to all other publications, Ducuing's magazine printed a large number of original images of the exposition. Moreover, the network visualization shows that *l'Exposition Universelle* sold copies of its illustrations all over Europe. An in-depth exploration into this publication can explain how it managed to publish such a large number of images and its sudden influence.

The title page of each issue of *l'Exposition Universelle* proudly points to the connection between its two publishers, Édouard Dentu (1830–1884) and Pierre Petit (1832–1909), and the Imperial Commission.[48] As its official publisher, Dentu acquired the right to publish and sell the authorized catalogue of the exposition, while Petit was the *concessionaire* of photography on the *champ de mars* and the official photographer of the commission.[49] An article in *l'Univers* tells of how Ducuing, referred to as the editor-in-chief on the title page of *l'Exposition Universelle*, claimed the exclusive right to publish a special illustrated newspaper on the basis of the monopolies of Dentu and Petit.[50] What did these *concessions* entail? And how can they explain the influence of *l'Exposition Universelle*?

The Imperial Commission sold all sorts of monopolies to control the representation of the 1867 exposition and make a profit at the same time. The *Illustrated London News* noted how it had:

> Farmed out its catalogues, its plans, and the right to seize and levy a tax upon all umbrellas and walking-sticks seeking to intrude within the building, together with the right to sell eatables and drinkables, to establish a theatre, baths, photographic studies, &c.[51]

Several other British newspapers outlined how Dentu bought his monopoly for 20,000 pounds, which granted him the exclusive right to publish the official catalogue of the exposition, and how, for 3,400 pounds, Petit became the owner of the right to take and distribute photographs of the exposition.[52]

The close ties between the French government and the Imperial Commission ensured that the French police enforced the monopolies. In January 1867, four months before the official opening of the exposition the French police raided the offices of the Parisian publisher Libigre-Duquesne after Dentu sued him for the 'novel offence of an anticipatory infringement of his copyright.'[53] Similarly, the police seized 'thousands of photographs of the exterior of the Exhibition building . . . in the interest of M. Pierre Petit.'[54] The strict enforcement continued after the opening and hindered the work of the special artists. Henry Vizetelly objected to how the monopolies made it extremely hard to obtain sketches of the exposition: 'Already more than one artist has been taken into custody for disregarding this arbitrary edict.'[55] Other illustrated newspapers complained that the monopoly wronged them. For example, the German *Illustrirte Zeitung* asked why the Imperial Commission thought it had the right to deny its special artist entrance to the ground and 'force the world to see it with only French eyes?'

In the final months of 1866, Ducuing hastily assembled a team of well-known French artists, including Lancelot, Gerlier, Gauldrau, and Blanaded, to work for

182 *Images of the world*

l'Exposition Universelle.[56] For 'anecdotes and observations,' he relied on writers with 'a sparkling style, which fizzles and blows the cork [of the bottle],' like Edmond About (1829–1885), Emmanuel Gonzalès (18150–1887), and Théophile Gautier.[57] Several members of the jury of the exposition also wrote for the publication, including 'the Saint-Simonian pen of the inevitable M. Michel Chevalier,' who covered the 'political economy,' pointing to the connections between the organizing committee, the French government and this school of economic thought.[58]

L'Exposition Universelle quickly became a success, selling 25,000 copies of its first issue within a few hours, necessitating a reprint of another 25,000 copies on the same day.[59] It is likely that Ducuing sold a substantial number of magazines on the exhibition grounds, as the monopolies of Dentu and Petit granted him the exclusive right to do so. However, advertisements in French newspapers revealed that he also hoped to make money from selling *clichés* of his exclusive illustrations to other illustrated newspapers: one such advertisement of Ducuing in *le Constitutionel* offered *clichés* to 'French and foreign publications.'[60]

Another advertisement in *le Constitutionel* reported how a Spanish and an Italian publisher founded foreign editions of *l'Exposition Universelle.*[61] The Italian version, *l'Esposizione Universale del 1867 Illustrato*, closely resembled the French original. François Ducuing, or rather the Italian equivalent of his name 'Francesco Ducuing,' is mentioned on its title page as being its 'redattore in capo' (editor-in-chief).[62] The Italian publisher, Edoardo Sonzogno (1836–1920), probably shipped the *clichés* of the French illustrations to Milan, where he owned a large printing firm. The reference to Ducuing as the editor-in-chief suggests that Sonzogno commissioned Italian translations of the original French articles, which were mostly written by Ducuing.

The set-up of the Spanish version of *l'Exposition Universelle* was entirely different. First of all, the title of the publication was not a literal translation of the French original but boasted a Spanish twist: *España en París. Revista de la Exposicion Universal de 1867*. Second, instead of referring to Ducuing, its first page stated that a certain Don Jose de Castro y Serrano (1829–1896), a Spanish writer living in Paris in 1867, wrote all the articles.[63] Most importantly, *España en París* was not printed in Spain. An advertisement on the last page of each issue mentions that the 'work was published periodically in Paris' and a line of fine print below this advertisement even details the exact location: 'Printing press of Ch. Lahure, Rue de Fleurus 9, Paris.'[64]

In contrast to Sonzogno's Italian version, *España en Paris* was not a foreign edition of *l'Exposition Universelle*. After noting that he had agreed upon an 'exclusive contract' with 'Dentu, Ducuing, and Petit,' De Castro y Serrano criticized their monopolies, which resulted in the fact that he could only buy 'French' illustrations of the exposition.[65] However, he promised his readers to refrain from 'slavishly following the footsteps of French papers' and asserted that *España en Paris* would also publish 'entirely new' illustrations of 'a national character,' made by 'young Spanish artists' who lived in Paris.[66] However, it proved difficult to deliver on these promises. Of the 67 illustrations that *España en París* published, only one, signed by a certain 'Rico,' had not previously appeared in *l'Exposition Universelle*.[67] Smaller illustrated newspapers often commissioned some original illustrations, because they were unhappy with the fact that the large illustrated newspapers only published a few images showing the exhibitions of their specific country. Rico's illustration, depicting the Spanish section of the first gallery of the exhibition palace, is a good example of this practice.

While Ducuing produced the largest number of original illustrations of the exposition, his images were not the most influential. As Figure 4.1 shows, smaller illustrated newspapers bought and reprinted illustrations from *le Monde Illustré* more often. In Chapter 2, I discussed the transnational roots of this French illustrated newspaper in the late 1850s. By 1867, the French publisher Paul Dalloz (1829–1887), who was closely connected to several powerful political figures of the Second Empire, owned *le Monde Illustré*. In contrast to its main competitor *l'Illustration*, the French state classified *le Monde Illustré* as a 'non-political' publication, meaning that it was tax-exempt and could sell for 35 centimes: 40 centimes cheaper than *l'Illustration*.[68] Marchandiau suggests that Napoleon III was involved in the foundation of *le Monde Illustré* and that this can explain the tax privilege.[69] The oldest French illustrated newspaper was furious about this unfair competition and declared in an editorial: 'The newspaper stamp for everybody or no stamp at all!'[70] The fact that *le Monde Illustré* never complained about the monopolies of Dentu, Petit, and Ducuing also suggests that Dalloz's contacts with the regime of Napoleon III enabled him to send special artists to the exhibition grounds without being harassed by the French police.

While many European and American publications contained at least one illustration that initially appeared in *le Monde Illustré*, one illustrated newspaper, the Spanish *el Globo Ilustrado*, purchased all its images of the exposition from Dalloz.[71] Its editor, Dionisio Chaulié y Ruiz (1814–1887), argued that it was almost impossible to surmount the 'seemingly insuperable difficulty of assembling a sufficient number of subscribers to cover the immense expenses' of an illustrated newspaper in Spain.[72] He solved this problem by ordering eight sheets filled with illustrations of *le Monde Illustré* in Paris and printing eight pages filled with articles by Spanish authors in Madrid.[73] The fact that the Spanish illustrated newspaper only published 30 issues suggests that, in the end, Chaulié was also unable to publish a successful illustrated newspaper in Spain.

L'Illustration, the *grande dame* of the French illustrated press, published 85 illustrations of the 1867 exposition. Besides the 24 images that it sold to the British *Illustrated Times*, it appears to have refrained from selling its illustrations in large batches. Likewise, for the *Illustrated London News*, which published 88 images of the exposition and only sold them to *l'Univers Illustré*. With 46 original illustrations, the German *Illustrirte Zeitung* was the fifth largest supplier of visual material of the 1867 exposition. In contrast to *l'Illustration* and the *Illustrated London News*, it sold its images on a much larger scale. First of all, the Dutch *Geïllustreerde Nieuws* bought all 46 illustrations of the exposition it published from the *Illustrirte Zeitung*. As outlined in Chapter 2, the Dutch publication bought printed sheets, filled with German illustrations in Leipzig: an arrangement

184   *Images of the world*

that was, as the cases of *España en Paris* and *el Globo Ilustrado* demonstrate, quite common at the time.

Two illustrated publications – *Tygodnik Illustrowany*, published by Józef Unger (1817–1874) in the Polish capital of Warsaw, and *Vasárnapi Ujság*, published in the Austro-Hungarian city of Pest by Gustav Hecknast (1811–1878) – bought all their images of the Universal Exposition from the *Illustrirte Zeitung*. As their names indicate, both men were part of the German-speaking diaspora in Eastern Europe. However, their publications were published in Polish and Hungarian rather than German and supported nationalist political movements. In contrast to the *Geïllustreerde Nieuws*, they also contained many original illustrations made by Polish and Hungarian artists. The fact that they both published the same illustrations of the Universal Exposition suggests that the *Illustrirte Zeitung* probably sold them in batches.

Illustrated newspapers were not the only suppliers of illustrations of the exposition. Large companies also commissioned and freely distributed images of their pavilions and products. A good example of this nineteenth-century form of native advertising is the image of the small 'perfumery cottage' of Eugène Rimmel (1820–1887). In his *Recollections of the Paris Exhibition* (1867), the British perfumer explained the 'various substances used in the manufacture of perfumery,' such as 'exotic flowers received in glycerin from Brazil' and 'alligator glands,' which visitors could admire inside the cottage.[74] Rimmel's book was published by Dentu in Paris, making it hardly surprising that the image of the cottage also appeared in his *l'Exposition Universelle*.[75] However, the same illustration also appeared in *l'Illustration*, *l'Univers Illustré*, and *l'Exposition Populaire*, three of Dentu's competitors (Figure 4.2).[76] In this case, it seems likely that Rimmel commissioned the illustration and distributed it to several illustrated newspapers, which gladly published this free material.

Of all the illustrated publications, *l'Exposition Populaire* depended the most on free images: of the total 54 illustrations of the exposition it published, 21 explicitly mention the name of a company. The newspaper often shared these images with other French illustrated newspapers, which further confirms that the companies distributed them. For example, *l'Illustration* and *l'Exposition Populaire* published an illustration showing a 'small living-room' filled with products of the French silverware manufacturer Christoffle.[77] The modestly priced illustrated publication shared an image of a showcase filled with fashionable lady's shoes from a certain M. Pinet with *l'Exposition Universelle*.[78] Finally, *le Monde Illustré* and *l'Exposition Populaire* published the same images showing the contributions to the exposition from five different French companies: the lace production of 'MM. Auguste Lefebure et fils,' the office supplies of Leglas Maurice, the coloured paper of M. Bezault, the porcelain from the house of Pillivuyt, and the musical instruments from MM. Gautrot.[79]

In addition to these private companies, some sources suggest that governments also provided illustrated newspapers with free images of their pavilions and exhibitions. An article in the British *Daily News* commented on how the Russian commission was anxious to obtain photographs of their national pavilion. However,

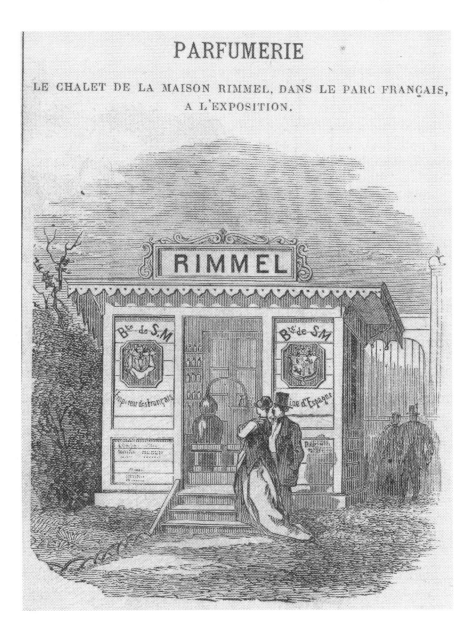

Figure 4.2 Rimmel's pavilion in the park (1867). 'Le Chalet de la Maison Rimmel dans le parc française à l'exposition,' *l'Illustration* (31 August 1867). The Hague, Royal Library of the Netherlands, T 1788 (1867–2).

186   *Images of the world*

they refused to hire Pierre Petit, the holder of the official monopoly, and commissioned Robert Jefferson Bingham (1824–1870), a British photographer working in France, to do the work. The *Daily News* noted that this seemed to be 'the first blow of a very petty war; where the war of the lenses will end it is not easy at the moment to predict.'[80]

A second example of this practice is found in the image 'Exterior view of the Swiss exposition,' published in *l'Exposition Populaire*.[81] The image, the only one in all 31 illustrated newspapers, shows the pavilion of Switzerland, housing a special art exhibition. Made by a certain 'Mariann,' whose signature only appears on this image, it contains all sorts of nationalist allegorical elements, such as the Swiss flag and a portrait of a Swiss artist. The accompanying description in *l'Exposition Populaire* is strikingly positive: 'It also shows that the Swiss Republic has not only produced good watchmakers and excellent shooters, but that she can also count distinguished painters and sculptors among her children.'[82]

More importantly, many images of national pavilions in the illustrated press were not based on the sketches of special artists but on architectural drawings supplied by organizing committees. For example, *l'Exposition Universelle* published an image of the Palace of the Bey of Tunis before it was finished. The caption of the illustration reveals that it was based on drawings by Alfred Chapon: the architect of the palace.[83] Because it received the plans for the pavilion, the illustrated newspaper could provide its readers with highly newsworthy illustrations without having to commission them. However, this arrangement was also beneficial for the organizing committees of the countries involved. By providing the illustrated newspaper with the plans of their pavilions, they could place them before the eyes of an international audience of readers.

A mixed image

The majority of smaller illustrated newspapers published *clichés* from several sources, where they remixed a selection of the original corpus of 1,103 illustrations and presented them in different combinations. As a result, these smaller publications were, to a certain extent, able to construct their own image of the exposition. Before turning to several more complex cases, an examination of *l'Univers Illustré* and the *Illustrated Times* will demonstrate how easy it was to fill a popular publication with cheap, foreign images. The British illustrated newspaper published 64 illustrations, 40 of which were purchased from *le Monde Illustré* and 24 from *l'Illustration*. It is likely that Henry Vizetelly acquired these *clichés* as he was the continental representative of both the *Illustrated Times* and the *Illustrated London News* at this time.

The case of *l'Univers Illustré* (1858–1912) is more complicated. Founded in 1858 by the influential publisher Michel Lévy (1821–1875) and selling for only 15 centimes per issue, it quickly became a formidable competitor of both *l'Illustration* and *le Monde Illustré*.[84] One might ask how Lévy's publication could sell for such a low price. Writing in 1863, Paul Schmidt, the German printer living in Paris, commented on how the 'extensive business connections of Mr

Images of the world 187

Levy provide him with as many *clichés*, which are unknown in France, as he could want.'[85] *L'Univers Illustré* commissioned 76 original images of the exposition but also bought 31 *clichés* from the *Illustrated London News* and 16 from the *Illustrirte Zeitung*.

Similar to *l'Univers Illustré*, the *Illustrirte Welt* and *Über Land und Meer*, both published by Eduard Hallberger in Stuttgart, produced original illustrations of the exposition but also purchased images from foreign sources. The *Illustrirte Welt* commissioned ten original illustrations and published eight images from several French sources: three from *l'Exposition Universelle*, three from *l'Illustration*, and two from *le Monde Illustré*. Similarly, *Über Land und Meer* published 35 original illustrations of the exposition and bought 15 images from French sources: five from *l'Exposition Universelle*, six from *le Monde Illustré*, and four from *l'Illustration*. It copied one illustration of the *Illustrated London News* by redrawing it.

Hallberger bought images from the same French sources, but the *Illustrirte Welt* and *Über Land und Meer* did not publish the same material. The intended audiences of the German publications played an important role in explaining the difference. While the German publisher marketed the *Illustrirte Welt* as containing 'pages on nature and life, science and art, for the *Unterhaltung* [entertainment] and instruction of the family,' he described *Über Land und Meer* as a 'general illustrated newspaper'.[86] Hallberger probably hoped that some readers would subscribe to both his publications: the one being focused on news and the other on *Unterhaltung*.

The French *le Journal Illustré* produced 23 original illustrations of the exposition. 'H de Hem,' Henri de Montaut's (1825–1890) pseudonym, the first illustrator of Jules Verne's *De la Terre à la Lune* (1865) and the editor-in-chief of the *Journal Illustré* since 1863, made almost all of them.[87] The French illustrated newspaper also purchased images from several foreign sources: seven from *l'Exposition Universelle* and one from *Über Land und Meer*. In contrast to Hallberger's publications, it also resold these illustrations to several foreign editions.

The Dutch *Hollandsche Illustratie*, one of the foreign editions of the *Journal Illustré*, published 19 illustrations of the Universal Exposition that had previously appeared in the French publication. However, five images, which originally appeared in *l'Exposition Universelle*, also found their way to the Dutch *Hollandsche Illustratie* via the *Journal Illustré*.[88] The captions of the illustrations in the *Hollandsche Illustratie* and the *Journal Illustré* are almost literal translations; meanwhile, they are similar in the two French publications, but not the same. Because the French publication did not contain a single image of the Dutch contribution to the exposition, the *Hollandsche Illustratie* had to buy four illustrations directly from *l'Exposition Universelle*: depicting a Dutch farmhouse, the Dutch café, the Dutch fine-art section, and the pavilion of the Amsterdam-based diamond seller Coster.[89]

The case of the *Hollandsche Illustratie* shows that the interest of national audiences in the contributions of their countries to the exposition shaped the transnational trade in illustrations of the news. If their usual source could not deliver

188 *Images of the world*

images of a specific subject, illustrated newspapers often commissioned new material or bought illustrations from a different foreign source. This practice is also evident in the Danish *Illustreret Tidende* and the Swedish *Ny Illustrerad Tidning*.

The Danish illustrated newspaper (published in Copenhagen since 1859) bought *clichés* from *le Monde Illustré* (7) and *l'Illustration* (3). However, because *le Monde Illustré* and *l'Illustration* did not publish images of the Danish exhibition, the *Illustreret Tidende* had to find them somewhere else and managed to purchase one illustration, 'The Danish section of the World Exhibition in Paris,' from *l'Exposition Universelle*.[90] Instead of hiding the foreign origin of this image, the caption proudly mentions the original French source. It also published the illustration, 'Farewell party for Danish workers in the *salle de families* at the World Exposition in Paris,' made by the Danish artist Niels Aagaard Lytzen (1826–1890): a regular contributor to the *Illustreret Tidende*.[91] A similar situation can be sketched for the Swedish *Ny Illustrerad Tidning* (1865–1900). It bought 6 of its 16 images of the exposition from *le Monde Illustré* and 5 from *l'Exposition Universelle*. The publication also commissioned four original illustrations, one representing the national pavilion of Norway on the *champ de mars* and three showing the Swedish section of different galleries in the exhibition palace, made by the Swedish architect, lithographer, and engraver Otto August Mankell (1838–1885).[92]

Pirates at the exposition

Not all publications bought copies of images from foreign sources. Many smaller illustrated publications copied images of larger illustrated newspapers by re-engraving them. As discussed in Chapter 2, in the mid-1850s, a technique was invented that could be used to transfer a photograph of an illustration directly on a woodblock. As these ways of copying did not necessarily entail any direct form of contact, illustrated newspapers that published photoxylographically copied and re-engraved images should be seen as a separate part of the transnational network. At the same time, their representation of the exposition was clearly a part of the transnational visual culture of the news in 1867. Just like the illustrated newspapers that did publish *clichés*, they contributed to the widespread dissemination of certain images of the exhibition.

The Portuguese *Archivo Pittoresco* (1857–1868), which was published in Lisbon but also found its way to the former colony Brazil, copied seven images of the exposition from *l'Exposition Universelle*.[93] The engraver 'Alberto' signed the only original illustration, depicting the national pavilion of Spain.[94] Similarly, *el Museo Universal*, published in Madrid between 1857 and 1869, copied nine illustrations from *le Monde Illustré*, eight from the *Illustrirte Zeitung*, seven from the *Illustrated London News*, four from *l'Illustration*, and two from *l'Exposition Universelle*. Enrique Laporta Valor (1842–1914) signed 12 of these images.[95] He sometimes even copied images line for line. The image 'Section of the United States – planetarium of Mr Barlow,' published on 14 September 1867 in *el Museo Universal*, is almost an exact copy of 'The United States section,'

Images of the world 189

published in the *Illustrated London News* of 6 July 1867 (Figure 4.3).⁹⁶ Besides being slightly smaller, the only difference between the two images is the signature of 'Laporta' in the lower-right corner. However, not all of the Spanish illustrations were direct copies. The first image *el Museo Universal* published of the Spanish national pavilion resembles illustrations in *l'Illustration*, *le Monde Illustré*, and *l'Exposition Universelle*; however, it is not an exact copy of any of these images.⁹⁷

The boundary between the smaller illustrated newspapers that published *clichés* and those that published re-engravings was sometimes blurry. The Italian *l'Emporio Pittoresco* owned by Eduoardo Sonzogno, who also published the Italian version of *l'Exposition Universelle*, contained re-engravings and copies. Three artists, 'Vajani,' 'Sartorio,' and 'Centenari,' signed the ten re-engraved images, which they based on illustrations of the *Illustrated London News* (1), *l'Illustration* (1), and *le Monde Illustré* (8). Sonzogno bought the two *clichés* from *l'Exposition Universelle*, which shows how he cleverly published these French copies in two different publications.

The images of the 1867 exposition in the American *Frank Leslie's Illustrated Newspaper* demonstrate that technological innovation started to play an essential role in the transnational visual culture of the news in the late 1860s. It published 94 images of the Universal Exposition, many more than several of the famous and well-established European illustrated newspapers such as the *Illustrated*

Figure 4.3 US exhibition at the exposition (1867). 'The United States Section.' *Illustrated London News* (6 July 1867). The Hague. Royal Library of the Netherlands. T 2258 (1867–2).

190   *Images of the world*

London News and *l'Illustration*. However, only four illustrations were originals: one showing the steamer *Mercury*, loading the American goods for the exhibition in the harbour of New York, and three representing the contributions of American companies to the exposition.[98] It copied all the other illustrations from major European publications: 27 from the *Illustrated London News*, 33 from *le Monde Illustré*, and 17 from *l'Illustration*.[99]

In contrast to standard practice at the time, *Frank Leslie's* did not hide the foreign origin of their European images from the American public. Making use of a photoxylographic technique, each issue of *Frank Leslie's* contained six illustrations of European illustrated newspapers printed in reduced form on a single page. As the short time between the publication date of the original image and the image in the American illustrated newspaper suggests, this special page, carrying the title 'The Pictorial Spirit of the European Illustrated Press', contained images that were copied as soon as the issues of several European publications arrived in New York.[100]

Mediation

Two years after the Universal Exposition of 1867, the Imperial Commission published a report, documenting its organization and success. In the introduction, General Commissioner Le Play proudly wrote: 'On the 1st of April 1867, the public, finding order established in the palace where confusion had still reigned the night before, understood the enormous efforts which such rapid transformation had required.'[101] The report summarizes the exposition in all sorts of statistics. For instance, Table 26 tells us that 36 physicians treated 6,750 visitors between 1 April and 3 November 1867; Table 27 shows how the exhibition police made 102 arrests on the grounds, three of which involved the crime of 'public indecency'; and Table 30 notes that visitors sent 4,537 international telegrams from the exhibition post office.[102]

For this chapter, Table 8 from the report, which indicates the exact number of square metres allotted to each participating country in the palace, the park, and the bank of the river Seine, is the most relevant (Table 4.3).[103] The Imperial Commission carefully considered the space they allotted to each state, and these choices structured the visitors' experience. In the total 329,678 square metres, a visitor was very unlikely to stumble upon the meagre 63 square metres allotted to the Kingdom of Hawaii; meanwhile, it would be almost impossible to avoid the 156,546 square metres taken up by France.[104] However, the choices made by the Imperial Commission did not entirely structure the experience of individual visitors. Unlike Queen Sophia of the Netherlands, who visited the exposition 18 times in a single month and could thus see almost all of the pavilions and exhibitions, most visitors could only come to the *champ de mars* a single time, making it possible to see only a part of the exposition.[105] As true *flâneurs*, they strolled through the palace and the park, amazed by what they encountered, and made their own summary of the exposition.

The illustrated press frequently invoked the figure of the *flâneur*, a strong nineteenth-century cultural trope. Scholar Jakob Stougaard-Nielsen observed how

Images of the world   191

Table 4.3 The percentage of square metres allotted to all participating countries on the exhibition ground and the percentage of space allotted to them in the illustrated press

Country	Percentage of square metres on the exhibition grounds	Percentage in the five main suppliers	Percentage in the smaller illustrated newspapers
Argentina	South America in figure eight	0.3	0.2
Austro-Hungary	5.3	4.4	3.5
Bade	0.2	0.3	0.0
Bavaria	0.7	0.7	0.0
Belgium	5.0	2.0	3.0
Brazil	0.1	0.3	0.5
Britain	11.3	7.6	8.6
Chile	South America in figure eight	0.1	0.2
China	0.7	2.5	4.2
Denmark	0.4	0.3	0.7
Egypt	2.0	6.8	10.9
France	47.8	25.0	17.9
Greece	0.2	0.1	0.0
Hesse	0.4	0.1	0.2
Italy	2.1	2.3	1.4
Japan	0.5	1.8	2.8
Mexico	Not listed	0.8	2.3
Morocco	0.5	1.1	1.2
Netherlands	2.1	1.5	3.0
North-Germany	6.6	4.9	10.5
Norway	0.7	2.1	2.8
Ottoman	1.3	5.2	9.5
Persia	0.0	0.3	0.2
Portugal	0.6	1.4	3.5
Rumania	0.8	1.4	0.7
Russia	1.9	8.3	14.9
Siam	0.1	0.6	1.2
South-America	0.2	0.3	0.2
Spain	1.0	3.2	5.1
Sweden	0.7	4.5	7.2
Switzerland	2.0	2.0	2.8
Tunisia	0.9	3.8	8.1
USA	2.7	2.0	4.0
Venezuela	Not listed	0.1	0.5
Wurtmeberg	0.7	0.4	0.0
Total	100%	100%	100%

the Danish *Illustreret Tidende* used the concept of the 'ørkesløse Tilskuer' (the idle spectator), drifting aimlessly around the exhibition grounds, to establish a modern sense of control over its content.[106] By embarking upon such 'strolls,' the *flâneur/flâneuse* rendered the exposition 'readable and knowable in its entirety.'[107] Other illustrated newspapers used similar concepts. Henry Vizetelly took readers

192 *Images of the world*

on imaginary tours, and *l'Illustration* published several 'Walks on the exhibition grounds.'[108] Similarly, the correspondent of *Über Land und Meer* noted how one of his aimless 'Spaziergangen' (leisurely walks) offered him the opportunity of making an 'ethnographic study' of all the different peoples serving meals in the restaurants of the outer ring of the palace.[109] Contrasting the figure of the journalist to that of the *flâneur*, journalist Victor Cosse (1831–1903) stated in *l'Exposition Universelle*: 'I know of nothing more agreeable than to leave aside the harness of journalism and walk through the wonders of the *camp de mars* as a true *flâneur* and tourist.'[110] He complained that, as a journalist, he had to subjugate his own 'inclinations and feelings' and ignore the most 'attractive spectacles' to satisfy the curiosity of his 'dreaded master,' by which he meant the general public.[111]

Despite their frequent invocation, the aimless strolls made by correspondents did not structure the image of the 1867 exposition in the illustrated press, and they almost always centred their textual descriptions on the available visual material, rather than the other way around. In sharp contrast to actual visitors, readers of illustrated newspapers could not personalize their experience of the exposition. As they were only able to visit certain parts through the images, which circulated in the network of European and American illustrated newspapers, the transnational trade in illustrations of the news undoubtedly structured their experience of the exposition. The following section of the chapter explores how the illustrated press offered readers in Europe and the United States a shared visual experience of the 1867 Exposition.

The image of the exposition in the five main suppliers of illustrations

How can the images of the Universal Exposition in the illustrated press be categorized? Because they depict all sorts of combinations of places, actors, and actions, I used three questions – what? who? and where? – to establish 12 different categories. The first three groups – national pavilions, sections of the palace, and sections of the agricultural exposition – mark a distinction between images of the national exhibitions in the three most important spaces of the exposition: the palace, the park, and a smaller agricultural park in the *bois de Boulogne*. The subsequent three categories – companies, entertainment, and other organizations – refer to images that depict the contributions to the exposition made by three non-state actors, corporations, entertainment entrepreneurs, and all sorts of other (often transnational) organizations, such as religions and the predecessor of the Red Cross. The category 'diplomatic' contains images of official ceremonies and visits to the exposition by (foreign) dignitaries. The ethnographic group includes illustrations of various 'national types' exhibited in Paris. The category 'views' holds general images of the exhibition palace and the park often described as panoramic. The final two categories – social and preparation – contain illustrations of the social initiatives of the Second Empire, an important part of the ideological programme of the Imperial Commission, and the preparations for the exposition respectively.

Table 4.4 shows the categorization of the illustrations of the five main illustrated newspapers. Of the total of 856 images, 21 per cent depict different national

Images of the world 193

Table 4.4 Percentage allotted to different categories in all the illustrated newspapers, the five main suppliers and the smaller illustrated newspapers

Category	Percentage in all illustrated newspapers	Percentage in the five main suppliers	Percentage in the smaller illustrated newspapers
Section	20.9	21	13
National Pavilion	20.7	21	36
Company	14.8	14.8	8
Ethnic	12.3	12	7
Entertainment	8.4	8	14
Diplomatic	7.6	8	6
Social	4.6	4	3
Views	4.1	4	5
Agriculture	2.7	3	1
Other actors	1.6	2	2
Preparation	1.5	1	3
Other	0.8	1	2
Total	100	100	100

pavilions, 20 per cent different national sections in the exhibition palace, 15 per cent refer to the exhibitions of companies, 8 per cent to all sort of entertainment on the exhibition grounds, and 12 per cent are ethnographic images. This general overview of the visual mediation of the 1867 exposition supports some conclusions from previous research, for example, the emphasis on national pavilions and exhibitions. However, other categories, such as the considerable number of images representing entertainment and the significant contribution of large companies, do not take a prominent place in research concerning nineteenth-century world exhibitions.

It is also possible to sort the original corpus of the five suppliers according to the state they refer to. As mentioned in the historiographical section of this chapter, we should not necessarily see all the pavilions and exhibitions as expressions of cultural self-definition. We can, therefore, divide them into three groups according to the measure of control that respective governments had over their final appearance. The first group concerns the pavilions and exhibitions of states that were organized by their own governments and presented self-defined notions about identity. The second group concerns the pavilions and exhibitions of states that ceased to exist in the tumultuous years before 1867, or, in that same year, were not yet fully accepted as sovereign states. These exhibitions were not organized by a government but by specific political interests. The last group concerns pavilions and exhibitions of mostly non-Western states that were built by French businessmen or political operatives.

The Netherlands is an excellent example of a country belonging to the first group. The official report from the Imperial Commission listed all the members of the national organizing committee and is a carefully considered representation of all the sectors of Dutch society. Besides its honorary president Prince William of Orange (1840–1879), we find representatives of the Dutch academies of

194 *Images of the world*

sciences and arts, director generals of several governmental departments, industrialists, and board members of colonial enterprises.[112] Two famous artists, Jozef Israëls (1824–1911) and Salomon Verveer (1813–1876), and the director of the acclaimed Boymans Museum in Rotterdam headed the commission responsible for the Dutch art exhibition.[113] Thus, the committee was able to present an image of the Netherlands sanctioned by its ruling elite. France, Britain, Belgium, Prussia and the North-German federation, the Austro-Hungarian Empire, Switzerland, Spain, Portugal, and the United States boasted similar commissions full of influential and powerful men.

The second group includes countries that were not officially recognized in 1867 but were present at the exposition. In the official report concerning the contribution of the Ottoman Empire, its commissioner Salaheddin Bey wrote: 'Strictly speaking, the exhibition of the Ottoman Empire, which does not include the exhibitions of some of its provinces, like Moldo-Valachie and Egypt, who have their own special exhibitions, is comprised of three constructions built in the park.'[114] The Ottoman Empire still considered Romania, formed by a unison of Ottoman provinces of Moldavia and Walachia in 1866, and Egypt, which only became a *Khedivate* (an autonomous tributary state of the Ottoman Empire) in June 1867, as parts of its empire. However, several European nations, especially France and Britain, which had loaned large sums of money to Egypt, supported their claims to independence, or at least their independence from the Ottoman Empire.[115]

Cosmin Minea has demonstrated that it was hard for Romania to assert its new role on the international stage. Alexandru Odobescu, the young general commissioner of this country, commissioned a truly 'Byzantine' monument that represented a uniquely Romanian national architectural style and was meant to place his country at the centre of attention in Paris.[116] However, French commentators were highly sceptical of Romania's national ambitions. *L'Exposition Universelle* commented on the newly formed state: 'The Danubian provinces have nothing in their own right, no language, no religion, no art, or government. . . . Romania doesn't exist by itself. It does not shine. . . . Is it meant to be Greek, Russian, French, or German?'[117] Another article remarked: 'Again, there is something of a mosque and the Kremlin in this architecture, half imported, half imposed; it is a lending art, if I can say so, that looks for its place but does not find it, in the same way as the country that it represents.'[118]

The critique of the Romanian pavilion is striking because many pavilions were neither commissioned nor built by the countries that they claimed to represent. The official report published in 1868 indicates that French political operatives and businessmen represented these countries, belonging to the third group. As a result, the pavilions mainly mirrored Western ideas about these countries, often of an orientalist nature. A small group of actors was especially influential in this respect. For example, the Imperial Commission appointed Baron Jules de Lesseps (1809–1887), the brother of Ferdinand, as the commissioner general of China, Japan, Morocco, and Tunisia.[119] His *secondant*, the architect Alfred Chapon (1834–1893), not only designed the pavilions of these four countries but is also listed as a member of the organizing committee for Brazil and Venezuela.

Images of the world   195

Jules de Lesseps seems to have been a power broker between France and several countries in Northern Africa. He used the Parisian expositions, especially the one of 1867, as an opportunity to expand both his own business and the colonial interests of the French state.[120] His main contribution to the exposition was the national pavilion of Tunisia, inspired by the Bardo Palace of the Bey of Tunis. An article in *l'Illustration* shows that it met the expectations of Western visitors: 'Do you recognize these halls and cabinets, the *koubas*, the *maxoures*, the mysterious *moucharabieh*, the Bey's apartments and the council chamber, the large reception-room with its dome, which resembles the vault of heaven?'[121] However, as one commentator proudly noted, it was not the mysterious 'magic of the servants of the [Aladdin's] lamp' that produced the dream-like oriental palace but Western scientific ingenuity:

> We must surrender and say: Yes, it is the same, in the smallest details, it is exactly right. But no, this palace is only a reproduction, a simple but admirable *facsimile*, the result of the efforts of the General Commissioner of the Bey, M. Jules de Lesseps, and the talent of the architect, M. Alfred Chapon. Magic no longer exists today, or rather, magic has entered reality through the door of science, the lamp of Aladdin of the nineteenth century.[122]

While many commentators must have known that Frenchmen built the Bardo Palace, they still attributed its fairy-tale character to the nature and inclinations of the Tunisian people. *L'Exposition Universelle* remarked how the Tunisian and Moroccan exhibitions did not represent 'the productive, agricultural, industrial, and commercial power of these two states,' which was the primary goal of 'normal' Western states at the exhibitions: 'In general, Muslims love fantasy, and we owe them a hospitality which accommodates their tastes.'[123] Of course, it was not the Tunisian love of fantasy but Western orientalism that was responsible for the Bardo Palace.

It was challenging for non-Western countries to present themselves at the Paris Exposition. When representatives of the Shogun of Japan reached Paris in April 1867, the Imperial Commission informed them that the domain of Satsuma, facilitated by Jules de Lesseps and the semi-official French diplomat Charles de Montblanc (1833–1894), already represented Japan.[124] Even if non-Western countries could present themselves at the exposition, the international (illustrated) press scarcely noticed these expressions of national identity. For example, in his article, Hoffenberg has claimed that nineteenth-century world exhibitions provided the independent Kingdom of Hawai'i with the opportunity of 'finding and claiming a place in the world' by 'watching others and being watched by them.'[125] However, the Imperial Commission hardly recognized these efforts and only allotted a scant 63 square metres on the exhibition grounds to the kingdom. More importantly for the context of this chapter, not a single illustrated newspaper published an image or article about the Hawaiian exhibition.[126]

Table 4.3 shows that the five main suppliers, three of which were French, devoted most of their attention to the French pavilions and exhibitions. Other

196 *Images of the world*

important countries, such as Russia, Britain, and the Ottoman Empire, were also represented fairly often. The relatively frequent appearance of some smaller countries, such as Sweden, and states that were not yet officially independent, such as Egypt, is more surprising. Table 4.3 compares the percentage of square metres of the exhibition grounds, noted in the official report of the Imperial Commission, to the portion of images in the five major suppliers of images and smaller illustrated newspapers. From this comparison, it becomes clear that some national pavilions and exhibitions were relatively more visible in the illustrated press than on the exhibition grounds, while others were less successful in attracting attention.

France is the most significant outlier. While the Imperial Commission allotted the organizing country almost half of the available exhibition space, only 25 per cent of the images of the five main illustrated newspapers directly refer to its exhibitions. Similarly, Britain and Belgium were given 11 and 5 per cent of the available exhibition space, while 7.5 and 2 per cent of the images in the five main illustrated newspapers refer to these countries. In contrast, other countries were more successful in attracting the attention of the illustrated press. While the Imperial Commission assigned a mere 2 per cent of the exhibition space to the Russian Empire, around 8 per cent of the images in the five main illustrated newspapers refer to its pavilions and exhibitions. The same applies to Egypt, the Ottoman Empire, Spain, and Portugal. Interestingly, Sweden and Tunisia, both of which were assigned less than 1 per cent of the exhibition space, managed a significant presence in the illustrated press, with 4.5 and 4 per cent of the images, respectively.

The five main suppliers also displayed differences in the extent to which their images refer to the exhibitions and pavilions of specific countries. For example, the *Illustrated London News* contained proportionally more illustrations concerning Britain: likewise for the *Illustrirte Zeitung* and images depicting the pavilions and exhibitions of the North-German federation. Other differences, however, are more problematic to explain. For example, the *Illustrirte Zeitung*, which had readers in all the German-speaking areas of Europe (see Chapter 1), did not publish a single image of the exhibitions of Baden, Bavaria, Hessen, and Württemberg: German states that were all present in 1867. It seems likely that political considerations played a role here. The *Illustrirte Zeitung* was published in Leipzig, annexed by Prussia the year before the 1867 exposition. While states like Baden sided with Prussia, or remained neutral, in the German-German War of 1866, their independence was still seen as a hindrance to a unified Germany under Prussian leadership. This might explain the fact that the *Illustrirte Zeitung* did not want to promote the national sentiments of these countries by publishing images of their pavilions and exhibitions.

Remediation: the Universal Exposition in smaller illustrated newspapers

Of the total 760 illustrations in the 25 smaller illustrated newspapers, 36 per cent depicted national pavilions, 14 per cent entertainment, 13 per cent national exhibitions in the palace, 8 per cent exhibitions of companies, and 7 per cent

Images of the world   197

ethnographical images (Table 4.4). A comparison between the categorization of the five main suppliers and the smaller illustrated newspapers shows that the latter devoted relatively more attention to the national pavilions in the park and the entertainment side of the exposition, while they focused less on the exhibitions located in the palace.

It is possible to make a similar comparison between the attention that the five major suppliers and the smaller illustrated newspapers paid to national pavilions and exhibitions of individual countries. With 18 per cent of the images, the 25 smaller illustrated newspapers published even fewer illustrations of the French exhibitions than the five major suppliers. Russia was allotted roughly 2 per cent of the available exhibition space; however, 8 per cent of the images in the five major suppliers referred to this country, and this figure had risen to almost 15 per cent in the 25 smaller illustrated newspapers. The same applies, to a lesser extent, for China (0.7 per cent exhibition grounds, 2.5 per cent suppliers, 4.2 per cent smaller illustrated newspapers), Spain (1 per cent exhibition grounds, 3.5 per cent suppliers, 5.1 per cent smaller illustrated newspapers), Sweden (0.7 per cent exhibition grounds, 4.5 per cent suppliers, 7.2 per cent smaller illustrated newspapers), Tunisia (0.9 per cent exhibition grounds, 3.8 per cent suppliers, 8.1 per cent smaller illustrated newspapers), the Ottoman Empire (1.3 per cent exhibition grounds, 5.2 per cent suppliers, 9.5 per cent smaller illustrated newspapers), and Egypt (2 per cent exhibition grounds, 2.5 per cent suppliers, 10.9 per cent smaller illustrated newspapers). The transnational trade in images thus amplified the effects of the original visual representation of the exposition in the five major illustrated newspapers.

The only exception to the trend sketched above is the visual representation of the national exhibitions of the North-German federation. The French organizers allotted the Prussian-led federation 6.5 per cent of the available exhibition space. Not very surprisingly, only 5 per cent of the images from the five major suppliers, three of which were French, referred to North-German exhibitions. However, this figure rose to almost 11 per cent of the images in the 25 smaller illustrated newspapers. This increase points to the importance of the transnational trade in images for the nature of the visual representation of the exposition. In comparison to its French competitors, the *Illustrirte Zeitung* did not publish an extraordinary number of images that concerned the exposition. However, it did sell these images very effectively. The central role of the German illustrated newspaper in the transnational trade can thus partly explain the increase in attention for the North-German federation.

The comparison in Table 4.4 gives a general impression of the image of the exposition in the illustrated press. However, the difference in the number of illustrations that the illustrated newspapers published distorts this overview. Another way of looking at how the exposition was represented is to study the dissemination of illustrations of specific buildings and elements of the exposition in the illustrated press. The French pavilions and exhibitions were the subject of many images in European and American illustrated newspapers, so it is not surprising that images of one specific building – the Imperial Pavilion – can be found in

198 *Images of the world*

20 different illustrated newspapers (Figure 4.4). Several French industrialists had commissioned this pavilion, or, as the *Illustrirte Welt* described it, this 'imperial tent,' to house the emperor when he visited the exposition.[127] According to *l'Exposition Universelle*, the outside of the pavilion looked like a 'dream from A Thousand and One Nights. What a taste! What a luxury!'[128] *L'Illustration* noted that the inside consisted of a central salon in Louis XIV style and two smaller salons: one decorated in Louis XVI style and the other in the 'Algerian' style.[129] Henry Vizetelly, probably confused by all the different French styles, noted that it was a mix between the Oriental, Renaissance, and 'Louis XV (sic)' styles. Despite this eclectic mix, the pavilion was 'certainly the chief object of attraction in the entire park, if one may judge from the numbers of people generally to be seen crowding the gallery that encircles it.'[130]

Besides the imperial pavilion, a large number of different illustrated newspapers also published images of other structures in the park. Illustrations of the several buildings of the Egyptian exposition – the Egyptian temple, the okel, or Egyptian stables, and the palace of the viceroy – appeared in 17, 11, and 10 different illustrated newspapers respectively. Twenty different illustrated newspapers published images of Jules de Lesseps' palace for the Bey of Tunis. While their grandeur and the mid-nineteenth-century interest in oriental exoticism might

Figure 4.4 The pavilion of the emperor (1867). 'The Paris International Exhibition: The Pavilion of the Emperor,' *Illustrated London News* (27 April 1867). The Hague, Royal Library of the Netherlands, T 2258 (1867–1).

explain the popularity of these pavilions, the frequent appearance of other buildings in different illustrated newspapers is more challenging to interpret.

Twenty-two different illustrated newspapers published images of the Russian national pavilion, a specific type of farmhouse called an *isbah* (Figure 4.5). There was, however, nothing exceptionally remarkable about the Russian contribution. *L'Exposition Universelle* and the *Illustrated London News* had described it as a typical Russian 'peasant hut,' although Henry Vizetelly questioned whether 'the recently emancipated serfs of Russia live in such ornamental though bizarre-looking habitations.'[131] In another article, the correspondent of the British illustrated newspaper wondered why the mighty Russian Empire exhibited this 'little apartment':

> The roof is low; the windows . . . are extremely small. Placed high up in one corner is the little altar with a picture of the . . . Virgin, and another of the 'eikon,' or patron saint. . . . It is towards these that the moujik turns before or after almost every aspect of his life. When he gets drunk, it is towards them that he holds his glass; when he beats his wife, he asks their permission, . . . as he knows they are too kindly disposed towards him ever to think of thwarting him, even in his most objectionable tastes and habits.[132]

According to British standards, the *isbah* was an unusual candidate to send to a competition where nations fought for their rightful place in the modern world.

Figure 4.5 The Russian *isbah* (1867). 'Les pavillons russes dans le parc.' *l'Illustration* (23 March 1867). The Hague, Royal Library of the Netherlands, T 1788 (1867–1).

200 *Images of the world*

Why did so many illustrated newspapers publish images of the *isbah*? On 1 June 1867, the Russian Tsar Alexander II (1818–1881) arrived in Paris with his two sons. The French public and the international press eagerly followed the visit, especially after the Polish nationalist Antoni Berezowski attempted to assassinate the Tsar on 6 June. According to Vizetelly, the Russian sections of the palace and the park attracted 'more attention than ever' after this failed assassination attempt.[133] The Russian restaurant in the outer ring of the exhibition palace, where the Tsar had breakfasted during his visit, was 'generally surrounded by a gaping crowd,' while it was 'almost impossible to wend one's way through it [the Russian court within the palace] at certain periods of the day, owing to the number of persons who congregate there.'[134] Similarly, *l'Exposition Populaire* noted in its sixth issue that it was happy to provide its readers with illustrations of the *isbah* at the moment when 'the visit of the Czar called the attention of the French public towards Russia.'[135]

The dissemination of images of the imperial pavilion, the Egyptian buildings, the palace of the Bey of Tunis, and the Russian *isbah* can be linked to their general popularity with actual visitors of the exposition. The widespread dissemination of images of three other pavilions – the Spanish, Swedish, and Portuguese – is harder to interpret, however. These countries were (respectively) assigned 1 per cent, 0.7 per cent, and 0.6 per cent of the available exhibition space. Although they were better represented in the illustrated press, especially in the smaller illustrated newspapers, with 5.1 per cent, 7.2 per cent, and 3.5 per cent of the images (respectively), these numbers still seem modest compared to the 17.9 per cent of the illustrations in the smaller illustrated newspapers that were devoted to French pavilions and exhibitions. However, if we do not look at the percentages but at the number of publications that contained at least one image of the national pavilions of Spain, Sweden, and Portugal, we find that these three structures were in fact among the most visible buildings of the exposition in the illustrated press: 23 titles published images of the Spanish pavilion, while the Swedish and Portuguese contributions could be seen in 20 different illustrated newspapers.

Just as with the Russian *isbah*, one might ask whether there was anything special about these pavilions that deserved this visual attention. Most commentators considered the Spanish pavilion to be a good but not very exciting example of a national architectural style (Figure 4.6). As *l'Exposition Universelle* noted: 'Because every [nation] has sought to recall the character of the national architecture in its pavilions, Spain also wanted other nations to know: "Here I am!"'[136] J. Deleiderrie, who 'had the honour of being the assistant architect' of the Spanish pavilion, underlined in *le Monde Illustré* that the architecture of the pavilion represented the *renaissance* of a 'truly Spanish style,' which visitors should not 'in any way' link to the Arabic influences for which many cities in Spain were famous.[137] However, other commentators did not recognize this specific characteristic of the Spanish design. Vizetelly wrote in the *Illustrated London News* that the Spanish pavilion mainly reminded him of a 'Moorish farmhouse.'[138]

Journalists often described the Portuguese pavilion in the same article as the Spanish contribution to the exposition, noting that the pavilions expressed similar

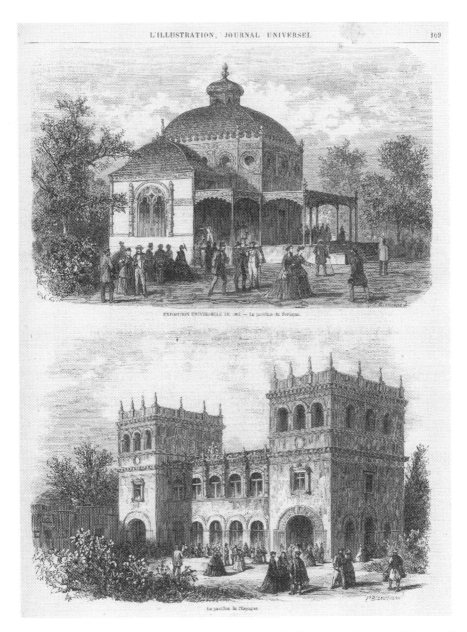

Figure 4.6 The Portuguese and Spanish pavilions (1867). 'Le pavillon de l'Espagne,' *l'Illustration* (16 March 1867). The Hague, Royal Library of the Netherlands, T 1788 (1867–1).

202   *Images of the world*

'Renaissance' styles.[139] While the Portuguese pavilion was built to showcase colonial products, most commentators did not even note this fact.[140] Descriptions of the Swedish pavilion, often referred to as 'Gustav Wasa's house,' were similarly minimal. The pavilion, entirely built from long wood beams, looked much like the Russian *isbah*. The *Illustrirte Zeitung* added that the Danish were probably not very happy with the pavilion, as Gustav Wasa ended the Danish control of Sweden in the sixteenth century.[141]

As the contemporaries themselves claim, there seemed to be nothing especially extraordinary about the Spanish, Portuguese, and Swedish pavilions; and yet, how can their widespread dissemination be explained? One clue can be found in the fact that 5 of the 31 illustrated newspapers studied for this chapter were published in Spain and 1 in Portugal. Although these illustrated newspapers did not publish many images concerning the exposition, it is not surprising that they contained illustrations of the pavilions of the countries in the Iberian peninsula.

The nature of the transnational trade in illustrations of the news is yet another clue that can partly explain their popularity. Images of the pavilions described above appeared in the five major suppliers, which provided smaller illustrated newspapers with the opportunity to re-publish them. Take for example the national pavilion of Portugal. Two illustrated newspapers, the *Archivo Pittoresco* and *España en Paris*, copied an image of this building from *l'Exposition Universelle*. Six others, *el Globo Ilustrado, el Museo Universal*, the *Emporio Pittoresco*, the *Universo Illustrato, Kłosy*, and the *Ny Illustrerad Tidning*, obtained their copy from *le Monde Illustré*. Four publications, the *Geïllustreerd Nieuws, Harpers' Weekly, Tygodnik Ilustrowany*, and *Vasárnapi Ujság*, copied an image from the *Illustrirte Zeitung*. And one, *Frank Leslie's Illustrated Newspaper*, reproduced an image from the *Illustrated London News*.

The five major suppliers published the images of the pavilions relatively early, sometimes even before the opening of the exposition, giving smaller illustrated newspapers ample opportunity to buy *clichés* or commission re-engravings. For example, the second issue of *l'Exposition Universelle* contained images of the Russian *isbah*, the Swedish house of Gustav Wasa, and the imperial pavilion.[142] In its third issue, it published illustrations of Spanish and Portuguese pavilions and the palace of the Bey of Tunis.[143] A similar situation occurred for *le Monde Illustré*: even before the official opening of the exposition in April, it had already published images of the Russian *isbah* (2 February), the palace of the Bey of Tunis and the Portuguese pavilion (2 March), Gustav Wasa's house (9 March), and the Spanish pavilion (23 March). Likewise, the *Illustrated London News* published images of the Egyptian temple, the Russian *isbah*, and the Swedish pavilion before the official opening.[144] Illustrations of other national contributions, such as those of Britain or the North-German federation, appeared much later.[145]

We can also link the prevalence of some pavilions in the illustrated press to the fact that many other buildings were still unfinished when the exposition opened its doors in April. In February 1867, Vizetelly noted that Spanish, Portuguese, Swedish, and Russian pavilions were almost ready, while the rest of the palace and park was nowhere near completion.[146] Ten days before the opening, he wrote:

Images of the world 203

'The park all around the Exhibition palace is still almost impassable with mud and heaps of sand, with piles of bricks, planks, or scaffold-poles, to be used in the various buildings erected by the different foreign commissions.'[147] Almost a month after the opening, he lamented the fact that many pavilions in the park, including the British ones, were still unfinished and would surely disappoint many visitors, especially the 'English excursionist[s]' who tended to flock to Paris during Easter.[148] In the issue of 4 May, he wrote that it was still not possible to say 'when the park will be clear of the many hundred workmen engaged on the various structures in the course of erection, . . . for almost every day one or more new buildings are erected.'[149] The Austrian section and the Swiss pavilion would 'not be completed for several weeks,' and the building of the Egyptian *okel* and the Chinese *pagoda* advanced, but slowly. Vizetelly even doubted if the palace of the Bey of Tunis would be ready 'in time for his Highness's reception when he honours the Exhibition with his presence.'[150]

The contrast between the images of the pavilions, showing beautiful structures, and their actual state of completion described by Vizetelly points to the complicated relationship between fact and fiction in the illustrated press. Illustrated newspapers supposedly based their images on eyewitness accounts, but Vizetelly's articles strongly contradict these claims. As we have seen, several national organizing committees provided illustrated newspapers with the architectural plans of their contributions. For example, the caption of the image of the imperial pavilion in the second issue of the *l'Exposition Universelle* notes that it was made 'on the basis of the plans of MM. Duval frères': it also used architectural plans for its images of the palace of the Bey of Tunis and the pavilions of Spain and Portugal.[151] While the caption of *le Monde Illustré*'s illustration of the Spanish pavilion failed to mention whether its artists used architectural plans, the article describing the image referred several times to J. Deleiderrie, the assistant architect of the Spanish commission, making it likely that the French publication also received plans of the pavilions, which could then be used to draw the illustrations.

Illustrated newspapers often contained what we today would describe as architectural renderings. In this regard, not only were the buildings depicted as finished but other elements, such as beautiful full-grown trees and groups of visitors, were added to convey the impression of completeness. The fictional nature of many images of the exposition in the illustrated press becomes clearer if we compare them to the small number of illustrations that show the pavilions in their unfinished state. On 9 February, *l'Univers Illustré* published an image of the 'State of the work on the western part of the *champ de mars*' by Riou.[152] Two months before the official opening of the exposition, most pavilions on the exhibition grounds were nowhere near completion. The discrepancy between the images of the pavilions in the illustrated press and their actual state can also be observed in the illustrations of Thomas Weber, the special artist of *Über Land und Meer*, published in April and May 1867. In one image, we see ladies manoeuvring through unpacked crates in the exhibition palace.[153] Another shows a family sitting on wooden beams in the park that looks unfinished.[154] His most interesting illustrations show workmen completing several national pavilions. In the first image, we

204 *Images of the world*

can see how crates are carried from the carriage of a mover to the pavilion of the Suez Canal Company.[155] A second image shows craftsmen decorating the 'Turkish' section of the park.[156] Another one shows workmen finishing the roof of the Swedish pavilion, which was supposedly one of the most completed buildings when the exposition opened its doors.[157]

Until now, this chapter has mainly focused on success stories: some buildings, such as the national pavilions of Spain and Portugal and the oriental fantasies of the De Lesseps brothers, were very successful in attracting the attention of the illustrated newspapers. Other contributors were far less successful in placing their exhibitions before the eyes of the readers of the illustrated press. For example, not a single image can be found of the contribution to the exposition of the independent Kingdom of Hawai'i. As Table 4.3 shows, the small German states, Baden, Bavaria, Hessen, and Württemberg; several relatively new Southern-American states; and Greece were equally ineffective in garnering attention. Historians using the world exhibition as sites of identity production have argued that aspiring nations contributed to the exhibitions in order to watch others and to be watched by them: the exhibition seemed to be a perfect environment to claim a place in the concert of nations. However, it has become clear that this process, at least as far as the mediation of the 1867 exposition in the illustrated press is concerned, is less straightforward than it is often presented to be. The fact that *l'Exposition Universelle* published not a single image of the exhibition of the Kingdom of Hawai'i demonstrates that its French and international readers were not interested in acknowledging the small island as a sovereign nation.

An underwater world: mediation and remediation of entertainment

In her book *Fairground Attractions* (2012), Deborah Philips has acknowledged that the pavilions were expressions of national architectural styles and can be related to the production of identity. Interestingly, she also connects them to the 'picturesque attractions of the landscaped garden, including the familiar attractions of the Swiss chalet, an Egyptian palace and an Indian temple.'[158] Similarly, Pieter van Wesemael has noted in *Architecture of Instruction and Delight* (2001) that 'instead of being instructive, the exhibition park appeared to be much more of a *jardin de plaisir*.'[159] National pavilions not only were sites of instruction and national competition but were also meant to entertain visitors. Indeed, Philips even argued that 'there is a direct lineage from the World's Fairs of the late nineteenth century to Walt Disney's first 1955 theme park, Disneyland.'[160]

The interest of the illustrated press in the entertainment side of the exposition substantiates the arguments put forward by Philips and Wesemael. Many 'national' pavilions were in fact highly commercial enterprises, started by French businessmen to entertain visitors to the exposition. The Mexican temple is a good example: many illustrated newspapers published images of the 'Mexican temple of Xochicalco,' referring to it as the national pavilion of Mexico. However, the South-American state did not build the temple. Three years before the exposition, Napoleon III ordered French soldiers to install the younger brother

Images of the world 205

of Austro-Hungarian emperor, Francis Joseph I, as Maximilian I of Mexico. The French intervention force included a team of scientists. One of them, the archaeologist and architect Léon-Eugène Méhédin (1828–1905), built the temple of Xochicalco on the basis of photographs he had taken of Mexican archaeological sites.

In an article concerning the temple, *l'Exposition Universelle* wondered: 'Why is the temple of Xochicalco the private exhibition of M. Méhédin and not of the scientific commission of Mexico? Why are there turnstiles instead of free tickets?'[161] This was a reasonable question. After all, the scientific commission already displayed Mexican antiquities in a large room in the pavilion of the French Ministry of Education.[162] Christiane Demeulnaere-Douyere has demonstrated that Méhédin built the temple from a commercial perspective, buying the rights to levy a separate entrance fee and sell coffee, ice cream, and other refreshments.[163] However, the Imperial Commission insisted that 'Mexicans' or people dressed in the 'national dress' of Mexico sold these refreshments.[164]

The Chinese pavilion, sometimes described as a 'pagoda,' is another good example of the commercial nature of these pavilions. On behalf of Jules de Lesseps, the official general commissioner of China, the French sinologist Marie-Jean-Léon Lecoq (1822–1892), and a certain M. de Meritens, described as the director of the customs office of China in Paris, commissioned the Chinese pavilion.[165] Hyungju Hur has noted how the Frenchmen served 'Chinese' food and presented 'Chinese' music, 'altered to suit the taste of Europeans.'[166] Vizetelly described how, besides tea, 'which visitors drink out of mere curiosity,' pale ale appeared to be the favourite beverage and '"biftick aux pommes" the *viand* most in request [*sic*].'[167] Next to the restaurant, three Chinese teenage girls, who had been 'bought in the province of Fo-Kien' and 'shipped to Paris quite regardless of their own feelings in the matter,' sold tea in packets and were made to pose for photographs with visitors.[168]

Next to the images of these commercial pavilions, many illustrations depicted the parts of the park that were more clearly meant to entertain visitors. For example, the Dutch café (where Vizetelly's favourite barmaid served drinks) could be seen by the readers of six different publications.[169] The Russian, Tunisian, 'Turkish,' and American restaurants and cafés were also represented. Van Wesemael has aptly concluded that this 'excess of restaurants, bars, *café-chantants* strewn across the park,' especially in the outer gallery of the exhibition palace, reinforced the entertainment side of the park and separated the 'serious' exhibitions in the palace from the amusement in the park.[170]

Philips has also substantiated his argument that the twentieth-century theme park developed from the landscaped garden by noting that the Imperial Commission built a separate part of the park, the *jardin réserve*, entirely in this tradition. As the *Illustrated London News* noted:

> Not the slightest trace can be discovered of the flat sandy plain of the Champ de Mars – the entire surface has been changed; valleys have been sunk, hills have been raised, rivulets haven been set running, lakes have been formed, and cascades made to play; grand old trees, and rare shrubs and flowers,

206 *Images of the world*

have been transplanted hither, and the sandy soil has been completely hidden beneath grassy slopes of the brightest green.[171]

Visitors had to pay an extra 50 centimes to enter this part of the exhibition grounds, where, as Gautier described it, 'the feverish activity of industry [was] followed by the peaceful tranquilly of nature.'[172] Its harmonious collection of 'groves, caves, waterfalls, and greenhouses' formed a 'rapid and complete contrast' with the exhibition palace.[173]

Several of the sights of the *jardin réserve* frequently appeared in the illustrated press. Seven different illustrated newspapers published images of the pavilion of the empress, while nine publications contained illustrations of the artificial waterfall in the reserved garden. However, its most popular attractions were a salt- and freshwater aquarium. Eighteen different illustrated newspapers contained images of both aquariums, and many of these publications contained views of both the interior and the exterior of these buildings. Similar to the minimal descriptions of the Spanish and Portuguese pavilions, most publications did not write a great deal about the aquariums but focused instead on spectacular visual representations of these novel structures. Only *l'Exposition Universelle* featured a somewhat longer article, which noted that both the salt- and freshwater aquariums, built by M. Guérard and M. Bétencourt respectively, tried to mimic the experience of standing on the bottom of the ocean or a river.[174] While *l'Exposition Universelle* complained that the use of glass made it 'unbearably hot' inside the aquarium, it did allow visitors to see the fish 'from top to bottom, from the front and *en profil.*'[175]

In contrast to other popular buildings of the exposition, images of the aquariums only appeared in two of the five major suppliers. The *Archivo Pittoresco* and *le Journal Illustré* re-published an illustration of the exterior of the saltwater aquarium from *l'Exposition Universelle*. The latter resold it to the *Hollandsche Illustratie* and *el Siglo Illustrado.*[176] Six different illustrated newspapers published *le Monde Illustré*'s beautiful illustration of the saltwater aquarium, which showed visitors walking around the grotto-like cave, while they admired all sorts of sea creatures. Because smaller illustrated newspapers bought most of their images from one of the five major suppliers, it is difficult to find the exact same illustration in more than two publications.

The illustration of inside the saltwater aquarium from *le Monde Illustré* is the single most widely reproduced image of the exposition (Figure 4.7). This demonstrates the centrality of *le Monde Illustré* in the network, but, significantly, it also points to the interest of smaller illustrated newspapers in the entertainment side of the exposition. *Le Monde Illustré* contained a relatively large number of images from this category, while other suppliers paid significantly less attention to it. This means that if smaller illustrated newspapers wanted to publish images of entertainment at the exposition, they ended up buying images from *le Monde Illustré*.

Three publications that contained the image – *Illustrerad Tidning, Illustreret Tidende, and Über Land und Meer* – regularly purchased images from *le Monde Illustré*. These regular customers of the French publication all published the image

Images of the world 207

Figure 4.7 The saltwater aquarium (1867). 'De Wereld-Tentoonstelling te Parijs: het zeewater-aquarium,' *Hollandsche Illustratie* vol. 3, no. 52 (1867). The Hague, Royal Library of the Netherlands, NBM Mfm MMT 0020 (1867).

relatively quickly after it had appeared. *Über Land und Meer*, which bought images of the exposition from all three major French producers, also bought the image of the aquarium. It is probably via this German connection that the image ended up in the *Hollandsche Illustratie*. As noted in Chapter 2, the German illustrated newspaper often resold images it had bought from other publications. All these images were clearly *clichés* of the original. This can be deduced from the fact that the images were of the same size and that most of the smaller illustrated newspapers published it in exactly the same way as *le Monde Illustré*, spread over two pages. Only the *Hollandsche Illustratie* published the image on a single page, but the large white border surrounding it reveals that it must have had the same size as the original (Figure 4.7).

Conclusion

This chapter opened with a quote from Théophile Gautier, pointing to the incoherent and often misleading representation of the Universal Exposition in the illustrated press. He criticized illustrated newspapers because they only published images of separate pavilions and exhibitions; thus, the newspapers provided only a fragmented impression, rather than conveying the true order of the exposition. It was precisely this order, or general idea, that Gautier and many contemporary

208 Images of the world

commentators tried to describe. This chapter has shown that the visual representation of the Universal Exposition was not without order as Gautier claimed; rather, the source of this order was not what Gautier had anticipated. The visual experience of readers of illustrated newspapers was structured – ordered – by the transnational trade in images of the news and not by the plans and the ideology of the organizers of the exhibition.

The first part of this chapter used the dissemination of images of the Paris Exposition of 1867 as a case study to demonstrate the existence of a transnational visual culture of the news in the mid-nineteenth century. The visualization of this network revealed the extensive and entangled connections between 31 European and American illustrated newspapers. Five publications – *le Monde Illustré, l'Exposition Universelle, l'Illustration, Illustrirte Zeitung*, and the *Illustrated London News* – were the central nodes of this network. In this regard, we can conclude that the first two French publications were especially influential: they supported foreign editions in other countries and sold images on a large scale to already established publications in smaller European countries. The strong ties these publications had to the regime of Napoleon III can, at least partly, explain their central position in the network. As we saw, Ducuing based his *l'Exposition Universelle* on monopolies, backed by the dictatorial regime of Napoleon III, and actively tried to control the visual representation of the exposition. Only *le Monde Illustré* was, thanks to the political connections of its publisher Dalloz, able to ignore Ducuing's monopoly and produce and sell images of the exposition on a large scale as well.

The visual representation of the Paris exposition in several smaller illustrated newspapers, like the *Hollandsche Illustratie* and the *Illusrtire Tidende*, exemplifies how two factors shaped the transnational dissemination of images of the exposition. First of all, economic considerations played a vital role. There was a large demand for illustrations of the 1867 exposition: everywhere in the world, people were eager to see what it looked like. Because producing original images was expensive and time-consuming, large illustrated newspapers tried to maximize their profits by either selling *clichés* to smaller illustrated publications abroad or starting their own foreign editions. In their turn, smaller illustrated newspapers bought *clichés* of images or redrew and re-engraved them for the same reason: their readers demanded authentic visual representations of the exposition, but producing original illustrations was expensive and (because of Ducuing's monopoly) generally difficult. Additionally, the many images of the exhibitions from private companies in all sorts of illustrated newspapers seem to have been at least partly the result of the fact that companies offered them for free. In short: many Europeans saw the same images of the 1867 exposition because the demand for this material was high and the supply limited.

This economic factor alone cannot explain why smaller illustrated newspapers re-published some images and ignored others. The interest of readers in the pavilions and exhibitions of their own country at the exposition also influenced which illustrations were disseminated. When smaller illustrated newspapers, including the *Hollandsche Illustratie* or the *Ny Illustrerad Tidning*, could not obtain images of their country's achievements from their regular source, they bought them elsewhere or commissioned new original illustrations. A second factor, therefore, must be introduced to explain this, which has to do with the almost universal interest of readers in the entertainment side of the exposition. This interest can explain the central place of *le Monde Illustré* in the network, because this was the only large publication that devoted considerable attention to the aquariums, bars, and restaurants that could be found in the park. Jointly, these two factors explain the complicated nature of the network: smaller illustrated newspapers mostly had a regular supplier of images, but they could also 'shop around.'

In *Fleeting Cities* (2010), Geppert has pointed to the importance of the mediation of nineteenth-century world exhibitions. While around 11 million visitors travelled to Paris in 1867, a large audience in Europe and America experienced the exposition through the press. Its mediation in illustrated newspapers is especially important because this medium allowed readers to not only read about it but also see it. By categorizing the illustrations of 31 illustrated newspapers, this chapter has shown how the image of the exposition, the content of its visual representation in the illustrated press, differed from the experience of actual visitors. Furthermore, it has argued that this mediated experience was, to a large extent, shaped by the nature of the transnational trade in illustrations of the news.

Significantly, the general impression of the exposition in the illustrated press was decidedly less 'French' than the exposition itself. While French exhibitors were allotted around 50 per cent of the available exhibition space, only 25 per cent of the images in the five major suppliers and 18 per cent of the illustrations in smaller publications referred to them. The exhibitions and pavilions of other industrial powers, like Britain and Belgium, also attracted less attention in the illustrated press than would be expected on the basis of the number of square metres allotted to them on the exhibition grounds. In contrast, some countries with small exhibitions benefited from the mediation and remediation in the illustrated press. Countries such as Russia, Tunisia, Sweden, and the Ottoman Empire were only allotted a small number of square metres on the exhibition grounds but were, nevertheless, very visible in the illustrated press. Finally, some countries, like several small German states and Greece, were entirely ignored in the European press, showing that the nature of the exposition was fundamentally changed by its mediation.

In a general sense, the mediation of the 1867 exposition in the illustrated press points to the increasing importance of mass media in the mid-nineteenth century. World exhibitions were staged as mass events and managed to attract millions of visitors. However, from the mid-nineteenth century onwards, their meaning can no longer be understood by only studying the intentions of organizers and the experiences of actual visitors. The image of the exposition in the illustrated press, which reached millions of readers, is the perfect example of this argument. Although each publication presented a different image of the exposition, the extensive transnational trade in illustrations made sure that this event was a part of a burgeoning transnational visual news culture.

210 *Images of the world*

Notes

1 "'Ou est l'Algérie? – Entre la France et les Pays-Bas. – Irons-nous, ce matin? – En Algérie soit! Puis au Brésil! C'est tout près. – En passant nous déjeunerons en Russie, pour y gouter du caviar. – Et chez les Chinois, si nous restons ce soir, nous prendrons le thé.'": Gautier, *Les curiosités de l'exposition universelle de 1867*, 1.
2 Greenhalgh, *Ephemeral Vistas*, 37; Limido, "L'Exposition universelle de 1867," 68.
3 "C'est une ville universelle": Gautier, Les curiosités de l'exposition universelle de 1867, 25.
4 "Vous souvient-il d'avoir vu quelquefois au frontispice de certains journaux illustrés un assemblage bizarre de tous les monuments des quatre points cardinaux, pèle mêle étages en amphithéâtre; en haut des dômes, des colonnes, des minarets, des phares et des clochers, en bas des temples antiques, des édifices européens, des kiosques chinois, des pagodes indiennes, des fontaines, des statues, tout un monde fantastique, désordonné, où se côtoient les architectures de tous les peuples, groupées au hasard par le caprice de l'artiste." : Ibid.
5 "Tous les journaux, grands ou petits, illustrés ou sans images, ont promis à l'avance des prodiges et des merveilles. Souhaitons modestement que la moitié se réalise [. . .].": Renaudin, *Paris-Exposition ou guide à Paris en 1867*, 329.
6 **BNA5**: "Paris and Parisians," *the Morning Advertiser* (26 February 1867).
7 The role of mass media in mediating world exhibitions to audiences all over the world is also noted by Wolfgang Kaiser: Geppert, Fleeting Cities, 6; Kaiser, "Vive La France!," 227.
8 Geppert, *Fleeting Cities*, 6.
9 "The Paris Exhibition," *Illustrated London News* (13 April 1867).
10 Geppert, *Fleeting Cities*, 7.
11 Wolfgang Kaiser is one of the few scholars who devotes a section of his article to how the message of the elites organizing the exhibition failed to achieve their audience. Kaiser, "Vive La France!," 237; Geppert, *Fleeting Cities*, 11.
12 Kaiser, "Vive La France!," 237.
13 Allwood, *The Great Exhibitions: 150 Years*, 16–17.
14 "The Paris Exhibition," *Illustrated London News* (13 April 1867).
15 Geppert, *Fleeting Cities*, 11; Auerbach, "Introduction," X; Greenhalgh, *Ephemeral Vistas*, 112; Hoffenberg, *An Empire on Display*, 20.
16 Greenhalgh, *Ephemeral Vistas*, 113; Hoffenberg, *An Empire on Display*, 20.
17 In the volume edited by Auerbach and Hoffenberg, chapters are devoted to future nations that were not yet formed in 1867, such as Ireland, Germany, and several former British colonies.
18 Çelik, *Displaying the Orient*, 2.
19 Gephi offers application of multiple algorithms. In this case the ForceAtlas algorithm was used.
20 Putnam, "The Transnational and the Text-Searchable," 377.
21 Brake, "London Letter," 246.
22 "Speaking to the Eye," *Illustrated London News* (24 May 1851).
23 Gautier, *Les curiositésde l'exposition universelle de 1867*, 5.
24 Renaudin, *Paris-Exposition ou guide à Paris en 1867*, 337; Gautier, *Les curiosités de l'exposition universelle de 1867*, 7; Guy, *Paris en 1867*, 1.
25 Guy, *Paris en 1867*, 1.
26 Allwood, *The Great Exhibitions: 150 Years*, 43.
27 "On trouvera dans ces établissements modèles des échantillons de tous les mets et de toutes les boissons de l'Univers.": Guy, *Paris en 1867*, 1.
28 Çelik, *Displaying the Orient*, 52.
29 Greenhalgh, *Ephemeral Vistas*, 42.
30 Kaiser, "Vive La France!," 237.

Images of the world   211

31   Gautier, *Les curiosités de l'exposition universelle de 1867*, 17.
32   "The Paris Universal Exhibition. Supplement," *Illustrated London News* (8 June 1867).
33   Greenhalgh, *Ephemeral Vistas*, 15; Allwood, *The Great Exhibitions: 150 Years*, 47.
34   Allwood, *The Great Exhibitions: 150 Years*, 47.
35   Gautier, *Les curiosités de l'exposition universelle de 1867*, 23–6.
36   Ibid., 35.
37   Ibid., 39.
38   Ibid., 44.
39   Ibid., 58.
40   Greenhalgh, *Ephemeral Vistas*, 35.
41   Kaiser, "Vive La France!," 235.
42   Ibid., 233.
43   Ibid., 232.
44   Greenhalgh, *Ephemeral Vistas*, 35.
45   Volkert Barth directs our attention to a darker side of the Saint-Simonian political ideology, by showing how it used the exposition of 1867 to normalize the growing power of the state over "every aspect of civil life." Barth, "Displaying Normalisation: The Paris Universal Exhibition of 1867," 463.
46   **GAL1:** "Et d'abord, prétend-il, il peut y avoir et il y a tous les jours méprise et confusion; les lecteurs peuvent à chaque instant prendre l'exposition populaire pour le journal de M. Ducuing qu'ils avaient l'intention d'acheter": "Chronique Judiciaire," *l'Univers* (24 August 1867).
47   **GAL1:** "L'immense exhibition de 1867 a été ouverte en vue d'une publicité sans limite; elle a donne une libre carrière à tous les modes de divulgation, à toutes les reproductions par la plume et par le dessin.": "Chronique Judiciaire," *l'Univers* (24 August 1867).
48   "Publication internationale autorisée par la commission impériale.": *l'Exposition Universelle*, vol. 1 (1867): 1.
49   Ibid.
50   "Chronique Judiciaire," *l'Univers* (24 August 1867).
51   "Foreign and colonial intelligence – France," *Illustrated London News* (23 February 1867).
52   **BNA5:** "The Paris Exhibition," *the London Daily News* (10 November 1867).
53   **BNA5:** "France," *The London Daily News* (19 January 1867).
54   **BNA5:** "The Paris Exhibition," *the London Daily News* (3 January 1867).
55   "The Paris Universal Exhibition," *Illustrated London News* (27 April 1867).
56   **GAL2:** "Chronique Judiciaire," *l'Univers* (24 August 1867).
57   Ibid.
58   Ibid.
59   **GAL2:** "L'Exposition Universelle de 1867 Illustrée," *le Figaro* (2 September 1867).
60   **GAL2:** "L'Exposition Universelle de 1867 Illustrée," *le Constitutionel* (29 March 1867).
61   **GAL2:** "L'Exposition Universelle de 1867 Illustrée," *le Constitutionel* (27 July 1867).
62   "Title page," *l'Esposizione Universale del 1867 Illustrato*, vol. 1 (1867).
63   "Introducción," *España en Paris* (15 April 1867).
64   "Esta obra se publica periódicamente en Paris."; "Imprenta de Ch. Lagure, Calle de Fleurus, o, Paris": "Revista Y Crónica de la Exposición Universal de 1867," *España En Paris* (30 April 1867).
65   "Advertencias," *España en Paris* (15 April 1867).
66   Ibid.
67   Rico, "Sección Española de la galería de la historia del trabajo en el Palacio," *España en Paris* (30 October 1867).
68   Wilson, *Paris and the Commune, 1871–1878: The Politics of Forgetting*, 34.
69   Marchandiau, *L'Illustration*, 15.

212   *Images of the world*

70 "Le timbre des journaux," *l'Illustration* (9 March 1867).
71 Based on a quick analysis of its first three volumes, which can be accessed online, it seems likely that the Italian publication *il Giornale Illustrato* also bought the majority of its images of the 1867 exposition from *le Monde Illustré*. However, I was unable to study the relevant volumes (6 and 7).
72 "La dificultad al parecer insuperada, de reunir un número suficiente de suscritores para sufragar los inmensos gastos que ocasionan este género de publicaciones": "Prospecto," *el Globo Ilustrado* (1 June 1867).
73 Ibid.
74 Rimmel, *Recollections of the Paris Exhibition of 1867*, 310.
75 "Parfumerie: M. Rimmel," *l'Exposition Universelle*, vol. 1, no. 21 (1867): 336.
76 "Le Chalet de la Maison Rimmel dans le parc française à l'exposition," *l'Illustration* (31 August 1867); "Exposition Universelle. Le chalet des parfums de M. Rimmel," *l'Exposition Populaire Illustrée*, vol. 1, no. 37 (1867): 289; "Exposition Universelle – Le chalet des parfums, à l'exposition Universelle," *l'Univers Illustré* (27 July 1867).
77 "Exposition Universelle – le petit salon de maison Christofle," *l'Illustration* (5 October 1867); "Exposition Universelle – le petit salon de maison Christofle," *l'Exposition Populaire Illustrée*, vol. 1, no. 51 (1867): 413.
78 "Les Chaussures: vitrine de M. Pinet," *l'Exposition Universelle*, vol. 2, no. 44 (1867): 244; "Les Chaussures: vitrine de M. Pinet," *l'Exposition Populaire Illustrée*, vol. 1, no. 45 (1867): 280.
79 "Exposition Universelle – Ateliers de fabrication de dentelles de MM. Auguste Lefebure et fils," *le Monde Illustré* (8 July 1867); "Exposition Universelle – Ateliers de fabrication de dentelles de MM. Auguste Lefebure et fils," *l'Exposition Populaire Illustrée*, vol. 1, no. 43 (1867): 356; "Exposition Universelle – Cabinet de travail et bibliothèque, en chêne, expose par M. Leglas Maurice," *le Monde Illustré* (1 July 1867); "Exposition Universelle – Cabinet de travail et bibliothèque, en chêne, expose par M. Leglas Maurice," *l'Exposition Populaire Illustrée*, vol. 1, no. 41 (1867): 108–9; "Exposition Universelle – Les papiers teints de M. Bezault," *le Monde Illustré* (22 July 1867); "Exposition Universelle – Les papiers teints de M. Bezault," *l'Exposition Populaire Illustrée*, vol. 1, no. 21 (1867): 173; "Exposition Universelle – Porcelaines de la maison Pillivuyt," *le Monde Illustré* (14 September 1867); "Exposition Universelle – Porcelaines de la maison Pillivuyt," *l'Exposition Populaire Illustrée*, vol. 1, no. 59 (1867): 465; "Exposition Universelle – vitrine de MM. Gautrot et Co, facteurs d'instruments de musique," *le Monde Illustré* (7 September 1867); "Exposition Universelle – vitrine de MM. Gautrot et Co, facteurs d'instruments de musique," *l'Exposition Populaire Illustrée*, vol. 1, no. 27 (1867): 209.
80 **BNA5:** "The Paris Exhibition of 1867," *London Daily News* (14 January 1867).
81 "Vue Exterieur de l'exposition Suisse," *l'Exposition Populaire Illustrée*, vol. 1. no. 2 (1867): 16.
82 "Elle apprend aussi que la République helvétique ne renferme pas seulement de bons horlogers et d'excellents tireurs, mais qu'elle compte aussi, parmi ses enfants, des peintres et des sculpteurs distingués.": "Exposition Suisse des Beaux-arts," *l'Exposition Populaire Illustrée*, vol. 1. no. 2 (1867): 15–16.
83 "Le Palais du Bey de Tunis et la tente de l'empereur du Maroc – Dessin de M. Gaildrau. M. Chapon, architecte," *l'Exposition Universelle*, vol. 1, no. 3 (1867): 40.
84 Bacot, *La presse illustrée au xixe siècle*, 79.
85 "Die ausgebreiteten Geschäftsverbindungen des Herrn Levy verschaffen ihm so viele in Frankreich unbekannte Clichés, als er nur wollte.": P. Schmidt, "Pariser Illustrirte Journale," *Journal für Buchdruckerkunst, Schriftgießerei und verwandte Fächer* (29 September 1863).
86 "Blatter aus natur und Leben, Wissenschaft und Kunst, zur Unterhaltung und Belehung fur die familie": "Allgemeine Illustrire Zeitung": "Title page," *Über Land und Meer*, vol. 18 (1867); "Title page," *Illustrirte Welt*, vol. 15 (1867).

Images of the world 213

87 Besides Henri de Montaut, Édouard Riou, who was mentioned earlier in this chapter, also illustrated several books of Verne. This substantiates the point made in this chapter about the thin line between reality and fantasy at the 1867 exposition. Bacot, *La presse illustrée au xixe siècle*, 113.

88 The five illustrations in the *Hollandsche Illustratie*: "Wereld-Tentoonstelling: de poort Rapp, ingang aan den oostelijken kant van het champ de mars," *Hollandsche Illustratie*, vol. 3, no. 33 (1867): 345; "Groote Galerij der machines van den kant der Oostenrijksche poort gezien," *Hollandsche Illustratie*, vol. 3, no. 45 (1867): 357; "Annexe van Spanje, waaron de voortbrengselen der Spaansche kolonien zijn tentoongesteld," *Hollandsche Illustratie*, vol. 3, no. 49 (1867): 392; "Aquarium van zoetwater," *Hollandsche Illustratie*, vol. 3, no. 52 (1867): 409; "De Wereld-Tentoonstelling te Parijs. Vervoerbaar landhuis," *Hollandsche Illustratie*, vol. 4, no. 8 (1867): 64. The five illustrations in the *Journal Illustré*: "Exposition Universelle: La porte Rapp, entrée à l'est du champ de mars," *Journal Illustré* (28 April 1867); "Exposition Universelle. Grande Galerie des machines. Vue prisé de la porte d'Autriche," *Journal Illustré* (5 May 1867); "Exposition Universelle: Annexe de l'Espagne contenant les productions des colonies espagnoles," *Journal Illustré* (26 May 1867); "Exposition Universelle: l'aquarium," *Journal Illustré* (19 May 1867); "Le chalet mobile," *Journal Illustré* (21 July 1867). The five illustrations in *l'Exposition Universelle*: "Port Rapp," *l'Exposition Universelle*, vol. 1, no. 16 (1867): 16; "Salle des Machines – Coupoles roumaines – Porte de Russie," *l'Exposition Universelle*, vol. 1, no. 4 (1867): 4; "Annexe de l'Espagne," *l'Exposition Universelle*, vol. 1, no. 3 (1867): 43; "Aquarium (Extérieur)," *l'Exposition Universelle*, vol. 1, no. 5 (1867): 77; "Chalet Mobile de M. Waaser," *l'Exposition Universelle*, vol. 1, no. 15 (1867): 237.

89 "Een diamantslijperij. Ingezonden door den Hr. M. E. Coster te Amsterdam. Teekening van den Hr. Metzelaar," *Hollandsche Illustratie*, vol. 3, no. 47 (1867): 369; "De Wereld-Tentoonstelling te Parijs in 1867: Afdeeling Nederland. De Hollandsche Boederij," *Hollandsche Illustratie*, vol. 4, no. 1 (1867): 1; "Het Hollandsche Koffiehuis," *Hollandsche Illustratie*, vol. 4, no. 3 (1867): 17; "De Wereld-Tentoonstelling te Parijs. De Hollandsche Afdeeling van Schoone Kunsten," *Hollandsche Illustratie*, vol. 4, no. 16 (1867): 128.

90 "Den danske afdeling på verdensudstillingen i Paris. efter 'l'Exposition Universelle'," *Illustreret Tidende* (27 October 1867); "l'Exposition du Danemark," *l'Exposition Universelle*, vol. 2, no. 35 (1867): 65.

91 "Afskedsfest for det danske Arbejder Tog i salle des familles Verdensudstillingenbygningen i paris. Efter en Skizze af N. A. Lytzen," Illustreret Tidende (4 Augustus 1867); Stolz, Steffen. Lytzen, Niels Aagaard. In Allgemeines Künstlerlexikon. 2017. Berlin, Boston: K. G. Saur. Retrieved 11 January 2018, from www.degruyter.com/view/AKL/_00148863.

92 "Frän Världsexpositionen: Ryska bondhus, uppförda i parken," *Ny Illustrerad Tidning* (6 April 1867); "Frän Världsexpositionen: Norska huset på Marsfaltet," *Ny Illustrerad Tidning* (18 May 1867); "Frän Världsexpositionen: Part af Svenska expositionen, med porslinsfabrikernas utställning i förgrunden. Efter fotografi tecknad af O. A. Mankell," *Ny Illustrerad Tidning* (6 June 1867); "Frän Världsexpositionen: Parti af Svenska utställningen, med malm-stapeln i fonden, tecknad af E. Jacobsson," *Ny Illustrerad Tidning* (13 June 1867); "Frän Världsexpositionen: Ingång till Svenska avdelningen i utställningsbyggnaden," *Ny Illustrerad Tidning* (29 June 1867).

93 Esteves, "Archivo Pittoresco," 123.

94 Alberto, "Anexo de Hespanha, na exposição universal de Paris," *Archivo Pittoresco*, vol. 10, no. 12 (1867): 12.

95 Sánchez Vigil, *Revistas ilustradas en España*, 77.

96 "Sección de los Estados Unidos – Planetario de Mr. Barlow," *el Museo Universal* (14 September 1867); "The United States Section," *Illustrated London News* (6 July 1867).

214 *Images of the world*

97 "Padellon de Espana," *el Museo Universal* (5 May 1867); "Le pavilion de l'Espagne," *l'Illustration* (16 March 1867), "Partie espagnole – Pavillon style renaissance, spécimen d'architecture nationale," *le Monde Illustré* (23 March 1867); "Annexe de l'Espagne – Dessin de M. Thorigny, M. De la Gandara, architecte," *l'Exposition Universelle*, vol. 1, no. 3 (1867): 43.

98 "The Ship Mercury, Loading at Pier no. 6, N.Y with Goods for the Paris Exhibition," *Frank Leslie's Illustrated Newspaper* (9 February 1867); "Walter A. Wood's New Jointed Bar Mower, on Exhibition at the Paris Exposition," *Frank Leslie's Illustrated Newspaper* (31 August 1867); "Messrs. Mason & Hamelin's Parlor Organs in Exhibition at the Paris Exposition: From a Photograph Taken Expressly for This Paper," *Frank Leslie's Illustrated Newspaper* (7 September 1867); "American Exhibitors at the Paris Exposition to Whom First Prizes Were Awarded: The Articles Exhibited in the Paris Exposition by the Tucker Manufacturing Company," *Frank Leslie's Illustrated Newspaper* (14 September 1867).

99 I could not establish the provenance of ten images of the exhibition in *Frank Leslie's Illustrated Newspaper*. However, the page on which they were published, "The Pictorial Spirit of the European Press," strongly suggests that they were copied from a European publication.

100 A quick comparison between the original publication dates of the European illustrated newspapers and the issue of *Frank Leslie's Illustrated Newspaper* containing the copy shows that it took around a month for an image to be copied in this way.

101 "Le public, en trouvant, le 1" avril 1867, l'ordre établi dans le Palais, où la veille encore régnait la confusion": Commission Impériale, *Rapport sur l'Exposition Universelle de 1867, à Paris*, III.

102 Ibid., 471–6.

103 Ibid., 440.

104 Ibid.

105 Figure 31 of the report notes all the visits of emperors, empresses, kings, and queens. Ibid., 471–6.

106 Stougaard-Nielsen, "The Idle Spectator," 147.

107 In traditional historiography, the concept of the flâneur has strong male gender connotations. Since Janet Wolff's 1985 essay "The Invisible flâneusse" the conceptualization of the flâneur as being necessarily male has been successfully challenged. The walks of oriental scholar and novelist Judith Gautier (1845–1917), daughter of Théophile Gautier, on the exhibition grounds substantiate the point that both men and women acted as "idle spectators" at world expositions. Janet Wolff, "The Invisible Flâneuse: Women and the Literature of Modernity," 36–46; Chagnon-Burke, "Tel Père, Telle Fille," 249; Richardson, *Judith Gautier*, 55.

108 "The Paris Universal Exhibition," *Illustrated London News* (1 June 1867); Achard, "Promenade a travers l'Exposition," *l'Illustration* (20 April 1867).

109 "Bilder von der Weltaustellung in Paris," *Über Land und Meer*, vol. 18, no. 47 (1867): 746.

110 "Je ne 'connais rien de plus agréable que de laisser une fois de côté les harnais du journalisme et de faire à travers les merveilles du Champ de Mars une véritable promenade de flâneur et de touriste.": Victor Cosse, "Le rue des Pays-Bas," *l'Exposition Universelle*, vol. 2, no. 42 (1867): 190.

111 Ibid.

112 Frédéric Le Play, *Rapport sur l'Exposition Universelle de 1867 à Paris*, 354–5.

113 Ibid.

114 "L'Exposition de l'Empire Ottoman proprement dit, dans laquelle ne doivent pas être comprises les Expositions de provinces telles, par exemple, que la Moldo-Valachie et l'Egypt, qui ont leur Expositions spéciale, se compisse de trois constructions élevées dans le Parc.": Bey, *La Turquie à l'Exposition Universelle de 1867*, 29.

Images of the world 215

115 Ajayi, *General History of Africa*, 137–9.
116 Minea, "An Image for the Nation," 1–2.
117 "Les provinces danubiennes n'ont rien en propre, ni langue, ni religion, ni art, ni gouvernement. Ce qui manque à la Roumanie, c'est de ne pas exister par elle-même. Elle ne rayonne pas. Elle reçoit la lumière de tous côtés, du nord comme du midi, du levant, du couchant aussi. Elle sera grecque, russe, française, allemande, quoi encore?" V. Cosse, "L'Exposition roumaine," *l'Exposition Universelle*, vol. 2, no. 39 (1867): 130–4.
118 "Encore une fois, il y a de la mosquée et du Kremlin dans cette architecture, mi-partie importée, mi-partie imposée; c'est un art mitoyen, si je puis ainsi parler, qui cherche son milieu et ne le trouve pas, comme le pays qu'il représente." Ducuing, "l'église roumaine," *l'Exposition Universelle*, vol. 1, no. 4 (1867): 52.
119 Frédéric Le Play, *Rapport sur l'Exposition Universelle de 1867 à Paris*, 365.
120 Although many books detail the life of Ferdinand de Lesseps and his Suez Canal, almost none of these refer to his brother Jules.
121 "Reconnaissez ces salles et ces cabinets, ces koubbas, ces maxoures, ce moucharabieh mystérieux, et les appartements du bey, et la salle du conseil, et le grand salon de réception avec son dôme, qui ressemble à la voûte du ciel; et dans ces diverses pièces, tout ce luxe, ces draperies somptueuses, ces divans, ces longs coffres incrustés d'or et d'ivoire, ces murs décorés de panoplies; ici les armes, là les pipes, et partout des étagères surchargées de poteries charmantes.": Doullay, "Tapis, Tapisseries et Costumes Russes," *l'Illustration* (12 October 1867).
122 "Il faut bien se rendre et dire: Oui, c'est cela même; dans les plus petits détails, c'est bien cela; le doute n'est plus possible. Et vous voyez bien que les serviteurs aériens de la lampe ont dû s'en mêler. Eh bien! Non, ce palais n'est qu'une reproduction, un simple, mais admirable fac-simile, dû aux soins du commissaire général du bey, M. Jules de Lesseps, au talent de l'architecte, M. Alfred Chapon. Il faut que les amis du merveilleux en prennent leur parti. Il n'y a plus de magie aujourd'hui, ou plutôt la magie a fait son entrée dans l'ordre naturel par la porte de la science, la lampe d'Aladin du dix-neuvième siècle!": Doullay, "Tapis, Tapisseries et Costumes Russes," *l'Illustration* (12 October 1867).
123 "En général, les musulmans aiment la fantasia, et nous leur devions une hospitalité selon leurs goûts.": "Exposition de Tunis et de Maroc," *l'Exposition Universelle*, vol. 1, no. 26 (1867): 413.
124 Lockyer, "The Problem of Sovereignty in an Age of Empire," 616.
125 Hoffenberg, "Displaying an Oceanic Nation and Society," 60.
126 Frédéric Le Play, *Rapport sur l'Exposition Universelle de 1867 à Paris*, 441.
127 "Bilder von der Weltaustellung," *Illustrirte Welt*, vol. 15, no. 36 (1867): 428.
128 "C'est un rêve des Mille et une Nuits! Quel goût! Quel luxe!": "Le pavillon imperial," *l'Exposition Universelle*, vol. 1, no. 2 (1867): 19–22.
129 Vigne, "Le pavillon imperial," *l'Illustration* (11 May 1867).
130 "The Paris Universal Exhibition," *Illustrated London News* (27 April 1867).
131 "Maisons russes," *l'Exposition Universelle*, vol. 1, no. 2 (1867): 26; "The Universal Exposition of 1867," *Illustrated London News* (16 February 1867).
132 "The Universal Exposition of 1867," *Illustrated London News* (8 June 1867).
133 "The Paris International Exposition," *Illustrated London News* (22 June 1867).
134 Ibid.
135 "Exposition Russe," *l'Exposition Populaire Illustrée*, vol. 1, no. 6 (1867): 42.
136 Plée, "Les annexes d'Espagne et du Portugal," *l'Exposition Universelle*, vol. 1, no. 3 (1867): 43–5.
137 Deleiderrie, "Pavilon Espagnol," *le Monde Illustré* (23 March 1867).
138 "The Paris Universal Exhibition of 1867," *Illustrated London News* (16 February 1867).

216 *Images of the world*

139 "Exposition Universelle de 1867. VII – Le pavillon espagnol et le pavillon portugais," *l'Illustration* (16 March 1867); "Partie espagnole – Pavillon style renaissance, specimen d'architecture nationale," *le Monde Illustré* (23 March 1867).

140 "Annexe du Portugal – Dessin de M. Thorigny. M. Pampin-Mayor, architecte," *l'Exposition Universelle*, vol. 1, no. 3 (1867): 43.

141 "Die Nationalpavilions auf dem Marsfelde," *Illustrirte Zeitung* (6 april 1867).

142 "Pavillon Imperial," *l'Exposition Universelle*, vol. 1, no. 2 (1867): 20; "Maison de Gustave Wasa," *l'Exposition Universelle*, vol. 1, no. 2 (1867): 21; "L'Izba Russe," *l'Exposition Universelle*, vol. 1, no. 2 (1867): 28.

143 "Le palais du Bey de Tunis et la tente de l'Empereur de Maroc. M. Chapon, architecte," *l'Exposition Universelle*, vol. 1, no. 3 (1867): 40; "Annexe du Portugal," *l'Exposition Universelle*, vol. 1, no. 3 (1867): 44; "Annexe de l'Espagne," *l'Exposition Universelle*, vol. 1, no. 3 (1867): 44.

144 "L'Isbah, modèle de maison Russe avec ses dépendances," *le Monde Illustré* (2 February 1867); "Pavillon destiné au bey de Tunis," *le Monde Illustré* (3 March 1867); "Pavillon d'exposition du royaume de Portugal," *le Monde Illustré* (3 March 1867); "Maison en bois construite sur le modèle de celle qu'habitait Gustavo Wasa," *le Monde Illustré* (9 March 1867); "Partie espagnole – Pavillon style renaissance, specimen d'architecture nationale," *le Monde Illustré* (23 March 1867).

145 "Cottage Anglais," *le Monde Illustré* (23 May 1867); "Vue generale des annexes et du jardin prussiens," *le Monde Illustré* (29 July 1867).

146 "The Paris Universal Exhibition of 1867," *Illustrated London News* (16 February 1867).

147 "The Paris International Exposition," *Illustrated London News* (22 March 1867).

148 "The Paris Universal Exhibition," *Illustrated London News* (27 April 1867).

149 "Foreign and Colonial Intelligence: France: The Exposition," *Illustrated London News* (4 May 1867).

150 Ibid.

151 "Pavillon Imperial, élevé d'après les plan et projets présentes par MM. Duval frères," *l'Exposition Universelle*, vol. 1, no. 2 (1867): 20; "Annexe de l'espagne – Dessin de M. Thorigny, M. De la Gandara, architecte," *l'Exposition Universelle*, vol. 1, no. 3 (1867): 43; "Annexe du Portugal – Dessin de M. Thorigny. M. Pampin-Mayor, architecte," *l'Exposition Universelle*, vol. 1, no. 3 (1867): 43; "Le Palais du Bey de Tunis et la tente de l'empereur du Maroc – Dessin de M. Gaildrau. M. Capon, architecte," *l'Exposition Universelle*, vol. 1, no. 3 (1867): 40.

152 "Exposition Universelle – Etat des travaux sur la partie occidentale du champ de mars. Dessin d'après nature par M. Riou," *l'Univers Illustré* (9 February 1867).

153 "Ein unkonzessionierter Fleckreiniger," *Über Land und Meer*, vol. 18, no. 29 (1867): 460.

154 "Vorläufige Ruhebaute," *Über Land und Meer*, vol. 18, no. 29 (1867): 461.

155 "Wie der Suez-Kanal seinen Einzug halt," *Über Land und Meer*, vol. 18, no. 29 (1867): 460.

156 "Pariser Weltausstellung. In der türkischen Abtheilung des Parkes," *Über Land und Meer*, vol. 18, no. 29 (1867): 424.

157 "Gustav Wasa's Haus," *Über Land und Meer*, vol. 18, no. 30 (1867): 476.

158 Philips, *Fairground Attractions*, 24.

159 Wesemael, *Architecture of Instruction and Delight*, 289.

160 Philips, *Fairground Attractions*, 24.

161 "Pourquoi le temple de Xochilcalco est-il l'exposition particulière de M. Méhédin et non celle de la commission scientifique du Mexique? Pourquoi y a-t-il là des tourniquets, au lieu d'entrées gratuites?": Ducuing, "Le temple de Xochicalco," *l'Exposition Universelle*, vol. 1, no. 3 (1867): 45.

162 "Exposition du ministère de l'instruction publique," *le Monde Illustré* (31 August 1867).

Images of the world 217

163 Demeulenaere-douyère, "Expositions Internationales et Image Nationale: Les Pays d'Amérique Latine Entre Pittoresque 'indigène' et Modernité Proclamée," 12.

164 Méhédin's temple was relatively popular, because the 1867 exposition coincided with the final days of the Second Mexican Empire. Refusing to abdicate, Maximilian I fought the Mexican republicans led by Benito Juárez (1806–1872) and, after his defeat, was executed on the morning of 19 June 1867, during the busiest month of the exposition. Ibid.

165 Ferrere, "Le Jardin chinois a l'Exposition," *l'Exposition Universelle*, vol. 1, no. 9 (1867): 134–8.

166 Hur, "Staging Modern Statehood: World Exhibitions and the Rhetoric of Publishing in Late Qing China, 1851–1910," 19.

167 "The Paris International Exhibition," *Illustrated London News* (22 June 1867).

168 Ibid.

169 "Dutch café at the corner of the rue des Pays-Bas," Illustrated London News (8 June 1867).

170 Wesemael, *Architecture of Instruction and Delight*, 289.

171 "The Paris Universal Exhibition," *Illustrated London News* (8 June 1867).

172 "L'activité fiévreuse de l'industrie succède le calme paisible de la nature": Gautier, Les Curiosités, 40.

173 Ibid.

174 The aquariums would inspire Jules Verne, who visited the exposition, to write his Vingt mille lieues sous les mers (1870). The aquarium also inspired the illustrator of his famous book Edouard Riou, who made an illustration of the aquarium for the *l'Univers Illustré*. E. About, "Le jardin réserve. Les aquariums," *l'Exposition Universelle*, vol. 1, no. 5 (1867): 73.

175 E. About, "Le Jardin réserve. Les aquariums," *l'Exposition Universelle*, vol. 1, no. 5 (1867): 73.

176 "Aquarium d'eau Douce," *l'Exposition Universelle*, vol. 1, no. 21 (1867): 332; "Exterior do aquário de aqua doce, na exposição universal de Paris," *Archivo Pittoresco*, vol. 10, no. 15 (1867): 105; "Exposition Universelle: l'aquarium," *le Journal Illustré* (19 May 1867); "Aquarium van zoetwater," *Hollandsche Illustratie*, vol. 3, no. 52 (1867): 409; "Exposición Universal – El aquarium," *el Siglo Illustrado* (19 October 1867).

Conclusion

During the writing of the thesis that formed the basis for this book, the photograph of Alan Kurdi, the drowned Syrian toddler of Kurdish ethnic background, reminded me of the power of *seeing* the news. For many months, newspapers had reported on the increasing brutality and death toll of the Syrian Civil War and the inhuman conditions of refugees trying to reach Europe. It took the photograph of Kurdi's lifeless body on a Turkish beach, a single victim among countless others, to make the devastating effects of the crisis inescapable. Newspapers simultaneously published the picture, provoking responses around the world. Both the 2015 Canadian federal election and Chancellor Angela Merkel's *Willkommenskultur*, a radical change in the German attitude towards refugees, are commonly seen as having been influenced by the public outcry that followed the publication of the photograph.

The almost universal impact of some pictures of the news, often described as *iconic*, is commonly connected to the medium of photography. Many people can easily picture Dorothea Lange's *Migrant Mother* (1936), the image of a Russian soldier planting a flag on the German *Reichstag*, that one portrait of Che Guevara, the somewhat grainy picture of the tank man on Tiananmen Square, or Nick Ut's 'Napalm girl.' However, the photograph of Kurdi, the latest image to become iconic, strongly reminded me of illustrations of the news in the nineteenth century.

This book argues that dissemination of popular illustrated newspapers and their images led to the formation of a transnational visual culture of the news in the nineteenth century. Two lines of inquiry support this main argument. First, well-known illustrated newspapers, such as the *Illustrated London News*, were distributed far beyond the borders of a specific nation-state. Second, the images of the news published by the nineteenth-century illustrated press were transnational products. Publications all over the world, in Europe, the United States, and Western colonies, sold them to each other.

Chapter 1 demonstrated how a transnational approach changes our perspective on the illustrated press: instead of being primarily directed at national audiences, the three most well-known illustrated newspapers of the nineteenth century – the *Illustrated London News*, *l'Illustration*, and the *Illustrirte Zeitung* – were transnational media corporations that targeted diverse audiences, from urban readers in London, Paris, and Leipzig to readers in British and French colonies and other nations. By transcending the limitations of most geographically inspired concepts, like the nation, the British Empire, or transatlantic print culture, Chapter 1 has shown how a transnational approach can incorporate all these different geographic levels and shed light on the genuinely global outlook of the nineteenth-century illustrated press.

While the first chapter focused on the transnational audiences of three famous illustrated newspapers, Chapter 2 described the transnational trade in illustrations of the news. We can trace two important developments in this trade between 1842 and 1870. First of all, the connections between the different nodes in the transnational network became increasingly complex. In the 1840s, only the original producer traded illustrations. For example, *l'Illustration* sold an image of Windsor castle to the Italian *il Mondo Illustrato* and the Russian *Illyustratsiya*. By the late 1860s, the increasing number of titles and the introduction of new photoxylographic techniques had made the transnational network more complex. In June 1867, the *Illustrated London News* published the image, 'The Thames embankment and subterranean London.' Two months later, a photoxylographic copy appeared in *Frank Leslie's Illustrated Newspaper* in New York. Almost 12 months after its original publication, German publisher Eduard Hallberger printed a re-engraving of the same image in *Über Land und Meer*. The French *le Journal Illustré* bought this German copy and re-used the illustration for its Dutch version: the *Hollandsche Illustratie*. The original producer of the image – the *Illustrated London News* – was not involved in any of the re-publications of the image.

Second, between 1842 and 1870 illustrations of the news became significantly cheaper as a result of several developments in reproduction techniques and increasing competition between several major suppliers. In the 1840s, illustrated newspapers had to produce their own images or buy them from the three major illustrated newspapers: the *Illustrated London News*, *l'Illustration*, or the *Illustrirte Zeitung*. In the 1850s, the founding of several new titles, like the *Illustrated Times* (1855) in Britain and *le Monde Illustré* (1857) and *l'Univers Illustré* (1858) in Paris, led to an increase in the availability of illustrations of the news. Newly founded illustrated newspapers, such as the Danish *Illustreret Tidende*, could buy images from several competing British, French, and German publications.

In addition to these two developments, we can also discern several themes. First of all, personal connections between important nodes in different national contexts shaped the transnational trade in illustrations. The Vizetelly family is a good example of this process. By acting as the central node in a large group of French and British artists and publishers, Vizetelly facilitated the exchange of medial formats, like the illustrated newspaper, and the trade in illustrations of the news.

The tension between the legal and illegal, or the controlled and uncontrolled trade in images, can be seen as the second theme. In the mid-1850s, the publication of more than one illustrated newspaper in the same country resulted in the fact that international copyright became an issue. In the early months of 1856, John Cassell sued his rival George Stiff of the *London Journal*, claiming that he published *clichés* of images in *l'Illustration* to which he had an 'exclusive

220   *Conclusion*

right.' Cassell not only paid *l'Illustration* for each copy but he also had to pay 500 pounds for the copyright of the French illustrations in Britain. *Cassell v. Stiff* became one of the first court cases dealing with international copyright on images of the news.

Even more than increasing competition, new photoxylographic techniques enabled a new way of copying images and, as a result, changed the nature of the transnational exchange of news illustrations. While transnational actors like Vizetelly were indispensable in the first phases of the trade, the new photoxylographic techniques eliminated the necessity of contact between the original producer of an image and the publication planning on reusing it. Especially American titles, such as *Frank Leslie's Illustrated Newspaper* and *Harpers' Weekly*, applied the techniques on a large scale and printed countless pirated images from several European illustrated newspapers.

The importance of nineteenth-century illustrated newspapers, especially if they targeted a massive audience, is often underestimated. Chapter 3 revealed that the reporting of *Cassell's Illustrated Family Paper* during the Crimean War is one of the best examples of this process. It sold around 500,000 copies at the height of the war, almost four times as many as the *Illustrated London News* and ten times the 50,000 copies of *The Times*. Despite these figures, which demonstrate that the publication was the most influential shaper of the Crimean War in Britain, it has hardly received any attention from historians.

Cassell's images of the Crimean War also undermine the pervading scholarly view of the national nature of illustrated newspapers. Although the publication purported to report the war first hand, it bought (almost) all its images from the French *l'Illustration*. This large-scale British re-publication of French images of the conflict shows that there was nothing specifically 'French' about the French images. More importantly, *Cassell's* also demonstrates that images of the news crossed not only national borders easily but also those of class. While *l'Illustration* marketed itself as a *bourgeois* publication, Cassel targeted the British working classes, selling his periodical for a single penny.

Cassell's publication not only used *l'Illustration*'s images but also borrowed its star reporter Henri Durand-Brager. This shows that the discourse surrounding the visual culture of the news was shaped in a transnational context. The *Illustrated London News* coined the term 'special artist,' a sketching eyewitness reporter, at the beginning of the war. *L'Illustration* quickly adopted this model of its British example and hired Durand-Brager, who was an embedded marine painter in the French navy when the war started, to be its eyes on the ground. Noticing the increasing popularity of special artists during the war, *Cassell's Illustrated Family Paper* adopted the Frenchman as its special artist. Unknowingly, a large part of the British audience thus became familiar with the new profession through French images and descriptions.

The fact that audiences from diverse social backgrounds in Britain and France shared the same images of the Crimean War underlines that illustrations of the news spoke a universal language. However, using Mitchell's concept of the composite work, Chapter 3 has also made clear that images should not be separated

Conclusion 221

from the titles, captions, and articles that accompanied them. Editors of *Cassell's Illustrated Family Paper*, like the journalist Thomas Frost, spent the majority of their time translating articles about the war from *l'Illustration*. They changed these textual elements if the combination of an image and text was thought to be offensive to a British audience: selective translation or the adding of new descriptions changed the meaning of the French images.

Chapter 4 captured the apotheosis of the two major developments of the transnational trade in images of the news between 1842 and 1870. The fact that more than 31 titles in 15 different countries published illustrations of the Universal Exposition of 1867 shows that illustrated newspapers had started to cater to all sorts of different audiences. This development is especially noticeable in France; in addition to the relatively expensive *l'Illustration*, the mid-range *le Monde Illustré*, and the cheap *l'Univers Illustré* and *le Journal Illustré*, three short-lived titles were especially established to report on the Universal Exposition. The visual representation of the Universal Exposition also points to the increasing entanglement of the transnational trade in illustration of the news. Thirty-one different titles published a total of 1,770 images of the exposition. One thousand, one hundred and three of these images can be designated as original, meaning that the publication in question was the first to publish it. Four hundred and ninety-five images were copies that previously appeared in another illustrated newspaper.

The representation of the exposition shows that the illegal copying of illustrations had become more important. Publications in Spain, Italy, and Germany re-engraved 80 of the total 1,770 images of the exposition. The Spanish artists of the *el Museo Universal* copied nine illustrations from *le Monde Illustré*, eight from the *Illustrirte Zeitung*, seven from the *Illustrated London News*, four from *l'Illustration*, and two from *l'Exposition Universelle*. Furthermore, the images of the exposition in the American *Frank Leslie's Illustrated Newspaper* demonstrate that technological innovation started to play an essential role in the transnational visual culture of the news in the late 1860s. Through clever use of the new photoxylographic technique, Leslie could publish more images than many well-established European illustrated newspapers, such as the *Illustrated London News*.

This book has shown that we can only understand the nineteenth-century illustrated press from a transnational perspective. This conclusion thus reconsiders previous research practices and opens up a range of new questions. Some of these reconsiderations and questions revolve around the extent of the transnational nature of the (illustrated) nineteenth-century press, while others are centred on the application of a transnational perspective and the benefits and pitfalls of using digital archives and digital methods.

The transnational nature of the nineteenth-century illustrated press sheds light on the complexity of Benedict Anderson's popular concept of the imagined community: a commonly used theoretical framework used to study nineteenth-century media. We have seen how readers of *l'Illustration* and *Cassell's Illustrated Family Paper* shared the experience of looking at the same images of the Crimean War. As a result, they became part of the same transnational visual culture: a shared discourse entailing notions and expectations about the objectivity and authenticity

222 *Conclusion*

of images of the news. However, not being aware of this shared experience, readers in one group would not feel directly connected to people in the other group. Although they were exposed to the exact same content, they did share a sense of togetherness or identity.

This book has made clear that if we want to use (nineteenth-century) media to describe the production of (national) identity, we should shift our focus from *representation*, a close reading of *content*, to the different *audiences* that consumed media. In my opinion, this does not mean that we have to discard Anderson's theory. However, we have to apply it in a different way: historians should primarily focus their research on the borders of the act of *imagining*, the audiences that were reached by a certain title, instead of on the borders of an identity as it was *represented* in the text and images of a publication.

Chapter 1 has shown that research in digital newspapers archives can reveal much about the diverse audiences of nineteenth-century illustrated newspapers. Without Trove, the Australian digital archives, it would have been impossible to get a clear image of the colonial audience of the *Illustrated London News*. While using digital archives, researchers should be aware that they provide selective access to the past. For example, readers of the *Illustrated London News* on the Indian subcontinent stay out of view because of the lack of a digital archive.

The same applies for the digital version of nineteenth-century illustrated newspapers. Although Chapter 2 has sketched the general outlines of the transnational trade in illustrations of the news between 1842 and 1870, there is undoubtedly still much more to discover. This study has exposed illustrated newspapers that were hidden, sometimes in plain sight, in national historiographies of the press. This raises the question of whether we can find more illustrated newspapers in other countries: Is there a French, German, or Italian equivalent of *Cassell's Illustrated Family Paper*? Did publishers outside the Western cultural zone also adopt the form of the illustrated newspaper? Just as there are Japanese and several Indian versions of *Punch*, can we find a non-Western version of the *Illustrated London News*?

On a methodological level, I hope that this book contributes to the debate concerning the connection between the digital and the transnational turn in history. Keyword searches in different digital collections give us the opportunity to chart transnational networks, enabling a single historian to control these vastly different national contexts and the large number of historical sources involved. Without digital archives and methods, it would have been impossible to find the colonial advertisements of the *Illustrated London News* in newspapers from Bermuda, Singapore, and Australia. Without digital versions, it would not have been feasible to look for copies of illustrations in different illustrated newspapers.

New digital archives can undoubtedly uncover more on the distribution of specific illustrated newspapers and the transnational trade in illustrations. Many national libraries are currently digitizing their collections at a rapid pace, and not all of these collections disappear behind paywalls. In April 2017, Digipress, the digital newspaper archive of the library of German province Bayern, began to put large numbers of German newspapers online. After only one year, the collection

Conclusion 223

now holds around 6.5 million newspaper pages. A quick keyword search for 'Illustrirte Zeitung' yielded almost 6,000 hits, which undoubtedly contain valuable information on the German illustrated newspaper. In contrast to other libraries, Digipress also makes publications in foreign languages available. We can find high-quality digital copies of *All the Year Round* and *Punch* but also of *l'Illustration* and the Russian illustrated newspaper *Illyustrirovannaya Gazeta*.

Working with digital archives, we run the risk of disregarding older pre-digital research methods. It is difficult to understand the form of the illustrated newspaper if we only look at a digital version of it. Additionally, keyword searches give us unprecedented access to the text but not to the specific structure of a medium. Finally, while many titles have been digitized, hundreds more exist only in a paper form because, consciously or not, digitization programmes often reproduce the prejudices of nineteenth-century national collection programmes. Widely distributed titles, such as *Cassell's Illustrated Family Paper*, are not likely to be digitized any time soon. This book demonstrates that we have to work in between publications that are available in digital and paper versions and apply methodologies associated with both these forms.

Finally, in a general sense, I hope that this book has laid the groundwork for future studies concerning the transnational nature of nineteenth-century media. In the first modern century, newspapers, periodicals, and magazines opened 'communicative spaces of every conceivable dimension,' as Osterhammel notes.[1] Although historians have long viewed them as purely national spaces, where national identity was represented and produced, this book has demonstrated that the dynamics of nineteenth-century media foreshadow the current highly connected and mediated reality in many ways.

Note

1 Osterhammel, *The Transformation of the World*, 69.

Bibliography

Ajayi, Jacob Festus Ade. *General History of Africa: Africa in the Nineteenth Century until the 1880s*. Oxford: Heinemann International, 1989.

Aldrich, Richard. *Greater France: A History of French Overseas Expansion*. Basingstoke: Palgrave Macmillan, 1996.

Allwood, John. *The Great Exhibitions: 150 Years*. London: Exhibition Consultants, 2001.

Altholz, Josef. *The Religious Press in Britain, 1760–1900*. New York: Greenwood Press, 1989.

Altick, Richard. *The English Common Reader: A Social History of the Mass Reading Public, 1800–1900*. Chicago: University of Chicago Press, 1957.

Anderson, Benedict. *Imagined Communities: Reflections on the Origin and Spread of Nationalism*. London: Verso, 2006.

Anderson, Patricia. *The Printed Image and the Transformation of Popular Culture, 1790–1860*. Oxford: Clarendon Press, 1991.

Armetta, Flora. "Cassell's (Illustrated) Family Paper (1853–1867) and Cassell's Magazine (1867–1932)." In *The Dictionary of Nineteenth Century Journalism*, edited by Laurel Brake and Marysa Demoor, 101. Ghent: Academia Press, 2009.

Auerbach, Jeffrey. "Introduction." In *Britain, the Empire, and the World at the Great Exhibition of 1851*, edited by Jeffrey Auerbach and Peter Hoffenberg, IX–XVII. Aldershot: Ashgate, 2008.

Bacot, Jean-Pierre. *La presse illustrée au XIXe siècle. Une histoire oubliée?* Limoges: Presses universitaires de Limoges, 2005.

———. "Le role des magazines illustres dans la construction du nationalisme au XIXe siecle et au debut du XXe siecle." *Réseaux* no. 107 (2007): 265–93.

Bantman, Constance, and Ana Cláudia Suriani da Silva. "Introduction: The Foreign Political Press in Nineteenth-Century London: Local and Transnational Context." In *The Foreign Political Press in Nineteenth-Century London: Politics from a Distance*, 1–15. London: Bloomsbury Academic, 2018.

Bardoel, Jo, and Huub Wijfjes, eds. *Journalistieke Cultuur in Nederland*. Amsterdam: Amsterdam University Press, 2015.

Bardon, Annie. "Militarmalerei Im Second Empire Am Beispiel Des Krimkrieges." Philipps-Universität Marburg/Lahn, 1980.

Barnham, Christopher. "John Dicks." In *Dictionary of Nineteenth-Century Journalism in Great Britain and Ireland*, edited by Laurel Brake and Marysa Demoor, 169. Ghent: Academia Press, 2009.

Barnhurst, Kevin, and John Nerone. "Civic Picturing vs. Realist Photojournalism: The Regime of Illustrated News, 1856–1901." *Design Issues* 16, no. 1 (2000): 59–79.

Barth, Volker. "Displaying Normalisation: The Paris Universal Exhibition of 1867." *Journal of Historical Sociology* 20, no. 4 (2007): 462–85.

Bibliography 225

Bayly, Christopher, Sven Beckert, Matthew Connelly, Isabel Hofmeyr, And Wendy Kozol, and Patricia Seed. "AHR Conversation: On Transnational History." *The American Historical Review* 111, no. 5 (2006): 1441–64.

Beegan, Gerry. *The Mass Image: A Cultural History of Photomechanical Reproduction in Victorian London*. Basingstoke: Palgrave Macmillan, 2008.

Beetham, Margaret. "Towards a Theory of the Periodical as a Publishing Genre." In *Investigating Victorian Journalism*, edited by Laurel Brake, Aled Jones, and Lionel Madden, 19–32. London: Palgrave Macmillan, 1990.

Beraldi, Henri. *Les graveurs du XIXe siècle: Guide de l'amateur d'estampes modernes*. Paris: Conquet, 1891.

Betz, Margret, and Andrew Nedd. "Irony, Derision, and Magical Wit: Censors as a Spur to Russian Abstract Art." In *Political Censorship of the Visual Arts in Nineteenth-Century Europe*, edited by Robert Goldstein and Andrew Nedd, 9–61. Basingstoke: Palgrave Macmillan, 2015.

Bewick, Thomas. *A Memoir of Thomas Bewick*. Newcastle-on-Tyne: Longman, Green, Longman, and Roberts, 1862.

Bey, Salaheddin. *La Turquie à l'Exposition Universelle de 1867*. Paris: Librairie Hachette & Cie, 1867.

Blanchon, Remi. *La gravure sur bois au XIXe siècle: L'âge du bois debout*. Paris: Les Editions de l'Amateur, 2001.

Blok, Gemma, Vincent Kuitenbrouwer, and Claire Weeda. "Introduction." In *Imagined Communities: Historical Reflections on the Process of Community Formation*, 2–14. Amsterdam: Amsterdam University Press, 2018.

Boardman, Kay. "'A Material Girl in a Material World': The Fashionable Female Body in Victorian Women's Magazines." *Journal of Victorian Culture* 3, no. 1 (1998): 93–110.

Boterman, Frits. *Moderne geschiedenis van Duitsland: 1800 – heden*. Amsterdam: De Arbeiderspers, 2011.

Boyer, Deborah. "Picturing the Other: Images of Burmans in Imperial Britain." *Victorian Periodicals Review* 35, no. 3 (October 2002): 214–26.

Brake, Laurel. "London Letter: Researching the Historical Press, Now and Here." *Victorian Periodicals Review* 48, no. 2 (2015): 245–53.

———. "'Time's Turbulence': Mapping Journalism Networks." *Victorian Periodicals Review* 44, no. 2 (2011): 115–27.

Brantlinger, Patrick. *The Reading Lesson: The Threat of Mass Literacy in Nineteenth-Century British Fiction*. Bloomington: Indiana University Press, 1998.

Briggs, Asa, and Peter Burke. *A Social History of the Media: From Gutenberg to the Internet*. Cambridge: Polity, 2005.

Broersma, Marcel. "Transnational Journalism History. Balancing Global Universals and National Peculiarities." *Medien & Zeit* 25, no. 4 (2010): 10–15.

Brown, Joshua. *Beyond the Lines: Pictorial Reporting, Everyday Life, and the Crisis of Gilded-Age America*. Berkeley: University of California Press, 2006.

———. "Reconstructing Representation: Social Types, Readers, and the Pictorial Press, 1865–1877." *Radical History Review* 1996, no. 66 (1996): 5–38.

Bryant, Arthur. "Foreword." In *The Illustrated London News' Social History of Victorian Britain*, edited by Christopher Hibbert, 9–11. London: Angus and Robertson, 1975.

Cantor, Geoffrey. "Reporting the Great Exhibition." In *Journalism and the Periodical Press in Nineteenth-Century Britain*, edited by Joanne Shattock, 182–200. Cambridge: Cambridge University Press, 2017.

Cathcart, Brian. *The News from Waterloo: The Race to Tell Britain of Wellington's Victory*. London: Faber & Faber, 2016.

226   Bibliography

Çelik, Zeynep. *Displaying the Orient: Architecture of Islam at Nineteenth-Century World's Fairs*. Berkeley: University of California Press, 1992.

Chagnon-Burke, Véronique. "'Tel Père, Telle Fille': Judith Gautier, Artist, Author, and Art Critic." In *Women Art Critics in Nineteenth-Century France: Vanishing Acts*, edited by Wendelin Guentner, 237–54. Newark: University of Delaware Press, 2013.

Chalaby, Jean. *The Invention of Journalism*. Basingstoke: Palgrave Macmillan, 1998.

Chevalier, Louis. *Labouring Classes and Dangerous Classes in Paris during the First Half of the Nineteenth Century*. London: Routledge & K. Paul, 1976.

Ciarlo, David. *Advertising Empire: Race and Visual Culture in Imperial Germany*. Cambridge: Harvard University Press, 2011.

Claassen, Ernest. "Het Nederlandsch Magazijn, Het Nederlandsch Museum En De Honigbij. Drie Geïllustreerde Tijdschriften in de Jaren Dertig En Veertig van de Negentiende Eeuw." *Jaarboek Voor Nederlandse Boekgeschiedenis* 5 (1998): 131–46.

Clarke, Peter. *European Cities and Towns, 400–2000*. Oxford: Oxford University Press, 2009.

Clauß, Carl. "Kretzschmar." In *Allgemeine Deutsche Biographie*. Vol. 17, 140–1. Leipzig: Historischen Kommission bei der Bayerischen Akademie der Wissenschaften, 1883.

Cockerham, Harry. "Gautier, Guys, le 'Palais de Cristal' et l'Illustrated London News en français de 1851." *Revue d'Histoire littéraire de la France* 94, no. 6 (1994): 959–74.

Codell, Julie. "Imperial Differences and Culture Clashes in Victorian Periodicals' Visuals: The Case of Punch." *Victorian Periodicals Review* 39, no. 4 (2006): 410–28.

Colclough, Stephen. "Readers and Readership: Real or Historical Readership." In *Dictionary of Nineteenth-Century Journalism*, edited by Laurel Brake and Marysa Demoor, 530. Ghent: Academia Press, 2009.

Collins, Irene. *The Government and the Newspaper Press in France, 1814–1881*. Oxford: Oxford University Press, 1959.

Cox, Howard, and Simon Mowatt. *Revolutions from Grub Street: A History of Magazine Publishing in Britain*. Oxford: Oxford University Press, 2014.

Cronqvist, Marie, and Christoph Hilgert. "Entangled Media Histories." *Media History* 23, no. 1 (2017): 130–41.

Cummins, Joseph. *The War Chronicles: From Chariots to Flintlocks*. Crows Nest: Allen & Unwin, 2008.

Darwin, John. *The Empire Project: The Rise and Fall of the British World-System 1830–1970*. Cambridge: Cambridge University Press, 2009.

Delafield, Catherine. *Serialization and the Novel in Mid-Victorian Magazines*. Farnham: Ashgate, 2015.

De la Motte, Dean, and J. Jeannene Przblyski. "Introduction." In *Making the News: Modernity & the Mass Press in Nineteenth-Century France*, edited by Dean De la Motte and Jeannene Przyblyski, 1–15. Manchester: Manchester University Press, 1999.

Demeulenaere-douyère, Christiane. "Expositions Internationales et Image Nationale: Les Pays d'Amérique Latine Entre Pittoresque "indigène" et Modernité Proclamée." *Diacronie. Studi Di Storia Contemporanea* 18, no. 2 (2014): 1–14.

Desmond, Robert W. *The Information Process: World News Reporting to the Twentieth Century*. Iowa City: University of Iowa Press, 1978.

De Vries, Boudien. *Een stad vol lezers: leescultuur in Haarlem 1850–1920*. Nijmegen: Vantilt, 2011.

———. "Lezende burgers. Cultuuridealen en leespraktijk in burgelijke kringen in de negentiende eeuw." *Groniek* 40, no. 176 bis (1997): 39–64.

Distad, N. Merrill. "The Origins and History of 'Victorian Periodicals Review', 1954–84." *Victorian Periodicals Review* 18, no. 3 (1985): 86–98.

Bibliography 227

Dowling, Peter. "Destined Not to Survive: The Illustrated Newspapers of Colonial Australia." *Studies in Newspaper and Periodical History* 3, no. 1–2 (1995): 85–98.

Engen, Rodney. *Dictionary of Victorian Wood Engravers*. Cambridge: Chadwyck-Healey, 1985.

Esteves, José Pereira. "Archivo Pittoresco." In *Dicionário Do Romantismo Literário Português*, edited by Helena Buescu Carvalhão, 23–4. Lisbon: Editorial Caminho, 1997.

Exposition internationale, ed. *Rapport sur l'Exposition Universelle de 1867 à Paris. Précis des opérations et listes des collaborateurs*. Paris: Imprimerie Impériale, 1869.

Faulstich, Werner. *Medienwandel im Industrie- und Massenzeitalter (1830–1900)*. Göttingen: Vandenhoeck & Ruprecht, 2004.

Fenton, Laurence. *Palmerston and the Times: Foreign Policy, the Press and Public Opinion in Mid-Victorian Britain*. New York: Tauris, 2013.

Figes, Orlando. *Crimea: The Last Crusade*. London: Penguin, 2011.

Flood, Catherine. "Contrary to the Habits of Their Sex? Women Drawing on Wood and the Careers of Florence and Adelaide Claxton." In *Crafting the Woman Professional in the Long Nineteenth Century: Artistry and Industry in Britain*, edited by Kyriaki Hadjiafxendi and Patricia Zakreski, 107–23. London: Routledge, 2016.

Fox, Celina. "The Development of Social Reportage in English Periodical Illustration during the 1840s and Early 1850s." *Past & Present* no. 74 (1977): 90–111.

Fraser, Hilary, Stephanie Green, and Judith Johnston. *Gender and the Victorian Periodical*. Cambridge: Cambridge University Press, 2003.

Frost, Thomas. *Forty Years' Recollections: Literary and Political*. London: Sampson Low, Marston, Searle, and Rivington, 1880.

———. *Reminiscences of a Country Journalist*. London: Ward and Downey, 1888.

Fyfe, Paul. "Illustrating the Accident: Railways and the Catastrophic Picturesque in the Illustrated London News." *Victorian Periodicals Review* 46, no. 1 (2013): 61–91.

Gallagher, Catherine, and Stephen Greenblatt. *Practicing New Historicism*. Chicago: The University of Chicago Press, 2007.

Gautier, Hippolyte. *Les curiosités de l'exposition universelle de 1867*. Paris: Delgrave et Cie, 1867.

Gebhardt, Hartwig. "Auf Der Suche Nach Nationaler Identitat. Publizistische Strategien in Der Leipziger 'Illustrirten Zeitung', Zwischen Revolution Und Reichsgrunding." In *Bilder Der Macht Und Macht Der Bilder. Zeitgeschichte in Darstellungen Des 19. Jahrhundert*, edited by Stefan Germer and Michael Zimmermann, 310–23. Berlin: Klinkhardt & Biermann, 1997.

Geppert, Alexander. *Fleeting Cities: Imperial Expositions in Fin-de-Siecle Europe*. Basingstoke: Palgrave Macmillan, 2010.

Gervais, Thierry. "Witness to War: The Uses of Photography in the Illustrated Press, 1855–1904." *Journal of Visual Culture* 9, no. 3 (2010): 370–84.

Gitelman, Lisa. *Always Already New Media, History, and the Data of Culture*. Cambridge: MIT Press, 2014.

Gitelman, Lisa, and Geoffrey Pingree, eds. *New Media, 1740–1915*. Cambridge: MIT Press, 2003.

Goldstein, Robert. *Political Censorship of the Arts and the Press in Nineteenth-Century Europe*. Basingstoke: Palgrave Macmillan, 1989.

Gouttman, Alain. *La guerre de Crimée: 1853–1856. La première guerre moderne*. Paris: Perrin, 2006.

Green, Abigail. *Fatherlands: State-Building and Nationhood in Nineteenth-Century Germany*. Cambridge: Cambridge University Press, 2001.

228   Bibliography

Greenhalgh, Paul. *Ephemeral Vistas: The Exposition Universelles, Great Exhibitions and World's Fairs, 1851–1939*. Manchester: Manchester University Press, 1988.

Gregory, Jeremy, and John Stevenson. *The Routledge Companion to Britain in the Eighteenth Century*. London: Routledge, 2012.

Gusman, Pierre. *La gravure sur bois en France au XIXe siècle*. Paris: Éditions Albert Morancé, 1929.

Guy, Pol de. *Paris en 1867: guide à l'Exposition universelle*. Paris: E. Rome, 1866.

Hanebutt-Benz, Eva-Maria. "Studien Zum Deutschen Holzstich Im 19. Jahrhundert." *Archiv Für Geschichte Des Buchwesens* 24 (1983): 581–1266.

Harris, Neil. *Cultural Excursions: Marketing Appetites and Cultural Tastes in Modern America*. Chicago: University of Chicago Press, 1990.

Hartzenbusch, Eugenio. *Apuntes para un catálogo de periódicos madrileños desde el año 1661 al 1870*. Madrid: Sucesores de Rivadeneyra, 1894.

Hemels, Joan. *De pers onder het juk van een fiscale druk*. Amsterdam: Otto Cramwinckel Uitgever, 1992.

Hemels, Joan, and Renée Vegt. *Het geïllustreerde tijdschrift in Nederland: bron van kennis en vermaak, lust voor het oog*. Vol. 1. Amsterdam: Cramwinckel, 1993.

Henkin, David. *The Postal Age: The Emergence of Modern Communications in Nineteenth-Century America*. Chicago: Chicago University Press, 2006.

Hibbert, Christopher. *The Illustrated London News: Social History of Victorian Britain*. London: Angus and Robertson, 1975.

Hill, Jason, and Vanessa Schwartz. *Getting the Picture: The Visual Culture of the News*. London: Bloomsbury Academic, 2015.

Hobbs, Andrew. "The Deleterious Dominance of the Times in Nineteenth-Century Scholarship." *Journal of Victorian Culture* 18, no. 4 (2013): 472–97.

———. "When the Provincial Press Was the National Press." *International Journal of Regional and Local History* 5, no. 1 (2009): 16–43.

Hobsbawm, Eric. *The Age of Capital, 1848–1875*. London: Abacus, 2008.

Hoffenberg, Peter. *An Empire on Display: English, Indian, and Australian Exhibitions from the Crystal Palace to the Great War*. Berkeley: University of California Press, 2001.

———. "Displaying an Oceanic Nation and Society: The Kingdom of Hawai'i at Nineteenth-Century International Exhibitions." In *Oceania and the Victorian Imagination: Where All Things Are Possible*, edited by Richard Fulton and Peter Hoffenberg, 59–79. London: Routledge, 2013.

Holloway, Laura. *Famous American Fortunes and the Men Who Have Made Them*. Philadelphia: Bradley & Company, 1884.

Houghton, Walter. *The Victorian Frame of Mind, 1830–1870*. New Haven: Yale University Press, 1985.

Hudson, Frederic. *Journalism in the United States, from 1690–1872*. New York: Harper & Brothers, 1873.

Hultzsch, Anne. "The Crowd and the Building: Flux in the Early Illustrated London News." *Architecture and Culture* 6, no. 3 (2018): 371–86.

Hur, Hyungju. "Staging Modern Statehood; World Exhibitions and the Rhetoric of Publishing in Late Qing China, 1851–1910." University of Illinois at Urbana-Champaign, 2012.

Jackson, Mason. *The Pictorial Press: Its Origin and Progress*. London: Hurst and Blackett, 1885.

Janet, Wolff. "The Invisible Flâneuse: Women and the Literature of Modernity." *Theory, Culture & Society* 2, no. 3 (1985): 37–46.

Bibliography 229

Janzen Kooistra, Lorraine. "Illustration." In *Journalism and the Periodical Press in Nineteenth-Century Britain*, edited by Joanne Shattock, 104–25. Cambridge: Cambridge University Press, 2017.

Jensen, Lotte. *"Bij uitsluiting voor de vrouwelijke sekse geschikt": vrouwentijdschriften en journalistes in Nederland in de achttiende en negentiende eeuw*. Hilversum: Verloren, 2001.

Jobling, Paul, and David Crowley. *Graphic Design: Reproduction and Representation since 1800*. Manchester: Manchester University Press, 1996.

John, Richard. *Spreading the News: The American Postal System from Franklin to Morse*. Harvard: Harvard University Press, 1996.

Johnston-Woods, Toni. "The Virtual Reading Communities of the London Journal, the New York Ledger and the Australian Journal." In *Nineteenth-Century Media and the Construction of Identities*, edited by Laurel Brake, Bill Bell, and David Finkelstein, 350–61. Basingstoke: Palgrave Macmillan, 2000.

Kaiser, Wolfram. "Vive La France! Vive La République? The Cultural Construction of French Identity at the World Exhibitions in Paris 1855–1900." *National Identities* 1, no. 3 (1999): 227–44.

Kay, Edward Ebenezer, and Henry Robert Vaughan Johnson. *Reports of Cases Adjudged in the High Court of Chancery, before Sir W.P. Wood, Vice-Chancellor. 1855 to 1856*. Vol. 2. London: W. Maxwell, 1856.

Keller, Ulrich. "Early Photojournalism." In *Communication in History: Technology, Culture, Society*, edited by David Crowley and Paul Heyer, 178–87. New York: Longman, 1999.

———. *The Ultimate Spectacle: A Visual History of the Crimean War*. Amsterdam: Amsterdam University Press, 2001.

King, Andrew. "Advertising." In *Dictionary of Nineteenth-Century Journalism*, edited by Marysa Demoor and Laurel Brake. Ghent: Academia Press, 2009.

———. *The London Journal, 1845–83: Periodicals, Production and Gender*. Aldershot: Ashgate, 2004.

King, Andrew, Alexis Easley, and John Morton. "Introduction." In *The Routledge Handbook to Nineteenth-Century British Periodicals and Newspapers*, edited by Andrew King, Alexis Easley, and John Morton, 1–15. Abingdon: Routledge, 2016.

Knight, Charles. *Passages of a Working Life during Half a Century*. Vol. 2. London: Bradbury & Evans, 1864.

Korey, Marie Elena, and Thomas Fisher. *Vizetelly & Compan(ies): A Complex Tale of Victorian Printing and Publishing: An Exhibition with Essays*. Toronto: University of Toronto Library, 2003.

Kreenen, Jan Jacob. *Beschrijving van Alle Landen, Staten En Rijken Der Aarde*. Zwolle: Van Hoogstraten & Gorter, 1867.

Law, Graham. "Distribution." In *The Routledge Handbook to Nineteenth-Century British Periodicals and Newspapers*, edited by Andrew King, Alexis Easley, and John Morton, 42–60. Abingdon: Routledge, 2016.

Leary, Patrick. "A Brief History of the Illustrated London News." *The Illustrated London News Histrical Archive* (blog). Accessed October 18, 2017. http://gale.cengage.co.uk/images/PatrickLeary.pdf.

Life, Allan. "The Periodical Illustrations of John Everett Millais and Their Literary Interpretation." *Victorian Periodicals Newsletter* 9, no. 2 (1976): 50–68.

Limido, Luisa. "L'Exposition universelle de 1867 Le Champ de Mars dans le sillage d'Haussmann." In *Les expositions universelles à Paris de 1855 à 1937*, edited by Myriam Bacha, 68–72. Paris: Action Artistique de la Ville de Paris, 2005.

230 Bibliography

Lockyer, Angus. "The Problem of Sovereignty in an Age of Empire." *Critical Asian Studies* 45, no. 4 (2013): 615–42.

Lückemeier, Kai. *Information als Verblendung. Die Geschichte der Presse und der öffentlichen Meinung im 19. Jahrhundert.* Stuttgart: Ibidem Verlag, 2001.

Maag, Georg, Wolfram Pyta, and Martin Windisch, eds. *Der Krimkrieg als erster europäischer Medienkrieg.* Berlin: LIT Verlag, 2010.

Mackay, Charles. *Forty Years' Recollections of Life, Literature, and Public Affairs.* Vol. 2. London: Chapman & Hall, 1877.

MacKenzie, John. *Propaganda and Empire.* Manchester: Manchester University Press, 1986.

Maidment, Brian. "Illustration." In *The Routledge Handbook to Nineteenth-Century British Periodicals and Newspapers,* edited by Andrew King, Alexis Easley, and John Morton, 102–24. Abingdon: Routledge, 2016.

Marbot, Bernard. "Durand-Brager (Jean-Baptiste-Henri)." In *After Daguerre: Masterworks of French Photography (1848–1900) from the Bibliothèque Nationale,* edited by Bernard Marbot, 58–9. New York: The Metropolitan Museum of Art, 1980.

Marchandiau, Jean-Noël. *L'Illustration: 1843/1944: vie et mort d'un journal.* Toulouse: Editions Privat, 1987.

Marcus, Sharon. "Reflections on Victorian Fashion Plates." *Differences* 14, no. 3 (2003): 4–33.

Markovits, Stefanie. *The Crimean War in British Imagination.* Cambridge: Cambridge University Press, 2009.

———. "Rushing into Print: 'Participatory Journalism' during the Crimean War." *Victorian Studies* 50, no. 4 (2008): 559–86.

Martin, Michèle. *Images at War: Illustrated Periodicals and Constructed Nations.* Toronto: Toronto University Press, 2006.

———. "Nineteenth Century Wood Engravers at Work: Mass Production of Illustrated Periodicals (1840–1880)." *Journal of Historical Sociology* 27, no. 1 (January 2014): 133–50.

Martin, Michèle, and Christopher Bodnar. "The Illustrated Press under Siege: Technological Imagination in the Paris Siege, 1870–1871." *Urban History* 36, no. 1 (2009): 67–85.

McKendry, Virginia. "The 'Illustrated London News' and the Invention of Tradition." *Victorian Periodicals Review* 27, no. 1 (1994): 1–24.

Merkle, Denise. "Vizetelly & Company as (Ex)Change Agent: Towards the Modernization of the British Publishing Industry." In *Agents of Translation,* edited by John Milton and Paul Bandia, 85–107. Amsterdam: John Benjamins Publishing, 2009.

Meulen, Rimmer van der. *Een veertigjarige uitgeversloopbaan. A.W. Sijthoff te Leiden.* Amsterdam: P.N. van Kampen & zoon, 1891.

Milligan, Ian. "Illusionary Order: Online Databases, Optical Character Recognition, and Canadian History, 1997–2010." *The Canadian Historical Review* 94, no. 4 (2013): 540–69.

Minea, Cosmin Tudor. "An Image for the Nation: Architecture of the Balkan Countries at the 19th Century Universal Exhibitions in Paris." Central European University, 2014.

Mitchell, William John Thomas. *Iconology: Image, Text, Ideology.* Chicago: University of Chicago Press, 2009.

———. *Picture Theory: Essays on Verbal and Visual Representation.* Chicago: Chicago University Press, 1994.

———. "There Are No Visual Media." *Journal of Visual Culture* 4, no. 2 (August 1, 2005): 257–66.

Bibliography 231

Mohrman, Gerhardus Thoman. *Hollandsche Illustratie? Neen, Fransche Kwakzalverij.* Amsterdam: Mohrman, 1865.

Mussell, James. "Digitization." In *The Routledge Handbook to Nineteenth-Century British Periodicals and Newspapers*, edited by Andrew King, Alexis Easley, and John Morton, 17–29. Abingdon: Routledge, 2016.

———. *Nineteenth-Century Press in the Digital Age.* Basingstoke: Palgrave Macmillan, 2014.

Naef, Weston. "The Beginnings of Photography as Art in France." In *After Daguerre: Masterworks of French Photography (1848–1900) from the Bibliothèque Nationale*, edited by Bernard Marbot, 15–71. New York: The Metropolitan Museum of Art, 1980.

Negri, Antonello, and Marta Sironi. "Censorship of the Visual Arts in Italy 1815–1915." In *Political Censorship of the Visual Arts in Nineteenth-Century Europe*, edited by Robert Goldstein and Andrew Nedd, 191–220. Basingstoke: Palgrave Macmillan, 2015.

Nicholson, Bob. "The Digital Turn." *Media History* 19, no. 1 (2013): 59–73.

Novás, Angeles Quesada. "'La Ilustración. Periódico Universal' (1849–1857): Panorámica General." *Anales de Literatura Española* no. 25 (2013): 239–51.

Nyrop, Camilus. "Hans Peter Hansen." In *Dansk Biografisk Lexikon: Tillige Omfattende Norge for Tidsrummet 1537–1814*, edited by Carl Frederik Bricka. Vol. 6, 633. Copenhagen: Gyldendal, 1892.

Olian, JoAnne. *Full-Colour Victorian Fashions: 1870–1893.* New York: Dover, 1999.

Osterhammel, Jürgen. *The Transformation of the World: A Global History of the Nineteenth Century.* Translated by Patrick Camiller. Princeton: Princeton University Press, 2014.

———. "A Transnational History of Society. Continuity or New Departure?" In *Comparative and Transnational History: Central European Approaches and New Perspectives*, edited by Heinz-Gerhardt Haupt and Jürgen Kocka, 39–52. New York: Berghahn Books, 2009.

Park, David. "Picturing the War: Visual Genres in Civil War News." *The Communication Review* 3, no. 4 (1999): 287–321.

Paul, Gerhard. *Bilder Des Krieges. Krieg Der Bilder.* Paderborn: Verlag Ferdinand Schoningen, 2004.

———. *Das visuelle Zeitalter: Punkt und Pixel.* Göttingen: Wallstein Verlag, 2016.

Pettegree, Andrew. *The Invention of News: How the World Came to Know about Itself.* New Haven, CT: Yale University Press, 2015.

Philips, Deborah. *Fairground Attractions: A Genealogy of the Pleasure Ground.* London: Bloomsbury Academic, 2012.

Piesse, Jude. "Dreaming across Oceans: Emigration and Nation in the Mid-Victorian Christmas Issue." *Victorian Periodicals Review* 46, no. 1 (2013): 37–60.

Pike, Holden. *John Cassell.* London: Cassel and Company, 1894.

Potter, Simon. "Webs, Networks, and Systems: Globalization and the Mass Media in the Nineteenth- and Twentieth-Century British Empire." *Journal of British Studies* 46, no. 3 (2007): 621–46.

Pritchard, Henry Baden. *The Photographic Studios of Europe.* London: Piper & Carter, 1882.

Puiseux, Hélène. *Les figures de la guerre: représentations et sensibilités, 1839–1996.* Paris: Gallimard, 1997.

Purbrick, Louise. "Defining Nation: Ireland at the Great Exhibition of 1851." In *Britain, the Empire, and the World at the Great Exhibition of 1851*, edited by Jeffrey Auerbach and Peter Hoffenberg, 47–75. Aldershot: Ashgate, 2008.

Putnam, Lara. "The Transnational and the Text-Searchable: Digitized Sources and the Shadows They Cast." *American Historical Review* 121, no. 2 (2016): 376–402.

232 Bibliography

Putnis, Peter. "The British Transoceanic Steamship Press in Nineteenth-Century India and Australia: An Overview." *Journal of Australian Studies* 31, no. 91 (2007): 69–79.

———. "News, Time and Imagined Community in Colonial Australia." *Media History* 16, no. 2 (May 2010): 153–70.

———. "Reuters in Australia: The Supply and Exchange of News, 1859–1877." *Media History* 10, no. 2 (2004): 67–88.

Quesada, Angeles Quesada. "La Ilustración. Periódico Universal (1849–1857). Panorámica General." *Anales de Literatura Española* no. 25 (2013): 239–51.

Reichardt, Rolf. "'Das Grosste Ereignis Der Zeit' Zur Medialen Resonanz Der Pariser Februarrevolution." In *Medienereignisse Der Moderne*, edited by Friederich Lenger and Ansgar Nunning. Darmstadt: WBG, 2008.

Remoortel, Marianne Van. "Woman Editors and the Rise of the Illustrated Fashion Press in the Nineteenth Century." *Nineteenth-Century Contexts* 39, no. 4 (2017): 269–95.

Remoortel, Marianne Van, Kristin Ewins, Maaike Koffeman, and Matthew Philpotts. "Joining Forces: European Periodical Studies as a New Research Field." *Journal of European Periodical Studies* 1, no. 1 (July 5, 2016): 1.

Renaudin, Edmond. *Paris-Exposition ou guide à Paris en 1867*. Paris: Ch. Delagrave et Cie, 1867.

Riall, Lucy. *Garibaldi: Invention of a Hero*. New Haven: Yale University Press, 2008.

Richardson, Joanna. *Judith Gautier: A Biography*. New York: F. Watts, 1987.

Rimmel, Eugene. *Recollections of the Paris Exhibition of 1867*. London: Chapman and Hall, 1868.

Robinson, Howard. *Britain's Post Office: A History of Development from the Beginnings to the Present Day*. London: Oxford University Press, 1953.

Rosenthal, Eric. *Heinrich Egersdörfer: 'n Outydse Sketsboek*. Cape Town: Nasionale Boekhandel, 1960.

Said, Edward. *Culture and Imperialism*. New York: Alfred A. Knopf, 1993.

———. *Orientalism*. New York: Pantheon, 1978.

Sala, George. *The Life and Adventures of George Augustus Sala*. Vol. 1. New York: Charles Scribner's Sons, 1896.

Sánchez Vigil, Juan Miguel. *Revistas ilustradas en España: del Romanticismo a la guerra civil*. Gijón: Trea, 2008.

Schäfer, Michael. *Bürgertum in der Krise: städtische Mittelklassen in Edinburgh und Leipzig 1890 bis 1930*. Göttingen: Vandenhoeck & Ruprecht, 2003.

Schwartz, Vanessa. *Spectacular Realities: Early Mass Culture in Fin-de-Siècle Paris*. Berkeley: University of California Press, 1998.

Schwartz, Vanessa, and Jeannene Przyblyski. *The Nineteenth-Century Visual Culture Reader*. New York: Routledge, 2009.

Sebe, Berny. "Justifying 'New Imperialism': The Making of Colonial Heroes, 1857–1902." In *Justifying War: Propaganda, Politics and the Modern Age*, edited by David Welch and Jo Fox, 46–71. Basingstoke: Palgrave Macmillan, 2012.

Seville, Catherine. *The Internationalisation of Copyright Law: Books, Buccaneers and the Black Flag in the Nineteenth Century*. Cambridge: Cambridge University Press, 2009.

Shannon, Mary. "Colonial Networks and the Periodical Marketplace." In *Journalism and the Periodical Press in Nineteenth-Century Britain*, edited by Joanne Shattock, 203–23. Cambridge: Cambridge University Press, 2017.

Shattock, Joanne. "Introduction." In *Journalism and the Periodical Press in Nineteenth-Century Britain*, edited by Joanne Shattock, 1–13. Cambridge: Cambridge University Press, 2017.

Bibliography 233

Shorter, C. "Illustrated Journalism: Its Past and Its Future." *The Contemporary Review* 75 (1899): 481–93.

Sinnema, Peter. "Around the World without a Gaze: Englishness and the Press in Jules Verne." *Victorian Periodicals Review* 36, no. 2 (2003): 135–52.

———. *Dynamics of the Pictured Page: Representing the Nation in the Illustrated London News*. Aldershot: Ashgate, 1998.

———. "Reading Nation and Class in the First Decade of the 'Illustrated London News'." *Victorian Periodicals Review* 28, no. 2 (July 1995): 136–52.

———. "Representing the Railway: Train Accidents and Trauma in the 'Illustrated London News'." *Victorian Periodicals Review* 31, no. 2 (1998): 142–68.

Smith, Francis Barrymore. *Radical Artisan: William James Linton 1812–97*. Manchester: Manchester University Press, 1973.

Smith, W. "The Early Days of 'The Illustrated London News'." In *Panorama 1842–1865: The World of the Early Victorians as Seen through the Eyes of the Illustrated London News*, edited by L. de Vries, 9–12. London: Murray, 1967.

Smits, Thomas. "Looking for the Illustrated London News in Australian Digital Newspapers." *Media History* 23, no. 1 (2017): 80–99.

———. "Making the News National: Using Digitized Newspapers to Study the Distribution of the Queen's Speech by W.H. Smith & Sons, 1846–1858." *Victorian Periodicals Review* 49, no. 4 (2017): 598–625.

———. "Problems and Possibilities of Digital Newspaper and Periodical Archives." *TS. Tijdschrift Voor Tijdschriftstudies* no. 36 (2014): 139–46.

———. "Teaching Transatlanticism: Resources for Teaching Nineteenth-Century Anglo-American Print Culture Ed. by Linda K. Hughes and Sarah R. Robbins (Review)." *Victorian Periodicals Review* 50, no. 2 (July 3, 2017): 437–40.

Sperber, Jonathan. *The European Revolutions, 1848–1851*. Cambridge: Cambridge University Press, 1994.

Spielmann, Harry. *The History of Punch*. London: Cassel and Company, 1895.

Springhall, John. "'Up Guards and at Them!': British Imperialism and Popular Art, 1880–1914." In *Imperialism and Popular Culture*, edited by John MacKenzie, 49–72. Manchester: Manchester University Press, 1986.

Stougaard-Nielsen, Jakob. "The Idle Spectator: Hans Christian Andersen's 'Dryaden' (1868), 'Illustrevet Tidende', and the Universal Exposition." *Scandinavian Studies* 78, no. 2 (2006): 129–52.

Tucker, Jennifer. "'Famished for News Pictures': Mason Jackson, the Illustrated London News, and the Pictorial Spirit." In *Getting the Picture: The Visual Culture of the News*, edited by Vanessa Schwartz and Jason Hill, 213–21. London: Bloomsbury Academic, 2015.

Van Lente, David. "Illustratietechniek." In *Geschiedenis van de Techniek in Nederland. De Wording van Een Moderne Samenleving 1800–1890*, edited by H.W. Lintsen. Vol. 2, 177–81. Zutphen: Walburg Pers, 1993.

Vaughan, Alden, and Virginia Vaughan. *Shakespeare's Caliban: A Cultural History*. Cambridge: Cambridge University Press, 1991.

Verhoogt, Robert. *Art in Reproduction: Nineteenth-Century Prints after Lawrence Alma-Tadema, Jozef Israels and Ary Scheffer*. Amsterdam: Amsterdam University Press, 2007.

Vizetelly, Ernest Alfred. *My Adventures in the Commune, Paris 1871*. London: Chatto and Windus, 1914.

———. *My Days of Adventure: The Fall of France, 1870–71*. London: Chatto and Windus, 1914.

234 Bibliography

Vizetelly, Henry. *Glances Back through Seventy Years: Autobiographical and Other Reminiscences.* Vol. 1. London: Kegan Paul, Trench, Trubner & Co., 1893.

————. *Glances Back through Seventy Years: Autobiographical and Other Reminiscences.* Vol. 2. London: Kegan Paul, Trench, Trubner & Co., 1893.

————. *Paris in Peril.* Vol. 1. London: Tinsley, 1882.

Watelet, Jean. "La presse illustrée en France. 1814–1914." Université Paris II: Panthéon-Assas, 1998.

Weber, Wolfgang. *Johann Jakob Weber. Ein Beitrag Zur Familiengeschichte.* Leipzig: Weber, 1929.

Weller, Toni. "Preserving Knowledge through Popular Victorian Periodicals: An Examination of the Penny Magazine and the Illustrated London News." *Library History* 24, no. 3 (2008): 200–7.

Wesemael, Pieter van. *Architecture of Instruction and Delight: A Socio-Historical Analysis of World Exhibitions as a Didactic Phenomenon (1798–1851–1970).* Rotterdam: 010 Publishers, 2001.

Wesseling, Henk. *Verdeel en heers. De deling van Afrika, 1880–1914.* Amsterdam: Bert Bakker, 1991.

Wiener, Joel. *Americanization of the British Press 1830s–1914: Speed in the Age of Transatlantic Journalism.* Basingstoke: Palgrave Macmillan, 2014.

Williamson, C. N. "Illustrated Journalism in England: Its Development: II." *Magazine of Art* (1890): 334–40.

Wilson, Charles. *First with the News: The History of W.H. Smith, 1792–1972.* London: Jonathan Cape, 1985.

Wilson, Colette. *Paris and the Commune, 1871–1878: The Politics of Forgetting.* Manchester: Manchester University Press, 2007.

Wolff, Michael, and Celina Fox. "Pictures from Magazines." In *The Victorian City: Images and Realities.* Vol. 2, 559–82. London: Routledge, 1973.

Wood, James. "Taxes on Knowledge." In *Dictionary of Nineteenth-Century Journalism,* edited by Marysa Demoor and Laurel Brake. Ghent: Academia Press, 2009.

Wuttke, Heinrich. *Die deutschen Zeitschriften und die Entstehung der öffentlichen Meinung: ein Beitrag zur Geschichte des Zeitungswesen.* Hamburg: Hoffmann und Campe, 1866.

Yukiko, Tatsumi. "Russian Illustrated Journals in the Late Nineteenth Century: The Dual Image of Readers." *Acta Slavica Iaponica* 26 (2009): 159–76.

Index

Aagaard Lytzen, Niels 188
Aberdeen Journal 139–40, 143
ABL (French engraving firm) 76, 84
About, Edmond 182
Ábrázolt Folyóirat 98
Age (the) 41, 43, 141
Algemeen Handelsblad 55–6, 113
Allanson, John 82, 84, 95, 107
Allgemeine Preußische Zeitung 34, 54
All the Year Round 2, 223
Andrew, John 82, 84
Archivo Pittoresco 188, 202, 206
Argus (the) 43, 141–2
Armstrong, Thomas 83–4
artistic freedom (of engraver) 76
Art Journal (the) 102, 175
Asmodée 113
Australian colonies 2, 22–3, 35, 41–3, 57, 84–5, 141–2
Austro-Hungarian Empire 13, 32–3, 53–4, 98, 137, 178, 184, 194, 205
Austro-Prussian War 33–4, 108

Bader, Friederich Wilhelm 82
Ballou's Pictorial Drawing-Room 2, 141, 146
Baudelaire, Charles 134
Bavaria 196, 204
Bayley, Frederick 79
Bazar (der) 109
Beck, August 73
Beets, Nicolaas 113
Belfast Mercury 141
Belgium 49, 52, 107, 194, 196, 209
Berezowski, Antoni 200
Berghaus, Heinrich 92
Bermuda 23, 36–7, 222
Best, Jean 82, 103
Bewick, Thomas 81–4, 116

Bey, Salaheddin 194
BHR (engraving firm) 84
Biblioteca Digital Hispánica 175
Bingham, Robert Jefferson 186
Blanc, Numa 75
Blanchard, Pharamond 90, 144, 159, 161–2
BLHR (French engraving firm) 58, 66
Bogue, David 87
Bonner, George Wilmot 82–4, 86
Bourdilliat, Achille 88, 106, 117
Bourdin, Ernest 99
Branston, Allen Robert 81–4
Braun, Kaspar 82
Brévière, Louis-Henri 82, 85
Brindesi, Giovanni Jean 145, 152
Britain 2, 5, 14, 23, 29–30, 34–5, 39, 41–4, 48–51, 54, 88, 99, 102–3, 106, 135, 141, 159, 162–4, 194, 196, 202, 209, 220
British colonies 23, 38, 50, 57
British Empire 10, 34, 37–8, 48, 50, 219
British Newspaper Archive 12, 23, 30, 71, 86
Brockhaus, F. A. 85, 109
Brown, Henry 107
Bulgaria 137
burin (engraving tool) 81, 115

California Illustrated News 84
Canada 41
Cassell, John 2, 102, 131, 141, 143, 156–7, 219
Cassell's Illustrated Family Paper 2, 11–12, 14, 99, 102–3, 117, 131–3, 135–43, 153–59, 163, 220–1
Cassell's Illustrated Family Paper and Melbourne Advertiser 2, 142
Chambers Journal 80
Chapon, Alfred 186, 194
Charivari (le) 100

236 *Index*

chartist 98
Charton, Édouard 69
Chaulié y Ruiz, Dionisio 182
Chevalier, Armand le 102
China 21, 40, 100, 194, 197, 205
cliché(s) 4, 13–14, 67, 70, 72, 80, 89, 93, 96–7, 99–101, 103–5, 109–15, 142, 154, 182, 186–9, 202, 207–8
collodion film 81
common reader 22
communication networks 5, 24
composite work 132, 135–6
Conan Doyle, Athur 139
Conrad, Joseph 139
Constitutionel (*le*) 182
Cosse, Victor 192
Crimean War 1–2, 9, 14, 87, 114, 117, 132–3, 136–9, 142–5, 151, 156–7, 162–3, 220
Croatia 53
Crystal Palace 175
Curacao 50
Czech Republic 32

daguerreotype(s) 81, 114
Daily News 91, 184, 186
Dalloz, Paul 183, 208
Danubian Principalities 137–8
De Bragelonne, Viscount 89
De Castro y Serrano, Don Jose 182
Deis, Carl August 82
Delbanco, Otto Herman 85
Delpher 12, 23, 44, 55, 72
Denmark 4, 12
Dentu, Pierre 175, 181–4
Derby, George 114
Dickens, Charles 2
Dicks, John 105
Didot, Firmin 82
Dietrich brothers 69, 107
digital archives 11–13, 22–3, 71, 221–3
discourse of (visual) objectivity 6, 11, 78, 146, 151–2, 154, 158, 163, 203
distribution 6, 22–4, 31–3, 38–9, 52–3, 56–7, 97, 141, 222
Doré, Gustav 88
Downpatrick Recorder 139
draughtsman 67, 70–7, 84, 88, 90, 110, 142–4, 151–2, 154–5
Dublin Evening Mail 78
Dubochet, Jacques-Julien 52
Ducuing, François 179–83, 208
Dulong, M. 145, 159
Dundee Courier 105

Durand-Brager, Herri 131, 135–6, 145–9, 151–2, 154–6, 220
Dutch colonies 50, 56–7

Edinburgh Weekly Register 77
Egersdörfer, Heinrich 85
Egypt 49, 179, 194, 196–8
electrotypes 80, 89, 114, 157
electrotyping 67, 72, 79–80, 104, 116
Elza Cook's Journal 31
Emporio Pittoresco (*l'*) 189, 202
engraver(s) 67, 70–7, 80–6, 90, 95, 97, 103, 107, 110–11, 142, 154, 180, 188
Enniskillen Chronicle and Erne Packet 139
España en París. Revista de la Exposicion Universal de 1867 182, 184, 202
Esposizione Universale del 1867 Illustrato (*l'*) 182
Exposition Populaire Illustrée (*l'*) 179–80, 184, 186, 200
Exposition Universelle (*l'*) 172, 179, 180–2, 186–9, 192, 194–5, 198–200, 202–6, 208

facsimile 76, 80
Family Herald (*the*) 31, 139–41
fashion magazines 68–70
Fenton, Roger 133–4, 148
Fernández de los Ríos, Ángel 69, 96
Figaro (*le*) 77
flâneur(s)/flâneuse(s) 134, 190–2
Flaubert, Gustav 91
Fliegende Blätter 82, 93–4
France 9, 12, 23, 32–4, 44, 48–9, 51–2, 54, 68–9, 71, 82, 91–2, 95–6, 99–100, 102–3, 105, 137, 148, 151–2, 159, 161, 163, 179, 194–6, 220–1
Franco-Prussian War 9, 32, 90, 109
freedom of press 98
French Colonial Empire 34
Frost, Thomas 140, 157–8, 221
Fuhri, Koenraad 108

Garibaldi, Giuseppe 73
Gartenlaube (*die*) 9
Gautier, Théophile 171, 173, 178, 182, 206–8
Gebroeders Binger 110–13
Gebroeders van Es 110–13
Geïllustreerde Courant 95, 108, 117
Geïllustreerd Nieuws 101, 108–10, 113, 183–4, 202
Gentleman's Magazine (*the*) 99, 103, 115, 142

Index 237

German Customs Union 32
German states 29, 32–4, 48, 50, 54, 67, 93, 196, 204, 209
Germany 9, 12, 23, 32, 44, 49, 50, 85, 95–6, 104–5, 109, 131, 196, 221
Gids (de) 109–10
Giornale Illustrato (il) 175
Gleason's Pictorial Drawing Room 50, 83
Globo Ilustrado (el) 183–4
Gonzalès, Emmanuel 182
Google Books 13, 71–2
Gracieuse (de) 109
Graphic (the) 74, 86, 115
Great Exhibition 4, 44–8, 55, 175
Greece 204, 209
Guys, Constantin 131, 134–5

Halifax Courier 140
Hall, Samuel Carter 175
Hallberger, Eduard 111–12, 187, 219
Hansen, Hans Peter 85
Harpers' Weekly 202, 220
Harrall brothers 88
Hawai'i 53, 190, 195, 204
Hecknast, Gustav 184
Herculano, Alexandre 69, 96–7
Hereford Times 142
Hessen 196, 204
Hollandsche Illustratie 58, 107, 110–13, 187, 206–8, 219
Home News (the) 41–2
Hong Kong 21
Hotelin, Laurent 84, 155
Hudson, Frederic 5, 67
Hungary 4, 12, 98

Illiustrirovannaia Gazeta 175
Illustração (a) 96–7, 117
Illustração do Brazil 5
illustrated journalism 5, 14, 87
Illustrated London News 3–4, 8, 11–13, 21, 23–5, 28–31, 34–51, 53–7, 67–9, 72–3, 75–6, 79–80, 81–4, 86–90, 91, 93, 95–8, 103–4, 108, 111–16, 134–5, 139, 163, 180, 183, 187–90, 196, 198–200, 202, 208, 218–22
Illustrated London News en Français 45, 49, 55
Illustrated London News Deutsches Supplement 46–8
Illustrated Midland News 103
Illustrated News of the World 103
illustrated press 4–5, 8–9, 11, 14, 67–9, 71–2, 74, 79, 86, 106, 108, 114–17, 131,

134–5, 142, 154, 163, 172–4, 183, 186, 190, 192, 196–7, 200, 202–4, 209, 218, 221
Illustrated Sydney News 84–5
Illustrated Tasmanian News 5
Illustrated Times 87–90, 99, 103, 111, 113–14, 117, 139, 141, 186, 219
Illustrated Weekly Times 102
Illustration (l') 1–4, 11, 13, 24–5, 27, 29, 31–2, 34–5, 43, 45, 48, 51–7, 70, 73, 75–8, 84–5, 88–93, 95–103, 106, 108, 110–11, 113–14, 117, 131–2, 135–5, 142–5, 147, 150–3, 155–9, 162–3, 180, 184–4, 186–90, 208, 218–21, 223
Illustreret Tidende 85, 188, 191, 206, 219
Illustrirte Welt 111, 187, 198
Illustrirte Zeitung 2–4, 9, 11, 13, 15, 21, 23–4, 26, 29, 31–4, 45, 48, 52–4, 56–7, 70, 73, 76, 84–5, 92–6, 98–101, 108–10, 119, 146, 180, 183–4, 187–8, 196, 202, 208, 221, 223
Illyustratsiya 82, 95–6, 117, 219
Ilustración (la) 2, 96, 146
Ilustración Española (la) 96
image-text 132, 136
imagined community 8–10, 174, 221–2
India 23, 37, 41, 74, 222
Indian Rebellion 4
Ingram, Herbert 37, 51, 70, 75, 86–9, 93, 106, 139
Ingram family 105, 117
intaglio printmaking 81
interpretative engraving 76
invented tradition 7–8, 174
Israëls, Jozef 194
Italian States 97
Italy 4, 12, 32, 49, 53, 70, 73, 97, 221

Jackson, Mason 4, 72
Janet, Gustave 88–90
Janet-Lange, Ange 89
Jersey Independent and Daily Telegraph 21, 141
Journal des Debats (le) 53
Journal für Buchdruckerkunst 93
Journal Illustré (le) 68, 88–9, 92, 106–7, 110–13, 117, 187, 206, 219, 221
Journal of the Photographic Society 81
Journées illustrées de la révolution de 1848 70

Képesujság 98–9
Kerry Examiner and Munster General Observer 2, 12

238 *Index*

Kłosy 202
Knight, Charles 37, 69, 79
Kretzschmar, Eduard 76, 85
Kukolnik, Nestor 95–6
Kunstkronijk 108

Laporta Valor, Enrique 188–9
Launceston Advertiser 37
Laveille, Jacques Adrien 84
Lecoq, Marie-Jean-Léon 205
Leicester Chronicle 141
Leloir, Isidore 82, 84, 90
Le Play, Frédéric 179, 190
Leslie, Frank 75, 83, 115–16, 221
Lesseps, Ferdinand de 179, 204
Lesseps, Jules de 194, 195, 198, 204
Letuaire, Pierre 145
Lévy, Michel 100, 103, 186
Linton, Henry 83, 88, 111
Linton, William James 82–3, 88
Literary World 105
Littell's Living Age 115
Lloyd's Weekly Newspaper 41
London Evening Standard 83
London Journal 10, 31, 102, 139, 141, 219
Lose, Carl Christian 85
Loudon, Robert 88
Love Match 31
Lyttelton Times 42–3

Mackay, Charles 51
Macniven & Cameron's Paper Trade Review 31
Manchester Times 30
Mankell, Otto August 188
Marc, Jean-Auguste 55
Mason, Abraham 84
Mason, Walter George 84–5
media (mass) 4–6, 9, 11, 13, 23, 70, 132–5, 146, 148, 157, 172, 209, 218, 221–3
media archaeology 6
media history 9–13, 68, 117
medium 4–6, 76, 80–1, 132, 134–6, 209, 218, 223
Méhédin, Léon-Eugène 205
Mexico 204–5
Millaud, Moïse Polydore 89, 106
Monde Illustré (*le*) 5, 52, 79, 88, 90, 99–100, 104, 106, 111, 113, 117, 145, 180, 183–4, 186–200, 202–3, 206–9, 219, 221
Mondo Illustrato (*il*) 70, 97, 219
Montaud, M. 73–4
Montaut, Henri de 187

Montblanc, Charles de 195
Morin, Edmond 88
Morning Advertiser 172
Morning Chronicle 31
Morning Post 77, 139, 143
Mount Alexander Mail 142
Mulattató Képesujság 98
Musée des familles (*le*) 107
Museo Universal (*el*) 188–9, 202, 221

Napoleon III 3, 33, 49, 53–5, 137, 145, 148, 158, 178–9, 183, 204, 208
Napoleonic Wars 34, 68, 133
Nederlandsche Maatschappij van Schoone Kunsten 107–8
Nederlandsche Spectator (*de*) 100
Nederlandsch Magazijn 107
Nelson Examiner and New Zealand Chronicle 43
Netherlands 2, 4, 13, 23, 44, 52, 54–7, 70, 107–13, 190, 193–4
network(s) (transnational) 10, 42, 52, 67–8, 70–2, 81–2, 86, 101, 116–17, 163, 174–7, 179–81, 188, 192, 206, 208–9, 219, 222
newsagents 24, 31, 39, 40, 41
newspaper stamp 30, 34, 37–42, 50, 87–8, 104, 139, 183
New World 114
New York Illustrated News 51, 83, 114
New York Tribune 141
New Zealand 41–3, 50
New Zealand Herald 42
Nicholls, William Alfred 82, 84
Nicholson, Thomas Henry 156
Niva 82
North-German federation 194–7, 202
Nottingham Review 93
Ny Illustrerad Tidning 188, 202, 208

Obermann, Franz Wilhelm 85
Oberungarische Illustrirte Zeitung 98
Odobescu, Alexandru 194
Orrin Smith, John 82–3, 86
Österreichische Illustrierte Zeitung 82
Ottoman Empire 53, 136–7, 151, 194–7, 209

Panorama (*o*) 96
paratext(s) 22
Paulin, Jean-Baptiste-Alexandre 102
Paulin, Victor 55, 146
Pelcoq, Jules 89–91
Pen and Pencil 88

Index 239

penny dreadful 105
Penny Illustrated News 105–6
Penny Illustrated Paper 105–6, 116
Penny Illustrated Weekly News 105
Penny Magazine 37, 67, 69, 71, 79, 96, 107
penny press 139–40
Petit, Pierre 181–3, 186
Pfennig-Magazin 107
Photographic Notes 81
photography 5–6, 14, 73, 80–1, 115, 133–5, 148, 181, 218
photojournalism 77, 133
photojournalist(s) 73, 133–4
photoxylography 80–1, 116
Pictorial Times 30, 51, 77, 87
Pictorial World 105
Piddington, William 42–3
piracy (of illustrations) 80–1, 92, 104, 113–16
Poland 4, 12, 32
Pomba, Giuseppe 69, 97
Porret, Henri Désiré 82, 84–5
Portugal 4, 12, 69–70, 194, 196, 200, 202, 204
Presse Illustrée (la) 107
Prior, Melton 95
Prior, William Henry 95
Prussia 32–4, 48, 53–4, 90, 92, 110, 179, 196–7
publisher(s) 4, 6, 9, 14–16, 24, 33–4, 37, 41, 51–2, 67, 69–72, 79–83, 86–8, 95–7, 102–5, 107–9, 116, 181–3, 186, 222
Punch 24, 41–2, 77–8, 134, 222–3

Queen Isabelle II 53
Queen Victoria 8, 48, 86, 95–6

reader(s) 2–4, 7, 13–14, 22–4, 29–58, 77, 79, 92, 95, 108, 139–43, 146, 151–4, 163, 172, 186, 192, 204, 209, 218
reader market 14, 95, 117
readership 14, 21–4, 29, 37, 50, 52, 54, 57, 87, 135, 140, 163
reception 22–3, 43–4, 173
Regnier, Isidore 84
Rehles, Johann 82
relief printing 81
reproduction technique(s) 11, 14, 67, 72, 79, 116, 219
Reynolds's Miscellany 105
Rico y Amat, Juan 96
Robertson, George 141
Romania 52–3, 137–8, 194

Russell, William Howard 131, 133, 155
Russia 1–2, 4, 44, 49, 52, 70, 95, 101, 104, 108, 136, 159, 162, 196–7, 199, 200, 209

Sachsen 48, 53, 69
Saint-Simonian(ism) 179, 182
Sala, George 91
Salisbury and Winchester Journal 142
Semanario pintoresco español (el) 96
Sijthoff, Albertus 108–10
Slovakia 32, 98
Slovenia 53
Smith, W. H. 31, 39
Society for the Diffusion of Useful Knowledge 37, 69
Society for the Suppression of Vice 51
Sonzogno, Edoardo 182, 189
Spain 4, 12, 49, 69–70, 96, 104, 131, 175, 182–3, 188, 194, 196–7, 200, 202–3, 221
special artist 72–4, 76–7, 131, 134–6, 142, 143–8, 152, 154–5, 158, 161, 163, 181, 203, 220
stereotype 4, 69, 79, 87, 104
Stiff, George 89, 102–3, 105, 143, 219–20
Strekoza 82
Sweden 4, 52, 196–7, 200, 202, 209
Switzerland 32, 49, 186, 194
Sydney Morning Herald 42–3

Tasmania 36–7, 141
taxes on knowledge 37–8, 105
Teatro Universale (il) 97
Teixeira de Vasconcelos, António Augusto 96–7
telephotography 6
Texier, Edmond 73
textual reader 22
Thomas, Joseph 51–2
Thompson, Charles 82
Tijd (de) 70
Tillotson, John 143, 157
Times (The) 21, 53, 131, 133, 135, 137, 163, 220
Tōkyō eiri shinbun 5
Tomahawk 90
Tour du Monde (le) 121
transatlantic journalism 10
transatlantic print culture 10, 219
transnational approach 10, 117, 218–19
transnational history 10–11
transnational perspective 9, 12–13, 131, 175, 221

240 *Index*

transnational trade in illustrations 67–72, 80, 91, 99–100, 114, 116, 131, 172–4, 177, 187, 192, 202, 209, 219, 222
Tsar Nicholas I 95, 137, 148, 200
Tunisia 178, 194–7, 205, 209
Tygodnik Illustrowany 184, 202

Über Land und Meer 111–13, 187, 192, 203, 206–7, 219
Ukraine 32
Unger, József 184
United Service Gazette 37
United States 2–4, 13, 50–2, 55, 83, 104, 108, 141, 188, 192, 194, 218
Universal Exposition 14, 78, 171, 173–4, 176–9, 184, 190, 192, 207–8, 221
Universel (l') 52, 106–7, 117
Univers Illustré (l') 52, 99–100, 103, 117, 183–4, 186–7, 203, 219, 221
Universo Illustrato (l') 202
Unzelmann, Friederich 85

Vasárnapi Ujság 184, 202
Verne, Jules 21, 187
Verveer, Salomon 194

visual (news) culture 3, 5–7, 11, 14, 58, 67, 80, 132, 134, 172, 188–9, 208–9, 218, 220–1
Vizetelly, Ernest Alfred 87, 89
Vizetelly, Frank 73, 88, 103
Vizetelly, Henry 30, 53–4, 83, 86–91, 103, 105, 111, 139, 178, 181, 186, 191, 198–200, 202–3, 205, 219
Voleur Illustré (le) 89
Von Humboldt, Alexander 92
Vsemirnaia Illyustratsiya 82

Waugh & Cox 41–2
Weber, Johan Jacob 24, 33–4, 69, 84–5, 101, 109
Weber, Thomas 203
Welcome Guest 88
Werfer, Károly (Carl) 98–9
wood engraving 5, 6, 13, 51, 69–72, 73–9, 81–6, 89–90, 96–7, 103–4, 106–8, 110, 114, 116, 134, 142, 144, 155, 202, 219
Worms, Jules 144, 155
Württemberg 196, 204

Zola, Émile 91

Printed in the United States
By Bookmasters